The Routle
in Science Education

This reader brings together a wide range of material to present an international perspective on topical issues in science education today. In order to identify what themes should be addressed in the book, 38 science educators from around the world responded to the question: 'What issues are currently important in science education in your country?' The outcome is this lively and authoritative Reader, which features topics as varied as:

- Globalisation
- Assessment
- Pupils' views on science education
- Environmental education
- Teaching approaches
- Teacher development
- Multimedia and ICT
- Constructivism

With a specially written introduction from the editor, providing a much-needed context to the current education climate, students of science education will find this reader an important route map to further reading and understanding.

John Gilbert is Professor of Education at the University of Reading and is Editor-in-Chief of the *International Journal of Science Education*.

Readers in Education

The RoutledgeFalmer Reader in Higher Education
Edited by Malcolm Tight

The RoutledgeFalmer Reader in Inclusion
Edited by Keith Topping and Sheelagh Maloney

The RoutledgeFalmer Reader in Language and Literacy
Edited by Teresa Grainger

The RoutledgeFalmer Reader in Multicultural Education
Edited by David Gillborn and Gloria Ladson-Billings

The RoutledgeFalmer Reader in Psychology of Education
Edited by Harry Daniels and Anne Edwards

The RoutledgeFalmer Reader in Science Education
Edited by John Gilbert

The RoutledgeFalmer Reader in Sociology of Education
Edited by Stephen J. Ball

The RoutledgeFalmer Reader in Teaching and Learning
Edited by Ted Wragg

The RoutledgeFalmer Reader in Science Education

Edited by
John Gilbert

RoutledgeFalmer
Taylor & Francis Group

LONDON AND NEW YORK

First published 2004
by RoutledgeFalmer
11 New Fetter Lane, London EC4P 4EE

Simultaneously published in the USA and Canada
by RoutledgeFalmer
29 West 35th Street, New York, NY 10001

RoutledgeFalmer is an imprint of the Taylor & Francis Group

© 2004 John Gilbert for editorial matter and selection

Typeset in Sabon and Futura by
Florence Production Ltd, Stoodleigh, Devon
Printed and bound in Great Britain by
TJ International, Padstow, Cornwall

British Library Cataloguing in Publication Data
A catalogue record for this book is available from the
British Library

Library of Congress Cataloging in Publication Data
A catalog record for this book has been requested

ISBN 0–415–32777–6 (hbk)
ISBN 0–415–32778–4 (pbk)

CONTENTS

ACKNOWLEDGEMENTS

Aikenhead, G. S. (2001) 'Science communication with the public: a cross-cultural event' in S. M. Stocklmayer, M. M. Gore and C. Bryant (eds) *Science Communication in Theory and Practice*, pp. 23–45, reproduced with kind permission of Kluwer Academic Publishers.

OECD (1999) 'Scientific Literacy' in OECD *Measuring student knowledge and skills 1999*, pp. 59–75, reproduced with kind permission of OECD.

Drori, G. S. (2000) 'Science education and economic development: trends, relationships, and research agenda' *Studies in Science Education* 35, 27–58, reproduced with kind permission of the author and the journal *Studies in Science Education*.

Scott, P. (1998) 'Teacher talk and meaning making in science classrooms: a Vygotskian analysis and review' *Studies in Science Education* 32, 45–80, reproduced with kind permission of the author and the journal *Studies in Science Education*.

Fullan, M. (2001) 'Planning, doing and coping with change' in M. Fullan *The New Meaning of Educational Change* (3rd edn.), pp. 95–112, reproduced with kind permission of Teachers College Press, New York.

The following are reproduced with kind permission of Taylor & Francis Books Limited

Black, P. (1997) 'Purposes' in P. Black *Testing: Friend or Foe?*, RoutledgeFalmer, pp. 24–36.

Bell, B. and Gilbert, J. K. (1996) 'A model for achieving teacher development' in B. Bell and J. K. Gilbert *Teacher Development: A Model from Science Education*, Falmer Press, pp. 5–37.

Burbules, N. C. and Torres, C. A. (2000) 'Globalization and Education: an introduction' in N. C. Burbules and C. A. Torres (eds) *Globalization and Education: Critical Perspectives*, Routledge, pp. 1–26.

The following are reproduced with kind permission of Taylor & Francis Journals. www.tandf.co.uk

Duit, R. and Treagust, D. (2003) 'Conceptual change – a powerful framework for improving science teaching and learning' *International Journal of Science Education* 25(6), 671–88.

Newton, P., Driver, R. and J. Osborne (1999) 'The place of argumentation in the pedagogy of school science' *International Journal of Science Education* 21(5), 553–76.

Buckley, B. C. (2000) 'Interactive multimedia and model-based learning in biology' *International Journal of Science Education* 22(9), 895–953.

Roth, W. M. and Alexander, T. (1997) 'The interaction of students' scientific and religious discourses: two case studies' *International Journal of Science Education* 19(2), 125–46.

Hodson, D. (2000) 'Time for action: science education for an alternative future' *International Journal of Science Education* 25(6), 645–70.

Gough, A. (2002) 'Mutualism: a different agenda for environmental and science education' *International Journal of Science Education* 24(11), 1201–15.

SCIENCE EDUCATION
Global or national?

John Gilbert

A preliminary enquiry

When invited to compile this Reader, I conducted a small-scale straw poll, e-mailing science education professionals throughout the world with one compound question:

> What do you perceive to be the most important current and future issues in science education, especially in your country?

Thirty-eight replies (out of 40 requests) were received from 14 countries. Some were very brief while others were extensive and reflective. I am very grateful to all those concerned; their names are listed on the Acknowledgements at the end of this chapter. They bear no responsibility for what has been done with their answers.

A total of 30 different issues were identified in the replies, to which I added some of my own. So on what basis was a selection to be made? Two criteria were used. First, was a particular issue likely to be of interest to a world-wide readership? This proved a poor discriminator, for all the issues seemed to be of general interest. Second, were high-grade articles available on an issue that combined thorough scholarship with a treatment that was not set too firmly in any one national context? This thinned the field considerably and enabled a choice to be settled upon.

This process of selection brought up two contrasting questions:

> Is science education a global phenomenon, with the similarities between curricula, teaching methods and assessment procedures far more important than their differences?

> Is science education distinctive in any one country, so that a world-wide perspective is the sum of national provisions?

These questions are now discussed as a framework within which to set the choice of articles made.

A global perspective on science education

Some similar elements can be seen in the reform of education in general across the globe in the last decade or so (Edwards and Usher, 2000). They involved the intentions of:

1   improving national economics by tightening the connection between schooling, employment, productivity and trade;

2   enhancing student outcomes in employment-related skills and competencies;
3   attaining more direct control over curriculum content and assessment;
4   reducing the costs of education to government;
5   increasing community input to education by more direct involvement in school decision taking and pressure of market choice (p. 4).

This trend has certainly applied to science education, not least because of the close connection believed to exist between educational attainment in science and industrial productivity and innovation (Drori, 2000).

The science curriculum has gradually evolved over time, with trends within diversity, as general reviews of the twentieth century for the USA illustrate (Krajcik, Mamlok and Hug, 2001; Bybee and DeBoer, 1994). However, in recent years the science curriculum in any one country has gradually become standardized for all schools because of the curriculum's prescription, to a greater or lesser degree, at regional, state or national level. Analyses of the situations in different countries show a high level of commonality, at least between the USA (Shiland, 1998), the UK (Millar and Osborne, 2000), Australia (Goodrum, Hackling and Rennie, 2001) and New Zealand (Hipkins et al., 2002).

This commonality consists of a set of concepts that are to be learned, a process that is helped by practical work. This convergence has been reinforced by the introduction of international testing regimes that have encouraged the drawing of comparisons between countries, even though the problems in doing so have been pointed out by experts in the field (Atkin and Black, 1997). The Third International Mathematics and Science Study (TIMSS) emphasised the attainment of content knowledge, while the OECD study (PISA) placed much more emphasis on the use of knowledge in everyday contexts.

Is it therefore true to say that there is a 'global science curriculum'? It sometimes feels like that, because modern communications and travel have made the transfer of ideas between countries much easier. As Ball (1998) observes:

> national policy making is inevitably a process of bricolage: a matter of borrowing and copying bits and pieces of ideas from elsewhere, drawing upon and amending locally tried and tested approaches, cannibalising theories, research, trends and fashions and not infrequently flailing around for anything at all that looks as if it might work.
>
> (p. 126)

However, the answer is probably 'no', for several reasons:

- The critical reviews of national situations written in English are almost exclusively of English-speaking countries. The trends elsewhere are not readily available. How, for example, does a monoglot anglophone community get to know what is going on in a monoglot francophone country and vice versa?
- The appearance of curricular stability is an illusion. Whilst some countries are 'catching up' on developments in the science curriculum elsewhere, it is often the case that the originator country is, at the same time, 'moving on'. For example, the UK currently has a rigid content-driven National Curriculum for Science in place for 5–16 year olds (DfEE, 1999). However, a recent governmental critique (Roberts, 2002: 69) has led to firm proposals for a considerable degree of choice in what is taught (QCA, 2002). New Zealand is in the process of reviewing its science curriculum, with a view to offering more choice (Hipkins et al., 2002). South Korea seems to be firmly fixed on a uniform prescribed-content curriculum (Han, 1995), while Brazil is actually introducing such a curriculum for 75 per cent of school time (Education, 2000). In the case of countries that were once colonies,

a clearer trend of influence can be seen. Thus, whilst the curriculum of Cyprus is still heavy influenced by that of the UK (Zembylas, 2002), the UK influence on the New Zealand curriculum seems to be waning rapidly (Hipkins *et al.*, 2002), and that on Australia is already largely historical (Goodrum *et al.*, 2001). Developing countries, lacking the expertise or infrastructure to develop their own science curricula, often adopt imported designs, to their detriment (Gray, 1999).

Many countries certainly share a degree of commonality between the science curricula, teaching methods and assessment procedures. The diffusion of ideas, discussed above, may be partially responsible. However, perhaps this convergence follows from the acceptance that 'science', as an intellectual activity, can be described with the aid of relatively few general principles (Matthews, 1994: 37–40). An agreement, however bounded, on the nature of 'science' would be reflected in similar views on the nature of science education. This would be particularly so where, as is usually the case, 'preparation to be a scientist' is the dominant (if covert) aim of the science education provided. However, in balancing this convergence there is still a considerable degree of divergence stemming from particular national concerns.

National perspectives on science education

One global trend that has unique national manifestations is a widespread commitment to 'scientific literacy for all'. This trend has resulted from the fact that scientists wish to build popular support for their activities, that economies are thought to be dependent on scientific knowledge and that individuals increasingly need access to scientific ideas in their private and social lives (Gregory and Miller, 1998: 10–12).

One impediment to progress in attaining 'scientific literacy for all' has been a lack of resources, possibly because governments have been seeking to reduce, rather than increase, their expenditure on education (Edwards and Usher, 2000). However, the main obstacle has been the failure among the science education community to agree on what 'scientific literacy for all' actually means. Laugksch proposed three 'levels' of scientific literacy, following a review of the field (Laugksch, 2000). I have defined and labelled these levels as follows:

- Level 1: scientifically literate as being able to function minimally in society. A person is able to use a restricted set of ideas derived from science when relating to others in some set of roles in a society, e.g. as a consumer or as a citizen.

- Level 2: scientifically literate as being competent. A person is able to draw on an existing body of knowledge derived from science in order to communicate successfully with others about scientific matters that are set within a restricted range of contexts, activities or problems.

- Level 3: scientifically literate as being learned. A person acquires a substantial body of scientific knowledge without a specific purpose for doing so, other than its intellectual value, and can relate that knowledge to contexts which seem appropriate, but without adopting any particular role in society.

Level 3 scientific literacy is that attained by those who study science for some time on a voluntary basis, for example science degree students. School science education has always been implicitly aimed at this group. The problem is that this focus has neglected the achievements of scientific literacy at Levels 1 or 2 in populations in general: hence the current priority to reverse this trend. In order to achieve a universal Level 1 or Level 2 scientific literacy, the processes, concepts and values of science have to be rendered compatible with each person's general cultural commitments. Unless this is done, science could be in a state of 'cognitive dissonance' with an individual's existing knowledge, beliefs and values (Festinger, 1957) and may well be discarded as a consonance of ideas is sought. Amongst the cultural commitments of individuals, the most important often relate to religion and distinctive worldviews derived from membership of an ethnic group – assuming that the two can be separated, if only for the purposes of discussion.

Science education and religion

Science education and religion can be in violent conflict, even today. The most visible example concerns Darwin's theory of evolution, especially in the USA, where the tradition of teaching 'evolution' is in direct conflict with 'creationism', to the extent that the USA National Academy of Sciences has had to publish a defence of teaching evolutionary theory to students (NAS, 1998). This conflict is spreading throughout the world, as Christian (and, no doubt, other) 'creationists' seek to evangelise their ideas.

The tensions between science and religion in countries that are nationally Christian can be obscured by presenting the theme of 'beliefs and values in science education' as being implicitly derived from a Christian ethic (Poole, 1995). This approach will be rejected by those seeking to provide science education for students with differing religious faiths, or with no religious faith at all. A more overt and universally applicable approach is set out by Reiss, who identified three ways of dealing with scientific ideas with students from any particular religious background or none:

- Advocacy: the teacher explicitly adopts either the religious view or the science view when dealing with a topic in the science curriculum.
- Affirmative neutrality: the teacher introduces the students to the range of interpretations possible, without revealing his/her personal views.
- Procedural neutrality: the teacher causes the students to become aware of the arguments involved and leaves them to draw their own conclusions.

Reiss states that he has used all three approaches and finds the last the most satisfactory (1993: 56). The three alternatives do provide a useful range of choice for a science teacher. It is, of course, open to a science teacher to take the view that science and religion are incompatible (Mahner and Bunge, 1996). However, this may lead to conflict with school managements.

What approaches to the relation between science education and religion are taken in societies where religions other than Christianity prevail? There seems to be little that has been written in English. An exception is the article by Loo, who identifies four traditions for science within Islam, each of which has implications for science education (Loo, 2001):

- Islamic science as modernist science within a Muslim polity. Science is conducted within societies dominated by Islamic values, but is not directly affected by them. This implies that science education, provided it deals solely with the material world, can be conducted as in other societies.
- Islamic science as revealed truth and knowledge. The acceptable discoveries of science are subsequently found to have been identified in the Koran. This implies a strong link has been made in science education between science and the Koran. This approach, however, rejects Darwin's ideas.
- Islamic science as a 'novum novum organum' [sic]. The basic assumption here is that the human intellect is divided into the rational, which deals with the external world, and the intuitive, which deals with religious ideas. A full understanding of the world can only

be attained by uniting the two components of the human intellect. The implications for science education are that religious ideas validate scientific ideas.

- Islamic science as science guided by environmental ethics. Islam is seen as exercising stewardship over nature and the socio-cultural environment. This sets the agenda for science. Science education would therefore focus on the protection of the environment and the perpetuation of sustainable development.

The existence of the four alternative views makes the science teacher's task especially difficult, for the approach taken will have to be set within the view of the Islam–science relationship that is most acceptable to the local Muslim community.

One consequence of the extensive migration that has taken place between countries in recent years is that a science teacher of one religious faith (or no religious faith) will often be called upon to teach students of another religious faith, or indeed of several faiths. It may well be that, in any one country, exemplary contexts of the religious affiliations of science teachers and students exist. If this is the case, then the approaches that are taken to the design and provision of the science curriculum may be unique to that country. Given the importance of maintaining and extending civic harmony in all countries, much more research is needed on this theme, not least into these exemplary contexts.

Science education in other world-views

It has been claimed that everybody has a 'world-view', which is:

> the culturally dependent, implicit, fundamental organisation of the mind. . . . It explains the how and why of things, and why things continue as they do. It validates goals, institutions, and values of a society. . . . It reinforces people at points of anxiety or crisis in life . . . and both encourages and prescribes behaviour. . . . Worldview helps one maintain a sense of mental order and the balance in a world of change'
> (Cobern, 2000: 8–9)

In short, it governs what knowledge a person is likely to find acceptable and therefore learn and use. The issue for school science education is that if the worldview of a student conflicts too sharply with what might be termed the 'worldview of science', it is science that will be rejected.

What can be done to avoid this rejection? Hipkins *et al.* (2002: para 8.4.4) outlines three responses that science education might make to the existence of potentially conflicting worldviews. These are to adopt:

- A cross-cultural perspective. This calls for the science curriculum to include the 'traditional ecological knowledge' (TEK) of other worldviews. The problem here is that the epistemological assumptions of TEK might be in irresolvable conflict.
- A multicultural perspective. Here both science and TEK are treated as problematic, such that science education involves a comparative interrogation of their epistemological similarities and differences.
- A pluralist perspective. Both science and TEK are taught, but entirely separately.

Inevitably, there is no agreement on which approach is in students' best interests long-term.

The adoption of any one of these approaches does depend on the teacher having in-depth knowledge of the epistemologies of both science and the relevant TEK. In a case study enquiry, Aikenhead and Huntley found that teachers:

- did not view science as a culture;
- did not appreciate that what students already knew could interact with new ideas;
- blamed students' 'personal defects' for their failure to learn science;
- did not perceive that evidence of cultural conflict in their classrooms could have an impact on the quality of learning taking place;
- valued memorisation, rather than understanding, of science, thus leaving worldview conflicts entirely alone;
- lacked the resources for an effective address to worldview issues

(Aikenhead and Huntley, 1999)

Pomeroy (1994) identified a range of strategies that could be incorporated into attempts to improve the learning of science by students with distinctive worldviews. These can be summarised as follows:

- provide role models from science with a programme of affirmative action;
- engage students in scientific enquiry that is local and relevant to their lives;
- use approaches to learning that have been validated by a particular worldview;
- cause teachers to raise their expectations in science of students from traditionally under-achieving groups;
- ensure that textbooks and other resources reflect the scientific achievements of people from a wide range of ethnic backgrounds;
- increase the emphasis on science as a human achievement;
- ensure that teachers can be effective in addressing the needs of students with limited language proficiency;
- explicitly introduce students to the genres of the discourse of the scientific community;
- wherever possible, show the relationship between science and TEK;
- encourage students to develop their own explanations of natural phenomenon, subsequently helping them to form a cognitive bridge to the scientific explanation;
- treat science as evolutionary, changing as new ideas are incorporated;
- explore the history and development of ideas in science.

It is likely that most countries will have exemplary contexts in which science teachers work with students of distinctive worldviews. Indeed, many teachers will have a range of worldviews represented in any school classroom. In these circumstances, it may be possible for a distinctly national resolution to the issues raised above to be reached. For example, New Zealand is making distinctive efforts to raise the achievement in science of its Maori/Pacific Islander population (Hipkins *et al.*, 2002).

The tensions between the global and the national positions in shaping the science curriculum, worked out within frameworks of religious and cultural affiliations, sets the scene for the articles selected.

Structuring the issues to be addressed

An analysis of the issues raised in the preliminary enquiry enables them to be placed into five groups.

Part I: some pressures being exerted on science education

This set of issues was not raised in the preliminary enquiry, but emerged from consideration of the broader context in which science education is set. Three issues are addressed: the impact of globalisation on the content of science education (Chapter 1); the role of science education in the economic development of nations (Chapter 2); the conduct of international assessment programmes in respect of science education (Chapter 3).

Part II: maintaining a continuity of achievement in science education

In the last 40 years or so a substantial international community of science education researchers and curriculum developers has grown up. This section celebrates its achievements and points to the challenges it faces.

A great deal has been achieved, building on the early work of Driver, Leach, Millar and Scott (1996) and others, on how to facilitate the acquisition and further development of understanding of the concepts of science. This issue emerged very directly from the preliminary enquiry. However, no succinct and comprehensive article on the achievements made could be found. So one was commissioned from Reinders Duit and David Treagust, initially for the 25th anniversary special issue of the *International Journal of Science Education*, and is reproduced here as Chapter 4.

Studies of the language of science and of the linguistic problems that students have in learning science have a long provenance, e.g. Lempke (1990). It therefore seemed appropriate to draw attention in Chapter 5 to the socio-cultural ideas of Vygotsky about the role of language in learning and in Chapter 6 to work on argumentation that utilises ideas from the philosophy of science.

Information and communication technologies (ICT) – what North Americans refer to simply as 'technology' (thus ignoring all the other technologies that their forebears gave to the world) – are playing an ever greater role in the teaching and learning of science. The paper by Barbara Buckley as Chapter 7 is a convincing account of how multi-media resources can be used in the classroom. Given the funding being invested in ICT – not least by the National Science Foundation in the USA – the good early work that has been done seems likely to explode in quantity within the next few years.

Part III: trends in science education at national level

'Scientific literacy for all' emerged as the most frequently and strongly expressed theme in the preliminary enquiry. It is an aspiration for most, if not all, countries. The theme was broken down into two allied issues. First, how to make science culturally credible to students from backgrounds that are very different from those commonly assumed by their teachers. In celebration of his sustained high quality work on 'border crossing' in science education, an article by Glen Aikenhead is included as Chapter 8. Second, the interface between science education and religion proved elusive, but Chapter 9 by Wolff-Michael Roth and Todd Alexander includes a most welcome empirical element that moves the issues away from politically correct rhetoric into the realities of the everyday classroom.

Ensuring that all students actually achieve some level of scientific literacy must entail the teacher in constantly monitoring what has been learnt and then in adjusting the lesson accordingly. This 'formative assessment' and its subsequent uses are the keys to supporting progression in the learning of science. The article by Paul Black, as Chapter 10, untangles the complex web of purposes to which assessment is put so that formative assessment can take its rightful place.

Part IV: some initiatives from within science education

The authorities overseeing the increased centralisation of decisions about the nature of the school curriculum in many countries sometimes seem to assume that the science education community exists just to implement the latest diktat. The realities of employment, and a natural wish to be supportive of the school system, led individuals to do what they are asked, even if they have, often grave, reservations. However, it is part of the intrinsic nature of universities that attitudes of criticism and autonomous creativity are maintained. It therefore seemed appropriate to follow through some of the ideas in science education that are currently largely being addressed in universities, confident that central bureaucracies will see their virtue is due time (usually over a decade hence).

Surprisingly, no clear agenda of radical ideas was readily found. Derek Hodson was invited to look down his 'philosophical telescope' in the article that appears here as Chapter 11, originally commissioned for the 25th anniversary issue of the *International Journal of Science Education*. There are other issues that, although formally approved by central ministries of education, seem to make slow progress towards the science classroom. One of these is environmental education. In Chapter 12, Annette Gough calls for the production of a common curriculum between science education and environmental education, to the betterment of both.

Part V: managing change in science education

School science education is in a process of change, whether it is headed towards a global uniformity or towards a celebration of legitimate national differences. In either case, the issue is how to 'manage change', meaning both how to bring about change and how to limit any adverse effects of that change. Chapter 13 is representative of Michael Fullan's extensive work on the strategic and tactical issues involved in curriculum change generally. These will only be addressed successfully if they are associated with a carefully thought out and followed-through programme of teacher professional development. Chapter 14 is from a book by Beverley Bell and myself based on a long-term professional development programme for science teachers in New Zealand. Its key finding is that professional development is progressive if accompanied by associated personal and social development.

The issues that are not addressed

The preliminary enquiry identified five themes that cannot be treated in this volume. This is because there is no suitable up-to-date literature available, or because the theme has risen to saliency too recently for a literature to have accumulated, or because suitable treatments already exist elsewhere.

Curriculum design

One consequence of the progressive centralisation of curriculum design in many countries is that the design of curricula is not open to academic account, critique and publication. There certainly is good material available on how to include the history and philosophy of science in the curriculum, e.g. Matthews (1994). However, there has been little written recently on curriculum design in science as a whole. For example, in soliciting research-based papers on chemical education for a recent book, the excellent work on 'curriculum for general chemical education' by the late Wobbe De Vos and his colleagues (2002) seemed to be one of the few pieces of such work available.

The preliminary enquiry suggested several issues on the theme of curriculum design that need more attention:

- the principles on which to update and reduce the content included, an issue that has been raised by White (1994)
- the relationships between the curriculum intended by the planners, the curriculum provided by the teachers, and the curriculum experienced by the pupils;

- the integration of the sciences (physics, chemistry, biology, etc.) in integrated science programmes;
- the transition from the compulsory science curriculum to the elective, pre-university science curriculum.

Teaching science

There has been recent work on the use of specific teaching methods in science, in particular the role of practical work (Leach and Paulsen, 1999; Psillos and Niedderer, 2002). Teacher demonstrations, small group work and games simulations have all received attention, yet nowhere does there seem to be an account of how to orchestrate these individual methods to provide an effective learning environment that addresses specific purposes. Although much has no doubt been written about the use of particular teaching methods in other school subjects, to what extent can that experience be transferred to the science classroom?

One consequence of the trend towards a centralised curriculum (where it did not exist before!) has been that the range of science textbooks in any one country has decreased, while the size of each such book has grown rapidly. Textbooks, often associated with detailed schemes of work, worksheets and CD-ROMs seem to play an ever-increasing role in the teaching of science, especially in the many countries where science teachers cannot be recruited and/or retained. Yet we have little evidence on the ways that textbooks are used by teachers and students or on the consequences of extensive reliance on them.

Teachers' subject knowledge and capacity to teach that knowledge

The work of Shulman (1987) drew attention to the central role played by teachers' knowledge of subject matter and their capacity to communicate it. Although his distinction between 'subject knowledge' and 'pedagogic content knowledge' has been much debated and efforts made to improve both in teacher, e.g. van Driel, Verloop and de Vos (1998), there is only general guidance on how to develop both *ab initio*.

The impact of assessment-driven teaching

National schemes of testing have only been used across different age ranges in some countries and then for only a decade or so. There is hearsay evidence that teachers are narrowing their vision to meet the requirements of the tests alone. However, the research in science education is scant.

Using the results of research to improve teaching

This theme has been addressed elsewhere, e.g. Gilbert, De Jong, Justi, Treagust and Van Driel (2002).

And finally

Let us not lose sight of the science education that we ought to want to provide. This has been admirably expressed by Leonie Rennie and her colleagues (Goodrum *et al.*, 2001: vii). The ideal picture can be described in nine themes:

1   The science curriculum is relevant to the needs, concerns and personal experiences of students.

2   Teaching and learning of science is centred on enquiry. Students investigate, construct and test ideas and explanations about the natural world.

3   Assessment serves the purpose of learning and is consistent with and complementary to good teaching.

4   The teaching–learning environment is characterised by enjoyment, fulfilment, ownership of and engagement in learning, and mutual respect between the teacher and students.

5   Teachers are life-long learners who are supported, nurtured and resourced to build the understandings and competencies required of contemporary best practice.

6   Teachers of science have a recognised career path based on sound professional standards endorsed by the profession.

7   Excellent facilities, equipment and resources support teaching and learning.

8   Class sizes make it possible to employ a range of teaching strategies and provide opportunities for the teacher to get to know each child as a learner and give feedback to individuals.

9   Science and science education are valued by the community, have high priority in the school curriculum, and science teaching is perceived as exciting and valuable, contributing significantly to the development of students and to the economic and social well-being of the nation.

Such aspirations must provide the fuel for our sustained endeavours.

Acknowledgements

Australia: Allan Harrison (University of Central Queensland), Ian Ginns (Queensland University of Technology), Léonie Rennie (Curtin University of Technology), Cam McRobbie (Queensland University of Technology), David Treagust (Curtin University of Technology). *Brazil*: Rosária Justi (University of Minas Gereis), *Canada*: Steve Alsop (York University), Derek Hodson (University of Toronto), Larry Yore (University of Victoria). *Germany*: Reinders Duit (University of Kiel). *Israel*: Avi Hofstein (Weizmann Institute of Science). *The Netherlands*: Jan Van Driel (University of Leiden). *New Zealand*: Dennis Burchill (Auckland College of Education), Richard Coll (University of Waikato), Beverley France (Auckland College of Education). *Portugal*: Helena Pedrosa de Jesus (University of Aveiro). *Spain*: Maria Pilar Jimenez Aleixandre (University of Santiago de Compostela). *Sweden*: Gustav Helldén (Kristianstad University). *Taiwan*: Huann-shyang Lin (Kaoshiung Normal University). *United Kingdom*: Mick Nott (Sheffield Hallam University), Robin Millar (University of York), Michael Reiss (University of London), D. Michael Watts (Roehampton University of Surrey). *United States of America*: Andy Anderson (University of Michigan), Doris Ash (University of California at Santa Cruz), William Cobern (Western Michigan University), Barbara Crawford (Penn State University), Zoubeida Dagher (University of Delaware), James Gallagher (University of Michigan), David Hammer (University of Maryland), Janice Gobert (Concord Consortium), Okhee Lee (University of Miami), Norman Ledermann (Illinois Institute of Technology), Kathleen Metz (University of California at Berkeley), Christina Schwarz (Michigan State University), James Wandersee (Louisiana State University), Carla Zembal-Saul (Penn State University). *Venezuela*: Mansoor Niaz (Universidade de Oriente).

References

Aikenhead, G. and Huntley, B. (1999). Teachers' views on Aboriginal students learning Western and Aboriginal science. *Canadian Journal of Native Education*, 23(2), 159–75.

Atkin, J. M. and Black, P. (1997). Policy perils of international comparisons. *Phi Delta Kappan* (Sept.), 22–8.

Ball, S. (1998). Big policies/small world: an introduction to international perspectives on educational policy. *Comparative Education*, 34(2), 119–32.

Bybee, R. W. and DeBoer, G. (1994). Research on the goals for science education. In D. L. Gabel (ed.), *Handbook of Research on Teaching and Learning of Science*. New York: Macmillan, pp. 357–87.

Cobern, W. W. (2000). *Everyday Thoughts about Nature*. Dordrecht: Kluwer.

De Vos, W., Bulte, A. M. W. and Pilot, A. (2002). Chemistry curricula for general education: analysis and elements of a design. In J. K. Gilbert, O. De Jong, R. Justi, D. F. Treagust and J. H. Van Driel (eds), *Chemical Education: Towards Research-based Practice*. Dordrecht: Kluwer, pp. 101–24.

DfEE (1999). *Science: The National Curriculum for England*. London: Department for Education and Employment.

Driver, R., Leach, J., Millar, R. and Scott, P. (1996). *Young People's Images of Science*. Buckingham: Open University Press.

Drori, G. S. (2000). Science education and economic development: trends, relationships and research agenda. *Studies in Science Education*, 35, 27–58.

Education, Brazilian Ministry of (2000). *The New Curricular Guidelines that Change Brazilian Secondary Learning*. Brazilian: Ministry of Education.

Edwards, R. and Usher, R. (2000). *Globalisation and Pedagogy: Space, Place and Identity*. London: RoutledgeFalmer.

Festinger, L. (1957). *A Theory of Cognitive Dissonance*. Evanston, IL: Row-Peterson.

Gilbert, J. K., De Jong, O., Justi, R., Treagust, D. F. and Van Driel, J. H. (2002). Research and development for the future of science education. In J. K. Gilbert, O. De Jong, R. Justi, D. F. Treagust and J. H. Van Driel (eds), *Chemical Education: Towards Research-Based Practice*. Dordrecht: Kluwer, pp. 391–408.

Goodrum, D., Hackling, M. and Rennie, L. (2001). *The Status and Quality of Teaching and Learning of Science in Australian Schools*. Canberra: Department of Education, Training and Youth Affairs.

Gray, B. V. (1999). Science education and the developing world: issues and considerations. *Journal of Research in Science Teaching*, 36(3), 261–8.

Gregory, J. and Miller, S. (1998). *Science in Public: Communication, Culture and Credibility*. New York: Plenum Trade.

Han, J. H. (1995). The quest for national standards in science education in Korea. *Studies in Science Education*, 26, 59–71.

Hipkins, R. *et al.* (2002). *Curriculum, Learning and Effective Pedagogy: A Literature Review in Science Education*. Wellington, New Zealand: Ministry of Education.

Krajcik, J., Mamlok, R. and Hug, B. (2001). Modern content and the enterprise of science: science education in the twentieth century. In L. Corno (ed.), *Education Across the Century: The Centennial Volume*. Chicago: University of Chicago Press, pp. 205–38.

Laugksch, R. C. (2000). Scientific literacy: a conceptual overview. *Science Education*, 84(1), 71–94.

Leach, J. and Paulsen, A. C. (eds) (1999). *Practical Work in Science Education: Recent Research Studies*. Roskilde: Roskilde University Press.

Lempke, J. (1990). *Talking Science: Language, Learning, and Values*. Norwood, NJ: Ablex.

Loo, S. P. (2001). Islam, science and science education: conflict or concord? *Studies in Science Education*, 36, 45–78.

Mahner, M. and Bunge, M. (1996). Is religious education compatible with science education? *Science and Education*, 5, 101–23.

Matthews, M. (1994). *Science Teaching: The Role of History and Philosophy of Science*. New York: Routledge.

Millar, R. and Osborne, J. (2000). *Beyond 2000: Science Education for the Future*. London: School of Education, King's College London.

NAS (1998). *Teaching about Evolution and the Nature of Science*. Washington, DC: National Academy of Sciences.

Osborne, J. (1996). Beyond constructivism. *Science Education*, 80(1), 53–82.

Pomeroy, D. (1994). Science education and cultural diversity: mapping the field. *Studies in Science Education*, 24, 49–73.

Poole, M. (1995). *Beliefs and Values in Science Education*. Buckingham: Open University Press.

Pope, M. and Keen, T. (1981). *Personal Construct Psychology in Education*. London: Academic Press.

Psillos, D. and Niedderer, H. (eds) (2002). *Teaching and Learning in the Science Laboratory*. Dordrecht: Kluwer Academic Press.

QCA (2002). *Science for the 21st Century*. London: Qualifications and Curriculum Authority.

Reiss, M. (1993). *Science Education for a Pluralist Society*. Buckingham: Open University Press.

Roberts, G. (2002). *SET for Success: The Supply of People with Science, Technology, Engineering and Mathematical Skills*. London: Her Majesty's Treasury.

Shiland, T. W. (1998). The atheoretical nature of the National Science Education Standards. *Science Education*, 82(5), 615–17.

Shulman, L. (1987). Knowledge and teaching: foundations of the new reforms. *Harvard Educational Review*, 57(1), 1–22.

van Driel, J. H., Verloop, N. and de Vos, W. (1998). Developing science teachers' pedagogical content knowledge. *Journal of Research in Science Teaching*, 35(6), 673–95.

Von Glasersfeld, E. (1985). Reconstructing the concept of knowledge. *Archives de Psychologie*, 53, 91–101.

Vygotsky, L. S. (1978). *Mind in Society: The Development of Higher Psychological Processes*. Cambridge, MA: Harvard University Press.

White, R. T. (1994). Dimensions of content. In P. J. Fensham, R. F. Gunstone and R. T. White (eds), *The Content of Science: A Constructivist Approach to its Teaching and Learning*. London: Falmer Press, pp. 255–62.

Zembylas, M. (2002). The global, the local, and the science curriculum: a struggle for balance in Cyprus. *International Journal of Science Education*, 24(5), 499–519.

PART I

SOME PRESSURES BEING EXERTED ON SCIENCE EDUCATION

EDITOR'S INTRODUCTION

The emphasis in Part I is on the intersection between trends towards the globalization of the science curriculum, the link between achievement in science education and economic development, and what is actually assessed in science education at world level.

In Chapter 1, Burbules and Torres outline the confluence of pressures towards economic globalisation, pointing out that their impact has, so far, been patchy. While recognising the more limited scope of response now possible by nation states, educational policy is still set at that level. They suggest that events can be monitored by examining: the use and meaning of educational 'buzz words'; the relative roles of national and international organisations in governing policy; the changing relationships between race, gender, social class and the state in the arena of educational provision. Educational initiatives that seem to run counter to globalization are: a concern with educational quality as the key to equity of provision; a direct address to the demands of sustainable ecological development; access to information and communication technologies for all; an emphasis on multiculturalism. Overall, they see the response of national educational systems to globalization to be a greater emphasis within the curriculum on the development of: flexibility and adaptation of response to changing circumstances; the skills of coexistence with others; the retention of a sense of identity in an ever-changing world.

Questions that you may care to address might include:

- What impact does globalisation seem to have had so far on the nation state in which you reside?
- What significance has this impact had so far for the curriculum, pedagogy and assessment used in science education?
- To what extent does science education, as currently provided and experienced, support a flexibility of response to changing circumstances, the ability to coexist with others, the development of a sense of identity?
- What are the likely consequences of currently planned changes in science education for these educational outcomes?

In Chapter 2, Drori looks at the relationship between science education and economic development. He notes that, since the 1970s, national states seem to have firmly believed in the efficacy of 'science education for development'. This has led to the global trend of more emphasis on science education. In general, the age range of students who receive science education has been expanded, the curriculum time devoted to the sciences has been increased, and the curriculum has been institutionalised at national or regional level. The expectation has been that this would lead directly to economic development. Drori, in reviewing many national and comparative studies, concludes that they show no clear relationship between achievement in science education, student enrolment in tertiary science education, the curriculum emphasis placed on science and indicators of economic development. He comments on the technical problems associated with the acquisition of suitable data on science education. While conceding that the relationship between science education and economic development may be complex, with many intervening variables, he suggests that one reason may be that 'loose coupling' is at work, i.e. central policy may not be fully reflected in classroom practice.

Some questions that you may care to address might include:

• Where, to what extent and in what way, do governmental statements about science education in your nation state assume a direct and positive relationship with economic development?
• What evidence can you assemble on the relationship between their economic success and earlier attainment in science education?
• What discrepancies known to you exist between curriculum policy and practice in science education?
• If you were seeking a greater impact on economic development, what changes would you make to both policy and practice in science education?

Chapter 3 is taken from an OECD publication that outlines the work in respect of science of the 'Programme for International Student Assessment' (PISA). The major global assessment in respect of science that is due to take place in 2006 will be focused on the level of 'science literacy' achieved by students. The testing will be of the processes of science applied to situations drawn from everyday life such that relevant concepts are used. The results will be scaled so that a full range of achievement can be demonstrated. The Third International Mathematics and Science Study (TIMSS) certainly caused nation states to become very concerned about their 'international ranking' in respect of the results shown. It might be hoped that PISA, by emphasising science literacy, will cause nation states to place a greater emphasis on everyday situations and the application of scientific knowledge and processes.

Some questions you might address could include:

• To what extent is the policy in respect of the assessment of achievement in science education in your nation state currently congruent with that outlined in the PISA scheme?
• What impacts on science curriculum policy in your nation state might the outcomes of the PISA science study have?
• Would any policy changes be welcomed by teachers?
• To what extent might such policy changes actually be implemented in the science classroom?

CHAPTER 1

GLOBALIZATION AND EDUCATION
An introduction

Nicholas C. Burbules and Carlos Alberto Torres

Globalization and Education: Critical Perspectives (2000) New York: Routledge, pp. 1–26

[. . .]
Economic restructuring and the trend toward globalization

> In order to capture the gist of social action, we must recognize the ontological complicity, as Heidegger and Merleu-Ponty suggested, between the agent (who is neither a subject or a consciousness, nor the mere executant of a role or the carrier of a function) and the social world (which is never a mere "thing" even if it must be constructed as such in the objectivist phase of research). Social reality exists, so to speak, twice, in things and in minds, in fields and in habitus, outside and inside of agents. And when habitus encounters a social world of which it is the product, it finds itself "as a fish in water;" it does not feel the weight of the water and takes the world about itself for granted?'[1]

The patterns of global economic restructuring, which emerged in the late seventies, went hand in hand with the implementation of neoliberal policies in many nations. At that time, capitalist management was caught in a profit squeeze, with labor fighting to keep wages high and foreign competitors pressing them to keep prices down. As the economy slowed, state revenues failed to keep pace with social expenditures, and taxpayers began to express resentment toward those who benefited the most from state revenues (the state bureaucracy, welfare recipients, institutions receiving state subsidies, and so on). This led to a breakdown of consensus around the viability and value of the welfare state. The state withdrew from its role as an arbiter between labor and capital, allying itself with capital and pushing labor into a defensive position.[2]

Economic restructuring reflected a world trend characterized by at least the following elements:

1. the globalization of the economy in the context of a new international division of labor and economic integration of national economies (such as emerging common markets and trade agreements);[3]
2. the emergence of new exchange relations and arrangements among nations, and among classes and social sectors within each country, and the emergence of new areas, especially in developed countries, where information and services are becoming more important than manufacturing;

3. the increasing internationalization of trade, reflected in the increasing capacity to connect markets on an immediate basis and to move capital across national frontiers (currently 600 major multinational corporations [MNCs] control 25 percent of the world economy and 80 percent of world trade);
4. the restructuring of the labor market, with the hourly wage being replaced in many settings by piecework remuneration, and the power of unions undermined by a relaxation or nonenforcement of labor legislation;
5. the decrease in capital-labor conflict, mainly due to such factors as the increase of surplus workers (unemployed or underemployed), the intensification of competition; the decrease of profit margins, less protective labor contracts, and the institutionalization of "team concept" strategies;
6. the shift from a rigid Fordist model of production to a model based upon increased flexibility in the use of the labor force, inventories, labor processes, and labor markets, and upon the declining costs and increasing speed of moving products and information from one location of the globe to another;
7. the rise of new forces of production, with industry shifting from an industrial-mechanical model to one governed by the microchip, robotics, and automatic, self-regulating machines, which in turn has led to the emergence of a high-tech information society based on the computer;
8. the growing importance of capital-intensive production, which results in the de-skilling or redundancy of large sections of the workforce, a situation that leads to a polarized labor market composed of a small, highly skilled, and well-paid sector on the one hand, and a large, low-skilled, and low-paid sector on the other;
9. the increase in the proportion of part-time and female workers, many of them now working out of their homes;
10. the increase in the size and importance of the service sector, at the expense of primary and secondary ones; and
11. the ever-increasing financial, technological, and cultural gap between more-developed and less-developed countries, with the only exception being the "newly industrialized countries" (NICs).[4]

[...]

What are the crucial characteristics of globalization?

[...] These seem to include, at the very least:

- in *economic terms*, a transition from Fordist to post-Fordist forms of workplace organization; a rise in internationalized advertising and consumption patterns; a reduction in barriers to the free flow of goods, workers, and investments across national borders; and, correspondingly, new pressures on the roles of worker and consumer in society;
- in *political terms*, a certain loss of nation-state sovereignty, or at least the erosion of national autonomy, and, correspondingly, a weakening of the notion of the "citizen" as a unified and unifying concept, a concept that can be characterized by precise roles, rights, obligations, and status [...];
- in *cultural terms*, a tension between the ways in which globalization brings forth more standardization and cultural homogeneity while also bringing more fragmentation through the rise of locally oriented movements. Benjamin Barber characterized this dichotomy in the title of his book, *Jihad vs. McWorld*;[5] however, a third theoretical alternative identifies a more conflicted and dialectical situation, with both cultural homogeneity and cultural heterogeneity appearing

simultaneously in the cultural landscape. (Sometimes this merger, and dialectical tension, between the global and the local is termed "the glocal.")[6]

Globalization and the state–education relationship

In *educational terms*, there is a growing understanding that the neoliberal version of globalization, particularly as implemented (and ideologically defended) by bilateral, multilateral, and international organizations, is reflected in an educational agenda that privileges, if not directly imposes, particular policies for evaluation, financing, assessment, standards, teacher training, curriculum, instruction, and testing. In the face of such pressures, more study is needed about local responses to defend public education against the introduction of pure market mechanisms to regulate educational exchanges and other policies that seek to reduce state sponsorship and financing and to impose management and efficiency models borrowed from the business sector as a framework for educational decisionmaking.[7] These educational responses are mostly carried out by teacher unions, new social movements, and critical intellectuals, often expressed as opposition to initiatives in education such as vouchers or publicly subsidizing private and parochial schools.

This poses a peculiar problem for analysis. Because the relationships between state and education vary so dramatically according to historical epochs, geographical areas, modes of governance, and forms of political representation, and between the differential demands of varied educational levels (elementary, secondary, higher education, adult, continuing, and non-formal education), any drastic alteration of modes of governance (for instance, the installation of a military dictatorship that may rule for several years before yielding hack to democracy) can have multiple, complex, and unpredictable effects on education. This situation calls for a more nuanced historical analysis of the state-education relationship. This problematic is made more difficult by the trend we have discussed above: the erosion in the autonomy of the nation-state in all matters, including educational policy matters.[8]

[. . .]

The dilemmas of globalization

[. . .]

Is it possible, then, to give general answers to the question of how globalization is affecting educational policy and practice worldwide? [. . .] We believe that there can be no single answer; national and local economic, political, and cultural changes are affected by, and actively responding to, globalizing trends within a broad range of patterns. Indeed, because education is one of the central arenas in which these adaptations and responses occur, it will be one of the most myriad of institutional contexts Hence, the answers developed will require a careful analysis of trends in education, including:

- the currently popular policy "buzz words" (privatization, choice, and decentralization of educational systems) that drive policy formation in education and prevailing research agendas based in rational organization and management theories [. . .];
- the role of national and international organizations in education, including teacher unions, parent organizations, and social movements [. . .];
- the new scholarship on race, class, gender, and the state in education (which raises concerns about multiculturalism and the question of identity in education,

critical race theory, feminism, postcolonialism, diasporic communities, and new social movements [. . .].

Questions about the role of participatory action research, popular education, and multicultural democratic struggle emerge as central in these debates. From these critical perspectives might emerge new educational models to confront the winds of change, including education in the context of new popular cultures and nontraditional social movements (and hence the role of cultural studies to understand them); new models of rural education for marginalized areas and the education of the poor; new models for migrant education, for the education of street children, for the education of girls and women, in general, but particularly in the context of traditional societies and cultures that have suppressed women's educational aspirations; new models of partnerships for education (between state, NGO, third-sector, and in some instances religious or private organizations); new models for adult literacy and nonformal education; new models of university/business relationships; and new models for educational financing and school organization (for instance, charter schools).

Some reform initiatives have been actively supported by UNESCO and other UN agencies. These include, for instance, reforms toward universal literacy and universal access to education; educational quality as a key component of equity; education as lifelong education; education as a human right; education for peace, tolerance, and democracy; eco-pedagogy, or how education can contribute to sustainable ecological development (and hence to an eco-economy); and educational access and new technologies of information and communication [. . .] . Thus, the influence of globalization upon educational policies and practices can be seen to have multiple, and conflicting, effects. Not all of these can be classified simply as beneficial or not, and some are being shaped by active tensions and struggles. [. . .]

Conclusion: dilemmas of a globalized education system

[. . .] At the economic level, because globalization affects employment, it touches upon one of the primary traditional goals of education: preparation for work. Schools will need to reconsider this mission in light of changing job markets in a post-Fordist work environment; new skills and the flexibility to adapt to changing job demands and, for that matter, changing jobs during a lifetime; and dealing with an increasingly competitive international labor pool. Yet, schools are not only concerned with preparing students as producers; increasingly, schools help shape consumer attitudes and practices as well, as encouraged by the corporate sponsorship of educational institutions and of products, both curricular and extracurricular, that confront students every day in their classrooms. This increasing commercialization of the school environment has become remarkably bold and explicit in its intentions. [. . .]

The broader economic effects of globalization tend to force national educational policies into a neoliberal framework that emphasizes lower taxes: shrinking the state sector and "doing more with less"; promoting market approaches to school choice (particularly vouchers); rational management of school organizations; performance assessment (testing); and deregulation in order to encourage new providers (including on-line providers) of educational services.[9]

At the political level, a repeated point here has been the constraint on national/state policy making posed by external demands from transnational institutions. Yet, at the same time that economic coordination and exchange have become increasingly well regulated, and as stronger institutions emerge to regulate global economic activity, with globalization there has also been a growing internationalization of global conflict, crime, terrorism, and environmental issues, but with an inadequate development of political institutions to address them. Here, again, educational institutions may have a crucial role to play in addressing these problems, and the complex network of intended and unintended human consequences that have followed from the growth of global corporations, global mobility, global communication, and global expansion. In part, this awareness may help to foster a more critical conception of what education for "world citizenship" requires.

Finally, global changes in culture deeply affect educational policies, practices, and institutions. Particularly in advanced industrial societies, for instance, the question of "multiculturalism" takes on a special meaning in a global context. How does the discourse of liberal pluralism—which has been the dominant framework for multicultural education in developed societies learning to live with others within a compact of mutual tolerance and respect—extend to a global order in which the gulf of differences becomes wider, the sense of interdependence and common interest more attenuated, and the grounding of affiliation more abstract and indirect (if it exists at all)? With the growing global pressures on local cultures, is it education's job to help preserve them? How should education prepare students to deal with the terms of local, regional, national, and transnational conflict, as cultures and traditions whose histories of antagonism may have been held partly in suspension by strong, overarching nation-states break loose when those institutions lose some of their power and legitimacy? To the degree that education can help support the evolving construction of the self and, at a more general level, the constitution of identities, how can multiculturalism as a social movement, as citizenship education, and as an antiracist philosophy in curriculum intervene in the dynamics of social conflict emerging between global transformations and local responses?

In this context, for example, current debates over bilingualism in the United States are surprisingly limited both in their theoretical content and their political foresight. From a theoretical perspective, it really makes no sense to argue *against* the teaching and learning of multiple languages; if anything, students need to develop even more proficiency than just bilingualism. The European experience with youth who are proficient in several languages finds that such skills facilitate interpersonal, academic, and social communication, expand intellectual horizons, and encourage appreciation and tolerance for different cultures.

In this and other respects, the global context presents a fundamentally different sort of challenge to education than in the Enlightenment framework. Whereas previously education was more focused on the needs and development of the individual, with an eye toward helping the person fit into a community defined by relative proximity, homogeneity, and familiarity, education for life in a global world broadens the outlines of "community" beyond the family, the region, or the nation. Today the communities of potential affiliation are multiple, dislocated, provisional, and everchanging. Family, work, and citizenship, the main sources of identification in Enlightenment education, remain important, certainly, but they are becoming more ephemeral, compromised by mobility (whether voluntary or diasporic) and competition with other sources of affiliation, including the full range of what can, be termed, in Benedict Anderson's phrase, "imagined communities."[10] Whereas schools or (before that) tutors acted in *loco parentis*, preparing learners for a relatively predictable range of future opportunities and challenges, schools today confront a series of conflicting, and changing, ad hoc expectations, directed to unpredictable alternative paths of development and to constantly shifting reference points of identification. As a result, educational aims that have more to do with flexibility and adaptability (for instance, in responding to rapidly changing work demands and opportunities), with learning how to coexist with others in diverse (and hence often conflict-riven) public spaces, and with helping to form and support a sense of identity that can remain viable within multiple contexts of affiliation, all emerge as new imperatives.

In closing, we believe that the manner in which such new educational imperatives get worked out in particular national and cultural settings depends upon two over-arching sets of issues. The first is whether, given the decreasing role and influence of the nation-state in unilaterally determining domestic policies, and given the fiscal crisis of public revenues in most societies, there will be a corresponding decline in the state's commitment to educational opportunity and equality, or whether there will simply be a greater turn toward the market, privatization, and choice models that regard the public as consumers who will only obtain the education they can afford. More broadly, will these changes produce an overall decline in the civic commitment to public education itself?

The second key issue is whether the troubles that educational systems experience today, which are not all related to the processes of globalization, signal a more deeply felt and decisive dilemma in developed and developing societies: the question of governability in the face of increasing diversity (and an increased awareness of diversity); permeable borders and an explosion in worldwide mobility; and media and technology that create wholly new conditions shaping affiliation and identification. What is the role of education in helping to shape the attitudes, values, and under-standings of a multicultural democratic citizen who can be part of this increasingly cosmopolitan world?

At least some of the manifestations of globalization as a historical process are here to stay. Even if the particular form of "globalization" presented by the neolib-eral account can be regarded as an ideology that serves to justify policies serving particular interests but not others, the fact is that part of this account is based in real changes (and to be fair, real opportunities, at least for certain fortunate people). The particular ways in which people talk about globalization today may end up being a passing fad. [. . .] At a deeper level something is changing in the areas of economy, politics, and culture that will fundamentally alter the terrain of public and private life. Public education today is at a crossroads. If it carries on as usual as if none of these threats (and opportunities) existed, it runs the risk of becoming increasingly superseded by educational influences that are no longer accountable to public governance and control. In our view nothing less is at stake today than the survival of the democratic form of governance and the role of public education in that enterprise.

Notes

[. . .]
1. Pierre Bourdieu, quoted in Loïc J. D. Wacquant, "Toward a Reflexive Sociology: A Workshop with Pierre Bourdieu," in *Social Theory and Sociology: The Classics and Beyond*, ed. Stephen P. Turner (Cambridge, Eng.: Basil Blackwell, 1996), 213–229.
2. Robert B. Reich, *Education and the New Economy* (Washington, D.C.: National Education Association, 1988); and Robert Reich, *The Work of Nations: Preparing Ourselves for 21st Century Capitalism* (New York: Vintage Rooks, 1992).
3. Andrew Sayer and Richard Walker, *The New Social Economy: Reworking the Division of Labor* (Cambridge and Oxford, Eng.: Blackwell, 1992).
4. Daniel Schugurensky and Carlos Alberto Torres, "Higher Education, Globalization and Exclusion: Latin America and the Caribbean in Comparative Perspective" (paper delivered at the Conference on Public Policy and Higher Education: Cuba, The

Dominican Republic, Puerto Rico, and New York, Centro de Estudios Puertor-riqueños, Hunter College of the City of New York and CUNY Dominican Institute, 22–26 April 1997); Daniel García Delgado, *Estado-Nacidn y Globalización. Fortalezas y Debilidades en el Humbral del Tercer Milenio* (Buenos Aires: Ariel, 1998); Roland Robertson and Habib Haque Khondker, "Discourses of Globalization: Preliminary Considerations," *International Sociology* 13, no. 1 (1998): 25–41; Ray Kiely, "Global-ization, Post-Fordism and the Contemporary Context of Development," *International Sociology* 13, no. 1 (1998): 95–116; and Peter Beyer, "Globalization Systems, Global Cultural Models and Religion(s)," *International Sociology* 13, no. 1 (1998): 79–94.

6. See Robert Arnove and Carlos Alberto Torres, eds., *Comparative Education: The Dialectic of the Global and the Local* (Lahman, Md.: Rowman and Littlefield, 1999).

7. Joel Samoff, *Coping with Crisis: Austerity, Adjustment, and Human Resources* (London and New York: Cassell, 1994); William C. Ayers and Janet L. Miller, eds., *A Light in Dark Times: Maxine Greene and the Unfinished Conversation* (New York: Teachers College Press, 1998); Fox and Brown, *The Struggle for Accountability.* [. . .]

8. Sousa Santos, *Reinventar a Democracia.* [. . .]

9. Geoff Whitty and Tony Edwards, "School Choice Policies in England and the United States: An Exploration of their Origins and Significance," *Comparative Education* 34, no. 2 (1998): 211–27.
[. . .]

10. Benedict Anderson, *Imagined Communities* (New York: Verso, 1991).

CHAPTER 2

SCIENCE EDUCATION AND ECONOMIC DEVELOPMENT

Trends, relationships, and research agenda

Gili S. Drori

Studies in Science Education (2000) 35, 27–58

[. . .]

The globalization of science education: trends and features

Directing global attention towards science education

The global expansion of mass (elementary and secondary) education has increasingly intensified since the 1950s.[1] Such an expansion is justified in human capital terms, by equating education with producing improved populations and by assuming that such improved populations are the basis for improved national progress (see Chabbott & Ramirez, 2000). Since the 1970s, global education policies redirected their focus from literacy and mass education towards science and mathematics education in particular. Two factors contributed to this change in education policy 'fashion.' First, due to the extensive expansion of mass education since the 1950s, many countries reached a 'ceiling effect,' especially in terms of access to primary education (see King, 1989b: 100). Second, the 1970s were the decade of greater international efforts to promote science and technology as the foundations for a prosperous national economy. Peaking with the declaration of 1980 as the Year of Science for Development, international policies – of development, education, and science – encouraged countries to centre their efforts of education expansion on the fields of science and technology. For the past three decades, therefore, the intersection between the policies, or discourses, of science and of education has been strengthened, especially because of their tight reliance on the framework of international economic development, or developmentalism.

As a result of such international policy initiatives, science education expands globally: greater attention is given to science and math education in various countries and more countries are centering their education efforts on these subjects. In addition, such global expansion is reflected through various monitors: evidence of science education expansion is provided in primary, secondary, or tertiary education; when reporting curricular emphasis or enrolment patterns; and, when focusing on 'input' (e.g., investment) or 'output' (e.g., achievement) measures.

In terms of an emphasis on a science curriculum in schools, this change is a part of a global change of 'fashions' in the field of education, or as summarized by Kamens *et al.*

(1996) – 'the rise and fall of curricular types.' This change entails the replacement of the old European classical programme (emphasizing classical languages and humanistic subjects) with a combination of the sciences (mathematics and science instruction) and the arts (humanities, arts, and modern languages). Science and math are, therefore, a fundamental part of what is regarded as a desirable modern curriculum (see, Meyer *et al.*, 1992).

This change in the nature of the modern curriculum established science and mathematics education as an integral feature of education systems worldwide. The dramatic changing point in curricular emphasis on science and mathematics is World War II, and by the 1980s these instruction subjects became essentially universal components of education (Kamens *et al.*, 1996).

Following trends of expansion

Assessing such trends with multiple indicators in various levels of education yields similar patterns of worldwide expansion. First, over time an increasing number of countries engage in science education activities. The number of countries having a ministry for science and technology affairs grew from 24 in 1970 to 73 in 1990 (Jang, 2000). Specifically to science education, '[s]ince the 1960s,' writes Aaron Benavot, 'virtually all developing countries have mandated some form of mathematics and science instruction in public elementary schools' (1992: 155).

Second, among those countries that institutionalize science education activities locally, there is greater emphasis over time on this education field. In other words, not only are more countries engaging in science education, but they also do so in intensifying rates. Such is the case of the instruction time devoted to science and mathematics education; it increases over time – in both primary and secondary schools and in both specialized science and mathematics programmes and in the comprehensive tracks (Kamens *et al.*, 1996: 130). Between 1960 and 1980 the proportion of official curriculum in primary schools devoted to mathematics and to science education rose worldwide by 9.6% (from 16.6 to 18.2) and 8.2% (from 7.3 to 7.9), respectively (N = 79 countries; Benavot, 1992: 156). Similarly, during this 20-year span the average annual hours of instruction of mathematics and science in primary education rose worldwide by 9.6% (from 146.5 hours to 160.6) and 5.1% (from 62.6 hours to 65.8), respectively (N = 55 countries; Benavot, 1992: 156). Overall, by the 1980s about one-third of the total instruction time in lower secondary schools was devoted to these instruction subjects (Kamens & Benavot, 1991: 145, Kamens *et al.*, 1996: 127–130).

This pattern of increase in science and mathematics education is repeated in all global regions, with the exception of Asia. In Asian countries there was a decline in both the proportion of official primary curriculum devoted to the sciences (–11.6%, from 8.6% to 7.6% in 14 Asian countries) and the average annual instruction hours devoted to the sciences in primary schools (–12.9%, from 71.9 hours to 62.6 in 11 Asian countries; Benavot, 1992: 156). Unlike a similar average decline in seven Latin American and Caribbean countries (only in the average annual hours, of 3%), this decline in Asian countries' emphasis on primary science education between 1960–1980 became a point of contention when assessing the effect that science education had on producing the Asian Miracle of the 1980s. A similar perplexing dilemma stems from the comparison between African and Asian countries: Benavot (1992) reports that whereas in 1980 African secondary schools devoted 16.5% (or 13.3 weekly hours) to mathematics, Asian countries devoted merely 14.9% (or 12.1 weekly hours) to this subject.

Last, focusing on enrolment information cross-national evidence again reveals the extent of global expansion in the field of science education. Paralleling an increase in the enrolment in tertiary education in general, enrolment in science education programmes grew dramatically since the 1950s and again since 1970 (Ramirez & Lee, 1995). Also, the number of science and engineering doctorates and the total of scientists and engineers doubles every 15 and 10 years since 1950 (Price and Cozzens, 1997: 135).[2]

Overall, then, science education is expanding globally – in terms of its proportion within education programmes, of its growing enrolments, and of its attractiveness to an increasing number of countries.[3] In other words, over time countries worldwide are expanding their educational efforts in the fields of science, mathematics and technology, while, in parallel, a growing number of countries are institutionalizing educational programmes for science, mathematics and technology. While this expansion trend is marked by obvious regional differences, even slow growing sub-Saharan African countries are expanding their local science fields and actively engaging in world science. This expansion trend is greatly supported by two inter-linked factors: (a) the sponsorship of international organizations and (b) the image of science education as the precursor for human-capital-based economic prosperity.

First, an increasingly dense web of international organizations encourages nation-states to institutionalize science education as an integral part of their education systems.[4] Varied group of organizations – from UNESCO to The World Bank to international associations of scientists and educators, from science- to education- to development-oriented international organizations, whether International Non-Government Organisations (NGOs) or International Government Organisations (IGOs) – all advise that science education is an important building block in preparing local populations for the demands of a globalized economy. To promote this agenda, international organizations sponsor the institutionalization of national programmes of science education, the training of local professionals, and the writing of local policies. In so doing, international organizations set an organizational base for science education and 'teach the norms'[5] that link between science education and economic development.

In addition to the sponsorship of such international organizations and their national clones, science education is also globalizing, due to the image of science education that these organizations are propagating. Therefore, second, science education is also expanding in hope that it encourages national economic development. The following section describes this common-wisdom, or belief, that science education is at the root of economic development.

Conceiving of a link between science, education, and development: the policy model of 'science education for economic development'

'More and more we see that competition in the international marketplace is in reality a "Battle of the Classrooms",' says Norman Augustine, the CEO and President of Lockheed & Martin Corporation[6]. This statement reflects the widespread belief that science, education, and lately science education are critical factors to achieving national economic development. Today the image of science education is inextricably dependent on its goal – preparing children to take their place in a prosperous, knowledge- and technology-based, globally-integrated, national economy. As mentioned earlier, this image is crystallized in numerous texts about science education – from policy statements to academic studies to news media articles. Such texts explicate the discourse of global science education, or the dominant perspective about science education. While this discourse has two variants[7], the overwhelmingly powerful image is the one that links science education with economic development. I label this image as the policy model, or discourse, of 'science education for development.'[8]

The 'science education for development' policy model praises education, and particularly science education, as a requirement for any modern, civilized, economically-vibrant nation-state. Standing at the junction of a few major global discourses – science, education, and national development – it refers to science education as paving several paths towards national development. While some researchers and policy-makers take a normative approach towards national progress[9], thus assuming that education sets a cultural base for a modern society, most discussions rest on a structural, instrumentalist perspective.[10] According to the structural-instrumental approach, science education brings about direct effects on the structure of the national economy, and, thus, shapes the economic trajectory of the countries that embrace it. Adopting this vision, policy-makers worldwide regard economic growth as dependent on the scientific and technological capabilities of the labour force, which are – in turn – dependent on the foundations provided by science education in primary and secondary schools.

Primary and secondary science education, it is conceived, set the foundation for skilfulness of the labour force. By stressing the importance of such education, providing access to scientific information and technical experiences, and introducing children to independent studies through science education, future members of the national labour force are prepared to assume in the tasks of sophisticated production roles. Such production roles involve both the fostering of local science and technology innovation and the effective transfer of imported technology. This science and technology base – either locally produced or transferred from Core countries – sets a secure foundation for an economy that is fully integrated into the global, modern economy. Even in Third World countries, where education is disjointed from production roles in the formal economy (King, 1989a; Strath, 1997), science education is conceived within the framework of practical education. In general, this model extends the notion of the 'scientific pipeline'[11] to its ultimate outcome in terms of national economic development. Figure 1 illustrates the principles of the 'science education for development' discourse model. Overall, then, while the effects of science education on national development are mediated by the skilfulness of the labour force, the science education – economic development link is still the foundation for a modern and active economy. Sarewitz (1996), when studying American science policy, refers to this belief in science's utility, as 'the myth of infinite benefit.'

Applied to science education, the pervasiveness of the 'science education for development' model implies that science education is judged by its production of, or at least by its relations with economic performance. In other words, science education is measured by its ability to shape the national trajectory in economic terms. As mentioned earlier, this judgement is at the core of recent reform initiatives. Davies and Guppy (1997) describe the tenets of this policy model, as well as considerations of global economic competition, as on the minds of education reformers. This mindset leads local leaders to transform education programmes (Torney-Purta, 1990). For example, explicitly expressing their hope of improving US student standing in international standardized tests, the governors of ten American states convened in 1999 to instate a new curriculum and rigorous exams to raise student performance (Archibold, 1999).

While education reform initiatives have such local dimension, most education initiatives draw from international organizations.[12] Numerous international organ-

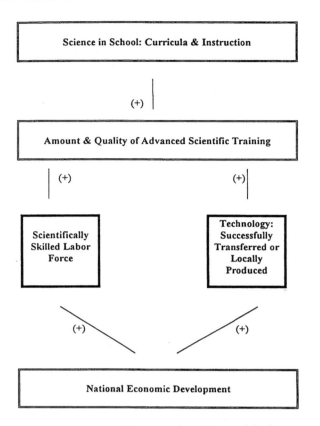

Figure 1 The image of science: the policy model of 'science education for development'

izations, IGOs and INGOs, are devoted to science education. Some IOs, such as UNESCO and the International Institute for Educational Planning (IIEP), have a direct link with the theme of science and mathematics education; other IOs, such as The World Bank and IMF, have an indirect link, which is mediated by the common belief that science education efforts shape economic potential. All such IOs, regardless of their formal goal, *build-up and transmit* the 'science education for development' model. They assist in the supply of science education needs (from teacher training material to laboratory equipment), in the drafting of science and mathematics curriculum (from the writing of school textbooks to setting science education priorities), and in the setting of expectations (from setting benchmarks for student achievement to implanting the rationale of the 'science education for development' model).[13] In setting both the normative and operational basis for this global diffusion process, IOs are pivotal to the field of science education. IOs are, therefore, as Martha Finnemore (1993, 1996) phrases, 'teachers of norms.'

One such IO-taught norm is that science education – in its role as the purveyor of economic prosperity – is a technical solution to a national problem, phrased in terms of efficiency, compatibility, and resource allocation. Yet, in spite of its portrayal as a neutral policy model, the 'science education for development' discourse is heavily laden with value-judgments. This model, essentially, promotes a vision of science education as (a) national, (b) systemically planned, (c) realist, (d) development-oriented, economic-centered, and (e) utilitarian.[14] As such, it infuses countries that adopt science education receipts with the notion that they should not only strive for economic development – a uni-dimensional measure of social progress, yet, nevertheless, an understandable goal considering the terrible conditions in which most of the world population lives in – but, more to my point, that they should judge the effectiveness of their education programmes by this uni-dimensional yardstick. In other words, science education initiatives are justified by their contribution to future economic prosperity and re-assessed by such future effects.

In spite of its faults, this imagery of science education is very powerful: as mentioned earlier, it sets the tone for international and national actions in the fields of science, of education, and of development. Furthermore, this image is built on the foundation set by the constructed tales of its validity, such as the explanation of the economic success of the Asian Tiger economies by their previous investment in science education. It is this image that encourages countries worldwide to embrace science education – to expand science-related curriculum, to increase enrolments in the sciences, and to emphasize the importance of student achievement in international standardized tests of science and mathematics. Policy-makers worldwide attribute economic success to their nation's foundation in the sciences. Yet, is this assumption valid? Does greater emphasis on science education result in greater economic prosperity? The following section addresses these questions by reviewing cross-national empirical studies of the relationships between science education and economic development.

Science education affecting economic development: a battle of the experts

The assumption regarding the link between science education and economic growth was well-established as a common wisdom, much earlier then any evaluation of such a link. Moreover, in spite of the wide acceptance of science education as an important contributor to establishing economic development, few are the empirical tests of this 'truth.' Much like the emphasis given to this topic in policy circles, early evaluation studies discuss the effect of education, in general, on economic development, and only recently – with the parallel change in the policy focus towards science education – do evaluation studies zero on the effects of science education in particular on economic development. Most importantly, throughout the past three decades researchers could not agree as for the direction of such effects: some studies confirm that science education contributes to greater economic development (i.e., positive effects), others contend that science education hinders economic development (i.e., negative effects), while some find no relationship (i.e., zero effect). Some of this discrepancy may be attributed to the methodological differences among the studies: they draw on different data, rely on cross-national comparative methods or case-studies, and employ various statistical methodologies. In the following Section I review comparative empirical studies of the effects of science education on economic development, addressing their different findings and their unique methodologies.

Previous research and theoretical positioning

Harbison and Myers' 1964 study, *Economics, Manpower, and Economic Growth*, paved the way for all cross-national efforts to assess the effect of education on economic development. Relying on the pioneering work of Thomas Schultz that laid out the foundations of human-capital theory (his 1963 book, *The Economic Value of Education*), Harbison and Myers reported a positive association between a country's level of education enrolment and economic development. Their conclusions relied on two types of empirical information: first, a set of simple cross-sectional tabulations between levels of national wealth and levels of secondary education enrolment, and second, some individual-level analyses showing that in many countries educated individuals receive higher salaries. These 'proofs' are obviously highly problematic. First, the cross-sectional nature of their tabulations prohibits them from truly assessing cause-and-effect relationship between education and national wealth; it may be that richer nations are those expanding education and not vice versa.[15] Second, drawing conclusions for cross-national patterns from individual-level analyses falsely assumes that aggregated salaries are any indication of national wealth. Last, their conclusions are drawn from bivariate analyses; as such, their models are unable to include the necessary control variables, which were adequately added to subsequent research. Indeed, their study quickly became the target of much criticism. In addition to pointing to these faults, early 1970s critics argued that education is a marker of status in a game of credentials and that education plays little or indirect role in determining overall productivity or national wealth (e.g., Spence, 1973; Boudon, 1974; Thurow, 1975; Anderson & Bowman, 1976).

In spite of these limitations of Harbison and Myers' research, other researchers offered empirical support for their general conclusions. These researchers found that national economic development is encouraged by an expanded scientific manpower (Blute, 1972; Inhaber, 1977), high student achievement levels (Inkeles, 1977), and a high number of 'publishing scientists' (Price, 1964 in Inhaber, 1977). Similarly, the general expansion of primary, secondary, and tertiary education was also shown to positively affect national economic standing: Meyer, Hannan, Rubinson, and Thomas (1977) focus on such effects by school enrolments between 1950–1970, Walters and Rubinson (1983) focus on secondary education in the United States between 1933–1969, Hage, Garnier and Fuller (1988) compare French and American secondary education's effects during 1950–1975, and, last, Ramirez and Lee (1995) observe cross-national effects of primary, secondary, and tertiary education enrolments on real GDP.[16] In general, these studies show that national economic growth is enhanced by both science and education indicators. These findings confirm the beliefs of early development theorists, adhering to the modernization theory and its neo-classical economic approach[17]: expanded education, with an emphasis on science, positively affects economic growth.

Dependency theorists attacked these findings, arguing that national emphasis on science and education, especially in less developed countries, carries the hidden agenda of perpetuating underdevelopment. They maintain that the current format (structures and themes) of education in general and of science education in particular further establish Western domination on the minds of people in underdeveloped countries and further cripples their national economies. Science education, therefore, assumes the role as mis-education; it is geared to educate local populations to their production roles in the margins of a global, capitalist economy, dominated by the core, industrialized countries. In other words, education in less developed countries provides the population with skills that are not applicable to the state and needs of their own economies, but rather suits the requirements set of the Core. In empirical terms, therefore, dependency theorists expect that the expansion of science education will negatively affect national economic growth in non-Core countries. Yet, while carefully crafting their theoretical arguments (e.g., Sagasti, 1973; Nandy, 1988), few are the studies that empirically show such a negative effect. Moreover, most of these studies were case studies (e.g. Stepan, 1978), leaving very few studies to rely on cross-national empirical evidence.

Among these few empirical comparative studies, Shenhav and Kamens (1991) report a negative cross-national effect of the national degree of scientific publication on subsequent economic performance. Such effect is most pronounced at the poorer countries: the effect is negative and significant with the group of 44 underdeveloped countries or 77 non-Western countries, yet the effect is positive and significant for 23 Western countries. These findings mean that whereas in Western countries greater rate of scientific publication enhances economic development, in poor countries such scientific efforts inhibit economic development. Moreover, the poorer the country is, the stronger the negative effect of science on economic development. In summary, their results show that science relates to its social context in unique ways in developed as in less developed countries and that in poor countries science cripples subsequent economic development. Yet, in spite of their findings, Shenhav and Kamens hesitate to fully embrace dependency arguments. Rather, they re-frame their findings within institutional terms and explain the observed negative effects of scientific activity on economic growth as evidence of the 'costs of isomorphism.' In other words, they stress that rather then regarding their findings as evidence for the direct manipulation by the powerful nations, the '[l]ack of economic efficiency can be considered a "legitimation cost"' (1991: 538).

Embracing their conclusions, Benavot (1992) examines the cross-national effects of curricular content (measured by the share of official curriculum devoted to a particular subject) on economic growth between 1960–1985. He concludes that since science education is the curricular subject 'most closely associated with a Western, rationalistic, cause-and-effect view of the world,' then its effect on economic growth 'may have more to do with "hidden" cultural rules, orientations, and worldview being transmitted than the specific scientific content being taught' (1992: 172–173). Yet unlike Shenhav and Kamens, Benavot finds positive effects of science education on economic growth. '[A]nnual hours of instruction devoted to science education,' he summarizes, 'has strong, positive effects in both additive and multiplicative models and in both samples examined [total 63 countries and 43 less developed countries; GD]' (1992: 171). This encouraging finding is rather perplexing, though, in light of its accompanying effects on economic growth: Benavot also finds consistent negative effects of prevocational education and positive effects of art and music education. Thus, while his findings and conclusions in regards to science education resonate with the general agenda of economic development, it is his findings regarding art, music and prevocational education and his resistance to confronting their role that is rather discouraging as a whole.

These two latest studies relating science and economic development join a growing tradition of cross-national studies, which emerged from the criticism of early, and rather methodologically primitive, cross-national studies. Since the mid-1980s theory and research in the area of science education and economic development changed in four major ways. First, from a technical standpoint, current research relies on multivariate and longitudinal statistical methodologies, thus it is able to determine the direction of causality, to control for intervening factors, and to allow sufficient time lags for such effects to occur. Second, current research acknowledges that the effects of science education on economic development are mediated by the nature of local society: the structure and themes of the local education system, the local economy, or the local polity in general. Stressing this point most clearly, Rubinson and Brown (1994) argue that education systems that are organized around status-maintenance through credential control are more likely to emulate schooling that is un-related with local economic needs. To date, unfortunately, there are no attempts to implement such insights into empirical cross-national research, by such techniques as introducing control variables into the multivariate analyses. Third, such recent comparative studies follow neo-institutional insights, emphasizing the central role of globalization pressures and world society in the diffusion of educational practices. This tradition, which is also anchored in empirical cross-national research, is well established in the field of comparative education.[18] Last, continuous and amplified interest in the effects of science education lead to an increase in data gathering efforts and such expanded data allow researchers (a) to observe changes over time and (b) to shift from a focus almost exclusively on enrolments (a quantity measure) to a focus on the *quality* of science education.

Latest research efforts

Until recently, cross-national measures of educational quality were indirect and unreliable. Such measures, as for example the investment in education, vary greatly, by definition, among nation-states and its cross-national gathering is, thus, unreliable. Other measures indicate science education only indirectly: evidence of scientific publication capacity, while indicating the contribution to the body of scientific knowledge, relates mostly to the quality of scientific activity rather then to the quality of science education in particular. Yet the efforts of the International Association for the Evaluation of Education (IEA) since the 1960s enable researchers to compare achievement information for reasonable samples of students, in various subjects, and in numerous countries. Early efforts to gather cross-national achievement information centered on merely 10 to 13 nation-states. Five such international tests of educational achievement in science and mathematics have been executed since 1964, by various agencies and they offer such comparative information for no more then thirty countries. While still suffering from problems of incompatibility and small sample size, these data offer a first chance to assess comparatively the effects of the quality of science education on economic development.

Hanushek and Kim (1996) employ these cross-national test scores in their admirable attempt to regress cross-national science and mathematics achievement scores on economic development in a causal manner. They find substantial positive effects of science and mathematics achievement levels on subsequent economic growth. Yet, in their effort to execute a panel model while still lacking longitudinal data and while having data for only a handful of countries, they create a composite score based on the five available international education tests. Assuming that national ranking of performance in these tests is consistent over time, they infer achievement scores for cases with missing data from national achievement scores at other tests or other time points.[19] Such stipulation and manipulation of the achievement data renders their information tautological and their conclusions unreliable. Similarly, Hanson *et al.* (1996), in an attempt to rely on SIMS data and to relate it with labour force placement, still employ cross-sectional, thus not causal, models and thus render their research findings problematic.

Today, the results of the Third International Mathematics and Science Study (TIMSS) allow for a more careful empirical examinational of curricular differences among nation-states. TIMSS offers an abundance of information: test scores in a variety of fields (science, mathematics and reading), for a variety of grades (4th, 8th and 12th graders), centralized administration that assures cross-national standardization of the tests and their conditions, and the prospects of repeated tests every few years (thus offering longitudinal data from a single source, which is crucial for panel analyses).[20] In addition, TIMSS findings changed the policy atmosphere in regards to science education: because it refutes the conclusions of such studies as the American Coleman Report and the British Plowden Report (which inferred that student achievement is attributed not to school environment, policy or curriculum, but rather to social background and family characteristics), TIMSS revived the interest in curricular reforms and school restructuring, and, as a result, it encouraged initiatives for gathering cross-national information on various education system features.[21] Most importantly for the study of student achievement and economic development, TIMSS offers, for the first time, achievement information for a reasonable number of countries; 45 countries participated in the first 1995/6 test.[22]

Taking a 'first shot' at these TIMSS data and investigating their effects on national economic development, Ramirez *et al.* (1998) still struggle to offer sound results. They find a positive relationship between test scores and economic growth (using two measures for test scores). They also find that neither scientization of the labour force nor increased scientific activities mediate between achievement and the economy, thus questioning the assumption of the 'science education for development' model that the quality, as well as quantity, of the labour force links science education and economic benefits. Rather, they find that the powerful intervening factors are those related to the structure of the polity and the economy; they point to such factors as previous level of economic development, the country's economic attractiveness (investment rate), and general literacy (level of secondary education). Moreover, since such factors may affect both student achievement and economic growth, they render their relationship as spurious. 'Test scores,' they conclude, 'may very well be the byproduct of effective national development policies, not a separate and distinct cause of economic growth.' (1998: 19).

Overall, then, the nature of the research on science education and economic development went through several fundamental changes: greater availability of cross-national measures, over a longer time period, and more sophisticated methodologies. Yet, in spite of these changes, cross-national empirical studies of the effects of science education on economic development are still plagued with methodological problems. Such methodological problems render any adjudication of the science education – economic development connection unreliable. The core problem currently is the availability of cross-national data, especially monitoring the quality of science education programmes.

[. . .]

Assessing the state of current research

In spite of the great interest among policy-makers and academicians in the effects of science education on economic development, current research does not offer clear answers for this question. Rather, current research suffers from both empirical problems and theoretical 'entrenchment.'

Empirical impediments

Currently, available cross-national data on student achievement are still inappropriate for the execution of proper modeling of the effects of science education on economic development. The history of collecting such data is too short to execute proper panel models and data are available for too few countries to execute the preferred multiple indicator methodologies. More appropriate data are available for other dimensions of science education, such as for enrolment into science education programmes. This data problem is the major impediment for current studies of science education and economic development.

In addition, the research tradition that examines the effects of science education on national economic development – much like the policy it sets to assess – is immersed in a debate over the technicalities of the models: measurement, indicators, control variables and appropriate time lags. Even these days, when TIMSS results finally provide comparative researchers with better measurement of cross-national variation in the quality of science education by specific topics, researchers still squabble over the validity of its measures, pointing to such potential problems as low cross-item correlation among TIMSS content items.

Moreover, most research on this topic employs 'quantity' measures, namely enrolments. While this data is abundantly available, cross-nationally, it ignores the dimension of the quality of education. To shape a country's economic future, however, science education programmes have to be effective not merely in drawing attention but also in providing the appropriate knowledge, namely the scientific and technical skills that are transferable into economic productivity. It is still debatable whether TIMSS data offer an indicator for such production-related skills. Even if so, comparative quality measures of science and mathematics education, such as achievement scores, are not available for tertiary education. Thus, all current analyses privilege primary and secondary schooling, while neglecting to assess the effects of science, mathematics and engineering education at the tertiary level.

Finally and most importantly, this research tradition has produced inconsistent results. In spite of the great improvements in the quality and availability of cross-national indicators of science education and of economic development, and in spite of the related advances in methodologies of comparative research, the direction of the effect – positive, negative or no effect – is still inconclusive, at best.

In summary, current empirical studies of the effects of science education on economic development suffer from multiple empirical problems: data availability, modeling ambiguity, and, thus, inconsistent results.

Theoretical impasse

On a theoretical sphere, advocates of each world-system theory – modernization or dependency – are entrenched within their perspective. They each repeatedly cite the findings – positive or negative effects, respectively – that support their assumptions. Their opinions also diverge on the explanations: for example, on what are the motivations or mediating factors – functional needs or capitalist interests. In this sense, these two theories reached an impasse: they offer competing function-based explanations but no way to adjudicate between them.

However, regardless of their diverging stands on the underlying mechanism and regardless of their findings of positive or negative effects, most researchers are immersed in a realist perspective over the whole issue. They not only investigate, but also expect that, science education has effects on economic development, rather then assessing the validity of the conceptual link itself. Such studies analyze, review and assess science education from within the framework of the 'human capital imperative'[23], thus accepting the 'science education for development' model as a taken-for-granted proposition. What unites the different neo-Marxist and neo-liberal theories is, thus, their utilitarian vision of the social institutions of science and education (see, Davies & Guppy, 1997: 444).

In general, the field of comparative science education studies is itself a captive of the myth of 'science education for development,' embracing the role of science education as a means for achieving economic progress. Even researchers finding no relationship or negative effects of science education on economic development, use their results as a platform for future reforms of the education system so to wield the expected economic benefits from it; they do not conclude from such findings that the conceptual connection itself should be re-examined. Overall, therefore, the realist perspective does not allow researchers to re-examine the conceptual connection itself, or question the link between science education, development and economics.

World polity perspective

Recent world polity studies, drawing attention to the global factors as driving the expansion of science education and re-directing attention to the role of education as a social institution, offer some re-examination of the assumptions and cultural forces behind this conceptual link. For example, advocates of this world polity perspective argue that '[B]road curricular outlines [and the increasing emphasis on science and mathematics education; GD] are less affected by economic development, political forces and the degree of educational expansion at the national level than by the broader currents of world history and the nation's location in that history' (Kamens *et al.*, 1996: 138).

This approach, demonstrated in numerous comparative studies of education, science and other national institutions[24], draws on the notion that education is a social institution and that ritual and myth are the major motivating factors in its global institutionalization. Building upon Meyer's canonized work defining education as an institution (Meyer, 1977), others continue to emphasize the cultural forces that drive the worldwide expansion of various educational forms – from mass education (Ramirez & Boll, 1982; Ramirez & Ventresca, 1992) to women's incorporation into education systems (Ramirez & Wotipka, 1999) to science education (Ramirez & Drori, 1992; Ramirez *et al.*, 1998). While sharing a global and comparative perspective with modernization and dependency theories, world polity theory differs from these realist theories in several essential ways. It relies on cultural and constructivist interpretation of progress and social change, rather than attributing power struggles among real actors; it traces linkages with the world polity, without assuming dependency on core-periphery continuum; it identifies global similarities, rather than focusing on differences and barriers; and, last, it regards legitimacy and authority as motivating factors, which are distinct from economic and political power.

Studies of science education adhering to this perspective focus on the features of its worldwide expansion. First, they note the intense levels of isomorphism across national science education programmes. Elizabeth McEneaney (1998) shows that science education curricula across the world take similar form: teaching similar subjects, but more importantly prescribing similar modes of thinking and acting, a similar range of pursuable questions and a similar notion of who may take the role of 'the scientist.' Analyzing the content of 265 science textbooks from 60 countries, published since the turn of this century, she shows that such similarities go beyond the changing of pedagogical 'fashions.' Rather, such similarities reflect an intensifying trend towards cross-national homogenization – of form and of content.

Second, this research tradition also notes the high degree of loose coupling among the various dimensions of science education. Loose coupling describes a structural condition of limited co-ordination among various spheres of activity within a single social field. Applied to science education, research shows that policy initiatives in science education are divorced from actual activity in this field, especially in developing countries (Ramirez & Drori, 1992). Such disjuncture between policy and practice in science education is attributed to the ritualistic nature of institutionalizing science education in these countries. In other words, in their haste to 'catch up' with the developed countries and with the understanding that science education results in greater prosperity, developing countries 'cut and paste' from international science education initiatives.

The criteria for such 'cut and paste' strategies are unclear: some countries follow their resource limits, while others follow in the tracks of their neighbouring or net-working countries. In this sense, science education policies based on best practice' do much to alienate (or loosely couple) education from its local context, or 'needs.' International organizations, again, contribute to this phenomenon of loose coupling: great differences in themes and 'styles' are evident between programmes originating from different institutions or sponsoring nations. Also, loose coupling best describes the gap between the general nature of policy statements originating from policy initiatives of IOs and the particular nature of the curriculum and materials available to teachers (see, Lewin 1995: 215). Overall, loose coupling becomes a feature of contemporary global conditions, especially among the poor and weak countries.

In summary, world polity research offers an opportunity to break the empirical and theoretical impasse in the current investigation of the effects of science educa-tion on economic development. Empirically speaking, the recent attempt by Ramirez *et al.* (1998) is a step in the right direction. Yet, they are still far from offering a proper empirical investigation and a conclusive answer to the current debate. Theoretically, by 'stepping outside' the realist perspective, world polity theory allows the assessment of the basic assumptions themselves.
[. . .]

Concluding comments

[. . .]

I do not offer a Luddite approach, suggesting that we revoke all science educa-tion initiatives merely because their effects on economic development are inconclusive. Also, it is not my intention to suggest that investigating the link between science education and economic development is futile merely because of methodological diffi-culties. These methodological points of contention will be solved by future, more sophisticated, comparative studies, relying on better data sources. Rather, I call for a more cautious application of science education policies, especially when such policies have the expectation of economic benefits as their underlying assumption.

Notes

1   For reviews and examinations of the global expansion of mass education, see Meyer *et al.*, 1977; Craig, 1981; Lockheed & Verspoor, 1990; Fuller & Rubinson, 1992.
2   Note that the overall expansion of science education enrolments parallels a decline in the *proportion* of science education enrolments within general enrolments. In other words, while the overall number of students in science, mathematics and technology programmes is growing, their proportion of the total number of students is declining.
3   Additional reviews of global over-time expansion of science and mathematics educa-tion can be found in UNESCO, 1986; McKnight *et al.*, 1987; Holmes & McLean, 1989; and Meyer *et al.*, 1992.
4   Numerous studies document the effects of international organizations on the global expansion of science policy (Finnemore, 1996), science ministries (Jang, 2000), mass education (Ramirez & Ventresca, 1992), tertiary science enrolments (Ramirez & Lee, 1995), and women's penetration into science education (Ramirez & Wotipka, 1999). See also King, 1989b for a thorough review of the involvement of internal organ-izations in science education programmes.
5   Martha Finnemore (1996) uses this term to describe the imprinting of local societies with the themes that are carried by international organizations. In particular, her research addresses UNESCO and science policy and The Red Cross and humanitar-ian norms.

6 Quoted in Ramirez *et al.*, 1998:5.

7 An alternative view of science, emerging in policy texts since the early 1990s, is that the social role of science is related to the global expansion of human rights. Such texts make plain that science should better human rights conditions by expanding the benefits of science: improving agricultural production or introducing better health care. Yet, these texts most often also reduce the notion of human rights to economic development, by defining 'the right for economic development' as a pivotal human right. This variant of the discourse about science is, therefore, not only marginal in policy circles, but also subsumed under the grand narrative of developmentalism.

8 I previously describe this policy model in regards to science education, Drori, 1998.

9 The normative approach proclaims that to national progress depends on the gradual change in the nature of the people who together compose nation-states rather then by structural changes. Social change is, therefore, caused by the change in the normative orientation of the members of society – changes in the values, motivations, and psychological forces of society's members. Rooted in Weberian notions, this perspective nourished the study of (a) normative effects on social change to consider the characteristics of the 'modern man' (e.g. Inkeles & Smith, 1974) and (b) the components of the 'mental virus' and the processes by which it 'transmits' modernity (e.g. McClelland, 1961, 1969).

10 The distinction between these two sociological perspectives to development – normative versus structural/instrumental – touches upon their diverging fundamental visions of social change and of the role of individuals and institutions. Essentially, the normative perspective locates the source of social change in individuals, their attitudes and values, while the structural/instrumental perspective focuses on change in the organizational frameworks. Yet, regardless of their stand in this fundamental sociological debate, both perspective are realist theories, which connect cause to effect – in this case, science education to changes in economic development – and accept this connection itself as self evident.

11 This term is used to describe the link between scientific training in various education levels and science placement in the labour market; see, Hanson *et al.*, 1996.

12 See, for example, Nagel & Snyder (1989) and Meyer, Nagel & Snyder (1993) for discussions of the global-local tensions in setting education programmes.

13 See King (1989b: 111–113) for a detailed description of the manpower planning undercurrents in education and technology policies, as prescribed by IIEP.

14 The five major assumptions of the 'science education for development' model are:

(1) Science education, as well as development, are *national* projects; in other words, their goal is to provide benefits for the nation as a whole, and they rely on national sponsorship (both financial support and societal legitimacy).

(2) National development through science education is achieved through the implementation of a particular plan, or systemic programme (unlike national policies for the support of, for example, the arts). This plan is explicit in its connections between science education and economic development.

(3) Its realist vision portrays science and education to be 'real' social institutions, rather than socially constructed phenomena. This realist vision places science within a concrete framework and hampers any attempt to consider it within a cultural framework.

(4) Most importantly, this vision subsumes all discussion of science education to the discursive regime of 'national development' (see, Fiala & Gordon-Lanford, 1987; Chabbot & Ramirez, 2000). Moreover, the vision of national development is reduced to economic development.

(5) This economy-based vision is also utilitarian in essence; meaning, it judges science soley by its end-products or consequences.

15 This problem of confusing cause-and-effect relationships due to reliance on cross-sectional data also plagues the findings of Inkeles (1977) that student achievements positively affect economic development.

16 For a review of the effects of education on economic development, see Chabbott & Ramirez, 2000.

17 See, for example, Smelser, 1963; Eisenstadt, 1966.

18   See, for example, Benavot *et al.* (1991) and Fuller & Rubinson (1992) for the application of this tradition – namely, world polity perspective – to comparative education and see Davies & Guppy (1997) for its review and assessment.
19   Hanushek and Kim inferred such data based on information about 34 countries to predict the missing information for an additional 66 countries. Overall, their conclusions rest on analyses of 100 nation-states, while their original, un-manipulated data are available for only 34 countries.
20   This abundance of data did not, however, dampen the heated debate around their interpretation. For the most forthright difference of opinion, see Gerald Bracey's and Harold Stevenson's exchange in *Educational Leadership*, 1993.
21   While TIMSS was designed to focus on curricular differences, TIMSS-R (the revised version of the comparative test run in summer 1999) acknowledges the additional contribution of other school characteristics, such as school organizational features and teachers' contributions.
22   For a discussion of the limitations of cross-national comparisons based on TIMSS scores and rankings, see Baker, 1993; Bracey, 1996.
23   Guthrie's term, describing science education as an imperative for nation-states to develop their skill resources 'as a strategic means . . . to gain or retain an economically competitive position in the global marketplace'; quoted in Ginsburgh *et al.*, 1991: 14.
24   To mark the central writings and trace the intellectual development of world polity perspective, see Meyer *et al.*, 1977; Thomas *et al.*, Meyer *et al.*, 1997.

References

Anderson, C.A. & Bowman, M.J. (1976) Education and economic modernization in historical perspective. In L. Stone (ed.) *Schooling and society*, Baltimore, MD: Johns Hopkins University Press, 3–19.
Archibold, R.C. (1999) Poor scores by US students lead to 10-State Math efforts, *New York Times*, 6 May 1999.
Baker, D. (1993) Compared to Japan, the US is a low achiever . . . really: new evidence and commentary on Westbury. (Response to Baker by Westbury and Rejoiner by Baker.) *Educational Researcher*, 19: 18–26.
Benavot, A., Yun-Kyung Cha, Kamens, D., Meyer, J.W. & Suk-Ying Wong (1991) Knowledge for the masses: world models and national curricula, 1920–1986. *American Sociological Review*, 56(1): 85–100.
Benavot, A. (1992) Curricular content, educational expansion, and economic growth. *Comparative Education Review*, 36(2): 150–174.
Blute, M. (1972) The growth of science and economic development. *American Sociological Review*, 37: 455–464.
Boudon, R. (1974) *Education, opportunity, and social inequality: changing prospects in western society*, NY: John Wiley.
Bracey, G.W. (1996) International comparisons and the condition of American education. *Educational Researcher*. 25: 5–11.
Chabbott, C. & Ramirez, F.O. (2000) Development and education. In Maureen T. Hallinan (ed.) *Handbook of sociology of education*, NY: Plenum.
Craig, J. (1981) The expansion of education. *Review of Research on Education*, 9: 151–213.
Davies, S. & Guppy, N. (1997) Globalization and educational reforms in Anglo-American democracies. *Comparative Educational Review*, 41(4): 435–459.
Drori, G.S. (1998) A critical appraisal of science education for economic development. In William W. Cobern (ed.) *Socio-cultural perspectives on science education: an international dialogue*, Dordrecht, Netherlands: Kluwer Academic Publishers, 49–74.
Eisenstadt, S.N. (1966) *Modernization: protest and change*, Englewood Cliffs, NJ: Prentice Hall.
Fiala, R. & Gordon-Lanford, A. (1987) Educational ideology and the world educational revolution, 1950–1970. *Comparative Education Review*, 31: 315–332.
Finnemore, M. (1993) International organization as teachers of norms: the United Nations Educational, Scientific, and Cultural Organization and science policy. *International Organization*, 47(4): 567–597.

Finnemore, M. (1996) *National interests in international society*, Ithaca, NY: Cornell University Press.

Fuller, B. & Rubinson, R. (eds.) (1992) *The political construction of mass education: school expansion, the state, and economic change*, NY: Praeger.

Ginsburg, M.B., Cooper, S., Rajeshwari Raghu & Zegarra, H. (1991) Educational reform: social struggle, the state and the world economic system. In Mark B. Ginsburg (ed.) *Understanding educational reform in global context*, NY: Garland Publishing, 3–48.

Hage, J., Garnier, M. & Fuller, B. (1988) The active state, investment in human capital, and economic growth. *American Sociological Review*, 53: 824–837.

Hanson, S.L., Schaub, M. & Baker, D.P. (1996) Gender stratification in the science pipeline: a comparative analysis of seven countries. *Gender and Society*, 10(3): 271–190.

Hanushek, E. & Kim, D. (1996) Schooling, labor force quality, and the growth of nations. unpublished paper.

Harbison, F. & Myers, C. (1964) *Education, manpower, and economic growth*, NY: McGraw-Hill.

Holmes, B. & Mclean, M. (1989) *The curriculum: a comparative perspective*, London: Unwin Hyman.

Inhaber, H. (1977) Scientists and economic growth. *Social Studies of Science*, 7: 517–524.

Inkeles, A. & Smith, D. (1974) *Becoming modern: individual change in six developing countries*, Cambridge, MA: Harvard University Press.

Inkeles, A. (1977) The International Evaluation of Education Achievement: A review. *Proceedings of The National Academy of Education*, 4: 139–200.

Jang, Yong Suk (2000) The worldwide founding of ministries of science and technology, 1950–1990. *Sociological Perspectives*, 43(2).

Kames, D. & Benavot, A. (1991) Elite knowledge for the masses: the origins and spread of mathematics and science education in national curricula. *American Journal of Education*, 99(2): 137–180.

Kames, D., Meyer, J. & Benavot, A. (1996) Worldwide patterns of academic secondary education curricula. *Comparative Education Review*, 40(2): 116–138.

King, K. (1989a) Primary schooling and developmental knowledge in Africa. *Studies in Science Education*, 17: 29–56.

King, K. (1989b) Donor aid to science and technology education: a state of the art review. *Studies in Science Education*, 17: 99–122.

Lewin, K.M. (1995) Development policy and science education in South Africa: Reflection on post-Fordism and praxis. *Comparative Education*, 31(2), 201–221.

Lockheed, M. & Verspoor, A. (1990) *Improving primary education in developing countries*, Washington DC: World Bank.

McClelland, D.C. (1961) *The achieving society*, NY: Free Press.

McClelland, D.C. (1969) *Motivating economic achievement*, NY: Free Press.

McEneaney, E.H. (1998) *The transformation of primary school science and mathematics*, unpublished Ph.D. Dissertation, Stanford University.

McKnight, C., crosswhite, F.J., Dossey, J. Kifer, E., Swafford, J., Travers, K.J. & Conney, T. (1987) *The underachieving curriculum: assessing U.S. school mathematics from an international perspective*, Champaign, IL: Stipes Publishing.

Meyer, J.W. (1977) The effects of education as an institution. *American Journal of Sociology*, 63: 55–77.

Meyer, J.W., Bolt, J., Thomas, G. & Ramirez, F. (1997) World society and the nation-state. *American Journal of Sociology*, 103(1): 144–181.

Meyer, J.W., Kamens, D.H. & Benavot, A. (1992) *School knowledge for the masses: national primary curricular categories in the twentieth century*. London: Felman.

Meyer, J.W., Ramirez, F.O. & Soysal, Y. (1992) World expansion of mass education, 1870–1980. *Sociology of Education*, 65(2): 128–149.

Meyer, J.W., Ramirez, F., Rubinson, R. & Boli-Bennett, J. (1977) The world education revolution. *Sociology of Education*, 50: 242–258.

Meyer, J.W., Nagel, J. & Snyder, C.W. Jr. (1993) The expansion of mass education in Botswana: local and world society perspectives. *Comparative Education Review*, 37(4): 454–475.

Meyer, J.W, Hannan, M., Rubinson, R. & Thomas, G. (1977) National economic development, 1950–1970: social and political factors. In John Meyer and Michael Hannan (eds.) *National development and the world system*, Chicago, IL: University of Chicago Press, 85–116.

Nagel, J. & Snyder, C.W. (1989) International funding of education development: external agendas and internal adaptation – the case of Liberia. *Comparative Education Review*, 33(1): 3–20.

Nandy, A. (1988) *Science, hegemony, and violence: a requiem for modernity*, New Delhi, India: Oxford University Press.

Ramirez, F.O. & Wotipka, C.M. (1999) Slowly but surely? The global expansion of womens participation in science and engineering fields of study. Paper presented at the Comparative and International Education Society meeting, Toronto, Canada, March 1999.

Ramirez, F.O. & Drori, G.S. (1992) The globalization of science: an institutionalist perspective. Paper presented at The American Sociological Association meeting, Pittsburgh PA, August 1992.

Ramirez, F.O. & Boli, J. (1982) Global patterns of educational institutionalization. In Phillip Altbach, R. Arnove, and G. Kelly (eds.) *Comparative education*, NY: Macmillan, 15–36.

Ramirez, F.O. & Ventresca, M. (1992) Institutionalizing mass schooling: ideological and organizational isomorphism in the modern world. In Fuller, Bruce and Richard Rubinson (eds.) *The political construction of education: school expansion, the state, and economic change*, NY: Praeger, 47–60.

Ramirez, F.O. & Lee, M. (1995). Education, science, and development. In Postiglione, Gerald and Lee Wing-On (eds.) *Social change and educational development in Mainland China, Taiwan, and Hong Kong, Hong Kong*: University of Hong Kong Cenre of Asian Studies, 15–39.

Ramirez, F.O, Xiaowei Luo, Schofer, E. & Meyer, J.W. (1998) Science and math achievement and economic growth. Paper presented at the American Educational Research Association meeting, San Diego, CA, April 1998.

Rubinson, R. & Brown, I. (1994) Education and the Economy. In Smelser, N. and R. Swedberg (eds.) *The handbook of economic sociology*, Princeton, NJ: Princeton University Press, 583–599.

Sagasti, F. (1973) Underdevelopment, science and technology: the point of view of the underdeveloped countries. *Science Studies*, 3: 47–59.

Sarewitz, D. (1996) *Frontiers of illusion: science, technology, and the politics of progress*, Philadelphia, PA: Temple University Press.

Shenhav, Y. & Kamens, D. (1991) The cost of institutional isomorphism: science in less developed countries. *Social Studies of Science*, 21: 527–545.

Schultz, T.P. (1963) *The economic value of education*, NY: Columbia University Press.

Smelser, N.J. (1963) Mechanics of change and adjustment to change. In B.F. Hoselitz and W.E. Moore (eds.) *Industrialization and society*, Paris: UNESCO/Mouton, 32–54.

Spence, M. (1973) Job market signaling. *Quarterly Journal of Economics*, 87(August), 355–75.

Stepan, N. (1978) The interplay between socio-economic factors and medical science: yellow fever research, Cuba and the United States. *Social Studies of Science*, 8(4), 397–423.

Strath, A. (1997) *Scientization and economic development*, unpublished Ph.D. Dissertation, Stanford University.

The Economist (1997) Who's top?. *The Economist*, 29 March, 15–16, 21–23.

Thomas, G.M., Meyer, J.W., Ramirez, F.O. & Boli, J. (1987) *Institutional structure: constituting state, society, and the individual*, Newbury Park, CA: Sage Publications.

Thurow, L. (1975) *Generating inequality*, New York: Basic.

Torney-Purta, J. (1990) International comparative research in education: its role in educational improvement in the US. *Educational Researcher*, 21: 32–35.

Unesco (1986) *The place of science and technology in school curricula: a global survey*, Paris: UNESCO.

Walters, P. & Rubinson, R. (1983) Educational expansion and economic output in the US, 1890–1969: A production function analysis. *American Sociological Review*, 48: 480–493.

CHAPTER 3

SCIENTIFIC LITERACY

Organisation for Economic Co-operation and Development

Measuring Student Knowledge and Skills (1999) Paris: OECD, pp. 59–75

An important life skill for young people is the capacity to draw appropriate and guarded conclusions from evidence and information given to them, to criticise claims made by others on the basis of the evidence put forward, and to distinguish opinion from evidence-based statements. Science has a particular part to play here since it is concerned with rationality in testing ideas and theories against evidence from the world around. This is not to say that science excludes creativity and imagination, which have always played a central part in advancing human understanding of the world. Ideas which sometimes appear to have "come out of the blue" have been seized upon by a mechanism which Einstein described as "the way of intuition, which is helped by a feeling for the order lying behind the appearance" (Einstein, 1933). Which ideas are "seized upon" at a particular time has depended historically upon their social acceptability, at that time, so that developments in scientific knowledge depend not only on the creativity of individuals but also on the culture in which they are proposed. But once the creative leap is made and a new theoretical framework for understanding has been articulated, then it has to be followed by painstaking testing against reality. As Hawking (1988) has written:

> A theory is a good theory if it satisfies two requirements: it must accurately describe a large class of observations on the basis of a model that contains only a few arbitrary elements, and it must make definite predictions about the results of future observations.
>
> (Hawking, 1988, p. 9)

Theories that do not meet these requirements – or cannot be tested – are not scientific theories and it is important for an educated citizen to be able to distinguish between the kinds of questions that can be answered by science and those which cannot, and between what is scientific and what is pseudo-scientific.

Definition of the domain

Current thinking about the desired outcomes of science education for all citizens emphasises the development of a general understanding of important concepts and explanatory frameworks of science, of the methods by which science derives evidence to support claims for its knowledge, and of the strengths and limitations of science in the real world. It values the ability to apply this understanding to real situations involving science in which claims need to be assessed and decisions made. For example,

Millar and Osborne (1998) have identified the focus of a modern science curriculum as being: "the ability to read and assimilate scientific and technical information and assess its significance". Their report continues:

> In this approach, the emphasis is not on how to 'do science'. It is not on how to create scientific knowledge, or to recall it briefly for a terminal examination. ... Thus, in science, students should be asked to demonstrate a capacity to evaluate evidence; to distinguish theories from observations and to assess the level of certainty ascribed to the claims advanced.
>
> (Millar and Osborne, 1998)

These should be the products of science education for all students. For some students, the minority who will become the scientists of tomorrow, this will be extended to in-depth study of scientific ideas and to the development of the ability to "do science".

With these points in mind, it is considered that the essential outcome of science education, which should be the focus OECD/PISA, is that students should be *scientifically literate*. This term has been used in different contexts. For example, the International Forum on Scientific and Technological Literacy for All (UNESCO, 1993) offered a variety of views, such as:

> The capability to function with understanding and confidence, and at appropriate levels, in ways that bring about empowerment in the made world and in the world of scientific and technological ideas.
>
> (UNESCO, 1993)

Included in the many different views of scientific literacy (reviewed by Shamos, 1995; see also Graeber and Bolte, 1997) are notions of levels of scientific literacy. For example, Bybee (1997) has proposed four levels, of which the lowest two are "nominal scientific literacy", consisting of knowledge of names and terms, and "functional literacy", which applies to those who can use scientific vocabulary in limited contexts. These are seen as being at levels too low to be aims within the OECD/PISA framework. The highest level identified by Bybee, "multidimensional scientific literacy", includes understanding of the nature of science and of its history and role in culture, at a level most appropriate for a scientific elite rather than for all citizens. It is, perhaps, the assumption that scientific literacy involves thinking at this level of specialisation that causes difficulty in communicating a more attainable notion of it. What is more appropriate for the purposes of the OECD/PISA science framework is closer to Bybee's third level, "conceptual and procedural scientific literacy".

Having considered a number of existing descriptions, OECD/PISA defines scientific literacy as follows:

> Scientific literacy is the capacity to use scientific knowledge, to identify questions and to draw evidence-based conclusions in order to understand and help make decisions about the natural world and the changes made to it through human activity.

The following remarks further explain the meaning condensed in this statement.

Scientific literacy . . .

It is important to emphasise not only that both *scientific knowledge* (in the sense of knowledge about science) and the processes by which this knowledge is developed are essential for scientific literacy, but that they are bound together in this understanding of the term. As discussed in more detail below, the processes are only *scientific processes* when they are used in relation to the subject matter of science. Thus, using scientific processes necessarily involves some understanding of the scientific subject matter. The view of scientific literacy adopted here acknowledges this combination of ways of thinking about, and understanding, the scientific aspects of the world.

. . . use scientific knowledge to identify questions and to draw evidence-based conclusions . . .

In the above definition, *scientific knowledge* is used to mean far more than knowledge of facts, names and terms. It includes understanding of fundamental scientific concepts, the limitations of scientific knowledge and the nature of science as a human activity. The questions to be identified are those that can be answered by scientific enquiry, implying knowledge *about science* as well as about the scientific aspects of specific topics. Drawing *evidence-based conclusions* means knowing and applying processes of selecting and evaluating information and data, whilst recognising that there is often not sufficient information to draw definite conclusions, thus making it necessary to speculate, cautiously and consciously about the information that is available.

. . . understand and help make decisions . . .

The phrase *understand and help make decisions* indicates first, that an understanding of the natural world is valued as a goal in itself as well as being necessary for decision-making and, second, that scientific understanding can contribute to, but rarely determines, decision-making. Practical decisions are always set in situations having social, political or economic dimensions and scientific knowledge is used in the context of human values related to these dimensions. Where there is agreement about the values in a situation, the use of scientific evidence can be non-controversial. Where values differ, the selection and use of scientific evidence in decision making will be more controversial.

. . . the natural world and the changes made to it through human activity

The phrase *the natural world* is used as shorthand for the physical setting, living things and the relationships among them. Decisions about the natural world include decisions associated with science related to self and family, community and global issues. *Changes made through human activity* refers to planned and unplanned adaptations of the natural world for human purposes (simple and complex technologies) and their consequences.

It is relevant to note here, and will be made more explicit later, that scientific literacy is not a dichotomy. That is, it is not suggested that people can be categorised as being either scientifically literate or scientifically illiterate. Rather, there is a progression from less developed to more developed scientific literacy. So, for example, the student with less developed scientific literacy might be able to identify some of the evidence that is relevant to evaluating a claim or supporting an argument or might be able to give a more complete evaluation in relation to simple and familiar situations. A more developed scientific literacy will show in more complete answers and the ability to use. knowledge and to evaluate claims in relation to evidence in less familiar and more complex situations.

Organisation of the domain

The OECD/PISA definition of scientific literacy comprises three aspects:

- *scientific processes* which, because they are scientific, will involve knowledge of science, although in the assessment this knowledge must not form the major barrier to success;
- *scientific concepts*, the understanding of which will be assessed by application in certain content areas; and
- *situations* within which the assessment tasks are presented (this aspect is often referred to in common usage as the "context" or "setting").

Although these aspects of scientific literacy are discussed separately it must be recognised that, in the assessment of scientific literacy, there will always be a combination of all three.

The first two of these aspects will be used both for the construction of tasks and for the characterisation of student performance. The third aspect will ensure that in the development of the assessment tasks due attention is paid to situating the science in a diverse range of relevant settings.

The following sections elaborate the three organising aspects. In laying out these aspects, the OECD/PISA framework has ensured that the focus of the assessment is upon the outcome of science education as a whole.

Scientific processes

Processes are mental (and sometimes physical) actions used in conceiving, obtaining, interpreting and using evidence or data to gain knowledge or understanding. Processes have to be used in relation to some subject matter; there is no meaning to a content-free process. They can be used in relation to a wide range of subject matter; they become *scientific processes* when the subject matter is drawn from scientific aspects of the world and the outcome of using them is to further scientific understanding.

What are commonly described as the processes of science range widely over the skills and understanding needed to collect and interpret evidence from the world around us and to draw conclusions from it. The processes relating to collecting evidence include those concerned with investigation in practice – planning and setting up experimental situations, taking measurements and making observations using appropriate instruments, etc. The development of these processes is included in the aims of school science education so that students can experience and understand the manner in which scientific understanding is built up and, ideally, the nature of scientific enquiry and of scientific knowledge. Few will require these practical skills in life after school but they will need the understanding of processes and concepts developed through practical, hands-on enquiry. Moreover, it has been strongly argued that what is traditionally regarded as the "scientific process", by which conclusions are drawn inductively from observations, and which is still reflected in much school science, is contrary to how scientific knowledge is developed (*e.g.* Ziman, 1980).

Scientific literacy, as identified here, gives higher priority to using scientific knowledge to "draw evidence-based conclusions" than to the ability to collect evidence for oneself. The ability to relate evidence or data to claims and conclusions is seen as central to what all citizens need in order to make judgements about the aspects of their life which are influenced by science. It follows that every citizen needs to know when scientific knowledge is relevant, distinguishing between questions which science can and cannot answer. Every citizen needs to be able to judge when evidence is valid, both in terms of its relevance and how it has been collected. Most important of all, however, every citizen needs to be able to relate evidence to conclusions based on it and to be able to weigh the evidence for and against particular courses of action that affect life at a personal, social or global level.

The distinctions that have just been made can be summarised briefly as giving priority to processes *about* science as compared with processes *within* science. It is important that the process skills listed in Figure 2 be read as being primarily about science and not primarily as they apply within science. All of the processes listed in Figure 2 involve knowledge of scientific concepts. In the first four processes this knowledge is necessary but not sufficient since knowledge about collecting and using scientific evidence and data is essential. In the fifth process the understanding of scientific concepts is the essential factor.

---

1. Recognising scientifically investigable questions.
2. Identifying evidence needed in a scientific investigation.
3. Drawing or evaluating conclusions.
4. Communicating valid conclusions.
5. Demonstrating understanding of scientific concepts.

Figure 2 Selected scientific processes

Some elaboration of these processes follows.

Recognising scientifically investigable questions

Recognising scientifically investigable questions can involve identifying the question or idea that was being (or could have been) tested in a given investigation. It may also involve distinguishing questions that can be answered by scientific investigation from those which cannot, or more openly suggesting a question that it would be possible to investigate scientifically in a given situation.

Identifying evidence needed in a scientific investigation

Identifying evidence needed in a scientific investigation involves identifying the information that is needed for a valid test of a given idea. This may require, for example, identifying or recognising what things should be compared, what variables should be changed or controlled, what additional information is needed, or what action should be taken so that relevant data can be collected.

Drawing or evaluating conclusions

Drawing conclusions or critically evaluating conclusions that have been drawn from given data may involve producing a conclusion from given scientific evidence or data or selecting from alternatives to the conclusion that fits the data. It may also involve giving reasons for or against a given conclusion in terms of the data provided or identifying the assumptions made in reaching a conclusion.

Communicating valid conclusions

Communicating to a specified audience valid conclusions from available evidence and data involves the production of an argument based on the situation and data given, or on relevant additional information, expressed in a manner that is appropriate and clear to the given audience.

Demonstrating understanding of scientific concepts

Demonstrating understanding of scientific concepts by applying appropriate concepts in a given situation involves explaining relationships and possible causes of given changes, or making predictions as to the effect of given changes, or identifying the factors that influence a given outcome, using scientific ideas and/or information which have not been given.

Some scientific knowledge is needed for all five processes. In the case of the first four, however, the knowledge is not intended to be the main "hurdle", since the aim is to assess the mental processes involved in gathering, evaluating and communicating valid scientific evidence. In the fifth process, on the other hand, it is the understanding of the scientific concept involved that is being assessed and this understanding is the main hurdle.

It is important to point out that, for each of the processes listed above, there is a wide range of task difficulties, depending upon the scientific concepts and situations involved. The OECD/PISA assessments will ensure that, through country feedback and the field trial, the items selected for the main study will be at the appropriate level of difficulty for 15-year-olds.

Concept and content

Concepts enable us to make sense of new experiences by linking them to what we already know. *Scientific concepts* are those which help to make sense of aspects of the natural and made worlds. Scientific concepts are expressed at many different levels, from the very broad labels of biological, physical, earth science, etc., under which they are presented in schools, to the long lists of generalisations such as often appear in statements of standards or curricula.

There are many ways of grouping scientific concepts to help the understanding of the scientific aspects of the world around. Sometimes concepts are labels indicating the range of characteristics that define a particular group of objects or events ("mammals", "acceleration", "solvent"); of these there must be several thousands. Concepts can also be expressed as generalisations about particular phenomena (the "laws" or theorems of physics or chemistry), of which there are many hundreds. They can also be expressed as major scientific themes which are more widely applicable and easier to operationalise for assessment and reporting purposes.

OECD/PISA uses four criteria for determining the selection of scientific concepts to be assessed:

– The first of these is relevance to everyday situations. Scientific concepts differ in the degree to which they are useful in everyday life. For example, although the theory of relativity gives a more accurate description of the relationships between length, mass, time and velocity, Newton's laws are more helpful in matters relating to the understanding of forces and motion encountered every day.
– The second criterion is that the concepts and content selected should have enduring relevance to life throughout the next decade and beyond. Given that the major assessment of science is planned to take place in the year 2006, the first cycle of OECD/PISA will focus on those concepts likely to remain important in science and public policy for a number of years.
– The third basis for selection is relevance to the situations identified as being ones in which scientific literacy should be demonstrated.
– The fourth criterion is that the concepts should require to be combined with selected scientific processes. This would not be the case where only recall of a label or of a definition was involved.

Figures 3 and 4 show the outcome of applying these criteria to the concepts and content of science. Figure 3 lists major scientific themes, with a few examples of the concepts relating to them. These broad concepts are what is required for understanding the natural world and for making sense of new experience. They depend upon and derive from study of specific phenomena and events but they go beyond the detailed knowledge that comes from study of these things. The concepts listed in Figure 3 are given to exemplify the meanings of the themes; there is no attempt to list comprehensively all the concepts which could be related to each theme.

The concepts given as examples in Figure 3 indicate that the knowledge that will be assessed relates to the major fields of science: physics, chemistry, biological sciences and earth and space sciences. Test items are classified by the major field of science as well as by the theme, area of application and process which they assess.

Figure 4 lists those areas of application of science that raise issues that the citizens of today and tomorrow need to understand and to make decisions about. It is these applications which guide the selection of content for tasks and items within them. Figure 4, therefore, indicates the areas of application in which the understanding of the concepts in Figure 3 will be assessed.

As indicated earlier, OECD/PISA will include important concepts that are relevant to the science curricula of participating countries without being constrained by the common denominator of national curricula. In accordance with its focus on scientific literacy, it will do this by requiring application of selected scientific concepts and the use of scientific processes in important situations reflecting the real world and involving ideas of science.

Situations

Besides the processes and concepts assessed, the third feature of assessment tasks which affects performance is the situation in which the issues are presented. This is often called the *context* or *setting* of the tasks, but here the word *situation* is used to avoid confusion with other uses of these words. The particular situations are known to influence performance, so that it is important to decide and control the

Structure and properties of matter
(thermal and electrical conductivity)

Atmospheric change
(radiation, transmission, pressure)

Chemical and physical changes
(states of matter, rates of reaction, decomposition)

Energy transformations
(energy conservation, energy degradation, photosynthesis)

Forces and movement
(balanced/unbalanced forces, velocity, acceleration, momentum)

Form and function
(cell, skeleton, adaptation)

Human biology
(health, hygiene, nutrition)

Physiological change
(hormones, electrolysis, neurons)

Biodiversity
(species, gene pool, evolution)

Genetic control
(dominance, inheritance)

Ecosystems
(food chains, sustainability)

The Earth and its place in the universe
(solar system, diurnal and seasonal changes)

Geological change
(continental drift, weathering)

Figure 3 Major scientific themes (with examples of related concepts) for the assessment of scientific literacy

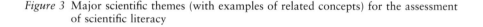

range of situations intended for the assessment tasks. It is not intended to report performance in relation to particular situations but they need to be identified in order to ensure a spread of tasks across those felt to be important and so that they can be controlled, as found necessary from field trials, from one survey to the next to ensure international comparability.

In selecting situations, it is important to keep in mind that the purpose of the assessment in science is to assess the ability of students to apply the skills and knowledge that they have acquired by the end of the compulsory years of schooling. OECD/PISA requires that the tasks should be framed in situations of life in general and not limited to life in school. In the school situation, scientific processes and concepts may be confined to the laboratory or classroom, but increasingly an attempt is being made also in countries' science curricula to apply these to the world outside the school.

Real-world situations involve problems which can affect us as individuals (*e.g.* food and energy use) or as members of a local community (*e.g.* treatment of the water supply or siting of a power station) or as world citizens (*e.g.* global warming,

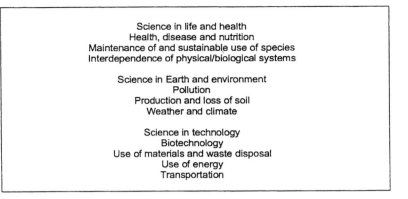

Figure 4 Areas of application of science for the assessment of scientific literacy

diminution of biodiversity). All of these are represented in the range of assessment tasks used in OECD/PISA. A further type of situation, appropriate to some topics, is the historical one, in which understanding of the advances in scientific knowledge can be assessed. In the framework of OECD/PISA the focus of the items will be on matters relating to the self and family (personal), to the community (public), to life across the world (global), and on those which illustrate how scientific knowledge evolves and affects social decisions associated with science (historical relevance).

In an international study it is important that the situations used for assessment items should be chosen in the light of relevance to students' interests and lives in all countries. They should also be appropriate for assessing scientific processes and concepts. Sensitivity to cultural differences has a high priority in task development and selection, not only for the sake of the validity of the assessment, but to respect the different values and traditions in participating countries. Feedback from field trials will be used to ensure that situations chosen for the survey tasks are relevant and appropriate across the different countries, whilst involving the combination of scientific knowledge with the use of scientific processes.

By setting test items in these situations OECD/PISA is seeking to assess the application of knowledge most likely to have been gained in the science curriculum (although some may be gained from other subjects and from non-school sources). However, although the knowledge that is required is curricular knowledge, in order to find out if this has gone beyond knowledge of isolated facts and is serving the development of scientific literacy, OECD/PISA is assessing the application of that knowledge in items reflecting real-life situations. Some of the examples of items presented below help to convey this point.

[. . .]

Assessment structure

As the examples illustrate, what is identified as a defined "task" will take the form of several items linked to some initial stimulus material. Between them the items within a task may assess more than one process and one scientific concept, whilst each item assesses one of the scientific processes listed in Figure 2.

One reason for this structure is to make the tasks as realistic as possible and to reflect in them to some extent the complexity of real-life situations. Another reason relates to the efficient use of testing time, cutting down on the time required for a student to "get into" the subject matter of the situation, by having fewer situations, about which several questions can be posed rather than separate questions about a larger number of different situations. The necessity to make each scored point independent of others within the task is recognised and taken into account. It is also recognised that it is all the more important to minimise bias which may be due to the situation when fewer situations are used.

The tasks will be extended ones incorporating up to about eight items, each independently scored. In the great majority of tasks, if not all, there will be both items eliciting knowledge and understanding of the concepts involved, and items requiring use of one or more of the processes of collecting and using evidence and data in a scientific investigation. As indicated earlier, OECD/PISA will not include practical ("hands on") tasks, at least in the years 2000 and 2003, when science is a "minor" domain.

For the overall assessment, the desired balance between the processes is given in terms of percentages of scored points in Table 1. This may be revised for the assessment in 2006, when science will be the major domain of OECD/PISA.

It may well be that the topics of some tasks mean that the balance is tipped more towards assessment of understanding (Process 5), with the opposite occurring within other tasks. Where possible, items assessing Processes 1–4 and items assessing Process 5 will occur within each task, both to achieve the aim of covering important scientific concepts that students are likely to have developed from their school science curricula or outside school, and because the ability to use processes is very highly dependent upon the situation in which they are used (hence the processes need to be assessed in relation to a range of concepts). The aims of OECD/PISA suggest that both conceptual understanding and the combination of scientific knowledge with the ability to draw evidence-based conclusions are valued learning outcomes. The recommended target of roughly equal numbers of score points assigned to these two main kinds of learning outcomes should serve these aims.

As already noted, all types of items will be concerned with the application of scientific concepts that are likely to be developed in students through their school science curricula. Where the OECD/PISA science items differ from some – but by no means all – school science assessment is in their requirement that the concepts be applied in real-life situations. Similarly, the ability to draw evidence-based conclusions appears among the aims of many school science curricula. The OECD/PISA assessment will require the application of the processes in situations which go beyond the school laboratory or classroom. The extent to which this is novel to students will depend on how far applications in the real world are part of the curriculum they have experienced.

In relation to the areas of application, Table 2 shows that there will be as even a spread as possible across the three main groups.

Table 1 Recommended distribution of score points across science processes

Scientific processes	% scored points
Recognising scientifically investigable questions	10–15
Identifying evidence needed	15–20
Drawing or evaluating conclusions	15–20
Communicating valid conclusions	10–15
Demonstrating understanding of science concepts	40–50

Table 2 Recommended distribution of score points across areas of application

Areas of application of science	% scored points
Science in life and health	30–40
Science in earth and environment	30–40
Science in technology	30–40

In relation to the selection of situations, OECD/PISA will aim to spread the items evenly across the four identified situations: the personal, the community, the global and the historical.

[. . .]

Reporting scales

Scales and sub-scales

To meet the aims of OECD/PISA, the development of scales of student achievement is essential. The process of arriving at a scale has to be iterative, so that initial proposals, based on past experience of assessing science achievement and findings from research into learning and cognitive development in science, are modified by empirical findings from the OECD/PISA field trials.

Existing research and past experience suggest that there will be a scale of scientific literacy indicating development:

from being able to use scientific concepts that are more easily grasped and being able to do things such as the following, in familiar situations:

- recognise questions that can and those that cannot be decided by scientific investigation;
- identify information that has to be obtained in order to test a claim or explore an issue in situations where there is one variable to change and one to control;
- state why conclusions or claims may not be tenable in situations where there is no control of a variable that should have been controlled;
- present some of the main points in relating evidence to conclusions in a way that can be understood by others;
- make predictions and suggest explanations in terms of more easily grasped concepts;

. . . to being able to apply concepts of greater cognitive demand and do the following things, in more complex situations:

- recognise the tentativeness of all scientific understanding and the fact that testing of theories can lead to revision and better understanding;
- identify the information that has to be collected and the conditions under which it should be collected to test an explanation or explore an issue in complex situations;
- criticise the adequacy of information given in support of a claim or argument; argue for and against a statement or conclusion in relation to the evidence available in cases where there is no simple, clear causal relationship;

- present a well-constructed argument for and against a particular conclusion using scientific knowledge and data or information provided;
- make predictions and provide explanations based on understanding of more complex and abstract scientific concepts.

Details of the scientific literacy scale will emerge from analyses of results from field trials. These will show which items can be grouped together and which are spread at different points on the scale. The empirical data will be used to test the progression proposed here on the basis of judgement and what is already known about cognitive development.

In the year 2006, when the testing time available will enable a comprehensive coverage of scientific concepts and areas of application, it may be possible, in addition, to report a sub-scale of understanding of scientific concepts (Process 5), to be assessed by application in the situations presented. Such a scale will describe development *from* demonstrating correct but incomplete understanding, often involving concepts that are easier to grasp *to* demonstrating more complete understanding, often involving concepts of greater complexity.

In 2006 there will be sufficient information available across the scientific processes listed in Figure 2 to consider reporting sub-scales, which might relate, for example, to performance in separate processes or in the major fields of science. Again, this will depend on statistical, conceptual and policy considerations. If it proves feasible to report sub-scales, countries will have the benefit of being able to compare the achieved outcomes of their science education in detail with what they consider desirable outcomes.

Reporting on the content of, and incorrect responses to, different items is an important accompaniment to item statistics. It is expected that these content categories will be generated from the field trial and related to the kinds of answers actually given by students. Reporting some types of answers to specific items will also be necessary in order to illustrate the scale(s) and to give meaningful labels to it (them). This will involve releasing some items from those used in OECD/PISA.

Further levels of reporting are desirable and may become possible after the major science survey in 2006. One of these is performance in groups of items across tasks relating to the separate areas of application of science. This information will be useful in considering whether sufficient and effective attention is being given to issues of current concern.

[. . .]

References

Almond, R.G. and Mislevy, R.J. (1998), *Graphical Models and Computerized Adaptive Testing*, TOEFL Technical Report No. 14, Educational Testing Service, Princeton, NJ, March.

Baker, L. (1991), "Metacognition, reading and science education", in C.M. Santa and D.E. Alvermann (eds.), *Science Learning: Processes and Applications*, International Reading Association, Newark, DE, pp. 2–13.

Bennett, R.E. (1993), "On the meanings of constructed response", in R.E. Bennett (ed.), *Construction vs. Choice in Cognitive Measurement: Issues in Constructed Response, Performance Testing, and Portfolio Assessment*, Lawrence Erlbaum Associates, Hillsdale, NJ, pp. 1–27.

Binkley, M. and Linnakyla, P. (1997), "Teaching reading in the United States and Finland", in M. Binkley, K. Rust and T. Williams (eds.), *Reading Literacy in an International Perspective*, US Department of Education, Washington, DC.

Bruner, J. (1990), *Acts of Meaning*, Harvard University Press, Cambridge, MA.

Bybee, R.W. (1997), "Towards an understanding of scientific literacy", in W. Grabe and C. Bolte (eds.), *Scientific Literacy – An International Symposium*, IPN, Kiel.

Council of Europe (1996), *Modern Languages: Learning, Teaching, Assessment. A Common European Framework of Reference*, CC LANG (95) 5 Rev. IV, Strasbourg.

Council of Ministers of Education, Canada (1994), *Student Achievement Indicators Program: Reading and Writing*, Toronto.

de Lange, J. and Verhage, H. (1992), *Data Visualization*, Sunburst, Pleasantville, NY.

de Lange, J. (1987), *Mathematics, Insight and Meaning*, OW and OC, Utrecht.

Devlin, K. (1994, 1997), *Mathematics, The Science of Patterns*, Scientific American Library, New York.

Dole, J., Duffy, G., Roehler, L. and Pearson, P. (1991), "Moving from the old to the new: Research on reading comprehension instruction", *Review of Educational Research*, 16 (2), pp. 239–264.

Ehrlich, M.F. (1996), "Metacognitive monitoring in the processing of anaphoric devices in skilled and less-skilled comprehenders", in C. Cornoldi and J. Oakhill (eds.), *Reading Comprehension Difficulties: Processes and Interventions*, Lawrence Erlbaum Associates, Mahwah, NJ, pp. 221–249.

Ehrlich, M.R., Kurtz-Costes, B. and Loridant, C. (1993), "Cognitive and motivational determinants of reading comprehension in good and poor readers", *Journal of Reading Behavior*, 25, pp. 365–381.

Einstein, A. (1933), "Preface to M. Plank", *Where is Science Going?*, Allen and Unwin, London.

Elley, W.B. (1992), *How in the World do Students Read?*, International Association for the Evaluation of Educational Achievement, The Hague.

Frederickson, N. (1984), "The real test bias", *American Psychologist*, 39, pp. 193–202.

Freudenthal, H. (1973), *Mathematics as an Educational Task*, Reidel, Dordrecht.

Freudenthal, H. (1983), *Didactical Phenomenology of Mathematical Structures*, Reidel, Dordrecht.

Graeber, W. and Bolte, C. (eds.) (1997), *Scientific Literacy – An International Symposium*, IPN, Kiel.

Gronlund, N.E. (1968), *Constructing Achievement Tests*, Prentice Hall, Englewood Cliffs.

Grünbaum, B. (1985), "Geometry strikes again", *Mathematics Magazine*, 58 (1), pp. 12–18.

Hawking, S.W. (1988), *A Brief History of Time*, Bantam Press, London.

Hubbard, R. (1989), "Notes from the underground: Unofficial literacy in one sixth grade", *Anthropology and Education Quarterly*, 20, pp. 291–307.

Jones, S. (1995), "The practice(s) of literacy", in *Literacy, Economy and Society: Results of the First International Adult Literacy Survey*, OECD and Statistics Canada, Paris and Ottawa, pp. 87–113.

Kirsch, I. (1995), "Literacy performance on three scales: Definitions and results", in *Literacy Economy and Society.' Results of the First International Adult Literacy Survey*, OECD and Statistics Canada, Paris and Ottawa, pp. 27–53.

Kirsch, I.S. and Mosenthal, P.B. (1989–1991), "Understanding documents. A monthly column", *Journal of Reading*, International Reading Association, Newark, DE.

Kirsch, I.S. and Mosenthal, P.B. (1994), "Interpreting the IEA reading literacy scales", in M. Binkley, K. Rust and M. Winglee (eds.), *Methodological Issues in Comparative Educational Studies: The Case of the IEA Reading Literacy Study*, US Department of Education, National Center for Education Statistics, Washington, DC, pp. 135–192.

Kirsch, I., Jungeblut, A. and Mosenthal, P.B. (1998), "The measurement of adult literacy", in T.S. Murray, I.S. Kirsch, and L. Jenkins (eds.), *Adult Literacy in OECD Countries: Technical Report on the First International Adult Literacy Survey*, US Department of Education, National Center for Education Statistics, Washington, DC.

Langer, J. (1995), *Envisioning Literature*, International Reading Association, Newark, DE.

Linnakylä, P. (1992), "Recent trends in reading literacy research in Finland", in P. Belanger, C. Winter and A. Sutton (eds.), *Literacy and Basic Education in Europe on the Eve of the 21st Century*, Council of Europe, Strasbourg, pp. 129–135.

Lundberg, I. (1991), "Reading as an individual and social skill", in I. Lundberg and T. Hoien (eds.), *Literacy in a World of Change*, Center for Reading Research/UNESCO, Stavanger.

MacCarthey, S.J. and Raphael, T.E. (1989), *Alternative Perspectives of Reading/Writing Connections*, College for Education, Institute for Research on Teaching. Occasional Paper #130, Michigan State University.

Millar, R. and Osborne, J. (1998), *Beyond 2000: Science Education for the Future*, King's College London School of Education, London.

Myers, M. and Paris, S.G. (1978), "Children's metacognitive knowledge about reading", *Journal of Educational Psychology*, 70, pp. 680–690.

Paris, S., Wasik, B. and Turner, J. (1991), "The development of strategic readers", in R. Barr, M. Kamil and P. Mosenthal (eds.), *Handbook of Reading Research*, Vol. II, Longman, New York.

Senechal, M. (1990), "Shape", in L.A. Steen (ed.), *On the Shoulders of the Giant – New Approaches to Numeracy*, National Academy Press, Washington, DC, pp. 139–182.

Shafer, M.C. and Romberg, T.A. (in press), "Assessment in Classroom that Promote Understanding", in E. Fennema and T.A. Romberg (eds.), *Mathematics Classrooms that Promote Understanding*, Erlbaum, Mahwah, NJ.

Shamos, M.H. (1995), *The Myth of Scientific Literacy*, Rutgers University Press, New Brunswick.

Smith, M.C. (1996), "Differences in adults' reading practices and literacy proficiencies", *Reading Research Quarterly*, 31, pp. 196–219.

Sticht, T.G. (ed.) (1975), *Reading for Working: A Functional Literacy Anthology*, Human Resources Research Organization, Alexandria, VA.

Stiggins, R.J. (1982), "An analysis of the dimensions of job-related reading", *Reading World*, 82, pp. 237–247.

Streefland, L. (1990), *Fractions in Realistic Mathematics Education, A Paradigm of Developmental Research*, Reidel Dordrecht.

Stuart, I. (1990), "Change", in L.A. Steen (ed.), *On the Shoulders of the Giant – New Approaches to Numeracy*, National Academy Press, Washington, DC, pp 183–218.

Taube, K. and Mejding, J. (1997), "A nine-country study: What were the differences between the low and high performing students in the IRA Reading Literacy Study?", in M. Binkley, K. Rust and T. Williams (eds.), *Reading Literacy the International Perspectives*, US Department of Education, National Center for Education Statistics, Washington, DC, pp. 63–100.

Taube, R.E. (1993), "On the equivalence of the traits assessed by multiple-choice and constructed-response tests", in R.E. Bennett (ed.), *Construction vs. Choice in Cognitive Measurement: Issues in Constructed Response, Performance Testing, and Portfolio Assessment*; Lawrence Erlbaum Associates, Hillsdale, NJ, pp. 29–44.

Travers, K.J. and Westbury I. (1989), *The IEA Study of Mathematics*, Vol. 1, Analysis of mathematics curricula, Pergamon Press, Oxford.

Treffers, A. (1986), *Three Dimensions*, Reidel, Dordrecht.

Treffers, A. and Goffree, F. (1985), "Rational analysis of realistic mathematics education", in L. Streefland (ed.), *Proceedings of the Ninth International Conference for the Psychology of Mathematics Education (PME)*, OW and OC, Utrecht, pp. 79–122.

UNESCO (1993), *International Forum on Scientific and Technological Literacy for All*, Final Report, UNESCO, Paris.

Ward, W.C., Dupree, D. and Carlson, S.B. (1987), *A Comparison of Free-response and Multiple-choice Questions in the Assessment of Reading Comprehension* (RR-87-20), Educational Testing Service, Princeton, NJ.

Werlich, E. (1976), *A Text Grammar of English*, Quelle and Meyer, Heidelberg.

Ziman, J.M. (1980), *Teaching and Learning about Science and Society*, Cambridge University Press.

PART II

MAINTAINING A CONTINUITY OF ACHIEVEMENT IN SCIENCE EDUCATION

EDITOR'S INTRODUCTION

The chapters in Part II address, in one way or another, some of the major achievements of scholarship, research and development in science education over recent years.

In Chapter 4, Duit and Treagust make a bold attempt to provide an overview of the achievements over the last 20 years or so in respect of 'the understanding and development of concepts'. They begin by observing that the early work was into the understanding held by students of specific concepts used in science, a field of enquiry that is still ploughed regularly. More recently, it has expanded to examine the understandings of the 'nature of science' held by students.

The work naturally progressed to attempts to develop the conceptions shown by students towards those accepted by science. The most widely used approach – the intra-psychological – sought to change the epistemological commitments of individual students, but has only proved to be of restricted success. This, they suggest, has been because it: has only been applied to a limited number of concepts; neglected the affective aspects of learning; failed to draw an appropriate balance between the personal and social aspects of learning; and assumed (contrary to experience) that conceptual change would be rapid. It is perhaps a recognition of this limited success that the outcomes are now discussed in terms of 'epistemological profiles', the holding of a range of understandings of any concept by an individual that are selectively applied. The limited work on the other major approach – the changing of ontological commitments – is also recorded. Duit and Treagust note that current work is framed by attempts to unify cognitive and affective approaches to conceptual development.

Most disturbingly, they review evidence that all the great volume of detailed work on this field has had very limited impact on classroom practice. Perhaps 'action research' – discussed in Chapter 18 – offers a way of overcoming this huge problem.

Questions that you may care to address might include:

- Do you have an overview of the range of understandings shown by students in respect of any one major concept used by science?

- What attempts that you know of are made in practice to identify students' understandings before they are taught a concept?
- What attempts that you know of are used in practice to change students' existing understandings?
- Why is it that science teachers pay so little attention to the great volume of research work on conceptual understanding and development?

In Chapter 5, Scott presents an elegant review of the implications of the socio-cultural theories of Vygotsky for the science classroom. This sees inter-psychological interactions, especially between a teacher and a student, as the key to learning. The rather elusive idea of 'zone of proximal development' is clearly presented, the text being made accessible by extracts from actual classroom interactions. Scott then reviews three aspects of socio-cultural theory: the forms of pedagogical intervention that are congruent with Vygotsky's ideas; the nature and function of talk, in general, in the classroom; the particular use of teacher talk to provide 'scaffolding' for student learning. Most telling of all, teaching is regarded as an act of persuasion, not as an act of indoctrination, as is all too often the case.

Questions you may care to address might include:

- What experience have you had, or do you know of, that has used a range of the pedagogical functions of talk that are outlined by Scott?
- How would you evaluate the effectiveness in promoting learning of an address to these functions?
- What do you think are the distinctive insights into learning that are made by the inter-psychological and intra-psychological approaches?
- What are the scope and limitations to a 'teaching as persuasion' approach?

In Chapter 6, Newton, Driver and Osborne take the analysis of classroom talk one stage further and discuss the role of argumentation in school science. They summarise Toulmin's analysis of the nature of an argument, interestingly the only one that is commonly used. After showing that argumentation is an integral part of science, they establish, by analogy, that it should be part of science education. They report the analysis of a series of science lessons and of a focus group of teachers in the UK. The results show that science lessons conform to what might almost be called a 'standard pattern'. While practical work occupied a major part of most lessons, the range of functions fulfilled by it was small. Of greatest concern, 'open investigation' lessons, in which argumentation would have played a major role, were infrequent. During all the lessons, 'listening' was the major activity for the students, with only a range of 8–13 per cent of class time being devoted to 'interaction', in which argument might have figured. Teachers gave a series of reasons why more argumentation did not take place: the limited time available, given the high content load of the curriculum; the problems of class management of discussion; their own skills of argumentation; and the views of science and science education that they held.

Questions you may care to address might include:

- What experience have you had, or do you know of, that supports the case that argumentation in class helps student learning?
- How might more time be found for argumentation in the existing science curriculum?
- What problems do you know of in managing discussions and how might these be addressed?
- Do you agree that science teaching is a conservative activity? If so, why is that?

In Chapter 7, Buckley presents a case study of the use of multi-media in the model-based learning of biology. It is of a classroom situation, observed over several weeks, that was set up with the expectation that a socio-cultural perspective on learning, supported by multi-media tools, would enable extensive argumentation and model-building to take place.

The case study reported in detail is of a student who, in a class organised into groups, chose to work on her own. It is interesting in that it warns that successful learning does not necessarily require extensive inter-psychological interaction. While the argumentation that took place is, due to these circumstances, not very evident, the case study student's selection and use of representations can be used as an indication of the thinking that took place. The study shows that a model-building theoretical framework can be used to successfully represent learning taking place.

Questions you may care to ask might include:

- Under what circumstances is a student working alone acceptable when a group working structure is the norm?
- How does the personal construction of knowledge relate to the social construction of knowledge?
- What value might visual representations have in the construction of arguments during the learning of science?
- How rich does a multi-media resource base have to be before self-directed project work can take place?

CHAPTER 4

CONCEPTUAL CHANGE – A POWERFUL FRAMEWORK FOR IMPROVING SCIENCE TEACHING AND LEARNING

Reinders Duit and David F. Treagust

International Journal of Science Education (2003) 25(6), 671–88

Development of the notion of conceptual change

Historical developments

Research on students' and teachers' conceptions and their roles in teaching and learning science has become one of the most important domains of science education research during the past three decades. Starting in the 1970s with the investigation of students' pre-instructional conceptions on various science content domains such as the electric circuit, force, energy, combustion, and evolution, the analysis of students' understanding across most science domains has been comprehensively documented in the bibliography by Duit (2002a). Two decades ago, research by Gilbert, Osborne and Fensham (1982) showed that children are not passive learners and the way they make sense of their experiences led to this intuitive knowledge being called 'children's science' (p. 623). Findings from many studies over the past three decades show that students do not come into science instruction without any pre-instructional knowledge or beliefs about the phenomena and concepts to be taught. Rather, students already hold deeply rooted conceptions and ideas that are not in harmony with the science views or are even in stark contrast to them. It is noteworthy that there are still a remarkable number of studies on students' learning in science that primarily investigate such students' conceptions at the content level. Since the middle of the 1980s investigations of students' conceptions at meta-levels, namely conceptions of the nature of science and views of learning (i.e., meta-cognitive conceptions) also have been given considerable attention. Research shows that students' conceptions here are also rather limited and naive.

The 1980s saw the growth of studies investigating the development of students' pre-instructional conceptions towards the intended science concepts in conceptual change approaches. Research on students' conceptions and conceptual change has been embedded in various theoretical frames over the past decades. Initially, Piagetian ideas were applied that drew primarily on stage theory on the one hand and on his clinical interview on the other. Also basic frameworks of the emerging theories of cognitive psychology were adopted. Later, constructivist ideas developed by merging various cognitive approaches with a focus on viewing knowledge as being constructed such as with the Piagetian interplay of assimilation and accommodation, Kuhnian

(Kuhn, 1970) ideas of theory change in the history of science and the radical constructivist ideas of people like von Glasersfeld (1989). However, certain limitations of the constructivist ideas of the 1980s and early 1990s led to their merger with social constructivist and social cultural orientations that more recently resulted in recommendations to employ multi-perspective epistemological frameworks in order to adequately address the complex process of learning (Duit & Treagust, 1998).

Recent studies in an edited volume by Sinatra and Pintrich (2003) emphasise the role of the learner's intentions in knowledge change. This volume brings together Bereiter and Schardamalia's (1989) ideas of the intentional learner and those of Pintrich, Marx & Boyle (1993) emphasizing that conceptual change is more than conceptual. It is this emphasis on the impetus for change being within the learner's control that forms the basis of the chapters in the text. The notion of intentional conceptual change is in some ways analogous to that of mindfulness (Salomon & Globerson, 1987, p. 623), a 'construct which reflects a voluntary state of mind, and connects among motivation, cognition and learning.

Sinatra and Pintrich acknowledge the important contributions to the study of conceptual change from the perspectives of science education and cognitive developmental psychology. However, what becomes increasingly evident in reviewing the literature on conceptual change in this text and others is the general polarisation of researchers in science education and cognitive psychology such that one can read excellent research in one domain that has little reference to research in the other domain. The text by Sinatra and Pintrich brings many of the researchers in these two domains together in one volume but this is not always the case. For example, in the very informative text by Limon and Mason (2002), based on a symposium as part of the activities of the Special Interest Group of the European Association for Research on Learning and Instruction, there are virtually no references to science education and science education researchers who have worked in this area. Our intention is that this review will help overcome this issue of researchers in two domains not referring to each others' work.

The concept of conceptual change

Research on the concept of conceptual change has developed a unique vocabulary because conceptual change can happen at a number of levels and different authors use alternative terms to describe similar learning. The most common analysis is that there are two types of conceptual change, variously called weak knowledge restructuring, assimilation or conceptual capture and strong/radical knowledge restructuring, accommodation or conceptual exchange. Some authors separate knowledge accretion from conceptual change while others include it as a third level. Various author's positions on these contrasting forms of conceptual change have been summarized by Harrison and Treagust (2000).

Consequently, because the term conceptual change has been given various meanings in the literature, the term change often has been misunderstood as being an exchange of pre-instructional conceptions for the science concepts. In this review, we do not use conceptual change in this way. Rather, we use the term conceptual change for learning in such domains where the pre-instructional conceptual structures of the learners have to be fundamentally restructured in order to allow understanding of the intended knowledge, that is, the acquisition of science concepts. In a general sense, conceptual change denotes learning pathways from students' pre-instructional conceptions to the science concepts to be learned (Duit, 1999).

Conceptual change has become the term denoting learning science from constructivist perspectives (Duit, 1999) and has been employed in studies on learning and instruction in a number of domains other than science (Guzetti & Hynd, 1998; Mason, 2001; Schnotz, Vosniadou, & Carretero, 1999; Vosniadou, 1994). An analysis of these studies on conceptual change shows that they primarily take an epistemological, an ontological or a social/affective position, with most studies adopting an epistemological position. As noted in this review, there are clear limitations to taking a single position to understand conceptual change.

An epistemological position

The classical conceptual change approach involved the teacher making students' alternative frameworks explicit prior to designing a teaching approach consisting of ideas that do not fit the students' existing ideas and thereby promoting dissatisfaction. A new framework is then introduced based on formal science that will explain the anomaly. However, it became obvious that students' conceptual progress towards understanding and learning science concepts and principles after instruction quite frequently turned out to be still limited (Duit & Treagust, 1998). There appears to be no study which found that a particular student's conception could be completely extinguished and then replaced by the science view. Indeed, most studies show that the old ideas stay alive in particular contexts. Usually the best that could be achieved was a 'peripheral conceptual change' (Chinn & Brewer, 1993) in that parts of the initial idea merge with parts of the new idea to form some sort of hybrid idea (Gilbert, et al., 1982; Jung, 1993).

The best known conceptual change model in science education, based on students' epistemologies, originated with Posner, Strike, Hewson and Gertzog (1982) and was refined by Hewson (1981, 1982, 1996), Hewson and Hewson (1984; 1988; 1992), Strike and Posner (1985, 1992) and applied to classroom instruction by Hennessey (1993). In the conceptual change model, student dissatisfaction with a prior conception was believed to initiate dramatic or revolutionary conceptual change and was embedded in radical constructivist epistemological views with an emphasis on the individual's conceptions and his/her conceptual development. If the learner was dissatisfied with his/her prior conception *and* an available replacement conception was intelligible, plausible and/or fruitful, accommodation of the new conception may follow. An intelligible conception is sensible if it is non-contradictory and its meaning is understood by the student; plausible means that in addition to the student knowing what the conception means, he/she finds the conception believable; and, the conception is fruitful if it helps the learner solve other problems or suggests new research directions. Posner et al. insist that a plausible conception must first be intelligible and a fruitful conception must be intelligible and plausible. Resultant conceptual changes may be permanent, temporary or too tenuous to detect.

In this learning model, resolution of conceptual competition is explained in terms of the comparative intelligibility, plausibility and fruitfulness of rival conceptions. Posner et al., claimed that a collection of epistemological commitments called the student's 'conceptual ecology' (Toulmin, 1972) mediated conceptual intelligibility, plausibility and fruitfulness. Strike and Posner (1992, pp. 216–217) expanded the conceptual ecology metaphor to include anomalies, analogies and metaphors, exemplars and images, past experiences, epistemological commitments, metaphysical beliefs and knowledge in other fields. The conceptual change model's use of constructs such as conceptual ecology, assimilation and accommodation suggests a constructivist notion built on Piagetian ideas. These conceptual change approaches have proven superior to more traditionally-oriented approaches in a number of studies.

However, a summarizing meta-analysis of the large number of studies available is still missing. A decade ago, Guzetti, Snyder, Glass and Gamas (1993) did provide such a meta-analysis but they only included studies that employed a treatment-control group design. At around the same time, Wandersee, Mintzes and Novak (1994) summarized their extensive analysis of conceptual change approaches with a cautious remark that their analysis gave the impression that conceptual change approaches usually are more successful than traditional approaches in guiding students to the science concepts. However, a problem with research on conceptual change is that it is rather difficult to compare the success of conceptual change approaches and other approaches. Usually different approaches to teaching and learning address different aims and hence it is only possible to evaluate whether the particular aims set have been adequately met. Nevertheless, in summary, if one takes into account attempts to identify key characteristics of efficient teaching and learning approaches based on reviews and meta-analyses of the relevant literature (e.g., Wang, Haertel & Walberg, 1993), it appears that features are relevant that are also at the heart of conceptual change approaches like cognitive activation. We therefore are convinced that conceptual change approaches are more efficient than so called traditional ones. This efficiency depends on the way the approaches are used in classroom practice and whether the potential they have in principle actually leads to the outcome expected.

Limits of the 'classical' conceptual change approaches

Research has revealed that the conceptual change approaches of the 1980s and the early 1990s may be more efficient compared to traditional approaches of teaching and learning science but these approaches are also limited in a number of other respects, the most important of which seem to be as follows.

First, conceptual change primarily has denoted changes of science concepts and principles, that is, cognitive development on the science *content* level. Often it has been overlooked that these changes usually are closely linked to changes of views of the underlying concepts and principles of the nature of science. The research has not been taken into consideration that understanding science includes knowledge of science concepts and principles and about this science content knowledge. In a recent review of science education research Fensham (2001) addressed this limitation by stating:

> Another weakness in the range of alternative conceptions is that the focus in most of the studies is on isolated concepts of science, rather than on the contexts and processes of conceptualisation and nominalisation that led to their invention in science.
>
> (p. 30)

Fensham also pointed to a certain restriction of the kind of content researched so far:

> Only a tiny fraction have been concerned with concepts that are associated with the environmental, technological, and socio-scientific content, that was beginning to be tried in the 1980s in STS-types of science curricula. Thus, there are few, if any studies of students' conceptions of green revolution, endangered

species, bio-diversity, ozone hole, greenhouse effect, noise pollution, shelf life, radiation risk, and toxic level.

(p. 29)

Second, there is a certain focus on the rational, that is, on issues following the logic of the science content structure. This rational approach, which holds for science education research and also cognitive science research on conceptual change, has limitations because it does not consider affective measures. This is the area of research that is addressed by the work on intentional conceptual change by Sinatra and Pintrich (2003) and their text contributors. In other words, learning of the science content embedded in learning environments that support the acquisition of these rational issues has been often neglected (Pintrich, Marx & Boyle, 1992). We discuss this issue in more depth later in the review.

Third, the epistemological orientation has been questioned because of the socio-cognitive ways in which individuals learn; for example, the radical constructivist approaches to learning involving an individual's cognition were overstated (cf. Matthews, 1993). Epistemological views merging radical and social-constructivist approaches appear to be more promising than monistic views proposed by the one or the other side. There have been developments during the past few years towards such inclusive epistemological views that seem to provide not only powerful frames for understanding learning processes as they happen in real learning situations but also may lead to more fruitful teaching and learning environments. There are powerful tendencies now towards theories of teaching and learning science paying equal attention to the individual and social aspects of learning (Duit & Treagust, 1998).

In a similar vein, Vosniadou and Ioannides (1998) provided a critique of classical conceptual change approaches. First, they argue that the conceptual change approaches as developed in the 1980s and early 1990s put too much emphasis on sudden insights facilitated especially by cognitive conflict (see also Limon, 2001). These authors claim that learning science should be viewed as a

gradual process during which initial conceptual structures based on children's interpretations of everyday experience are continuously enriched and restructured.

(p. 1213)

They also point out that conceptual change involves 'metaconceptual' awareness of the students. In other words, students will be able to learn science concepts and principles only if they are aware about the shift of their initial metaconceptual views towards the metaconceptual perspectives of science knowledge – again the same notion taken up by Sinatra and Pintrich. Finally, Vosniadou and Ioannides argue in favour of a theory of science learning that includes the individual cognitive development and the situational and cultural factors facilitating it.

Metacognition is seen by Georghiades (2000) as a potential mediator in improvement of conceptual change learning with primary school children, especially in terms of their inability to transfer their conceptions from one domain to another and the short durability of their conceptions. Both of the inability to transfer and the short duration of conceptions give rise to problems faced by classroom practitioners. His model of learning draws upon four overlapping areas: conceptual change sets the epistemological background; transfer and durability of scientific conceptions are the problems to be addressed and metacognition as the potential mediator for improving learning.

Alternative approaches to analysing conceptual change

Conceptual change at the content level is closely linked to changes at meta-levels such as views about the nature of science knowledge (McComas, 1998) and meta-cognitive views about learning. However, to date little is known about the *interactions* of these conceptual changes. Research should put more emphasis on that in the coming years.

Student conceptual status

Hewson appears to understand dissatisfaction as a product of the intelligibility-plausibility fruitfulness interaction between competing conceptions. The conceptual status construct which classifies a conception's status as intelligible, plausible or fruitful (Hewson, 1982; Hewson & Lemberger, 2000; Hewson & Thorley, 1989) is particularly useful for assessing changes to students' conceptions during learning. When a competing conception does not generate dissatisfaction, the new conception may be assimilated alongside the old, which Hewson (1981) called 'conceptual capture'. When dissatisfaction between competing conceptions reveals their incompatibility (Hewson & Hewson, 1984), two things may happen. If the new conception achieves higher status than the prior conception, accommodation, which Hewson calls conceptual exchange, may occur. If the old conception retains higher status, conceptual exchange will not proceed for the time being. It should be remembered that a replaced conception is not forgotten and the learner may wholly or partly reinstate it at a later date. Both Posner et al. and Hewson stress that it is the student, not the teacher, who makes the decisions about conceptual status and conceptual changes. This position harmonises with constructivist learning theory and the highly personal nature of mental models (Norman, 1983).

Studies utilising the notion of conceptual status include that by Treagust, Harrison, Venville and Dagher (1996) which set out to assess the efficacy of using analogies to engender conceptual change in students' science learning about the refraction of light. Following instruction by the same teacher, two classes of students, one of which was taught analogically and one which was not, were interviewed three months after instruction using an interview-about-instances protocol. Factors related to status were identified from the interview transcripts to help in the process of classifying each students' conception of refraction as being intelligible, plausible or fruitful. Descriptors described by Hewson and Hennessey (1992, p. 177) were used as a guide during this process. For example, Hewson and Hennessey explained that for a concept to be intelligible, students must know what the concept means and should be able to describe it in their own words. For a concept to be plausible, the concept must first be intelligible and students must believe that this is how the world actually is, and that it must fit in with other ideas or concepts that students know about or believe. Finally, for a concept to be fruitful, it must first be intelligible and plausible and should be seen as something useful to solve problems or a better way of explaining things.

Most of the evidence from this study indicated that conceptual change which meets the criteria of dissatisfaction, intelligibility, plausibility and fruitfulness is not necessarily an exchange of conceptions for another but rather an increased use of the kind of conception that makes better sense to the student. This research has shown that while increased status of a conception is possible by means of analogical teaching, it does not necessarily lead to different learning outcomes as measured on traditional tests.

Ontology and conceptual change

Posner et al., Strike and Posner, and Hewson primarily use epistemology to explain conceptual changes and also comment upon in the way that students view reality which is an ontological position. Others, however, use specific ontological terms to explain changes to the way students conceptualise science entities (Chi et al., 1994; Thagard, 1992; Vosniadou, 1994). In showing that 'some of the child's concepts are incommensurable with the adults', Carey (1985, p. 269) argued for strong knowledge restructuring during childhood and Vosniadou called similar changes radical restructuring and explains that revisions to central 'framework theories' (pp. 46–49) involve ontological and epistemological changes. Chi et al. called their strongest ontological changes 'tree swapping' and Thagard (1992) also has a strongest change which he calls 'tree switching.' Two candidates for these types of change are, heat needs to change from a flowing fluid to kinetic energy in transit and a gene from an inherited object to a biochemical process. There are many other concepts where scientists' *process* views are incommensurable with students' *material* conceptions and the desired changes to students' ontologies are not often achieved in school science. Despite this pessimistic view, this chapter argues that school students' material conceptions can be successfully challenged. However, scientific concepts are very complex and what may be suitable for optimising of school science is not always the currently held science view. For example, in modern physics there are two ways of modelling heat – a process way and also a way that draws on change and conservation of 'thing like entities'.

Consistent with our position is the research of Chiu, Chou and Liu (2002) who adopted Chi's ontological categories of scientific concepts to investigate how students perceived the concept of chemical equilibrium. These authors argue that 'although Posner's theory is widely accepted by science educators and easy to comprehend and apply to learning activities, . . . it does not delineate what the nature of a scientific concept is, which causes difficulty in learning the concept (p. 689).'

Student modelling ability

Models of every kind are used to communicate science outcomes, plan and implement its methods, and models are science's major learning and teaching tools (Gilbert, 1993; Gilbert & Boulter, 1998). However, many students find the diverse models that are used to explain science challenging and confusing (Bent, 1984; Carr, 1984; Garnett & Treagust, 1992; Gilbert & Boulter, 1998) although some researchers (Russell, Kozma, Jones, et al. 1997) advocate that learning with diverse models prevents students developing alternative conceptions that are hard to change. This problem is particularly severe for young students and for those students whose abstract reasoning is poorly developed. Grosslight et al. (1991) investigated student/expert modelling abilities in terms of changes to students' *beliefs* about a model's structure and purpose. They classified many lower secondary students as level 1 modellers because these students believe that there is a 1:1 correspondence between models and reality (models are small incomplete copies of actual objects). Some secondary students achieve level 2 where models remain real world entities rather than representations of ideas, and a model's main purpose is communication rather than idea exploration. Experts alone satisfied level 3 criteria that models should be multiple; are thinking tools; and can be manipulated by the modeller to suit his/her epistemological needs. Some students fell into mixed level 1/2 and 2/3 classifications. Because the levels are derived from the way students describe, explain and use models, the levels provide information about the status of students' conceptions and modelling level changes may provide useful evidence for conceptual changes.

The differences between Grosslight et al.'s three modelling levels also may reflect different ontologies as students need to change the way they think about reality in order to advance from one level to the next. Modelling ability is a particularly useful tool for identifying changing epistemologies and ontologies during science learning. There is a Piagetian flavour to modelling levels because Grosslight et al.'s levels appear to be linear, age and experience dependent. Conceptual status is strongly epistemological and only conceptions that are at least plausible or fruitful are likely to support higher modelling levels. Useful educational similarities seem to exist between conceptual status and modelling levels 1, 2 and 3 (see Harrison & Treagust, 1999) Grosslight et al.'s work suggests that instruction that ignores a student's epistemological status appears futile and monitoring student epistemology is essential if students are to be led along the modelling level 1 to level 3 learning path.

Epistemological and conceptual profiles

A different but useful way to understand students' conceptualising of multiple models is to use Bachelard's (1968) epistemological profile which is based on the notion that people possess more than one way for describing objects and processes and this is especially so in science. For example, mass can be described in everyday terms of 'bigness', measured instrumentally using a spring balance, expressed in dynamic terms like $F = ma$ or relativistically. Scientists use different methods depending on context so why should students not do likewise? What may appear to be a change in conception by a scientist or a student could simply be a different way of describing a conception based on the context in which it is presented and the preference for one conceptualisation or model over another. For instance, many secondary teachers and textbooks simultaneously use the electron shell or Bohr model when discussing atomic structure, use balls or space-filling models to explain kinetic theory and Lewis electron-dot diagrams for bonding; the particular conceptualisation or model often depends upon the context.

Consequently, while the ability to select intelligible, plausible and fruitful representations or conceptions for a specific context is itself a measure of expertise, researchers need to be aware that apparent conceptual changes may in fact be context-driven choices rather than conceptual status changes. In learning settings, Mortimer (1995) proposed the use of conceptual profiles to help differentiate conceptual changes from what are contextual choices.

Affective factors

Several authors, including Posner et al. (1982) and more recently Sinatra and Pintrich (2003), have emphasised to lesser or greater extents the importance of affective factors in conceptual change. The affective factor of motivation involves establishing conducive learning environments and most teachers value social and group learning. It was with these ideas in mind that Pintrich et al. (1993) proposed that a 'hot irrational' explanation for conceptual change is as tenable as cold cognition and argued that students' self-efficacy and control beliefs, classroom social context, 'individual's goals, intentions, purposes, expectations [and] needs' (p. 168) are as important as cognitive strategies in concept learning. Similarly, Dykstra et al. (1992) claim that group factors can advantage concept learning and Vygotsky's theories (van der Veer & Valsiner, 1991) highlight the importance of social and motivational influences.

Pintrich et al.'s review of the social and motivational literature highlights the importance of interest, personal and situational beliefs to students' engagement in learning activities. Indeed, they claim that teachers who ignore the social and affective aspects of personal and group learning may limit conceptual change.

Towards multi-perspective views of science learning and instruction

Conceptual change approaches as developed in the 80s and early 90s contributed substantially to improving science learning and teaching. However, as outlined there are a number of limitations and one-sidedness that have to be overcome the next years. There are promising tendencies towards new approaches that are multi-perspective in several ways:

Towards merging the cognitive and affective domains

There is ample evidence in research on learning and instruction that cognitive and affective issues are closely linked. However, the number of studies on the interaction of cognitive and affective factors in the learning process is limited. There are, for instance, many studies on the relations between interests and acquisition of science concepts. However, these studies are usually restricted to correlations between interests and cognitive results of learning. The interplay of changes of interests and conceptual change is investigated only in a small number of studies. The multi-dimensional framework for interpreting conceptual change by Tyson, Venville, Harrison and Treagust (1997) includes, for instance, an affective domain, but this domain has not been fully elaborated so far. It appears that it is fruitful to merge ideas of conceptual change and theories on the significance of affective factors. It also seems to be most valuable to view the issue of interests in science and science teaching from the perspective of conceptual change. Clearly, it is an important aim of science instruction to develop interest in much the same way as to develop students' pre-instructional conceptions towards the intended science concepts.

Towards merging moderate and social-constructivist views of learning

Most studies on learning science so far have been oriented towards views of learning that are monistic to a certain extent. Only recently there are powerful developments towards admitting that the complex phenomenon learning needs pluralistic epistemological frameworks (Greeno, Collins, & Resnick, 1997) in order to address the many facets emphasized by different views of learning adequately. In science education there is a growing number of multi-perspectives views which appear to be rather promising to improve science teaching and learning (Duit, 1998; Duit & Treagust, 1998).

Briefly summarized, multi-perspective frameworks have to be employed in order to adequately address the complexity of the teaching and learning processes. Only such frameworks allow to model teaching and learning processes sufficiently and to address the ambitious levels of scientific literacy briefly presented in the following.

The research papers discussed so far have largely remained committed to one theoretical perspective of conceptual change as a framework for their data analysis and interpretation. In contrast to this approach, Venville and Treagust (1998) utilised four different perspectives of conceptual change to analyse different classroom teaching situations in which analogies were used to teach biology concepts. The perspectives they used are Posner, et al.'s (1982) conceptual change model, Vosniadou's (1994) framework theory and mental model perspective, Chi, et al.'s (1994) ontological category perspective and Pintrich, et al.'s (1993) motivational perspective. They found that each of the perspectives of conceptual change had explanatory value and contributed a different theoretical perspective on interpreting the role that analogies played in each of the classroom situations.

Conceptual change views and scientific literacy

The 1990s saw an intensive debate about scientific literacy inspired by concerns about the educational demands of the 21st century (DeBoer, 2000; Gräber & Bolte, 1997). Later in the 1990s, these discussions were further fuelled by the results of the TIMSS project (Third International Mathematics and Science Studies) that uncovered striking deficiencies in the state of scientific literacy in many countries. More recently, PISA 2000 (Programme for International Student Assessment) (OECD/PISA, 1999) also showed that students' performance in many countries was less than expected. These results provided another impetus for discussion on scientific literacy concepts and on attempts to improve science teaching and learning.

The major features of scientific literacy will be briefly outlined in the following. Driver and Osborne (1998) provided the following four arguments for the need to improve scientific literacy: (1) The economic argument – modern societies need scientifically and technologically literate work-forces to maintain their competencies; (2) The utility argument – individuals need some basic understanding of science and technology to function effectively as individuals and consumers; (3) The cultural argument – science is a great human achievement and it is a major contributor to our culture; (4) The democratic argument – citizens need to be able to reach an informed view on matters of science related public policies in order to participate in discussions and decision-making.

The conceptions of scientific literacy in PISA is of particular interest here as cross curricular competencies and science processes are given particular emphases (Fensham & Harlen, 1999; Harlen, 2001). Scientific literacy is seen as the capacity to identify questions and to draw evidence-based conclusions in order to understand and help make decisions about the natural world and the changes made to it through human activity. The foci are the following science processes and cross-curricular competencies: Science processes: (1) recognizing scientifically investigable questions; (2) identifying evidence needed in a scientific investigation; (3) drawing or evaluating conclusions; (4) communicating valid conclusions; (5) demonstrating understanding of science concepts. Cross-curricular competencies: (a) self-regulated learning; (b) ability to solve problems; (c) communication and cooperation.

Briefly summarized, the conceptions of scientific literacy include a broad spectrum of different facets and competencies. These 'visions' are rather ambitious. The more advanced levels of scientific literacy such as Bybee's (1997) multidimensional level demand a large complexity of teaching and learning processes and conceptual changes as outlined above. It appears that only multi-perspective conceptual change approaches as outlined above are suited to meet these demands.

Improving scientific literacy has become a major concern of science education research and development during the 1990s, in many respects driven by public awareness about the urgent need for a sufficient level of scientific literacy. In a number of countries the disappointing results of students in TIMSS and PISA studies have alarmed a broader public, as well as politicians and school administrators, who demand that school science instruction become more effective. Recently initiated quality development projects (e.g. Beeth, 2001; Prenzel & Duit, 2000; Tytler & Conley, 2001) share the following characteristics (Beeth, Duit, Prenzel, Ostermeier, Tytler & Wickman, 2003): (1) Supporting schools and teachers to rethink the representation of science in the curriculum. (2) Enlarging the repertoire of tasks, experiments, and teaching and learning strategies and resources. (3) Promoting strategies and resources that attempt to increase students' engagement and interest. (4) Setting constructivist principles into practice. These characteristics imply that a teacher is a reflective practitioner with a non-transmissive view of teaching and learning. Similarly, these characteristics imply that students are active, self-responsible, co-operative and self-reflective learners. Consequently, quality development programs are based on constructivist views of teaching and learning that are at the heart of conceptual change approaches as discussed in the present chapter.

The impact of research on school practice

Educational research in general appears to be in danger of being viewed as irrelevant by many teachers (Lijnse, 2000). Kennedy (1997) for instance, argued that the 'awful reputation of educational research' (Kaestle, 1993) is due to the domination of basic research by cognitive psychology. Such studies are usually carried out in laboratory settings in order to allow strict control of variables. The price to be paid for a large degree of experimental 'cleanness' is that the results often do not inform the actual practice of teaching and learning. Wright (1993) provided similar arguments to explain that science education research is frequently viewed as irrelevant by policy makers, curriculum developers, and science teachers. He also claims that most science education researchers have little interest in putting into practice what is known.

Mainstream research in the domain of conceptual change, however, is substantially different from the basic research that Kennedy (1997) criticised.

> Constructivist research on conceptual change in science education, for instance, has been of an applied research type from the very start in the early 1980s. It is also most fortunate that there was a turn towards applied research in cognitive psychology in the 1990s (Vosniadou, 1996). Hence, most research on conceptual change in principle addresses the needs of educational practice more adequately than traditional forms of educational research. This research also provides powerful means to improve science teaching and learning. However, it has to be taken into account that every research community develops a particular research culture that defines what counts as good research and this may not be in accordance with what teachers expect and need. Hence, there is always a tendency for the research culture to alienate teachers. This also holds for research in the domain of conceptual change.
>
> (Duit, 2002b)

Research on teachers' views of teaching and learning and their actual teaching behaviour

There is substantial research available on possibilities to set the visions of scientific literacy as outlined above into practice. Anderson and Helms (2001) point to the crucial issue of changing teachers' views of teaching and learning from transmissive towards constructivist orientation. However, research has also shown that a constructivist view, for example, as revealed in interviews, does not necessarily guarantee teaching behaviour that is constructivist oriented (Fischler, 1994). In other words, there may be a substantial gap between teachers' views (their subjective theories) and actions. It is necessary to change teachers' views *and* actions.

More recent video-studies like the TIMSS video study on mathematics instruction in the U.S., Japan and Germany (Stigler, et al., 1999) or the TIMSS-R video studies on science (Roth, et al., 2001) allow to investigate teachers' actual teaching behaviour in 'normal' practice and compare that to teachers' views about teaching and learning. In order to find out which teaching and learning scripts are dominating in German physics instruction a video-study comprising a sample of 14 teachers was carried out. Data sources comprise video documents of about 90 lessons on the introduction to electric circuits and the force concept, in-depth interviews with every teacher (including stimulated recall) and various student questionnaires. Only preliminary results are available so far (Prenzel, et al., 2002). However, with regard to the impact of visions of scientific literacy, contemporary constructivist views of teaching and learning, and conceptual change strategies, it turns out that the teachers in this study are not familiar with these issues of science education literature. Their views of the aims of physics instruction are rather limited. It also appears that most of them do not hold explicit theories about the teaching and learning process (Widodo & Duit, 2002; Widodo, Duit & Müller, 2002). Their view of learning seems to be transmissive rather than constructivist. It is particularly remarkable that most of the teachers are not even familiar with the kind of students' pre-instructional conceptions that have to be taken into account when the concepts of the electric circuit and force are introduced. Their views about dealing with pre-instructional conceptions are not informed by conceptual change ideas. Some teachers are aware that students' pre-instructional conceptions have to be taken into consideration but usually they do not explicitly see them as 'goggles' that guide observation and interpretation of everything presented in class by the teacher or the textbook. The teaching behaviour of several teachers meets a number of features that are characteristic for constructivist informed science classrooms (Widodo, Duit & Müller, 2002). They provide, for instance, certain cognitive activation (e.g., by addressing thought provoking problems) or certain features of 'conceptual change supporting conditions' (such as dealing with everyday phenomena). However, the teachers do not employ conceptual change teaching and learning strategies presented in the literature such as Driver's (1989) constructivist strategy, the learning cycle (Lawson, Abraham & Renner, 1989) or the more recent CONTACT-2 strategy by Biemans, Deel & Simons (2001). The dominating way of thinking about teaching physics may be called subject specific. The teachers have a quite substantial and well-organized repertoire of the kind of experiments available and of how to introduce a certain concept. But this subject specific thinking is only rather loosely based on more general views of good science teaching. Briefly summarized, the impact of more recent research ideas and research findings on teachers' views and classroom actions appears to be rather limited in this study. Of course, the small sample investigated may not be representative for German physics teachers as a whole. However, the major findings on teachers' scripts are in accordance with results of other studies on German physics instruction (Baumert & Köller, 2001). Further analysis will be carried out to prove the preliminary findings.

Bridging the gap between research findings on conceptual change and instructional practice

The rather ambitious competencies affiliated with recent conceptions of scientific literacy demand the kind of multi-perspective conceptual change approaches outlined above. If a substantial part of the students shall achieve at least a minimum of scientific literacy that is needed to address the challenges of the future these approaches should be taken into account. Research, namely, has shown that conceptual change informed teaching usually is superior to more traditional means of teaching. Hence, conceptual change may still be a powerful frame for improving science teaching and learning.

The state of theory building on conceptual change has become more and more sophisticated and the teaching and learning strategies developed have become more and more complex the past 25 years. These developments are, of course, necessary in order to address the complex phenomena of teaching and learning (science) more and more adequately. However, the gap between what is necessary from the researcher perspective and what may be set into practice by 'normal' teachers has increased more and more also. In other words, there is the paradox that in order to adequately address teaching and learning processes research alienates the teachers and hence widens the 'theory-practice' gap. The views of teaching and learning developed in our field are far from normal classroom teachers' ways of thinking about instruction. The instructional strategies developed by us are far from the routines of normal classes. As research has clearly shown it is rather difficult to change (in the sense of a conceptual change) teachers' views and teachers' classroom practice. It may be argued that many conceptual change strategies have been developed and evaluated in actual classrooms and often in close co-operation with teachers (e.g., Biemans et al., 2001; Vosniadou, Ioannides, Dimitrakopoulou & Papademitriou, 2001). However, what works in special arrangements does not necessarily work in everyday practice.

The major message of the present paper is that it is necessary to close the gap between theory and practice at least to a certain extent. What research on conceptual change has to offer classroom practice can not be set into normal practice to a substantial extent. Of course, teacher development programs are essential in order to change teachers' views of teaching and learning and their practice. However, it appears to be also necessary to make these theories more simple and describe conceptual change strategies in such a way that they may become part of teachers' routines.

References

Anderson, R. D. and Helms, J. V. (2001) The ideal of standards and the reality of schools: needed research. *Journal of Research in Science Teaching*, 38, 3–16.

Bachelard, G. (1968) *The Philosophy of No. A philosophy of the new scientific mind.* New York: The Orion Press.

Baumert, J. and Köller, O. (2001) Unterrichtsgestaltung, verständnisvolles Lernen und multiple Zielerreichung im Mathematik- und Physikunterricht der gymnasialen Oberstufe [Instructional patterns, insightful learning and achieved literacy in upper secondary mathematics and physics instruction]. In J. Baumert, W. Bos & R. Lehmann, (Eds.), *TIMSS/III. Dritte Internationale Mathematik- und Naturwissenschaftsstudie. Mathemacische und naturwissenschaftliche Bildung am Ende der Schullaufbahn. Band 2: Mathematische und physikalische Kompetenzen am Ende der gymnasialen Oberstufe* (pp. 271–316) Opladen, Germany: Leske & Budrich.

Beeth, M. (2001) Systemic reform in mathematics and science education in Ohio (USA): 1991–2000. In D. Psillos, P. Kariotoglou, V. Tselfes, G. Bisdikian, G. Fassoulopoulos,

E. Hatzikraniotis and M. Kallery, (Eds.), *Proceedings of the Third International Conference on Science Education Research in the Knowledge Based Society, Vol. 1* (pp. 198–200). Thessaloniki, Greece: Aristotle University of Thessaloniki.

Beeth, M., Duit R., Prenzel, M., Ostermeier, C., Tytler, R., and Wickman, P. O. (2003) Quality development projects in science education. In D. Psillos, P. Kariotoglou, V. Tselfes, G. Fassoulopoulos, E. Hatzikraniotis & M. Kallery, (Eds.), *Science Education research in the knowledge based society.* Dordrecht, The Netherlands: Kluwer Academic Publishers (in press).

Bent, H. (1984) Uses (and abuses) of models in teaching chemistry. *Journal of Chemical Education*, 61,774–777.

Biemans, H. J. A., Deel, O. R., and Simons, R. J. (2001) Differences between successful and less successful students while working with the CONTACT-2 strategy. *Learning and Instruction*, 11, 265–282.

Bybee, R. W. (1997) Towards an understanding of scientific literacy. In W. Gräber & K. Bolte (Eds.), *Scientific literacy* (pp. 37–68). Kiel, Germany: IPN – Leibniz Institute for Science Education at the University of Kiel.

Carey, S. (1985) *Conceptual change in childhood.* Cambridge, MA: A Bradford Book. The MIT Press.

Carr, M. (1984) Model confusion in chemistry. *Research in Science Education*, 14, 97103.

Chi, M. T. H., Slotta, J. D., and de Leeuw, N. (1994) From things to process: A theory of conceptual change for learning science concepts. *Learning and Instruction*, 4, 27–43.

Chiu, M-H, Chou, C-C, and Liu, C-J (2002) Dynamic processes of conceptual change: Analysis of constructing mental models of chemical equilibrium. *Journal of Research in Science Teaching*, 39, 713–737.

Chinn, C. A. and Brewer, W. F. (1993) The role of anomalous data in knowledge acquisition: A theoretical framework and implications for science education. *Review of Educational Research*, 63, 1–49.

DeBoer, G. E. (2000) Scientific literacy: another look at its historical and contemporary meaning and its relationship to science education reform. *Journal of Research in Science Teaching*, 37, 582–601.

Driver, R. and Osbourne, J. (1998, April) Reappraising science education for scientific literacy. Paper presented at the annual meeting of the National Association for Research in Science Teaching (NARST), San Diego.

Driver, R. (1989) Changing conceptions. In P. Adey, (Ed.), *Adolescent development and school practice* (pp. 79–103). London: Falmer Press.

Duit, R. and Treagust, D. (1998) Learning in science – From behaviourism towards social constructivism and beyond. In B. Fraser & K. Tobin (Eds.), *International handbook of science education* (pp. 3–26). Dordrecht, The Netherlands: Kluwer Academic Publishers.

Duit, R. (1998, April) Towards multi-perspective views of science learning and instruction. Paper presented at the annual meeting of the American Educational Research Association in San Diego.

Duit, R. (1999) Conceptual change approaches in science education. In W. Schnotz, S.Vosniadou, & M. Carretero (Eds.), *New perspectives on conceptual change* (pp. 263–282). Amsterdam, NL: Pergamon.

Duit, R. (2002a) *Bibliography STGSE: Students' and teachers' conceptions and science education,* Kiel, Germany: IPN – Leibniz Institute for Science Education (*us*http://www.ipn.uni-kiel.de/*us*)

Duit, R. (2002b) Visions, research, and school practice. In R. Cross, (Ed.), A vision for science education: Responding to the work of Peter Fensham (pp. 155–169). London: RoutledgeFalmer.

Dykstra, D. I. (1992) Studying conceptual change: Constructing new understandings. In R. Duit, F. Goldberg, & H. Niedderer (Eds.), *Research in physics learning: Theoretical issues and empirical studies* (pp. 40–58). Proceedings of an international workshop. Kiel, Germany: IPN – Leibniz Institute for Science Education.

Fensham, P. and Harlen, W. (1999) School science and public understanding of science. *International Journal of Science Education*, 21, 755–763.

Fensham, P. (2001) Science content as problematic – Issues for research. In H. Behrendt, H. Dahncke, R. Duit, W. Gräber, M. Komorek, A. Kross & P. Reiska, (Eds.), *Research in science education – Past, present, and future* (pp. 27–41). Dordrecht, The Netherlands: Kluwer Academic Publishers.

Fischler, H. (1994) Concerning the difference between intention and action: Teachers' conceptions and actions in physics teaching. In I. Carlgren, G. Handal & S. Vaage, (Eds.), *Teachers' minds and actions: Research on teachers' thinking and practice* (pp. 165–180). London: The Falmer Press.

Garnett, P. J. and Treagust, D. F. (1992) Conceptual difficulties experienced by senior high school students of electrochemistry: electric circuits and oxidation reduction equations. *Journal of Research in Science Teaching*, 29, 121–142.

Georghiades, P. (2000) Beyond conceptual change learning in science education: focusing on transfer, durability and metacognition. *Educational Research*, 42(2), 119–139.

Gilbert, J. K. and Boulter, C. J. (1998) Learning science through models and modeling, In. In B. Fraser & K. Tobin (Eds.), *International handbook of science education* (pp. 53–66). Dordrecht, The Netherlands: Kluwer Academic Publishers.

Gilbert, J. K. (Ed.) (1993) *Models and modeling in science education*. Hatfield, Herts, UK: Association for Science Education.

Gilbert, J. K., Osborne, R. J., and Fensham, P. (1982) Children's science and its implications for teaching. *Science Education*, 625–633.

Gräber, W. and Bolte, K. (Eds.) (1997) *Scientific literacy*. Kiel, Germany: IPN Leibniz-Institute for Science Education.

Greeno, J. G., Collins, A. M., and Resnick, L. B. (1997) Cognition and learning. In D. C. Berliner & R. C. Calfee, (Eds.), *Handbook of educational psychology* (pp. 15–46). New York: Simon & Schuster Macmillan.

Grosslight, L., Unger, C., Jay, E. and Smith, C. (1991) Understanding models and their use in science: Conceptions of middle and high school students and experts. *Journal of Research in Science Teaching*, 28, 799–822.

Guzetti, B. and Hynd, C., (Eds.) (1998) *Perspectives on conceptual change*. Mahwah, NJ: Lawrence Erlbaum.

Guzetti, B. J., Snyder, T. E., Glass, G. V. and Gamas, W. S. (1993) Promoting conceptual change in science: A comparative meta-analysis of instructional interventions from reading education and science education. *Reading Research Quarterly*, 28, 116–159.

Harlen, W. (2001) The assessment of scientific literacy in the OECD/PISA project. In H. Behrendt, H. Dahncke, R. Duit, W. Gräber, M. Komorek & A. Kross, (Eds.), *Research in Science Education – past, present and future* (pp. 49–60). Dordrecht: The Netherlands: Kluwer Academic Publishers.

Harrison, A. G. and Treagust, D. F. (2000) Learning about atoms, molecules and chemical bonds: A case-study of multiple model use in grade-11 chemistry. *Science Education*, 84, 352–381.

Hennessey, M. G. (1993, April) *Students' ideas about their conceptualisation: Their elicitation through instruction*. Paper presented at the Annual Meeting of the American Educational Research Association. Atlanta, GA.

Hewson, P. W. (1981) A conceptual change approach to learning science. *European Journal of Science Education*, 3, 383–396.

Hewson, P. W. (1982) A case study of conceptual change in special relativity: The influence of prior knowledge in learning. *European Journal of Science Education*, 4, 61–78.

Hewson, P. W. (1996) Teaching for conceptual change. In D. F. Treagust, R. Duit & B. J. Fraser (Eds.), *Improving teaching and learning in science and mathematics* (pp. 131–140). New York: Teachers College Press.

Hewson, P. W. and Hewson, M. G. A'B. (1984) The role of conceptual conflict in conceptual change and the design of science instruction. *Instructional Science*, 13, 1–13.

Hewson, P. W. and Hewson, M. G. A'B. (1988) An appropriate conception of teaching science: A view from studies of learning. *Science Education*, 72(5) 597–614.

Hewson, P. W. and Hewson, M. G. A'B. (1992) The status of students' conceptions. In R. Duit, F. Goldberg, & H. Niedderer (Eds.), *Research in physics learning: Theoretical issues and empirical studies* (pp. 59–73). Proceedings of an international workshop. Kiel, Germany: IPN – Leibniz Institute for Science Education.

Hewson, P. W. and Lemberger, E. (2000) Status as the hallmark of conceptual change. In R. Millar, J. Leach, & J. Osborne, (Eds.), Improving science education (pp. 110–125). Buckingham, UK: Open University Press.

Hewson, P. W, and Thorley, N. R. (1989) The conditions of conceptual change in the classroom. *International Journal of Science Education*, 11, Special Issue, 541–553.

Hewson, P., and Hennessey, M. G. (1992) Making status explicit: A case study of conceptual change. In R. Duit, F. Goldberg, & H. Niedderer (Eds.), *Research in physics learning: Theoretical issues and empirical studies* (pp. 176–187) Proceedings of an international workshop. Kiel, Germany: IPN – Leibniz Institute for Science Education.

Jung, W. (1993) Hilft die Entwicklungspsychologie dem Physikdidaktiker [Does developmental psychology help the physics educator?]. In R. Duit & W Gräber (Eds.), *Kognitive Entwicklung und naturwissenschaftlicher Unterricht* (pp. 86–107). Kiel, Germany: IPN – Leibniz Institute for Science Education.

Kaestle, C. F. (1993) The awful reputation of educational research. *Educational Researcher*, 22(1), 23–31.

Kennedy, M. M. (1997) The connection between research and practice. *Educational Researcher*, 26(7), 4–12.

Khun, T. S. (1970) Structure of scientific revolutions. 2nd edition. Chicago: University of Chicago Press.

Lawson, A. E., Abraham, M. R., and Renner, J. W. (2001) *A theory of instruction: Using the learning cycle to teach science concepts and thinking skills*. NARST Monograph Number One. University of Cincinnatti: National Association for Research in Science Teaching.

Lijnse, P. (2000) Didactics of science: The forgotten dimension in science education research. In R. Millar, J. Leach, & J. Osborne (Eds.), *Improving science education* (pp. 308–326). Buckingham, UK: Open University Press.

Limon, M. and Mason, L. (Eds.) (2002) *Reconsidering conceptual change: Issues in theory and practice*. Dordrecht, The Netherlands Kluwer Academic Publishers.

Limon, M. (2001) On the cognitive conflict as an instructional strategy for conceptual change: a critical appraisal. *Learning and Instruction*, 11, 357–380.

Mason, L., (Ed.) (2001) Instructional practices for conceptual change in science domains. *Learning and Instruction*, 11, 259–429 (Special Issue).

Matthews, M. (1993) Constructivism and science education: Some epistemological problems. *Journal of Science Education and Technology*, 2, 359–369.

McComas, W. F., (Ed.) (1998) *The nature of science in science education – rationales and strategies*. Dordrecht, The Netherlands: Kluwer Academic Publishers.

Mortimer, E. F. (1995) Conceptual change or conceptual profile change? *Science & Education*, 4, 267–285.

Norman, D. A. (1983) Some observations on mental models. In D. Gentner & A. L. Stevens (Eds.), *Mental models* (pp. 7–14). Hillsdale, NJ: Lawrence Erlbaum Associates, Publishers Inc.

OECD-PISA (1999) Measuring student knowledge and skills: A new framework for assessment. Paris: OECD.

Pintrich, P. R., Marx, R. W., and Boyle, R. A. (1993) Beyond cold conceptual change: The role of motivational beliefs and classroom contextual factors in the process of conceptual change. *Review of Educational Research*, 63, 167–199.

Posner, G. J., Strike, K. A., Hewson, P. W., and Gertzog, W. A. (1982) Accommodation of a scientific conception: Toward a theory of conceptual change. *Science Education*, 66, 211–227.

Prenzel, M. and Duit, R. (2000, April) Increasing the efficiency of science and mathematics instruction: report of a national quality development programme. Paper presented at the annual meeting of the National Association for Research in Science Teaching (NARST), New Orleans.

Prenzel, M., Duit, R., Euler, M., Geiser, H., Hoffmann, L., Lehrke, M., Müller, C., Rimmele, R., Seidel, T., and Widodo, A. (2002) Eine Videostudie über Lehr-Lern-Prozesse im Physikunterricht [A video-study on teaching and learning processes in physics instruction]. *Zeitschrift für Pädagogik*, 48 [45. Beiheft], 139–156.

Roth, K. J., Druker, S., Kawanaka, T., Okamoto, Y., Trubacova, D., Warvi, D., Rasmussen, D., and Gallimore, R. (2001, March) Uses of video-based technology and conceptual tools in research: the case of the TIMSS-R Video Study. Paper presented at the annual meeting of the National Association for Research on Science Teaching (NARST), St. Louis, MO.

Russell, J. W., Kozma, R. B., Jones, T., Wykoff, J., Marx, N., and Davis, J. (1997) Use of simultaneous-synchronised macroscopic, microscopic and symbolic representations to enhance the teaching and learning of chemical concepts. *Journal of Chemical Education*, 74(3), 330–334.

Salomon, G., and Globerson, T. (1987) Skill may not be enough: the role of mindfulness in learning and transfer. *International Journal of Educational Research*, 11, 623–637.

Schnolz, W., Vosniadou, S. and Carretero, M., (Eds.) (1999) *New perspectives on conceptual change*. Amsterdam, NL: Pergamon.

Sinatra, G. M., and Pintrich, P. R., (Eds.) (2003) *Intentional conceptual change*. Mahwah, NJ: Erlbaum.

Stigler, J. W, Gonzales, P., Kawanaka, T, Knoll, S., and Serrano, A. (1999) *The TIMSS Videotape Classroom Study. Methods and findings from an exploratory research project on eighth-grade mathematics instruction in Germany, Japan, and the United States.* Washington, DC: US Department of Education.

Strike, K. A. and Posner, G. J. (1985) A conceptual change view of learning and understanding. In L. West & L. Pines (Eds.), *Cognitive structure and conceptual change* (pp. 259–266). Orlando. FL: Academic Press.

Strike, K. A., and Posner, G. J. (1992) A revisionist theory of conceptual change. In R. A. Duschl & R. J. Hamilton (Eds.), *Philosophy of science, cognitive psychology, and educational theory and practice* (pp. 147–176). New York: State University of New York Press.

Thagard, P. (1992) *Conceptual revolutions*. Princeton, NJ: Princeton University Press

Tobin, K. (Ed.) (1993) *The practice of constructivism in science education*. Washington, DC: American Association for the Advancement of Science Press.

Toulmin, S. (1972) *Human Understanding: Vol. I.* Oxford: Oxford University Press.

Treagust, D. F., Harrison, A. G., Venville, G. J., and Dagher, Z. (1996) Using an analogical teaching approach to engender conceptual change. *International Journal of Science Education*, 18, 213–229.

Tyson, L. M., Venville, G. J., Harrison, A. G., and Treagust, D. F. (1997) A multidimensional framework for interpreting conceptual change in the classroom. *Science Education*, 81, 387–404.

Tytler, R., and Conley, H. (2001) The science in schools research project: improving science teaching and learning in Australian schools. In D. Psillos, P. Kariotoglou, V. Tselfes, G. Bisdikian, G. Fassoulopoulos, E. Hatzikraniotis & M. Kallery, (Eds.), *Proceedings of the Third International Conference on Science Education Research in the Knowledge Based Society. Vol. 1* (pp. 204–206). Thessaloniki, Greece: Aristotle University of Thessaloniki.

van der Veer, R. and Valsiner, J. (1991) *Understanding Vygotsky: A quest for synthesis*. Oxford, UK: Blackwell.

Venville, G. J. and Treagust, U. F. (1998) Exploring conceptual change in genetics using a multidimensional interpretive framework. *Journal of Research in Science Teaching*, 35, 1031–1055.

von Glasersfeld, B. (1989) Constructivism in education. In T. Husen & T. N. Postlethwaite, (Eds.), *The international encyclopaedia of education* (pp. 162–163). New York: Pergamon Press.

Vosniadou, S. and Ioannides, C. (1998) From conceptual change to science education: a psychological point of view. *International Journal of Science Education*, 20, 1213–1230.

Vosniadou, S. (1994) Capturing and modelling the process of conceptual change. *Learning and Instruction*, 4, 45–69.

Vosniadou, S. (1996) Towards a revised cognitive psychology for new advances in learning and instruction. *Learning and Instruction*, 6, 95–109.

Vosniadou, S., Ioannides, C., Dimitrakopoulou, A., and Papademetriou, E. (2001) Designing learning environments to promote conceptual change in science. *Learning and Instruction*, 11, 381–419.

Wandersee, J. H., Mintzes, J. J., and Novak, J. D. (1994) Research on alternative conceptions in science. In D. Gabel (Ed.), *Handbook of research on science teaching and learning* (pp. 177–210). New York: Macmillan.

Wang, M. C., Haertel, G. U., and Walberg, H. J. (1993) Towards a knowledge base for school learning. *Review of Educational Research*, 63(3), 249–294.

Widodo, A. and Duit, R. (2002, June) Conceptual change views and the reality of classroom practice. Paper presented at the Third European Symposium on Conceptual Change. Turku, Finland.

Widodo, A., Duit, R., and Müller, C. (2002, April) Constructivist views of teaching and learning in practice: Teachers' views and classroom behaviour. Paper presented at the Annual Meeting of the National Association for Research in Science Teaching, New Orleans.

Wright, B. (1993) The irrelevancy of science education research: perception or reality? *NARST News*, 35(1), 1–2.

CHAPTER 5

TEACHER TALK AND MEANING MAKING IN SCIENCE CLASSROOMS
A Vygotskian analysis and review

Philip Scott

Studies in Science Education (1998) 32, 45–80

Introduction: the discursive turn in psychology

In his book *Acts of Meaning* Jerome Bruner (1990) develops a case in support of what he refers to as a 'culturally oriented psychology'. Central to this psychology is *meaning* and the processes and transactions involved in the construction of meanings. Bruner contrasts this kind of approach with that based on computational or information processing models of the mind and maintains that the very shape of our lives is understandable to ourselves and to others only by virtue of the cultural systems of interpretation; that is, through the symbolic systems of the culture – 'its language and discourse modes, the forms of logical and narrative explication, and the patterns of mutually dependent communal life' (Bruner, 1990, p. 34).

Just four years later Harré and Gillett (1994, p. 27) refer to the 'new cognitive psychology' that represents the 'discursive turn' and identify core principles to characterise it. They suggest that many psychological phenomena are to be interpreted as properties or features of public or private discourse. As public discourse, it is behaviour, as private discourse, it is thought. Furthermore, individual and private uses of symbolic systems are derived from interpersonal discursive processes that are the main feature of the human environment.

The roots of this cultural or discursive psychology can be traced to a number of sources which include the later writings of Wittgenstein (1953), the symbolic interactionist approach to human studies developed from the work of G.H. Mead (1934) and the sociocultural psychology developed by Lev Vygotsky (Vygotsky, 1962, 1978) and his colleagues Alexander Luria and Alexei Leontiev.

In recent years the influence of discursive or cultural psychology on research in science education has been reflected in a gradual development of interest in studies of how meanings are developed through language and other semiotic means in the classroom. This 'new direction' for science education research (see Solomon, 1994; Sutton, 1996) signals a move away from studies focussing on individual student understandings of specific phenomena towards research into the ways in which understandings are developed in the social context of the science classroom (Duit and Treagust, 1998); this new direction also signals a revived interest in the role played by the teacher in the science classroom (Ogborn *et al.*, 1996).

This review examines one aspect of the discursive turn in science education research by focussing on a selection of studies which investigate the ways in which meanings are developed in the interactions within science classrooms. The field covered in the review is confined to research into interactions between teacher and students, although there is an extensive literature dealing with analysis of meaning making through student-student interactions (see, for example, Howe *et al.*, 1990). The review is organised in terms of basic Vygotskian principles and these are addressed in the following section.

A framework for the review, based on Vygotskian principles

As indicated in the previous section, Vygotsky's writings have been highly influential in the development of a culturally-oriented or discursive psychology. In fact, Vygotsky's sociocultural perspective on development and learning has become increasingly prominent in educational circles over the last ten years or so, particularly in North America where scholars such as James Wertsch have contributed a great deal to interpreting the Vygotskian position and bringing it to the attention of researchers in education. A number of articles (for example: Bruner, 1985; Hicks, 1995; Hodson and Hodson, 1998; Howe, 1996; Shepardson, 1997), edited collections (for example: Daniels, 1996; Forman *et al.*, 1993; Hicks, 1996; Moll, 1990) and introductory texts (for example: Kozulin, 1990; Newman and Holzman 1993; Tharp and Gallimore, 1988; Wertsch, 1985a, 1985b, 1991, 1998), now exist in which various aspects of Vygotsky's sociocultural perspective are considered. In this chapter, I draw upon Vygotskian theory in setting out an organising framework for the review.

Central to Vygotsky's sociocultural approach is the claim that higher mental functioning in the individual derives from social life. This claim predates, and overlaps with, Harré and Gillet's principles for a 'new' cognitive psychology and is summarised in Vygotsky's frequently cited 'General Genetic Law of Cultural Development' which outlines how higher psychological structures (such as scientific conceptual knowledge) appear, 'first between people as an interpsychological category and then inside the child as an intrapsychological category' (Vygotsky, 1978, p. 128). On the interpsychological, or social, plane language and other semiotic mechanisms are used to develop and rehearse meanings between individuals and provide the tools or mediational means that enable individual cognition.

In considering the question of how students develop 'new' understandings or meanings in science classrooms, the Vygotskian perspective therefore leads to an analytical approach which recognises the importance of the interactions of the interpsychological plane and in particular the nature of teacher-student discourse in the classroom. According to the Vygotskian perspective the teacher, or some other knowledgeable figure, has a key role to play in mediating and 'passing on' existing public knowledge (such as scientific knowledge) to students. Bruner (1985) draws attention to this central role of the teacher, stating that:

> Vygotsky's project [is] to find the manner in which aspirant members of a culture learn from their tutors, the vicars of their culture, how to understand the world. That world is a symbolic world in the sense that it consists of conceptually organised, rule-bound belief systems about what exists, about how to get to goals, about what is to be valued. There is no way, none, in which a human being could master that world without the aid and assistance of others for, in fact, that world is others.
>
> (Bruner, 1985, p. 32)

Vygotsky's analysis of the teacher's role is based on a conceptualisation of teaching as 'assisting performance'; this notion of assisting performance is linked to individual student learning through the concept of the 'Zone of Proximal Development' (ZPD) (Vygotsky, 1978). Thus, the teacher assists the student in achieving a level of performance within the ZPD which the student would be incapable of whilst acting independently and will subsequently be able to achieve alone (see Tharp and Gallimore, 1988, p. 33). More recently the ways in which performance might be assisted in the ZPD have been characterised in terms of the 'scaffolding' metaphor (Wood *et al.*, 1976).

Bearing in mind these basic aspects of Vygotskian sociocultural theory, this review will focus on activity of the interpsychological plane of the classroom and in particular on research studies into the ways in which teachers guide the discourse of the interpsychological plane to support student learning. Specifically, this review is framed around the following three features:

i.   *The forms of pedagogical intervention*
     These are the different forms of intervention made by teachers to support students in developing an understanding of scientific knowledge (acknowledging the fact that teachers make interventions in the classroom for many purposes other than promoting the understanding of scientific knowledge). The principal focus here will be upon the ways in which researchers characterise different forms of discursive intervention by teachers (acknowledging the fact that other forms of mediational means are simultaneously in operation in the classroom).

ii. *The authoritative and dialogic functions of the discourse*
     The second feature concerns the nature of the talk of the interpsychological plane and draws on the distinction between authoritative and dialogic discourse. In the classroom, the relationship between teacher and students is clearly subject to an asymmetry in authority with regard to knowledge of subject matter. It is the teacher who is recognised as having responsibility for providing guidance in learning and it is to be expected that this is reflected in the way in which the teacher controls the discourse of the classroom. The authoritative-dialogic distinction offers one means for distinguishing between situations where the teacher tends to approach this task from an authoritative stance (transmitting knowledge), and where the teacher adopts a more dialogic approach (encouraging exploration and development of meanings).

iii. *Teacher talk and scaffolding*
     The final feature concerns the ways in which teacher interventions on the social plane of the classroom might be conceptualised in terms of the notion of 'scaffolding' introduced by Wood *et al.* (1976).
[. . .]

Approaches to analysing discourse and meaning-making on the interpsychological plane of the science classroom

In Chapter 6 of *Thinking and Speech* (Vygotsky, 1987) Vygotsky introduces his ideas on how the forms of teacher-student interpsychological functioning, encountered in the institutional setting of formal schooling, provide a framework for the development of students' conceptual thinking. This analysis was developed in the year that Vygotsky died, thus removing the opportunity for any elaboration of ideas; the analysis was also (of course) rooted in the social and cultural context of Soviet schooling in the 1930s. Wertsch has pointed out the lack of detailed analysis, by Vygotsky, of the social and cultural contexts in which the interactions of the interpsychological plane are played out, arguing that: 'Instead of recognising that interpsychological functioning itself is always situated with regard to cultural, historical and institutional setting, Vygotsky often treated it as if it always occurs in essentially the same form' (Wertsch and Toma, 1991).

Whilst it is certainly the case that the Vygotskian sociocultural perspective provides an important template for theorising and organising research into meaning-making in the classroom, what it does not (and clearly cannot) offer is any developed and detailed analysis of how meanings are developed on the interpsychological plane of the classroom in the institutional setting of Western schools towards the end of the twentieth century. Here we turn to research which has been carried out to address this particular issue focussing on each of the three features of discourse set out earlier.

The forms of pedagogical intervention

The ways in which one teacher intervened in the classroom to make a scientific explanation (based on the concept of air pressure) available to his students were outlined earlier. Attention is now given to examining how such pedagogical interventions have been conceptualised in the research literature.

A frequently cited and influential study in this area of research is that of Edwards and Mercer (1987), presented in the book 'Common Knowledge'. The central issue dealt with by Edwards and Mercer is the relationship between the thematic content of the lessons, and the practical activities and discourse which constitute the lessons themselves. The study is based on detailed analyses of teaching and learning episodes taken from lessons in various subject areas including science and mathematics.

From their analyses Edwards and Mercer identify how teachers *control* the teaching and learning events of the classroom 'maintaining a tight definition of what became joint versions of events, and joint understandings of curriculum content' (Edwards and Mercer, 1987, p. 129) and develop an inventory of the ways in which the teachers are able to do this. The pedagogical interventions identified are presented in terms of the level of control exerted by the teacher and include, starting with the lowest level of teacher control, the following:

Elicitation of pupils' contributions: which, in the classes observed, often fell into the familiar initiation-response-feedback (IRF) structure (Sinclair and Coulthard, 1975); *Marking knowledge as significant and joint*: where expressed knowledge is given special prominence by discursive practices such as special enunciation, repetition and the use of formulaic phrases; *Cued elicitation of pupils' contributions*: which are IRF types of discourse where the teacher asks questions whilst simultaneously providing explicit clues to the information required, a process which may be accomplished with the help of teacher intonation, pausing, gestures or physical demonstrations.

Edwards and Mercer (*ibid.* p. 143) suggest that through cued elicitation, 'the pupils are neither being drawn out of themselves, in the *e-ducare* sense, nor simply being taught directly in the "transmission' sense". Rather they argue that the pupils are 'being inculcated into what becomes for them a shared discourse with the teacher'; they suggest that this form of intervention can be interpreted in terms of the teacher providing assistance and scaffolding in the ZPD, requiring the pupils to 'actively participate in the creation of shared knowledge, rather than merely sit and listen to the teacher talking' (*ibid.*, p. 143). At the same time they identify the problematic nature of cued elicitation where it is 'difficult to avoid the impression that the pupils were essentially trying to read all the signals available in a guessing game in which they had to work out . . . what it was that the teacher was trying to get them to say' (*ibid.*, p. 145).

Further interventions identified by Edwards and Mercer (at an increasing level of teacher control) include *Paraphrasing pupils' contributions, Offering reconstructive recaps and Direct Lecturing.* By 'offering reconstructive recaps', the teacher is able to redefine what the pupils said and what occurred in the lesson in a way which is 'neater and closer to the intended lesson plan' (*ibid.*, p. 146). In addition, 'by presupposing certain things are known or understood the teacher was able to forestall disagreement, and shape the direction of the discourse and interpretations put upon experience'. In 'direct lecturing', little or no contribution is asked of, or offered, by pupils.

Anyone who has spent time in schools will recognise the forms of pedagogical intervention outlined above. Indeed some of these interventions are represented in the teaching episode given earlier, where the teacher: *marked the significance* of the air pressure explanation through *repetition* and by clear and deliberate intonation of the voice; and *summarised* the air pressure explanation, marking it as 'joint knowledge'. What Edwards and Mercer offer in this study (further developed in Mercer, 1995) is a description of the ways in which teachers frame and guide classroom discourse to introduce, and promote shared understanding of, the thematic content of the lessons.

The aim of characterising teacher talk on the interpsychological plane of the classroom is also addressed by Jay Lemke in *Talking Science: Language, Learning and Values* (1990), a book which has proven to be widely influential in the area of language, teaching and learning in science. The basic thesis which Lemke proposes is that learning science involves learning to talk science: 'it means learning to communicate in the language of science and act as a member of the community of people who do so' (Lemke, 1990, p. 1); the basic question which is addressed in the book concerns *how* students learn to talk science through classroom discourse.

Lemke's analysis of classroom discourse is made in terms of two components: an 'activity structure' which demonstrates the organisational patterns of social interaction in the discourse; and the 'thematic pattern' of semantic relationships which constitutes the scientific content of the discourse. Lemke (*ibid.*, p. 100) addresses the question of how teachers use language to build up thematic patterns, that correspond to the conceptual systems of science, by identifying various activity structures (or 'thematic development strategies') commonly used by teachers. These strategies include what Lemke refers to as 'Dialogue and Monologue Strategies'.

The first Dialogue Strategy introduced by Lemke is the *Teacher Question Series* which is a sequence of thematically closely-related teacher questions in triadic dialogue (IRF structure) that construct a series of linked semantic relations. Lemke (*ibid.*, p. 101) suggests that this form of intervention is a transposition of a teacher lecture into dialogue form and provides effective exposition of thematic relations so long as the students provide thematically correct answers. There are clear similarities between the 'teacher question series' and the interactions which Edwards and Mercer describe as functioning through 'cued elicitation'. Lemke draws attention to various interventions which the teacher might employ in the event of students not providing the required answers. These include: *Selection and modification* of student answers to fit a thematic pattern; *Retroactive recontextualisation* of student answers which involves teacher elaboration of a student answer to place it in a different thematic context, retrospectively changing its meaning. A further Dialogue Strategy involves *Joint construction*, where a thematic pattern is constructed jointly by contributions to dialogue from both teacher and students, with one completing or extending clauses begun by the other.

Lemke also presents a range of teacher Monologue Strategies. *Logical exposition* is where a series of thematically related logical connections are made between various thematic items and semantic relations. *Narrative* involves an account of a set of events or actions which establishes chronological and often causal relations among them. *Selective Summary* involves summarisation of prior discourse which includes only selected thematic elements and relations. *Foregrounding and backgrounding* involves a repeat or summary of prior discourse in which certain themes are overtly marked as of greater importance and others implicitly as of lesser importance.

As with Edwards and Mercer, the interventions which Lemke identifies are distinctive and easily related to the activity of high school classrooms. In the 'air pressure' episode presented earlier, the teacher *selects* Michael's muttered comments so that they can be restated to all students on the interpsychological plane. He then rehearses the scientific explanation as a *joint construction* with Michael, thereby breaking down the explanation into its key component parts and making it available to all students. Finally the teacher offers a *summary* of the air pressure explanation.

There are significant overlaps between the list of 'classroom communications' identified by Edwards and Mercer and the 'thematic development strategies' identified by Lemke. In the analysis developed by Edwards and Mercer a key theme is the authority of the teacher and the control exercised by the teacher in shaping and guiding the discourse on the interpsychological plane, whereas Lemke's work is based on detailed analyses of classroom discourse drawing on the theoretical base of Social Semiotics'. It is interesting that both studies lead to similar outcomes in terms of the patterns of discourse which are identified; perhaps this should not be altogether surprising given the similarity in social and cultural contexts (schools in the UK and North America) in which each research project was carried out.

More recently the present author has developed a framework, based on empirical research, in which five forms of pedagogical intervention are identified (Scott, 1997b). These five forms of intervention are conceptualised as forming a 'Teaching Narrative' or teaching performance through which the teacher directs and sustains interactions to make the scientific view available to students. The concept of the Teaching Narrative is intended to provide an overarching theoretical structure which acknowledges the fact that teaching and learning science in the classroom occur over an extended time line with beginning and end points, and involve the teacher in laying a 'language trail' from students' cognitive starting points towards the learning goal of the scientific

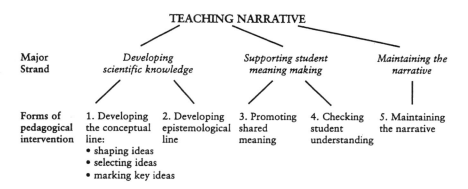

Figure 5 The teaching narrative, major strands and forms of pedagogical intervention

view. This aspect of the extended timeline is given prominence neither by Edwards and Mercer, nor by Lemke. The five categories of pedagogical intervention identified in the framework are grouped into three major strands; Developing scientific knowledge; Supporting student meaning making; Maintaining the teaching narrative.

The first strand of the Teaching Narrative consists of those interventions directed towards making scientific knowledge available on the interpsychological plane and is sub-divided into 'Developing the conceptual line and 'Developing the epistemological line' of the narrative.

Developing the conceptual line includes pedagogical interventions directed towards, 'Shaping Ideas', where the teacher might: guide students through the steps of an explanation by means of a series of key questions; paraphrase students' ideas; differentiate between ideas. In 'Selecting Ideas', the teacher might: select a student idea or part of a student idea; retrospectively elicit a student idea; overlook a student idea. In 'Marking Key Ideas', the teacher might: repeat an idea; ask a student to repeat an idea; enact a confirmatory exchange with a student; validate a student idea; pose a rhetorical question; use a particular intonation of voice.

Developing the epistemological line consists of teacher interventions which are aimed at introducing to students aspects of the nature of the scientific knowledge (such as the generalisability of scientific explanations) which is being taught. In the associated classroom-based research very few examples of interventions to contribute to the Epistemological Line of the narrative were observed, but nevertheless it can be argued that learning the science way of knowing involves not only learning how to use the conceptual tools of science but also coming to appreciate the epistemological framing of those tools Scott (1997b).

In the classroom episode presented earlier, the teacher does make an intervention which contributes to the Epistemological Line of the narrative when he makes the distinction between 'old' (everyday) and 'new' (scientific) ways of explaining. The teacher used this epistemological marker throughout the lessons (also see the postscript at the end of this chapter).

The second strand of the Teaching Narrative consists of those interventions directed towards making the science point of view available to all of the students in the class and checking the meanings and understandings that they subsequently develop. It is sub-divided into 'Promoting shared meaning' and 'Checking student understanding'. The teacher interventions to Promote shared meaning follow from the practicalities of the classroom where one teacher works with over twenty students; the teacher needs to organise the presentation of the scientific view in ways which make it available to all students. In *Promoting shared meaning* the teacher might: present ideas to the whole class; share individual student ideas with the whole class; share group findings with the whole class; jointly rehearse an idea with a student in front of the whole class; provide a spoken commentary to make explicit the thinking behind a specific activity that they are engaged in. In making interventions to *Check student understanding* the teacher might: ask for clarification of student ideas; check individual student understanding of particular ideas; check consensus in the class about certain ideas.

The third and final strand 'Maintaining the narrative' consists of those interventions by which the teacher provides a commentary on the unfolding teaching narrative with a view to helping students follow the development of the 'science story' (thematic content or pattern). This is talk *about* the narrative rather than 'talking the narrative'. In *Maintaining the narrative* the teacher might: state aims/purposes for the next part of the narrative; look ahead to anticipate possible outcomes; review progress of the narrative; refocus discussion. These various interventions to maintain the narrative help establish lines of *continuity* (Mercer 1995) in the discourse from one part of the teaching narrative to another.

An important point to bear in mind in considering these various strands of the teaching narrative is that a single teacher intervention can serve more than one goal or purpose. For example, the teacher asking a student to repeat an idea can act to 'mark a key idea' and also to 'promote shared meaning', making the idea available to other students. Wertsch (1998, p. 32) makes the general point when he argues that, 'mediated action typically serves *multiple* purposes ... multiple goals, often in interaction and sometimes in conflict, are typically involved'.

Each of the studies referred to here contribute to Vygotsky's project of characterising the discourse of the interpsychological plane of the classroom (or at least the discourse of this particular kind of classroom). In Bakhtinian terms, the studies contribute to describing the prevailing *speech genre* of the classroom (Bakhtin, 1986). A significant feature of the interventions identified is the way in which they contribute to, and constitute, a coherent 'performance' as the teacher is engaged in guiding the development of discourse on the interpsychological plane so that the scientific view is made available to all students. Some students become directly involved in the performance of the scientific view (as did Michael through the 'joint construction' of the air pressure lesson), others sit back and watch and listen as the performance of the scientific view unfolds. The challenge for the teacher is to guide the presentation of the scientific 'story' in such a way that it remains accessible and coherent to all of the students.

Further studies in this area include work by: Mortimer (1995), who investigates, from a social negotiation perspective, how ideas about the particle model of matter develop in a Brazilian classroom (14–15 years); Boulter and Gilbert (1996), who examine the talk of a primary (9–11 years) classroom and propose a framework for analysing teacher and pupil participation in modelling; Watt (1996) who analyses teacher questioning behaviour in constructivist primary science classrooms using a modification of a descriptive system designed by Barnes and Todd (1977).

Ogborn, Kress, Martins and McGillicuddy (1996) have taken a slightly different approach to analysing the pedagogical interventions of the interpsychological plane of the classroom by focussing on the ways in which high school science teachers construct and present *explanations* in the classroom. The main outcome of the research is a theoretical framework which has three components (Ogborn *et al.*, 1996, p. 8):

1. Scientific explanations as analogous to 'stories'
2. An account of meaning-making in explanation consisting of four main parts:

    - creating differences
    - constructing entities
    - transforming knowledge
    - putting meaning into matter

3. Variation and styles of teacher explanation.

In developing the notion of scientific explanations being analogous to stories (see also: Arnold and Millar, 1996; Stinner, 1995; Sutton, 1996), Ogborn *et al.* suggest that the vital features of a scientific story are that: firstly there is a cast of *protagonists*, each of which has its own capabilities which are what makes it what it is (protagonists might include entities such as electric currents, germs, magnetic fields and also mathematical constructions such as harmonic motion and negative feedback); secondly the members of this cast enact one of the many series of events of which they are capable; lastly these events have a consequence which follows from the nature of the protagonists and the events they happen to enact.

Ogborn *et al.* (*ibid.*, p. 137) maintain that the first step in meaning making in explanation is to create a need for that explanation and suggest that this can be achieved through identifying a difference to be bridged or resolved. In the classroom, *Creating Differences* might be achieved through: promises of clarification; eliciting differences of opinion; using stories to suggest ideas; displaying counter-intuitive results and creating expectations. In the episode given earlier, the teacher 'creates differences' by demonstrating a counter-intuitive phenomenon; the balloons expand when air is removed from the bell jar. The excited reaction of the pupils suggests that the demonstration was successful in sparking interest and creating the need for an explanation.

Having created an opening for the explanation, the teacher is now faced with the fact that the worlds of protagonists, which constitute scientific explanations, are often removed from everyday common sense and that scientific explanations can make no sense to the learner until they know what the entities involved are supposed to be able to do, or have done to them. Thus there is the need for students to *Construct Explanatory Entities* or to 'talk into existence' (Ogborn *et al.*, 1996, p. 14) these entities. The process of talking into existence explanatory entities involves transformation of meaning by students. Thus, 'every discussion gives an entity new possibilities and transforms its meaning. The pupil's knowledge is constantly being transformed' (*ibid.*, p. 15). This personal transformation of knowledge corresponds to the process of internalisation (Vygotsky, 1962) in which learners reorganise and reconstruct experiences played out on the interpsychological plane. In addition to this personal transformation of knowledge, Ogborn *et al.* point out the ways in which knowledge is transformed as it is presented in the classroom. The authors cite the narrative form as being one way to *transform knowledge* and also point to the crucial role of analogy and metaphor in transforming knowledge in the classroom (with, for example, the eye seen as a camera and the control of the hormone system by the pituitary gland seen as a conductor keeping an orchestra together, *ibid.*, p. 15).

Ogborn *et al.* (1996, p. 141) claim that their description of explaining science in the classroom provides a framework to 'give accounts of many different ways of explaining; accounts which can bring out similarities and differences between them'. In terms of what has been laid out in this review so far it can be seen that this work on explanations contributes to an understanding of what might be involved in developing the 'Conceptual Line' of a teaching sequence.

A central feature of each of the studies referred to so far is that they all focus on the analysis of discourse and meaning making in whole-class teaching situations. A separate group of research studies can be identified in which there is a similar focus on classroom discourse and meaning making, but which involves rather different classroom teaching practices. Here, the students are encouraged to take part in the 'authentic practices' (Brown, Collins and Duguid, 1989) of the discipline which is being taught and learning is considered to occur through immersion in the language and activities of those practices.

Interestingly, a key influence in this field of research studies (which has developed principally in North America) has been the previously reviewed work of Jay Lemke (1990). *Talking Science* provides an analysis of discourse from 'traditional' North American classrooms. Through analysing that empirical data Lemke points to various shortcomings in prevailing approaches to teaching and learning and offers alternative pedagogical strategies. As outlined earlier, Lemke suggests that scientific reasoning is learnt 'by talking to other members of the community, we practice it by talking to others, and we use it in talking to them, in talking to ourselves, and in writing and other forms of more complex activity' (*ibid.*, p. 122). This research field has also been influenced by Vygotsky's sociocultural perspective, it draws on the principles of situated cognition (see: Brown, Collins and Duguid, 1989; Lave and Wenger, 1991; Rogoff, 1990) and has had considerable impact in both science education (see, for example: Eichinger, Anderson, Palincsar and David, 1991; Roth, 1995, 1996; Moje, 1995; Roychoudhury and Roth, 1996) and mathematics education (see, for example: Lampert, 1990; Cobb, Wood and Yackel, 1991; Cobb, Perlwitz and Underwood-Gregg, 1998).

In the studies cited here students are directly involved in 'doing' science or 'doing' mathematics. Roychoudhury and Roth (1996), for example, investigate interactions in an 'open-inquiry' physics laboratory involving junior high school students. They describe the 'open-inquiry' laboratory as being one in which, 'the activities are open-ended ... there is no recipe-type, step-by-step procedure available for conducting the experiments' (*ibid.*, p. 425); the students 'have decision-making power over what to investigate and how to investigate within the constraints of available resources' (*ibid.*, p. 426). The purpose of this study was to find out about the nature of student–student interactions, the nature of the peer group-teacher interactions and the students' views of collaborative work in the context of the open-ended laboratory activities.

In their analysis Roychoudhury and Roth develop a categorical scheme for characterising the verbal interactions among students which is based on the degree of participation by the members of the group. The teacher in the study is described as acting either as a 'Socratic interlocutor who helped students with guiding questions to construct their own meaning or as a 'coach' who provided scaffolding through explicit explanation in areas that were unfamiliar to the students' (*ibid.*, p. 442).

The educational rationales underlying 'explicit instruction' and 'inquiry-based' approaches are fundamentally different (Gee, 1996) and this difference leads to different patterns of classroom discourse. In this respect the observations and descriptions of language-use offered by, for example, Roychoudhury and Roth (1996), where the students work in groups and the teacher acts as coach, are significantly different to those presented by Ogborn *et al.* (1996) where the focus is on teachers working to develop explanations with whole classes of students. The two patterns of language-use exemplify and follow from different approaches to instruction.

In this section a range of studies has been referred to which characterise the ways in which teachers 'talk into existence', and make available to students, scientific subject matter on the social plane of the classroom. Attention is now turned to a complementary form of analysis of that discourse; this focusses on the ways in which discourse might be framed to serve both 'authoritative' and 'dialogic' functions.

The authoritative and dialogic functions of classroom discourse

Although patterns and practices of classroom activity vary both across and within cultures a shared, and fundamental, starting point is that the teacher is charged with the responsibility of introducing students to a particular way of knowing about some event or phenomenon. Given this situation, then it is clear that, in terms of teaching and learning, the teacher occupies a position of *authority* in the classroom. Wertsch makes the point that 'sociocultural settings inherently involve power and authority' and that any analysis that focusses on cognitive-instrumental rationality alone would have to be viewed as having essential shortcomings' Wertsch (1998, p. 64). In this section attention is focussed upon ways in which classroom discourse can be analysed in terms of its authoritative and dialogic functions.

In authoritative discourse the teacher's interventions are intended to convey information, the emphasis is on the transmissive function of teacher talk, whilst the dialogic function of teacher talk is realised as the teacher encourages students to put forward their ideas, to explore and to debate points of view. This approach to analysing discourse is discussed by Wertsch (1991), who draws attention to the distinction made by Lotman (1988) between two purposes of written and spoken texts: the univocal and dialogic functions. These two functions which Lotman sees texts fulfilling are 'to convey meanings adequately' and 'to generate new meanings' (Lotman, 1988, p. 34). The first of these, the 'univocal' function, is very similar to that assumed by a simple transmission model of communication. In contrast, the second 'dialogic' function of a text:

> ... is to generate new meanings. In this respect a text ceases to be a passive link in conveying some constant information between input (sender) and output (receiver). Whereas in the first case a difference between the message at the input and that at the output of an information circuit can occur only as a result of a defect in the communications channel ... in the second case such a difference is the very essence of a text's function as a thinking device.
>
> (Lotman, 1988, pp. 36–37)

A fundamental point in Lotman's account of functional dualism is that communication is best understood *not* in terms of *either* a univocal or dialogic model in isolation; instead, virtually every text is viewed as involving *both* univocal, transmission aspects and dialogic, thought generating aspects.

This concept of the functional dualism of texts is closely tied to the distinction made by Bakhtin between 'authoritative' (corresponding to univocal) and 'internally persuasive' (corresponding to dialogic) discourse. In Bakhtin's (1981) view authoritative discourse is based on the assumption that utterances and their meaning are fixed, not modifiable, as they come into contact with new voices:

> The authoritative word demands that we acknowledge it, that we make it our own; it binds us, quite independent of any power it might have to persuade us internally; we encounter it with its authority fused to it.
>
> (Bakhtin, 1981, pp. 342–343)

Instead of functioning as a generator of meaning or as a thinking device, an authoritative text 'demands our unconditional allegiance' (*ibid.*, pp. 342–343). In contrast to authoritative discourse, 'the internally persuasive word is half-ours and half-someone else's. Indeed:

> Its creativity and productiveness consist precisely in the fact that such a word awakens new and independent words, that it organises masses of our words from within, and does not remain in an isolated and static condition ... the semantic structure of an internally persuasive discourse is open ... this discourse is able to reveal ever new ways to mean.
>
> (ibid., pp. 345–346)

Wertsch (1991) suggests that the functional dualism of texts has major implications for the analysis of classroom discourse; Wertsch and Toma (1991), for example, present an analysis of pupil discourse from an elementary school classroom, based on the univocal/dialogic functions. They suggest that to identify the different functions, an observer should ask the question, '*Why* did the pupil make that utterance?'. In one episode taken from their observations, Wertsch and Toma surmise that the pupils 'wanted to convey information about their beliefs' (interpreted as contributing to the authoritative function); in a further episode they suggest that the pupils 'wanted to respond to another's utterance, or to construct an idea in collaboration with others' (interpreted as contributing to the dialogic function). [. . .]

In the same paper, Wertsch and Toma (1991) make an explicit link between activity on the interpsychological and intrapsychological planes in suggesting that, 'the styles of interpsychological functioning employed in the classroom discourse will be reflected in subsequent intrapsychological functioning'. Thus if the dialogic function of discourse is dominant in the classroom, then it might be expected that pupils, 'will treat the utterances of others and of themselves as thinking devices. Instead of accepting them as information to be received, encoded, and stored, they will take an active stance toward them by questioning and extending them, by incorporating them into their own external and internal utterances. When the univocal function is dominant, the opposite can reasonably be expected to be the case' (*ibid.*, 1991). This line of argument follows Vygotsky's General Genetic Law of Development and leads to the implication that if meaningful learning is to occur in classrooms, then there is the need for increased opportunities for pupils to engage in forms of discourse grounded in the dialogic function. That is, such good habits as questioning and making explicit links between ideas rehearsed on the social plane, might then form the basis of active, analytic, individual thought.

Mortimer (1998) draws directly upon the distinction between the univocal and dialogic functions of texts in analysing three episodes from a Brazilian Year 8 classroom. He identifies both authoritative and internally persuasive discourse in the classroom talk and draws attention to the alternating representation of the two forms: 'While the internally persuasive discourse allows alternative explanations and contradictory versions to be considered through argumentation and justification, the authoritative discourse stresses [recapitulations of] the shared knowledge already constructed' (Mortimer, 1998, p. 79). Mortimer suggests that such an alternation in function of discourse is important for developing conceptual thinking on the intrapsychological plane. Elsewhere, I have called this alternation in function of classroom talk the 'rhythm of the discourse' (Scott, 1997a) and argue that 'it seems reasonable to suggest that learning in the classroom will be enhanced through achieving some kind of balance between presenting information and allowing opportunities for exploration of ideas' (p. 227). There needs to be an appropriate 'rhythm' to the discourse.

Van Zee and Minstrell (1997) introduce their notion of 'reflective discourse' in examining ways of speaking in the classroom that foster the communication of physics principles. They contrast reflective classroom discourse with the discourse of traditional classrooms in which the authority of the teacher is central, and define reflective discourse as classroom discussions in which three conditions are frequently met. The three conditions are that: i. students express their own thoughts, comments and questions, ii. the teacher and individual students engage in an extended series of questioning exchanges that help students better articulate their beliefs and conceptions, iii. student/student exchanges involve one student trying to understand the thinking of another (Van Zee and Minstrell, 1997, p. 209). This conceptualisation of 'reflective discourse' maps directly onto what Lotman and Bakhtin refer to as 'dialogic' or 'internally persuasive' discourse.

Van Zee and Minstrell identify further characteristic features of reflective discourse. A key aspect is that teachers envision themselves as developing shared understandings with students through a process 'similar to negotiation' rather than 'transmitting information or confronting misconceptions' (ibid., p. 213). They identify various teacher interventions to *follow the students' lead in thinking*. These include: restating student utterances in a neutral manner; using reflective questioning; acknowledging and encouraging students as conversational partners; invoking silence to foster student thinking.

In addition Van Zee and Minstrell identify teacher interventions which involve, *structuring the discussion to foster and monitor changes in student conceptions*. These interventions include: soliciting students' initial conceptions; guiding the discussion; and engaging students in monitoring changes in conceptions. There is obviously overlap between these various interventions identified by Van Zee and Minstrell and the pedagogical interventions of the 'teaching narrative' (Scott, 1997b). One additional aspect introduced by Van Zee and Minstrell is the intended metacognitive outcome of the teacher prompts to engage students in monitoring changes in their own conceptions.

Taking the ideas presented above, and drawing on analyses of empirical classroom data, the present author has developed (Scott, 1997b) a characterisation of authoritative and dialogic discourse which is set out below. The characterisation is in terms of: the general features of the discourse; the nature of teacher utterances; the nature of student utterances, Following Lotman's point referred to earlier, these characterisations do not imply a dichotomous analysis of discourse into either authoritative or dialogic functions; rather they represent patterns of discourse which lie at the extreme ends of a continuous dimension, and 'real' discourse will contain elements of both.

General features of discourse

Authoritative discourse	*Dialogic discourse*
• focussed principally on the 'information transmitting' voice	• involving several voices
• 'closed': new voices not acknowledged, unless supporting message to be transmitted	• 'open': new voices contribute to the act of developing meaning
• fixed intent: outcome controlled	• generative intent: outcome may not be anticipated.

Thus, in dialogic discourse several voices are represented and the interaction between voices leads to an outcome which may not be anticipated, whilst in authoritative discourse the outcome is fixed in advance by the information transmitting voice and there is little interaction between voices.

Nature of teacher utterances

Authoritative discourse	*Dialogic discourse*
• invested with authority which tends to discourage interventions	• framed in such a way as to be open to challenge and debate
• intended to convey information	• intended to act as 'thinking devices' or 'generators of meaning'

• often based on instructional questions (to which the teacher already has the answer)	• often based on open or genuine questions where the answer is not obvious
• often involving formal reviews or factual statements which offer few 'invitations' to dialogue	• directed towards sustaining dialogue
• selectively drawing on other voices	• representing other voices

In dialogic discourse the teacher's interventions encourage thought and debate: Now, what do people think of that idea?' ... often involving genuine questions, possibly relating to matters of personal opinion. In authoritative discourse, the teacher's contributions are intended to convey information, offer few invitations to genuine dialogue and often involve instructional questions to guide students through a particular argument or explanation.

Nature of student utterances

Authoritative discourse	*Dialogic discourse*
• often in response to teacher questions	• often spontaneously offered (not elicited by teacher) and triggered by comments from other students.
• often consisting of single, detached words interspersed in teacher delivery.	• often consisting of ideas expressed in whole phrases and in the context of on-going dialogue
• often direct assertions	• often tentative suggestions open to interpretation and development by others

In dialogic discourse the students offer ideas spontaneously, quite often in whole phrases and sentences and in a tentative manner which invites comment from others. Thus, for example, a student might suggest: 'Could it be that the air is pushing in from the outside?'. Barnes and Todd (1995, p. 161) capture this tentativeness eloquently when they refer to making a suggestion which 'carries with it the grounds of its own challenge'. In authoritative discourse the students' contributions are usually in response to the teacher's instructional questions and are short, often single word answers.

The concepts of the authoritative and dialogic functions of texts, as a means for analysing classroom discourse, complement the framework of forms of pedagogical intervention set out in the previous section. As the conceptual line of the teaching narrative is developed, the teacher's interventions contribute to both authoritative and dialogic functions.

Pedagogical interventions as scaffolding

This final part of the chapter focusses on the ways in which teacher interventions might be conceptualised in terms of the concept of 'scaffolding (Wood *et al.*, 1976). Scaffolding is often associated with the concept of assisted performance which is central to Vygotsky's sociocultural perspective on development and learning. In this section the origins and substance of the concept of scaffolding are briefly reviewed and the *potential* of scaffolding as an analytical tool for describing teacher–pupil interactions in the science classroom is considered.

Firstly, the point should be made that although there is a clear link between the concept of scaffolding and Vygotsky's work, the notion of scaffolding did not originate with Vygotsky. The scaffolding metaphor was first introduced by Wood, Bruner and Ross (1976) in their analysis of the role of tutoring in problem solving. Their seminal study refers to a task in which a tutor seeks to teach children aged 3, 4 and 5 years to build a three-dimensional structure that requires a degree of skill which is initially beyond them. Wood *et al.* describe the intervention of the tutor as involving:

> a kind of 'scaffolding' process that enables a child or novice to solve a problem, carry out a task or achieve a goal which would be beyond his unassisted efforts. The scaffolding consists essentially of the adult 'controlling' those elements of the task that are initially beyond the learner's capacity, thus permitting him to concentrate upon and complete only those elements that are within his range of competence. The task thus proceeds to successful conclusion. We assume, however, that the process can potentially achieve much more for the learner than an assisted completion of the task. It may result, eventually, in development of task competence by the learner at a pace that would far outstrip his unassisted efforts.
>
> (Wood, Bruner and Ross, 1976, p. 90)

In this first specification of scaffolding there are no direct references to the work of Vygotsky, although it is clear that the approach is consistent with Vygotsky's notion of assisted performance. Bruner (1985) later makes the link explicit when he refers back to the Wood *et al.* paper, 'a study that I am only beginning to understand' and writes of the implications of the tutor 'acting as a support for the child's foray into the zone of proximal development' (Bruner, 1985, p. 29).

A key feature for Vygotsky of learning in the ZPD is that it involves a process in which 'consciousness and control appear only at a late stage of development of a function' (Vygotsky, 1934, p. 90). Bruner addresses this point when he suggests that learning in the ZPD without conscious awareness, is made possible by the actions of a tutor or peer who:

> serves the learner as a vicarious form of consciousness until such a time as the learner is able to master his own action through his own consciousness and control.
>
> (Bruner, 1985, p. 24)

When the learner achieves that conscious control over a new function or conceptual system, it is then that they are able to use it as a tool:

> Up to that point, the tutor in effect performs the critical function of scaffolding the learning task to make it possible for the child to internalise external knowledge and convert it into a tool for conscious control.
>
> (Bruner 1985, p. 25)

It is clear that the concept of scaffolding relates closely to the zone of proximal development in specifying the kinds of support which a tutor might provide to assist a learner in firstly completing a particular task and thereby developing the competence to perform the task independently.

The concept of scaffolding has been explored in various areas of informal out-of-school learning, focussing on problems which include, for example, weaving a piece of cloth, making a basket, or putting away the shopping (Rogoff and Gardner, 1984). Griffin and Cole (1984, p. 47) outline the kinds of activities which might be involved in scaffolding and suggest that: Sometimes the adult directs attention. At other times the adult holds important information in memory. At still other times the adult offers simple encouragement. Rather less clear is the extent to which 'scaffolding' might be useful in describing teaching and learning in the classroom. Maybin *et al.* (1992, p. 187) suggest that the metaphor of scaffolding is tremendously appealing in principle but at the same time elusive, or at least problematic, in practice.

A major problem which arises in using the concept of scaffolding to describe teaching and learning in classroom situations, follows from the number of students involved. Wood *et al.* originally developed the notion of scaffolding in the context of a tutor working with a single child; this is a rather different situation to that of the school teacher working with thirty children. Casual use of the term scaffolding is common. Within the last year the author of this chapter has read, or heard stated, how: 'the teacher scaffolded the introduction of "chemical reactions" with a series of class demonstrations'; 'the pupils working in small groups scaffolded each other's progress'; 'the teacher used a CD-ROM programme to scaffold learning of the kinetic theory of gases'; 'the teacher scaffolded the class through the theory by means of a series of instructional questions'. Statements such as these are commonplace and have led to a situation where indiscriminate usage has almost rendered the term 'scaffolding' meaningless.

In attempting to bring some clarity to this situation, Mercer (1995, pp. 74, 75) suggests that the 'essence of the concept of scaffolding as used by Bruner is the sensitive, supportive intervention of a teacher in the progress of a learner who is actively involved in some specific task, but who is not quite able to manage the task alone . . . it is the provision of guidance and support which is increased or withdrawn in response to the developing competence of the learner'. Scaffolding thus involves a gradual withdrawal of assistance, a gradual handover (Bruner, 1985) of responsibility from teacher to learner.

This notion of 'sensitive intervention' has been further developed to suggest that it is teacher *responsiveness* to student learning which lies at the heart of scaffolding (Scott, 1997b); this is teacher assistance (as envisaged by Vygotsky) during teaching and learning in the ZPD which is responsive to *differences* between the present level of student performance and the level of performance specified by the learning goal. This teacher responsiveness is such that as learning proceeds and progress is made towards the learning goal (changing the current level of performance) then the nature of the teacher assistance is modified appropriately.

The notion of 'responsiveness' is further broken down into three elements (Scott 1997b). *Monitoring*: monitor the present performance of the learner. *Analysing*: analyse the nature of any underlined differences between present performance and the target performance. *Assisting*: respond with an appropriate intervention to support the learner in progressing from present to target performance. These three elements can be represented in terms of an action cycle shown in Figure 6.

In an extended intervention to scaffold learning the teacher moves around the elements of the cycle: monitoring the student's performance; analysing how that level of performance relates to the goal level; taking action to help the student towards

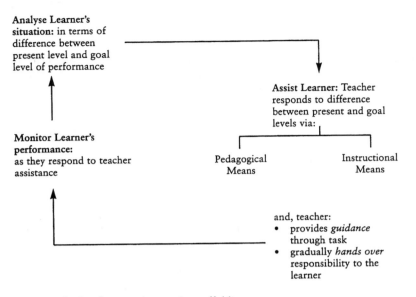

Figure 6 Cycle of responsiveness in scaffolding

the goal; monitoring the student's new performance . . . and so on. In taking action to assist the student in moving towards the target performance, the teacher might employ *pedagogical means* and/or *instructional means*. Pedagogical means consist of the discursive interventions made by the teacher in spontaneous response to the student's performance; instructional means are the teaching activities which are planned ahead of the instruction. As the child progresses in capability towards the learning goal then the level of assistance is reduced; if the child indicates through its performance that more help is needed then the teacher responds accordingly to provide greater assistance. Scaffolding thus consists of continuous cycling around the three elements with the teacher varying the type and amount of assistance according to the learner's needs.

It is possibly with this kind of teacher responsiveness in mind that Tharp and Gallimore (1988) refer to scaffolding as a 'metaphor to describe the ideal role of the teacher' (my emphasis). Given such a view of scaffolding, then perhaps it should come as no surprise that Askew *et al.* (1995) report very few, if any, instances of teacher interventions which might be termed scaffolding following observation of 105 primary school lessons. Nevertheless, there are certainly examples in the literature of teacher interventions which are described in terms of scaffolding and which entail the kind of 'responsiveness' which is referred to above. Again not surprisingly, virtually all of these examples (see, Mercer, 1995; Cazden, 1988) involve the teacher working with individual, or pairs of, children.

In conclusion, it would appear that there is a role for the concept of scaffolding in describing teacher interventions on the interpsychological plane of the classroom, but that it is limited. As described in earlier sections, teachers spend much of their time in making the scientific 'story' or 'themes' available to students; they might achieve this through overlooking a student response, paraphrasing a student idea, presenting new ideas and not pausing to check student understanding. All of these interventions are directed towards making the scientific story available on the interpsychological plane. They are not concerned with supporting individual meaning making on the intrapsychological plane and cannot therefore be interpreted as contributing to the scaffolding of learning. Herein lies the fundamental tension for the teacher between, on the one hand, making the scientific view available to all of the students in the class and, on the other hand, acting to resolve personal difficulties to support individual meaning making.

Discussion

The studies referred to in this review contribute to an alternative approach to science education research in focussing on the ways in which teacher talk can support student meaning making in the science classroom, rather than on specific instructional approaches where 'key activities' (demonstrations, experiments, models, analogies) are developed to promote conceptual change (see, for example: Andersson and Bach, 1996; Schwedes and Dudeck, 1996). The research studies reviewed *do* refer to specific instructional activities; however the analyses presented suggest that the way in which the teacher 'talks around the activity' is at least as important as the activity itself.

Clive Sutton (1996) refers to science learning as 'learning to talk in new ways' and sees science lessons as offering 'access to new conversation'. He also suggests that part of the job of the science teacher is 'to persuade pupils of the value and reasonableness of those new ways'. This notion of *persuading* pupils resonates with much that has been presented in this review, where teachers introduce arguments, establish lines of continuity in the way that they talk about phenomena, develop points through anecdotes, review and summarise ideas, and repeat important ideas time and time again. In the terms introduced earlier, the teacher guides the performance of a 'teaching narrative' over an extended period of time, encouraging exploration of ideas through internally persuasive discourse, to support students in developing an understanding of the scientific view.

Sutton's perspective helps draw attention to a view of learning science which involves taking on new ways of talking and thinking about the world. Here teachers have a key role to play in acting as the 'vicars of their culture' (Bruner, 1985, p. 32) and presenting the scientific view through extended and elaborate talk in the classroom. At times the teacher may well feel that she or he is persuading students to try this new way of talking about the world and indeed if there are major differences between everyday and scientific views in a particular concept area, then this is precisely what the teacher will need to do.

Joan Solomon (1994) offers a metaphor for learning which has a great deal in common with the ideas developed here. In it Solomon imagines a child sitting outside the family circle; listening to the words and phrases used; building up ideas; trying out the sense of those ideas with elders; receiving new and helpful explanations; gradually having ideas accepted by others; being encouraged to use those ideas in new ways. This is a picture of learning which brings to the fore the importance of talk in exploring new ideas and learning how to use them in appropriate contexts and in appropriate ways.

The theoretical ideas for analysing classroom discourse which are presented in this review offer a starting point for talking and thinking about classroom-based science teaching and learning, in ways which are consistent with the ideas sketched out by Sutton and Solomon. A perspective is offered in which the focus is no longer upon isolated instructional activities to promote conceptual change but is shifted towards viewing such activities in the critically influential context of an ongoing flow of discourse, which runs back and forth, between teacher and learners. The importance of various 'key activities' in supporting learning is not being denied here; what is being argued is that the effects on learning might be better understood if such activities are considered in the context of the talk which surrounds them.

When learning science is conceptualised as 'learning to talk science' or in terms of 'learning to talk in new ways' then the act of learning can appear deceptively straightforward; isn't it the case that the student simply learns how to talk about familiar phenomena in new ways? This sounds remarkably straightforward but, as all teachers are very well aware, learning science often creates difficulties. The learning outcomes which follow from instruction are often disappointing in terms of how much students understand, how much they are able to apply, how much they are able to remember. Why should this be the case?

An obvious point here is that the process of 'internalisation', as envisaged by Vygotsky, cannot simply involve direct transfer of 'ways of talking' from social to personal planes; there must be a step of personal interpretation or personal sense-making. The point is made by one of Vygotsky's contemporaries, Leontiev who states that, 'the process of internalisation is not the transferral of an external activity to a pre-existing, "internal plane of consciousness": it is the process in which this plane is formed' (Leontiev, 1981, p. 57). That is, individual learners must make sense of the talk which surrounds them, relating that talk to their existing ideas and ways of thinking; learners must reorganise and reconstruct the talk and activities of the social plane. In this respect Vygotskian theory brings together social and personal perspectives, sharing common ground with constructivist perspectives in recognising that the learner cannot be a passive recipient of knowledge and instruction.

In addition, this reconstructive step to be taken by the individual learner is consequent upon shifts in ways of knowing which follow from the differences between everyday and scientific views (see Leach and Scott, 1995). These shifts may be due to: differences in the conceptual tools used; differences which relate to basic assumptions about the nature of the world – ontological assumptions (see Chi *et al.*, 1994); differences which relate to the nature of the knowledge being used – epistemological assumptions (see Driver *et al.* 1996); and to differences in patterns of reasoning (see Halliday and Martin, 1993).

Returning to the teaching and learning episode given earlier, learning an air pressure explanation for a 'simple' phenomenon such as drinking through a straw might involve the learner in: using the concept of 'air pressure' rather than that of 'sucking' (a conceptual shift); coming to accept that air is a substantial material which can exert large pressures (an ontological shift); appreciating that the air pressure explanation can be applied to a whole range of different phenomena, i.e. that it is generalisable (an epistemological shift). In this case learning the scientific view involves the learner ('surely it can't be the air which is pushing the juice up through the straw') in making significant changes to fundamental personal assumptions about the nature of the world. It is clear that, in this case and in many others, 'learning to talk science' runs rather deeper than 'simply' learning to articulate the words and phrases of a new speech genre. There are implications here for the 'lines of discourse' which need to developed and sustained in science lessons. This involves not only focussing on the introduction of new conceptual tools but also acknowledging differences in the 'epistemological framing' of those tools and differences in basic assumptions about the natural world (ontological assumptions) which arise out of using the tools.

Wertsch (1998) draws upon Bakhtin in making the point that cultural tools are often not easily and smoothly appropriated by agents. In Bakhtin's words:

... not all words submit equally easily to this appropriation, to this seizure and transformation into private property: many words stubbornly resist, others remain alien, sound foreign in the mouth of the one who appropriated them and who now speaks them; they cannot be assimilated into his context and fall out of it, as if they put themselves in quotation marks against the will of the speaker.

(Bakhtin, 1981, pp. 293–294)

Wertsch (1998, p. 55) suggests that, 'whenever we speak we must "buy into" an existing set of linguistic terms and categories'. In learning to talk science we must buy into, and learn to work with, the conceptual tools, epistemological framing, ontological perspectives and forms of reasoning of the scientific community.

In the earlier sections of this review, a range of theoretical constructs, for describing and characterising teacher interventions in science classrooms, have been introduced. These constructs offer a framework which might be used in reflecting upon and evaluating existing instructional practices; they offer a means for thinking and talking about teaching. Wertsch and Toma (1991) suggest that such constructs or tools 'have major implications for understanding how classroom discourse does and could occur'.

The analyses presented in the review point to the extraordinarily skilled ways in which teachers can engage whole classes of children in learning activity. These discursive teaching skills have tended to remain invisible as research and pedagogical attention have been focussed on student thinking and instructional activities. However, once some level of insight and expertise has been achieved in describing and interpreting existing practices, then the means are provided to bring that practice to the attention of others, and to consider how it might be refined. There is potential for using the kinds of theoretical frameworks presented in this chapter as tools (in the contexts of both teacher pre-service and in-service training) to explicate current practice and to raise awareness of the range of classroom discursive approaches which might be employed. Of course there is also potential for refining the analytical tools themselves. Kress *et al.*, for example, have broadened the scope of their analysis of meaning making in the classroom (as presented in Ogborn *et al.*, 1996) to include 'visual communication in learning science' (Kress *et al.*, 1997) and subsequently an even more broadly based approach focussing on the 'multimodal rhetorics of the science classroom' (Kress *et al.*, 1998).

The central focus of this review has been on the ways in which teachers can act upon the *subject matter of science*, through a range of mediational means (focussing on language), to make the scientific view available on the interpsychological plane of the classroom in ways which promote and sustain student learning. As outlined earlier the genesis of this research can be traced back to Vygotsky's work of the 1930s. It is clear that there remains great potential for extending the line of development of work in this area, both in terms of putting to work existing theoretical tools, in analysing and developing instructional practices, and in further developing the analytical frameworks.

[. . .]

References

Andersson, B. and Bach, F. (1996) Developing new teaching sequences in science: the example of 'gases and their properties. In: *Research in Science Education in Europe*. G. Welford, J. Osborne, P. Scott (Eds.), pp. 7–21. London: Falmer Press.

Arnold, M. and Millar, R. (1996) Learning the scientific 'story': A case study in the teaching and learning of elementary thermodynamics. *Science Education*, 80(3), pp. 249–281.

Askew, M., Bliss, J., and MaCrae, S. (1995) Scaffolding in mathematics, science and technology. In: P. Murphy, M. Selinger, J. Bourne, M. Briggs (Eds.) *Subject learning in the primary curriculum: Issues in English, Science and Mathematics* (pp. 209–218). Routledge, London.

Bakhtin, M.M. (1981) *The dialogic imagination: four essays by M.M. Bakhtin*, Ed. Michael Holquist, trans. Caryl Emerson and Michael Holquist. University of Texas Press, Austin.

Bakhtin, M.M. (1986) *Speech genres and other late essays*. Eds. C. Emerson and M. Holquist, trans. V.W. McGee. Austin: University of Texas Press, Austin.

Barnes, D. and Todd, F. (1977) *Communication and learning in small groups.*, Routledge and Kegan Paul.

Barnes, D. and Todd, F. (1995) *Communication and learning revisited: Making meaning through talk*. Boynton/Cook, Portsmouth.

Boulter, C. and Gilbert, J. (1996) Texts and contexts: Framing modelling in the primary science classroom. In: *Research in Science Education in Europe*. G. Welford, J. Osborne, P. Scott (Eds.), pp. 177–188. London: Falmer Press.

Brown, J.S., Collins, A., and Duguid, P. (1989) Situated cognition and the culture of learning. *Educational Researcher*, 21(5), 31–35.

Bruner, J. (1923) *Child's talk: Learning to use language*. New York: Norton.

Bruner, J. (1985) Vygotsky: A historical and conceptual perspective. In: J. Wertsch (Ed.), *Culture, communication and cognition: Vygotskian Perspectives* (pp. 21–34). Cambridge University Press, England.

Cazden, C. (1988) *Classroom discourse*. Portsmouth, NH: Heinemann.

Chi, M.T.H., Slotta, J.D., and de Leeuw, N. (1994) From things to processes: A theory for conceptual change for learning science concepts. *Learning and Instruction*, 4, pp. 27–43.

Cobb, P., Perlwitz, M., and Underwood-Gregg, A. (1998) Individual construction, mathematical acculturation, and the classroom community. In: *Constructivism and education*. Eds: M. Larochelle, N. Bednarz, J. Garrison, pp. 63–80. Cambridge University Press, Cambridge, UK.

Cobb, P., Wood, T., and Yackel, E. (1991) Analogies from the philosophy and sociology of science for understanding classroom life. *Science Education* 75, 23–44.

Daniels, H. (Ed.) (1996) *An introduction to Vygotsky*. London: Routledge.

Driver, R., Leach, J., Millar, R., and Scott, P. (1996) *Young people's images of science*. Buckingham: Open University Press.

Duit, R. and Treagust, D. (1998) Learning in science – From behaviourism towards social constructivism and beyond. In: *International Handbook of Science Education*, Editors, B.J. Fraser and K.G. Tobin, pp. 3–25. Kluwer Academic Publishers, Dordrecht.

Edwards, D. and Mercer, N.M. (1987) *Common Knowledge: The development of understanding in the classroom*. Methuen, London.

Eichinger, D.C., Anderson, C.W., Palincsar, A.S., and David, Y.M. (1991) An illustration of the roles of content knowledge, scientific argument, and social norms in collaborative problem solving. Paper presented at the annual meeting of AERA, Chicago.

Forman, E., Minick, N., and Stone, C. (Eds.) (1993) *Contexts for learning*. New York: Oxford University Press.

Gee, J.P. (1996) Vygotsky and current debates in education. In: D. Hicks (Ed.), *Discourse, learning and schooling*. Cambridge University Press.

Griffin, P. and Cole, M. (1984) Current activity for the future: The Zo-ped. In: B. Rogoff & J.V. Wertsch (Eds.), *Children's learning in the zone of proximal development* (New directions for child development, No. 23) pp. 45–64. San Francisco: Jossey-Bass.

Halliday, M.A.K. and Martin, J. (1993) *Writing science*. London: Falmer Press

Harré, R. and Gillett, G. (1994) *The discursive mind*. Thousand Oaks, California: Sage Publications.

Hicks, D. (1995) Discourse, learning and teaching. In: M.W. Apple (Ed.) *Review of Research in Education* (No. 21), pp. 49–95. AERA.

Hicks, D. (Ed.) (1996) *Discourse, learning and schooling*. Cambridge University Press.

Hodson, D. and Hodson, J. (1998) From constructivism to social constructivism: a Vygotskian perspective on teaching and learning science. *School Science Review*, 79 (289): 33–41.

Howe, A.C. (1996) Development of science concepts within a Vygotskian framework. *Science Education*, 80(1): 35–51.

Howe, C., Tolmie, A., and Rodgers, C. (1990) Physics in the primary school: peer interaction and the understanding of floating and sinking. *European Journal of Psychology of Education*, 4, pp. 459–475.

Kozulin, A. (1990) *Vygotsky's psychology: a biography of ideas*. Cambridge, MA: Harvard University Press.

Kress, G., Ogborn, J., and Martins, I. (1997) Visual communication in the learning of science. Final report to the ESRC. Institute of Education, University of London.

Kress, G., Ogborn, J., Jewitt, C., and Tsatsarelis, C, (1998) Rhetorics of the science classroom: a multimodal approach. Mid-project consultative meeting texts. Institute of Education, University of London.

Lampert, M. (1990) When the problem is not the question and the solution is not the answer: Mathematical knowing and teaching. *American Educational Research Journal*, 27, pp. 29–64.

Lave, J. and Wenger, E. (1991) *Situated learning: legitimate peripheral participation*. New York, Cambridge University Press.

Leach, J. and Scott, P. (1995) The demands of learning science concepts: Issues of theory and practice. *School Science Review*, 76 (277), pp. 47–51, Association for Science Education, Hatfield.

Lemke, J.L. (1990) *Talking Science: Language, learning and values*. Ablex Publishing Corporation, Norwood, New Jersey.

Leontiev, A.N. (1981) The problem of activity in psychology. In: J.V. Wertsch (Ed.) *The concept of activity in Soviet Psychology*. Armonk, N.Y., Sharpe.

Lotman, Yu.M. (1988) Text within a text. *Soviet Psychology*, 26(3): 32–51.

Maybin, J., Mercer, N., and Stierer, B. (1992) Scaffolding learning in the classroom. In: K. Norman (Ed.), *Thinking voices: The work of the National Oracy Project*. pp. 186–195, Hodder and Stoughton, London.

Mead, G.H. (1934) *Mind, self and society*. Chicago: University of Chicago Press.

Mercer, N.M. (1995) *The guided construction of knowledge*. Multilingual Matters, Clevedon, UK.

Moje, E.B. (1995) Talking about science: an interpretation of the effects of teacher talk in a high school classroom. *Journal of Research in Science Teaching*, Vol. 32(4), pp. 349–71.

Moll, L.C. (Ed.) (1990) *Vygotsky and Education: Instructional implications and applications of sociohistorical psychology*. Cambridge University Press.

Mortimer, E.F. (1995) Addressing obstacles in the classroom: An example from the theory of matter. Paper presented at the European Conference on Research in Science Education, Leeds, 7–11 April.

Mortimer, E.F. (1998) Multivoicedness and univocality in classroom discourse: an example from theory of matter. *International Journal of Science Education*, Vol. 20, No. 1, pp. 67–82.

Newman, F. and Holzman, L. (1993) *Lev Vygotsky: Revolutionary scientist*. London and New York: Routledge.

Ogborn, J., Kress, G., Martins, I., and McGillicuddy, K. (1996) *Explaining science in the classroom*. Open University Press, Buckingham.

Rogoff, B. (1990) *Apprenticeship in thinking: Cognitive development in social context*. Oxford, England: Oxford University Press.

Rogoff, B. and Gardner, W. (1984) Adult guidance of cognitive development. In: B. Rogoff and J. Lave (Eds.), *Everyday Cognition*. Cambridge, MA: Harvard University Press, pp. 95–117.

Roth, W.-M. (1995) *Authentic school science. Knowing and learning in open-inquiry science laboratories*. Netherlands: Kluwer Academic Publishers.

Roth, W.-M. (1996) Teacher questioning in an open-inquiry learning environment: interactions of context, content and student responses. *Journal of Research in Science Teaching*, Vol. 33(7), pp. 709–36.

Roychoudhury, A. and Roth, W.-M. (1996) Interactions in an open-inquiry physics laboratory, *International Journal of Science Education*, 18, No. 4, pp. 423–445.

Schwedes, H. and Dudeck, W-G. (1996) Teaching electricity by help of a water analogy (how to cope with the need for conceptual change). In: *Research in Science Education in Europe*. G. Welford, J. Osborne, P. Scott (Eds.), pp. 50–63. London: Falmer Press.

Scott, P.H. (1997a) Teaching and learning science concepts in the classroom: talking a path from spontaneous to scientific knowledge. Paper presented at an international seminar held at Universidade Federal de Minas Gerais, Belo Horizonte, Brazil. March 1997.

Scott, P.H. (1997b) Developing science concepts in secondary classrooms: an analysis of pedagogical interactions from a Vygotskian perspective. Unpublished PhD thesis, University of Leeds, UK.

Shepardson, D.P. (1997) A Vygotskian Perspective on Teaching and Learning Science. Paper presented at the Annual Meeting of the National Association for Research in Science Teaching, Chicago.

Sinclair, J. McH., and Coulthard, R.M. (1975) *Towards an analysis of discourse: The English used by teachers and pupils*. London: Oxford University Press.

Solomon, J. (1994) 'The rise and fall of constructivism', *Studies in Science Education*, 23, pp. 1–19.

Stinner, A. (1995) Contextual settings, science stories and large context problems: toward a more humanistic science education. *Science Education*, 79(5).

Sutton, C. (1996) The scientific model as a form of speech'. In: *Research in Science Education in Europe*. G. Welford, J. Osborne, P. Scott (Eds.), pp. 143–152. London: Falmer Press.

Tharp, R.G. and Gallimore, R. (1988) *Rousing minds to life. Teaching, learning, and schooling in social context*. Cambridge University Press.

Van Zee, E.H. and Minstrell, J. (1997) Reflective discourse: developing shared understandings in a physics classroom. *International Journal of Science Education*, Vol. 19, No. 2, pp. 209–228.

Vygotsky, L.S. (1934) Thinking and speech: psychological investigations. Moscow and Leningrad: Gosudarstvennoe Sotsial'no – Ekonomicheskoe Izdatel'stvo.

Vygotsky, L.S. (1962) *Thought and Language*. Cambridge, MA: MIT Press.

Vygotsky, L.S. (1978) *Mind in Society: The development of higher psychological processes*. Cambridge, MA: Harvard University Press.

Vygotsky, L.S. (1987) *The collected works of L.S. Vygotsky*, Volume 1, R.W. Rieber and A.S. Carton (Eds.), N. Minick (trans.). New York: Plenum.

Watt, D. (1996) An analysis of teacher questioning behaviour in constructivist primary science education using a modification of a descriptive system designed by Barnes and Todd (1977). *International Journal of Science Education*, Vol. 18, No. 5.

Wertsch, J.V. (1985b) *Vygotsky and the social formation of mind*. Harvard University Press.

Wertsch, J.V. (1991) *Voices of the mind: A sociocultural approach to mediated action*. Harvester Wheatsheaf.

Wertsch, J.V. (1998) *Mind as action*. New York: Oxford University Press.

Wertsch, J.V. (Ed.) (1985a) *Culture, communication and cognition: Vygotskian Perspectives*. Cambridge University Press.

Wertsch, J.V. and Toma, C. (1991) Discourse and learning in the classroom: A sociocultural approach. Presentation made at the University of Georgia Visiting Lecturer Series on 'Constructivism in Science Education'

Wittgenstein, L. (1953) *Philosophical investigations* (trans. G.E.M. Anscombe). Oxford: Blackwell.

Wood, D.J., Bruner, J.S., and Ross, G. (1976) The role of tutoring in problem solving. *Journal of Psychology and Psychiatry*, (17), pp. 89–100.

CHAPTER 6

THE PLACE OF ARGUMENTATION IN THE PEDAGOGY OF SCHOOL SCIENCE

Paul Newton, Rosalind Driver and Jonathan Osborne

International Journal of Science Education (1999) 21(5), 553–76

Theoretical developments in perspectives on learning

We believe that argumentative practices are central both to education and science. Moreover, we believe that pedagogies which foster argument lie at the heart of an effective education in science. Our chapter begins with an expansion of this position.

Over the last couple of decades, a major shift has been taking place in the way learning is viewed, away from seeing it as a process confined to the individual mind towards recognizing it as also involving social and cultural processes. Research undertaken from an anthropological perspective has highlighted the way in which learning is framed by social and institutional contexts, and is assisted by culturally produced artefacts (Lave 1988). Furthermore, studies undertaken from a socio-linguistic perspective indicate the way in which language plays a critically important role in learning, as it is through language that the cultural tools and 'ways of seeing' of a community are made available to learners (Vygotsky 1978, Lemke 1990, Wertsch 1991). As Lemke (1988: 81) has pointed out, 'the mastery of academic subjects is the mastery of their specialised pattern of language use'. From this socio-linguistic perspective, learning within a discipline requires adopting the forms of the language of that discipline. For young people learning science, this requires their participation, through talk and writing, in thinking through and making sense of the scientific events, experiments and explanations to which they are being introduced (Driver *et al.* 1994). Active participation by learners in the discourse of lessons is therefore central to providing an enabling learning environment. Talking offers an opportunity for conjecture, argument and challenge. In talking, learners will articulate reasons for supporting particular conceptual understandings and attempt to justify their views. Others will challenge, express doubts and present alternatives, so that a clearer conceptual understanding will emerge. In such a manner, knowledge is co-constructed by the group as the group interaction enables the emergence of an understanding whose whole is more than the sum of the individual contributions. The extent to which such a learning environment is provided in secondary science lessons is the focus of the empirical study which is reported later in this chapter.

What is argument?

A particularly valuable way of looking at science classroom discourse is in terms of argument. Krummheuer (1995: 231) provides a helpful definition of argument as 'the intentional explication of the reasoning of a solution (during its development or after it'. In some cases, this 'explication of reasoning' will be in terms of a single line of thought: this is often referred to as *monological argument*. In other cases, particularly where a number of people are involved in the reasoning process, there will be a number of contrasting lines developed: this is often referred to as *dialogical argument*. Although we occasionally draw a further subtle distinction between 'argument' and 'discussion' – proposing that 'argument' is the sub-set of 'discussion' which is focused upon the resolution of a specific controversy – we have used the terms relatively synonymously in the present chapter.

Toulmin (1958) developed a model of argument that has been drawn upon by educators, and science educators in particular, to identify the components and complexities of students' arguments (e.g. Krummheuer 1995, Druker *et al.* 1996, Jiménez-Aleixandre *et al.* 1997). He identified four main types of statements which contribute to an argument: *claims*, assertions or conclusions whose merits are to be established; *grounds* or data which are the facts that are appealed to in support of the claim; *warrants* which are the reasons justifying the connection between particular data and the knowledge claim; and finally, *backings* which are basic assumptions that provide the justification for particular warrants, We find this to be a useful structural account of argument, although one that needs to be supplemented by a social psychological account when 'real-life' arguments are being analysed (e.g. Richmond and Shriley 1996, Alexopoulou and Driver 1997).

Since Toulmin's seminal work (1958), it has become increasingly apparent that what counts as 'a good argument' is relative to the context in which it takes place: the validity of an argument is a matter of 'informal' rather than 'formal' logic and different areas of human activity (e.g. legal systems, evangelical meetings, domestic interactions, etc.) will have their own distinctive forms of argumentation. Putting it simply different communities address different types of issues and are satisfied by different kinds of solutions. Forms of argumentation that are typically valued by the scientific community include: the development of simplifications, e.g. taxonomies, laws and mathematical formulae; the postulation of causal-explanatory theories which generate novel predictions; the presentation of evidence from observation and experiment, etc.

It is interesting to note the convergence between recent advances in educational theory (inspired by socio-cultural models of learning) and advances in the field of argumentation (inspired by the work of Toulmin). In both cases, the centrality of the community of practice has been emphasized: the community of practice is ultimately 'the measure of all things', and learning 'the measure of all things' requires active participation within that community.

The place of argument in science and science education

Argument in science

The importance of argument in science can be illustrated on a number of levels. Firstly, argument is central to the philosophy of science. There has been a general trend over the last half century away from the view that science is predominantly an empirical process, where claims to truth are grounded in observation and where conclusions are seen as unproblematic deductions from those observations. The shift in position has been towards a view of science as a social process of knowledge construction which involves conjecture. This perspective recognizes that observations are theory laden (Hanson 1958, Kuhn 1962) and, therefore, that it is impossible to ground claims for truth in observation alone. Instead, claims are seen to be grounded through processes of argumentation, where the function of argument is to construct plausible links between the imaginative conjectures of scientists and the available evidence. Moreover, the notion of 'evidence' itself is open to scrutiny, both in terms of the way that it is framed conceptually and in terms of the trust that can be placed in its reliability. The key activity of science, therefore, is the evaluation of conjecture in the light of available evidence; the *raison d'être* of the scientist is to determine which conjectures present the most convincing explanations for particular phenomena in the world.

At an institutional level, argument is manifest in the establishment of scientific knowledge. Science is the product of a community and new scientific conjectures do not become public knowledge until they have been checked, and generally accepted, by the various institutions of science. Thus, papers are reviewed by peers before being published in journals; claims made in published papers are scrutinized and criticized by peers; sometimes experiments are repeated and checked; alternative interpretations are put forward and debated. The rational processes of argument are the foundation of these institutionalized practices. However, it should always be remembered that – even in science – argument is not a purely objective and unproblematic activity. Scientists are humans, after all, and are influenced by factors, e.g. social commitments and personal values, as well as by the wider culture of ideas and technological capabilities evident in society at any one time.

Through this discussion of science as the production of socially constructed knowledge, we have indicated that the argumentative practices of the scientific community are pivotal in the establishment of knowledge claims. Observation and experiment are not the bedrock upon which science is built; rather they are handmaidens to the rational activity of constituting knowledge claims through argument. It is on the apparent strength of arguments that scientists judge competing knowledge claims and work out whether to accept or reject them.

Argument in the learning of science

As we commented earlier, learning science involves becoming socialized into the languages and practices of the scientific community. It is necessary for students to develop an appreciation for both the kinds of questions, and the types of answers that scientists value. Moreover, to become scientists, they must make these forms of argument their own. This process of enculturation into science comes about in a very similar way to the manner in which a foreign language is learned, i.e. through use. It is not enough for students just to hear explanations from experts (e.g. teachers, books, films, computers); they also need to practise using the ideas for themselves. 'The' answers to 'the' questions need to become their' answers to 'their' questions. Through practice in posing and answering scientific questions, students become active participants in the community of science rather than just passive observers.

Furthermore, through taking part in activities that require them to argue the basis on which knowledge claims are made, students also begin to gain an insight into the epistemological foundations of science itself.

Over the last few decades, there have been various studies undertaken which have highlighted the importance of talk in enabling students to develop their understandings of scientific ideas. Seminal work was undertaken by Barnes (1977), and Barnes and Todd (1977). More recently, Lemke (1990) and Sutton (1992) have extended our understanding of the significance of language in science and our appreciation of the centrality of linguistic practices for the induction of students into science. Ways of achieving this end have been explored in science classrooms across the world. The rise of constructivist learning approaches – which have stressed the importance of active participation by learners for making meanings – has led to frequent calls for discussion and group work to be given higher priority in science lessons (e.g. CLIS 1987, Driver 1987, Duit *et al.* 1991). The literature on constructivist teaching continues to be an important source of information about appropriate strategies for promoting discussion and argument in order to develop students' conceptual understandings.

Finally, we would argue that science education also has an important contribution to make to the general education of students by developing their ability to understand, construct and evaluate arguments (both as individuals and as contributors to a group). The discussion of socio-scientific issues (whether or not to eat meat; how domestic waste should be disposed of; the ethics of the new genetics, etc.) give students opportunities in lessons to consider relevant evidence, develop appropriate arguments and come to reasoned conclusions about issues that impinge directly upon their own lives.

Traditionally, science teaching has paid little attention to argument and controversy. This has given a false impression of science as the unproblematic collation of facts about the world, thereby rendering disputes between scientists, whether historical or contemporary, puzzling events (Geddis 1991, Driver *et al.* 1996). It has also failed to empower students with the ability to argue scientifically through the kinds of socio-scientific issues that they are increasingly having to face in their everyday lives (Solomon 1991, Norris and Phillips 1994). If pupils are genuinely to understand scientific practice, and if they are to become equipped with the ability to think scientifically through everyday issues, then argumentative practices will need to be a prominent feature of their education in science.

[. . .]

Teachers' views on argumentation in science lessons

In order to throw more light on the reasons why discussions were such a minor feature of pupils' experience, either in whole class or small group settings, two focus group interviews with a total of 14 experienced science teachers, some of whom were Heads of Department, were conducted. In addition, these were supplemented by five individual interviews. All the interviews were transcribed and then coded for recurrent themes. There is no suggestion that the findings from these interviews are representative, rather that they provide an initial insight into four factors which constrain or limit discussions, and lastly, some of the ways in which discussion in school science classrooms might be promoted.

Time constraints and the National Curriculum

The main reason which was mentioned by all participants was the problem of time.

> Time is a major problem and there certainly is a large contingent of teachers who see discussion as a luxury that can be dispensed with.

> The average teacher will not want to run discussion groups, the main reason is time.

In many cases, teachers commented that the National Curriculum, with its heavy content load, had exacerbated the problem of finding time for discussion.

What has happened is that the National Curriculum has forced us down the road of 'we've got to get everything done' and so we have lost that feeling of luxury of time, cos we have to get through things and we are even struggling to get through the investigative work that we have to do.

We use discussion infrequently because . . . the pressure of the curriculum really, we've got to get the content across most of the time.

Discussion is slowly being pushed out of the curriculum became of time constraints.

I think the National Curriculum keeps us from doing a lot of this because we have to push on and it's a lot to recap a class discussion that lasts a lot of time.

Parents' concerns about their children's progress through the National Curriculum were also mentioned as a factor.

One of the problems is that parents want to be sure that their children are learning and if kids come home with nothing in their books they want to know why.

The difficulties of managing discussion

Teachers were also clear that managing discussion effectively is a difficult pedagogical task.

Many things can go wrong that you are not expecting, putting wrong children together, having wrong seating arrangements.

Discipline is a major issue, it is very easy for a discussion to degenerate.

Kids need to have information to be able to discuss the pros and cons of an argument.

It is quite difficult to get full motivation, to get everyone taking part – it has to be an issue or a problem (in which they) have an interest.

The main thing is that pupils are deeply interested in the problem.

Teachers also recognized that the published materials that they used were not helpful in supporting discussion activities.

We rely on published materials and so although books say 'now discuss' the kids just don't discuss it. Or the teacher can say 'I want you to discuss the answers with one another' . . . the odd little argument can go on then, but that is not really what it is about.

Teachers' skills and views of science

Teachers in our interviews were clear that, because of the difficulty of using discussion in teaching, many teachers (usually but not always the less experienced) did not have the necessary pedagogical skills or the confidence that comes with them.

> We do have average and below average teachers who actually don't have the skills to run discussion groups. I think that it is quite a high level skill for teachers.

> Much depends on whether the teacher feels confident enough to take off on a tangent if the need arises, particularly if this means the exclusion of covering other content areas.

> Teachers need to be confident enough to accept that they may not know the answers, this may ... discourage some teachers from allowing the situation to occur in the first place.

The epistemological orientation of science teachers was also commented on as a reason for not using discussion.

> If they are scientists who believe in black and white and firm answers they may not see the significance of discussion.

Even the experienced science teachers we talked with admitted to feeling unskilled at organizing and leading effective group discussions. All of them commented that they had had problems from time to time with discussion activities. There were a number of comments about the need for more training in the skills required to manage discussions and the importance of initial teacher training was underlined.

> Where are teachers meant to know about the possibility of doing this sort of thing if they don't pick it up during their teacher training?

Pupils' views of learning science

Teachers commented that pupils hold views about what activities are and are not appropriate in science lessons.

> Many children are not happy when they don't fill their course books up.

> The children are often not used to discussion during science lessons – while they might be quite happy doing so in an English lesson.

> Teachers in English classes do not have the same kind of problem in running discussions – perhaps because they have been trained to do it. Also the students actually see discussion as part of English and therefore seem happy to engage in it, but not in science.

These accounts indicated the recognition of both internal and external factors which affect the use of discussion and argument in science lessons. The internal factors related to the teachers' pedagogical skills, pupils' views and, to a lesser extent, to available materials. External factors concerned the pressure of time that teachers experience in 'covering' the National Curriculum.

Promoting discussion in classrooms

The data from the interviews would suggest that the development of discussion within school science is dependent on four constraints – advanced planning, appropriate time slots, a prerequisite knowledge base, and establishment of clear procedures for running group discussions. For instance, teachers commented:

> I think if we are going to carry out these kind of activities, I think basically kids need quite a bit of time to prepare in advance, maybe not in class time but maybe at home, to bring in information and so that they can argue certain points. I mean, I think what makes it difficult is students together in the classroom unprepared.

Existing resources, particularly SATIS (ASE 1986) were criticized for being too 'time consuming', whereas spending 'three or four minutes coming up with ideas' and then moving on should be one way of developing its use. Teachers were also aware that 'this isn't the kind of thing you can drop out of nowhere' and that the first few times might result 'in a complete pig's ear'. In short, the need for children to be prepared and prepare themselves was emphasized as indicated by the following comment.

> And it starts with kids being able to express anything, and not necessarily being able to argue well, but to express themselves well, what they have learnt and openly. And that comes first I feel. I mean, before you argue, you have to have a sound basis of what you understand. And I think the most important thing is for students to get up and just talk about their science – and that may be the first step.

Investigative good for this .

Discussion in science was problematic because school science predominantly deals in ideas which are perceived to be right or wrong, whereas good discussion requires the participants to propose thoughts that are half-formed or simply flawed. Therefore, teachers need to 'impress on them that it doesn't matter if what they think is wrong'. Furthermore, groups may encourage careful initial selection and monitoring to ensure successful interaction – both of which are recommendations highlighted by Bulman (1985) and Dillon (1994), and not reinforced by the published materials. For as one teacher commented:

> Although the books say 'Now discuss bla, bla, bla . . .' the kids don't now discuss it, well they may discuss it to some extent but . . . and the odd little argument can then go on but that's not really what it's about . . . So probably because this isn't tackled in the published materials then people are not doing it.

[. . .]

The relationship between educational theory and practice

At this point, we consider three different models of teaching and learning, and reflect on how these relate to the results from our study. The models we will consider are the *transmission* model, the *discovery* model and the *social constructivist* model. In Figure 7 below, we characterize each of these models along a number of dimensions.

In the light of evidence from our observation study, we now consider which of these models of teaching and learning are reflected in teachers' pedagogical practices. We do not envisage these models as explicit theoretical frameworks that are held by teachers and that direct their method of teaching. Science teachers are rarely explicit about theories which guide their practice and, indeed, are often cynical about the value of such theories. Instead, we see the models as characterizing underlying features of sets of pedagogical practices; they are more descriptive of what teachers *do* than of what they *think*.

	Transmission model	Discovery model	Serial constructivist model
Nature of science (for students)	Science as a fixed body of facts primarily accessed through authoritative sources (e.g. teacher).	Science as a body of facts, laws and theories primarily accessed through personal experience.	Science as plausible explanations for phenomena primarily accessed through argument.
Method of learning science	Paying attention to authoritative sources in order to acquire scientific knowledge from them via *absorption*.	Paying attention to personal observations in order to draw general scientific principles from them via *induction*.	Collaborating (with authoritative sources) to arrive at convincing scientific explanations via the co-construction of knowledge.
Teaching approaches	Telling pupils the facts of science.	Organizing practical activities that will furnish pupils with appropriate observations from which appropriate conclusions may be drawn.	Negotiating experiences and explanations with pupils to persuade them of the value of accepted scientific ideas.

Figure 7 Models of teaching and learning science

The social constructivist model strongly recommends opportunities for reflective interaction (e.g. through discussion and argument) to support the co-construction of knowledge. As we have noted, few opportunities were given in lessons for activities where this can take place. An exception was open-ended practical work which did provide opportunities for the personal and social construction of knowledge. The extent to which this can actually take place depends on the degree of openness of the task and the extent to which pupils are encouraged to reflect and negotiate interpretations of their findings. In general, apart from the limited evidence of open-ended practical work, there appeared to be little indication of a social constructivist perspective on science teaching being put into practice.

There was more evidence of teachers being guided by a discovery model. The fact that the majority of lessons included some pupil practical work indicates the value that teachers place on giving pupils first hand experiences. However, a closer inspection of the way the closed practical activities were conducted shows that they gave little opportunity for pupils to reflect and make their own generalizations. In fact, the practical activities tended to serve as illustrations of principles which the teacher wished to promote, thus reflecting more of a transmission view. Open-ended investigations, on the other hand, did provide opportunities for pupils to undertake experiments, to make their own generalizations and to negotiate appropriate interpretations. They may reflect, therefore, a discovery or social constructivist perspective depending on the way that they are implemented.

Overall, the dominant model appears to be a transmission model with emphasis being given to teacher exposition, focused question and answer interactions, and closed practical work. Whilst such procedures might superficially offer the appearance of whole class discussion, research has shown that teachers' questions are overwhelmingly closed (Edwards and Mercer 1987) and whose primary function is evaluative and a mechanism for controlling classroom talk (Lemke 1990). Rather than assisting the development of understanding and co-construction of knowledge as learners contribute their half-formed understandings, such procedures invariably lead to 'guessing what is in teacher's mind'. Thus, one of us was perhaps somewhat premature in cautioning about social constructivist approaches that placed an over-reliance on discussion and co-construction whilst ignoring the importance of 'telling' (Osborne 1996). For as Hacker and Rowe's (1997) recent study suggests, within English and Welsh classrooms, it is the teacher as informer and not teacher as facilitator which is the predominant role model.

Exploring reasons for the persistence of traditional pedagogical practices

Social constructivist perspectives on learning science (e.g. Johnson 1990) have been current in England since the mid 1980s when they were the focus of the Secondary Science Curriculum Review (SSCR 1987). Since then, they have featured in many initial teacher training courses and in-service programmes. Yet, although social constructivist perspectives may predominate in the thinking of science educators, they are not reflected in classroom practice. Why do we still find the transmission model dominating science classroom teaching?

We suggest that there are two key explanations. The first, which is internal to schools and classrooms, relates to the fact that pedagogy is essentially a conservative activity; the skills and practices that make up the craft of teaching are learned through experience and changes in such practices are difficult to bring about. The second explanation is external to schools and classrooms; it relates to the pressures which teachers and schools are increasingly being subjected to as a consequence of accountability and the marketization of education (e.g. Ball 1990, Apple 1992).

Training old dogs to do new tricks?

The patterns of pupil and teacher interaction observed in our study (e.g. the predominance of teacher exposition and question–answer sequences) are not novel; they have been documented across countries and across decades in time. For example, our observation that deliberative interactions occupied less than 2% of total class time on average was mirrored in an observation study of 1000 elementary and secondary classrooms, undertaken in the USA by Goodlad (1984), where open discussion occupied an average of 4–7% of total class time.

Our conclusions also mirror those from research conducted in England nearly two decades ago. In a study of group work in science lessons undertaken by Sands (1981), the activities of pupils in 18 mixed ability classes, from the first 3 years of secondary schooling, were observed. Her findings resonate with our own to a remarkable degree. In particular she noted the following.

(i)   All the observed groups were undertaking practical work. In no lessons were groups used for other activities.

(ii)   No opportunities were given for groups to design experiments or interpret results.
(iii)   Any imaginative, analytical or enquiry-based thinking was done by the teacher with the whole class.
(iv)   Rarely were there follow-ups to the practical group work which involved the sharing of experiences.
(v)   Pupil talk during group practical work involved no reasoning activity (e.g. the evaluation of an experiment, interpretation of an observation, or relating of an investigation to a theory).

In her summary, Sands (1981: 768) commented:

> What happened to the idea of groups in which children exchanged views and ideas, where teachers initiated and encouraged discussion, or where the teacher's questions were designed to stimulate and not only to elicit facts? ... And what about the idea of groups existing which, even in the context of a traditional practical lesson, are allowed to grow so that ... one sees the development of initiative and leadership, cooperation, decision-making and responsibility?

The pressure of the National Curriculum

The second key explanation relates to the socio-political climate in which schools are currently operating. Apple (1992: 782) offers an 'analysis of the economic and ideological influences on schools in terms of a conflict between a previous liberal consensus and an emergent zeitgeist centred on education for economic utility. He comments:

> No longer is education seen as part of a social alliance ... A new alliance has been formed, one that has increasing power in educational and social policy. This power bloc ... aims at providing the educational conditions believed necessary both for increasing profit and capital accumulation.

This new alliance, which can be described as reflecting a *technocratic orientation*, views education as a commodity to be bought and sold in the market place. The technocratic orientation to education sees learning not as the development of critical faculties of individuals, but as the mastery of given bodies of knowledge and skills selected to serve the interests of the political/industrial world. Evaluation and assessment is an essential part of this orientation to education: it is necessary to find out the extent to which learners have achieved specified learning goals in order to determine the efficiency of aspects of the system.

Such a system of accountability is having a major impact on education in England and Wales: pupils are now faced with far more formal assessment than ever before and the results of these assessments are used, not only for ranking individual pupils, but for ranking local authorities, schools, departments and individual teachers. The institutional importance of the results of assessment tests means that schools and teachers place great emphasis on learning activities that enhance test scores. The consequences of this technocratic orientation for science education can be seen in the results of our observation study as elaborated through the teachers' comments. Science teachers are under pressure to emphasize the recall of unrelated ideas and concepts of science, and to give priority to 'covering the syllabus'. They feel that the time pressures they are working under mean that they are unable to pay attention to broader issues, e.g. how scientific and technological knowledge is created, or to discuss the social and ethical implications of scientific developments (Cross and Price 1992).

In short, we argue that the technocratic orientation to education is leading to a regressive pedagogy that emphasizes rote learning at the expense of deeper understanding. This is the antithesis of our vision for a science education with argumentation at its heart. Bearing in mind that few science teachers have so far developed the skills necessary to include argumentation in their pedagogical repertoire (Boulter and Gilbert 1995), the conservatism of pedagogy combined with a technocratic orientation to education does not augur well for the hopes of social constructivist educators. To realize such hopes will require a highly concerted effort.

The genesis of change?

There has always been opposition to change as far as pedagogy is concerned. Now, in the UK, where more responsibility for initial teacher education rests with teachers in schools, the inertial effect of 'current practice' is likely to be even more restrictive. To provide more opportunities for discussion and activities in which pupils themselves took responsibility for their own learning would, indeed, constitute a major change in pedagogy. Some indication of the foundations on which relevant practices could be developed is offered by the comments of the teachers recorded earlier. More fundamentally, change is impossible without a widespread recognition that current practices offer little or no opportunity for the discussion of socio-scientific issues. In reiterating the findings of Sands (1981), and Lunzer and Gardner (1979), therefore, the findings of this research support the argument that the impact of the national curriculum in the UK has been conservative and regressive.

Yet, modern societies require future citizens with a different set of competencies. The European Commission's White Paper on Education (1995) and training argues that sustaining a healthy and participatory democracy requires citizens 'who are capable of making considered decisions' by 'enabling them to fulfil an enlightened role in making choices which affect the environment'. Similarly, the UK government's Advisory Group for Education for Citizenship (1998) argues that schools should provide young people with 'an armoury of essential skills: listening, arguing, making a case; and accepting the greater wisdom or force of an alternative view'. Yet, how can young people learn how to make considered decisions and discuss issues of a socio-scientific nature if their education in science fails to provide them with the opportunity to practise the skills associated with argument by considering issues of a controversial nature? Moreover, if the recurrent stress by employers for schools to produce individuals who are 'flexible', adaptable' and 'good communicators', rather than individuals with a detailed knowledge of science curriculum *per se* is a true reflection of the current needs of society, then are existing curricula in danger of becoming an anachronism, irrelevant both to society and to our children? In short, science education persists with the fallacy of miscellaneous information – the belief in the usefulness of disparate, but unrelated facts – the force that holds us to the Earth, the order of the planets, the nature of chemical bonds (Cohen 1952). The need for such specific information becomes increasingly questionable in a society which offers information on tap when, in contrast, the ability to sift, sort and interrogate information, and the ability to assess its import and significance becomes an evermore important skill.

Changing the current orientation of the ship of science education will never be easy, however, the first task of those working within the vessel is to continue to warn, and stridently at that, not only of the irrelevance of the current direction but that the ship is in danger of foundering on the rocks. Such initiatives and arguments can be found within recent reports published in both the UK and America (American Association for the Advancement of Science 1998, King's College London 1998). Sowing the seeds of dissatisfaction both within the body politic of science education and with the wider public is, therefore, an *a priori* necessity for any reform initiative. Similarly, overcoming the strong conservative influence of pedagogical culture will require convincing teachers of the necessity for change. Importantly, this will also require equipping new science teachers with the skills necessary for applying social constructivist principles. Teachers require enculturation into the practice of science teaching just as their students need enculturation into the practice of science. In particular, we must ensure that appropriate resource materials are available for scaffolding teachers' initial attempts at adopting new techniques, e.g. those that involve argument.

To borrow an evolutionary metaphor, without a mechanism for systematically encouraging innovation and curriculum development, existing curriculum frameworks do not encourage adaptation and the growth of diversity. Consequently, new forms cannot evolve and be tested to see if they offer improvement. As a result, the system cannot easily accommodate any changes in the social context which may require a different set of competencies and skills compared to those fostered by existing curricula. The strong message of evolution is that lifeforms that fail to adapt merely become extinct. Hence, the consistent failure of science education to transform and adapt from its extant 19th century origins now places it under threat. It is our view, then, that the changes in the pedagogy argued for in this chapter are of great educational importance for the health, vitality and relevance of science education, and the struggle to promote change is therefore a mantle of responsibility that falls on us all.

References

Advisory Group for Education for Citizenship (1998) Education, Citizenship & Teaching Democracy. Report No 98/155, Qualifications and Curriculum Authority, London.

Alexopoulou, E. and Driver, R. (1997) Small group discussions in physics: peer interaction modes in pairs and fours. *Journal of Research in Science Teaching*, 33, 1099–1114.

American Association for the Advancement of Science (1998) *Blueprints for Reform: Science, Mathematics and Technology Education* (New York: Oxford University Press).

Apple, M. (1992) Educational reform and educational crisis. *Journal of Research in Science Teaching*, 29, 779–789.

Association for Science Education (1980) *Science and Technology in Society: General Guide for Teachers* (Hatfield: Association for Science Education).

Ball, S. (1990) *Politics and Policy Making in Education: Explorations in Policy Sociology* (London: Routledge).

Barnes, D. (1977) Talking and writing in science lessons. *Cambridge Journal of Education*, 7, 138–447.

Barnes, D. and Todd, F. (1977) *Communication and Learning in Small Groups* (London: Routledge & Kegan Paul).

Boulter, C. J. and Gilbert J. K. (1995) Argument and science education. In P. S. M. Costello and S. Mitchell (eds) *Competing and Consensual Voices: The Theory and Practice of Argumentation* (Clevedon: Multilingual Matters).

Bulman, L. (1985) *Teaching Language and Study Skills in Science* (London: Heinemann Educational Books).

CLIS (1987) *CLIS in the Classroom* (Leeds: Centre for Studies in Science and Mathematics Education, University of Leeds).

Cohen, I. B. (1952) The education of the public in science. *Impact of Science on Society*, 3, 78–81.

Cross, R. T. and Rice, R. F. (1992) *Teaching Science for Social Responsibility* (Sydney: St. Louis Press).

Dillon, J. T. (1994) *Using Discussion in Classrooms* (Buckingham: Open University Press).

Driver, F. (1987) Theory into practice: a constructivist approach to curriculum development. In P. Fensham (ed.) *Development and Dilemmas in Science Education*, London: Falmer Press, pp. 133–149.

Driver, F., Asoko, H., Leach, J., Mortimer, E. and Scott, P. (1994) Constructing scientific knowledge in the classroom. *Educational Researcher*, 23, 5–12.

Driver, R., Leach, J., Millar, R. and Scott, P. (1996) *Young People's Images of Science* (Buckingham: Open University Press).

Druker, S. L., Chen, C. and Kelly, G. J. (1996) Introducing content to the Toulmin model of argumentation via error analysis. Paper presented at NARST meeting, Chicago, USA.

Duit, R., Goldberg, F. and Niedderer, H. (1991) Research in physics learning: theoretical issues and empirical studies. *Proceedings of an International Workshop*, Kiel, IPN.

Edwards, D. and Mercer, N. (1987) *Common Knowledge: The Development of Understanding in the Classroom* (London: Methuen).

European Commission (1995) White paper on education and training: Teaching and learning – Towards the learning society (White paper). Office for Official Publications in European Countries, Luxembourg.

Geddis, A. (1991) Improving the quality of classroom discourse on controversial issues. *Science Education*, 75, 169–183.

Goodlad, J. (1984) *A Place Called School* (New York: McGraw-Hill).

Hacker, R. J. and Rowe, M. J. (1997) The impact of National Curriculum development on teaching and learning behaviours. *International Journal of Science Education*, 19, 997–1004.

Hanson, N. R. (1958) *Patterns of Discovery* (Cambridge: Cambridge University Press).

Jiménez-Aleixandre, M. P., Gugallo-Rodriguez, A. and Duschl, R. (1997) Argument in High School genetics. Paper presented at the NARST Conference. March.

Johnson, K. (ed.) (1990) *Interactive Teaching in Science: Workshops for Training Courses* (Hatfield: Association for Science Education).

King's College London (1998) *Beyond 2000: Science Education for the Future* (London: King's College London).

Krummheuer, G. (1995) The ethnography of argumentation. In P. Cobb and H. Bauersfeld (eds) *Emergence of Mathematical Meaning* (Hillsdale, NJ: Lawrence Erlbaum).

Kuhn, T. S. (1962) *The Structure of Scientific Revolutions* (Chicago, IL: University of Chicago Press).

Lave, J. (1988) *Cognition in Practice: Mind, Mathematics and Culture in Everyday Life* (Cambridge: Cambridge University Press).

Lemke, J. L. (1988) Games, semantics and classroom education. *Linguistics and Education*, 1, 81–99.

Lemke, J. L. (1990) *Talking Science: Language, Learning, and Values* (Norwood, NJ: Ablex).

Lunzer, E. and Gardner, K. (1979) *The Effective Use of Reading* (London: Heinemann Educational).

Norris, S. P. and Phillips, L. M. (1991) Interpreting pragmatic meaning when reading popular reports of science. *Journal of Research in Science Teaching*, 31, 947–967.

Osborne, J. F. (1996) Beyond constructivism. *Science Education*, 20, 53–82.

Richmond, G. and Shriley, J. (1996) Making meaning in classrooms: social processes in small group discourse and scientific knowledge building. *Journal of Research in Science Teaching*, 33, 839–858.

Sands, M. (1981) Group work in science: myth and reality. *School Science Review*, 62, 765–769.

Secondary Science Curriculum Review (1989) *Better Science: making it happen* (London: ASE/Heinemann).

Solomon, J. (1991) Group discussions in the classroom. *School Science Review*, 72, 29–34.

Toulmin, S. (1958) *The Uses of Argument* (Cambridge: Cambridge University Press).

Vygotsky, L. (19/8) *Thought and Language* (Cambridge, MA: MIT Press).

Wertsch, J. (1991) Voices on the mind: *A Socio-Cultural Approach to Mediated Action* (Cambridge: Cambridge University Press).

CHAPTER 7

INTERACTIVE MULTIMEDIA AND MODEL-BASED LEARNING IN BIOLOGY

Barbara C. Buckley

International Journal of Science Education (2000) 22(9), 895–935

Introduction

This chapter describes the prior knowledge, goals, interactions with representations and resulting knowledge of one student who used 'Science for Living: the Circulatory System' (SFL). The case is drawn from a larger project that developed SFL and examined its use in a technology rich, tenth grade biology class while the class of 27 students created multimedia projects over the course of three weeks. This case is significant because it dissects the knowledge of the learner as well as the representations and interface of SFL and examines the learning activities of the learner as she interacted with those representations. Her knowledge and activities are contrasted with those of her classmates. This learner was chosen because her performance at the end of the study was judged by the teacher and researcher to be superior to those of her classmates, thus offering an opportunity to investigate an example of effective biology learning. The model-based learning framework emerged from the analysis of this case of model-building in biology.

To facilitate the reading of this chapter, working definitions and the model-based learning framework are presented as background information. For the purposes of this chapter, representations are defined as external representations of ideas, events, objects, or systems (Boulter and Buckley 2000, Buckley and Boulter 2000). Representations are considered expressions of mental models, i.e. expressed models (Gilbert 1995) created for particular purposes such as communicating, negotiating understanding, reasoning and problem-solving (Kindfield 1993–1994, Larkin and Simon 1987). Mental models are internal, cognitive representations used in generating external representations and in reasoning of many kinds (Brewer 1987, Rouse and Morris 1986). Mental models, like prior knowledge, influence our perceptions of phenomena and our understanding of representations. Interactions with phenomena and representations, in turn, influence our mental models (Gentner and Stevens 1983, Johnson-Laird 1983). As researchers we also construct mental models and representations of the mental models of others (Norman 1983). Model-based learning is a dynamic, recursive process of learning by building mental models. It involves the formation, testing and subsequent reinforcement, revision, or rejection of mental models of some phenomenon (see Figure 8).

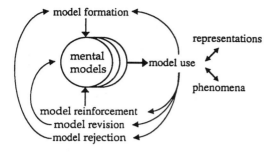

Figure 8 Expressed model of model-based learning

During *mode formation* a learner – drawing on existing knowledge, new information and the demands of the task, constructs a mental model of some phenomenon (Buckley 1992, Kozma *et al.* 1992). When the model is used successfully to accomplish that task or to interact with and reason about phenomena or representations, the model is reinforced (Clement 1989) and may eventually become a precompiled, stable model (Vosniadou and Brewer 1992). However, if inconsistencies and/or deficiencies in the model are noted (Bransford *et al.* 1986), the learner may reject the model and form a new one, or revise and/or elaborate the initial model so that the new model better supports completion of the task (Chinn and Brewer 1993, Clement 1989, Schauble *et al.* 1991). *Model revision* involves modifying parts of an existing model while *model elaboration* involves adding to or combining existing models. Embedding a model in a larger model is an example of elaboration (deKleer and Brown 1983, Monaghan and Clement 1994, Stewart and Hafner 1991). Thus the mental model evolves through multiple recursions as it is made increasingly complex and, hopefully, more accurate (Johnson-Laird 1983, White and Frederiksen 1990).

The difficulty in understanding biological phenomena

Understanding biological phenomena such as the circulatory system is difficult for a number of reasons. It is a complex interactive system that ranges in scale from the heart or blood vessels visible through the skin to blood cells circulating in capillaries much smaller than the human visual range. At lower levels of organization the tissues and cellular structures that enable the functioning are too small to see unaided and thus are inaccessible to learners without visualization tools (Chi *et al.* 1991).

Since most of the system is embedded invisibly throughout the body and its functioning generally hidden from view, children trying to make sense of their bodies often develop misconceptions about the circulatory system and how it works. Their direct observations and experiences are mediated by interactions with parents, peers and medical personnel. Phrases such as 'feel your pulse' may lead children to infer that the pulse is an object, 'just like the other parts the doctor wants to feel' (Gellert 1962), or another pumping system (Quiggin 1977). Children initially give psychological explanations for what they observe, but older children are more likely to provide biological explanations (Carey 1985). The influence of textbooks, illustrations and other representations encountered in the classroom becomes evident in their drawings but misconceptions abound (Porter 1974).

Arnaudin and Mintzes (Arnaudin 1983, Arnaudin and Mintzes 1985, Arnaudin and Mintzes 1986) investigated conceptions about the circulatory system held by

495 students at the fifth (10 years old), eighth (13 years old) and tenth (15 years old) grade level and first year college undergraduates. The researchers identified and described seven circulatory system concepts including: the structure of blood, the function of blood, structure of the heart, function of the heart, circulatory pattern, circulatory/respiratory relationships and closed circulation. Misconceptions about the last three were still prevalent among college freshmen.

In their study of causal reasoning among medical students, Patel *et al.* (1991) noted errors in problem solving that arose when students reasoned about changes in blood pressure caused by a blood clot in a blood vessel of the respiratory system. Students failed to take into account the closed nature of the circulatory system and the anatomy of the blood vessels that supply blood to the lungs.

In contrast to the studies of individual conceptions just cited, Feltovich *et al.* (1988) systematically investigated the networks of conceptions held by medical students about heart failure. They demonstrated that students' misconceptions contained component misconceptions that reinforced each other, resulting in reciprocating misconceptions that persist even among experienced cardiologists. In congestive heart failure the heart cannot maintain blood flow at rates sufficient to support the needs of the body. The ways in which the cardiac muscle fails at the subcellular level are not yet fully known, but involve inadequate contraction due to insufficient metabolic energy and other biochemical defects. Misconceptions about heart failure focused on anatomical mechanisms involved in skeletal muscle contraction, but not in cardiac muscle. In skeletal muscle decreased force is generated when the muscle is overstretched and the sliding filaments of actin and myosin cannot 'get a good grip'. Yet cardiac muscle contracts more strongly when it is filled with a larger volume of blood. The misconception contained four components:

(1)   The mechanism that causes an individual isolated skeletal muscle fibre to produce different contracting forces at different lengths of stretch is mechanical.
(2)   Individual cardiac muscles are like individual skeletal muscle fibres.
(3)   The increased force produced by an intact heart when it is filled with increased blood volume results from the same mechanism.
(4)   When the heart becomes too big, cardiac muscles are overstretched and cannot generate adequate force and hence fail for the same reason that individual skeletal muscle fibres fail when they are overstretched.

Such misconceptions, they assert, arise from oversimplification among teachers, students and researchers. Perhaps the representations of sliding filament theory were more memorable as well.

When learners are unable to observe or experience phenomena directly, representations can play a crucial role in helping them understand those phenomena. The complexity and multiple levels of organization of the circulatory system are difficult to represent without simplification. One of the challenges posed by illustrations of the circulatory system is the difficulty of discerning the parts of the system depicted. Dwyer, in his extensive work on different kinds of illustrations in texts about the heart, documented difficulties in learning from realistic drawings and photographs. He concluded that simple diagrams of the relevant structures were more effective than realistic images because the parts could be more easily seen and identified (Dwyer 1972, Dwyer 1978, Joseph and Dwyer 1982). In studies of the role of conceptual models in understanding scientific prose, Mayer (1989a, 1989b) demonstrated that the use of conceptual models in instructional materials decreases verbatim or rote recall but increases creative solutions on transfer problems. Mayer's conceptual models represent the major objects, actions and causal relations in a system, using 'words and/or diagrams that are intended to help learners build mental models of the system' (1989a: 43) Conceptual models thus make the parts of the system clear. Salomon (1980) asserts that visual media sequences, such as zooming in on relevant detail, facilitate development of internal modes of representation and model cognitive operations, i.e., attending to those details. Goldsmith (1984) suggests that these function by making the entity clear and by providing relevant details that enable recognition of the entity.

However clear the representation, there remain wide variations in interpretations by users. Nature does not come with labels and outlines. This is often true of realistic representations of natural phenomena as well. The novice may not see the parts of the phenomena while the expert sees them easily and knows the behaviour of those parts as well as the causes of the behaviour. Goldsmith (1984) characterizes this continuum between novice and expert reading of illustrations in terms of semiotic levels. The syntactic level involves being able to discern the image or set of images. The semantic level involves recognizing what the image represents based on relevant detail. The pragmatic level involves recognizing not only the image and what it represents but also the wider context.

The use of interactive multimedia enables new ways of overcoming some of the challenges of representing biological phenomena It allows the inclusion and integration of different kinds of representations linked and structured in a multitude of ways, presumably supporting learners with diverse aptitudes and preferences for particular representational modes. However, research has shown that it also presents cognitive and metacognitive challenges because learners must direct their own learning as well as understand the various representations and how they relate to each other (Marchionini 1988).

Researchers also need to tease apart a variety of factors beyond representations and learning strategies, not the least of which is grappling with how previous research can be brought to bear on understanding what and how students learn when they have access to interactive multimedia resources (Trumbull *et al.* 1991). Many of the early media studies focused on the effectiveness of a particular piece of interactive multimedia courseware in comparison with other methods of instruction (for example, Bunderson *et al.* 1984, Smith and Lehman 1988) or of variations within interactive video courseware (Gay 1986). But as Clark and Salomon (1986) noted, the instructional strategy embodied in a piece of interactive courseware must also be embodied in the instruction used for the control group in order for such research to be a study of the media or technology *per se.*

Most of the multimedia studies provide little evidence indicating how the representations within the interactive multimedia operate in the learning of the students. One of the few studies to do so demonstrated that use of an interactive multimedia resource designed to help veterinary medicine students relate abnormal heart sounds to the cardiac cycle was more effective than traditional methods. They showed that students initially used audio of the heart sounds and the relevant EKG trace simultaneously, but as they became more knowledgeable, they used only the audio (Branch *et al.* 1987). This suggests that in their development of expertise they had integrated the heart sounds with the heart cycle as represented by the EKG.

Understanding living things can be challenging. The problem lies not only in the difficulty of observing some biological phenomena directly but also in the difficulty of creating and interpreting representations of phenomena that occur over a wide range of physical and temporal scales.

'Science for Living' project

The 'Science for Living' project, from which data the current chapter is drawn, was established to explore the potential of interactive multimedia for addressing the persistent problem of fragmented, inert and often inaccurate science knowledge among learners. An interdisciplinary team of faculty, students and staff at Stanford University developed an interactive multimedia resource prototype entitled 'Science for Living: The Circulatory System' (SFL) with the assistance of Apple Computer and the Carnegie Corporation. After two rounds of formative evaluation and revision, the third version of SFL was introduced into an Apple Classroom of Tomorrow (ACOT). A classroom-based cognitive case study sought to address the questions: What is the nature and extent of student learning about the circulatory system when they have access to SFL? How do they go about their learning? What role do the representations in SFL and its interface play?

'Science for Living': the circulatory system

SFL was designed to provide access, only on demand, to a wide range of information about the circulatory system and to tools for manipulating that information to create multimedia presentations. Computer software controls a videodisc player whose images are processed by a video board before being displayed on a colour television screen. This allows the user to interact with the videodisc images and to access additional information about the image or parts of it. Information is available on the computer screen as well as the television screen. The bar across the top is the main navigation panel providing access to laboratories (simulations), the video notebook and information. The panel at the bottom of the screen provides access to experts who present lectures and demonstrations on selected topics. These presentations often include animations in addition to explanatory narration and can be stopped at any time.

As a result of formative evaluations of 'Science for Living' (Buckley 1989) and research in biomedical education (Patel *et al.* 1988, Patel *et al.* 1991) information in SFL is structured around an anatomical hierarchy. That is, at the main level, information is available about the circulator system as a whole. At a lower level, information is available about the heart, blood vessels or blood, etc. The diagram of the circulatory system on the left side of the screen serves as a map of and route to the different levels. When a level such as the heart is selected, the heart is highlighted on the map and an expanded diagram of the heart is displayed while the first video for that level plays on the television screen.

At each level the user has access to multiple pieces of information from the videodisc which may include video of live phenomena, photographs, slides or drawings. Each video segment displayed on the television screen is accompanied by a text caption displayed on the computer screen. A video control panel displayed on the television screen allows the user to stop or slow play back of the video segment. The user can also access additional information about the image by clicking on a pre-defined portion of the image. That portion of the image is highlighted and a text box pops up indicating the name of the part and/or what is happening. SFL's experts are available to provide lectures or demonstrations on topics related to the selected part of the circulatory system Some topics include short pieces of animation from *Hemo the Magnificent* (Capra 1957).

The user may, at any time, access the laboratory simulations or the NoteBook provided in SFL. The simulations include the Pump Lab for exploring and experimenting with valves in a single chamber pump and the Life Lab for exploring and experimenting with risk factors associated with heart disease. The NoteBook allows the user to select video segments and create note cards linked to the segment. Note cards may be annotated with text and/or graphics and sequenced for linear presentation. SFL generates a log that traces the user's path through the information and indicates lapsed time and buttons clicked.

Methods

The research design drew on case study methods (Merriam 1991) augmented with techniques from cognitive psychology (Cronbach 1985, Cronbach 1991, Ericsson and Simon 1984) and other interpretative traditions in educational research (Erickson 1986, Jaeger 1988). The preconceptions test, the unit test, projects and presentations were collected from the entire class with additional data collected for selected students.

The classroom

The classroom was one of several participating in an ACOT long term research project. Situated in a large urban Midwestern high school, the classroom was well equipped with computers, scanners, videodisc players and printers. Each of the students and the teacher also had a computer to use at home. The teacher created a template of the SFL NoteBook so that students could enter information into their projects at home, but they could not access the full version of SFL since that requires a workstation with a special video processing board and a laser disc player. The classroom was selected for several reasons. There was enough hardware to set up four multimedia workstations. In addition, the students and teacher were experienced users of the technology and accustomed to the presence of researchers. This minimized both training time and novelty effects.

The students

By design of the long-term research study (Fisher *et al.* 1996) the 28 students in the class mirrored the composition of the high school in ethnicity and socioeconomic status. They had been in the program for almost two years at the time of the study. Prior to entering the program in the ninth grade, some of the students had elected to take a general studies curriculum but, upon admission to the program, were required to take the college prep curriculum that serves as the core of the ACOT curriculum.

Data collection

The operational framework of the study (see Figure 9) displays the diverse data sources gathered to provide evidence of learning and learning activities. Descriptions of the data sources are integrated into the chronological description of the study, which took place over a three week period when students spent 90 minutes a day in this class.

Preconceptions test

At the beginning of the study a written *preconceptions test* was given to all students. The pencil and paper test was an adaptation of the instrument developed by Arnaudin and Mintzes (1985, 1986) to survey conceptions about the circulatory system held

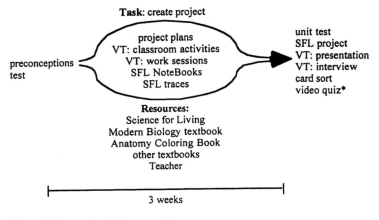

Figure 9 Operational framework
*Video quiz was given two months later

by students ranging from primary school to college level. The test poses four open-ended and 11 multiple choice questions that often use diagrams as choices. It was modified for this study by asking students to justify their choices in the multiple choice questions and by providing an opportunity for students to create their own drawings in answer to the questions. The teacher then introduced SFL to the class and provided a series of 'get acquainted' exercises.

The task

Results from the preconceptions test indicated that half of the students believed that the digestive system and the circulatory system were not connected. Since the class had just studied the digestive system, the teacher and researcher decided to assign students the *task* of using the SFL NoteBook to create a multimedia project that 'tells how digestion and circulation are tied together and how the food that you take in ends up coming up here to this little finger cell.' To get them started, the teacher delivered a 45 minute lecture that explained – with the help of video clips from SFL and diagrams from *The Anatomy Colouring Book* (Kapit and Elson 1977) – how food is absorbed from the small intestine into the blood.

Data on learning activities

Most students worked in teacher-assigned groups of three or four but one student, Joanne, negotiated with the teacher and researcher to work alone. After the get-acquainted exercises and project assignment, the students were instructed to begin by creating *project plans*. The teacher provided blank storyboards[1] so that students could plan what would appear on the computer and video screens during their presentations. Project plans were collected, copied and returned to the students. The second week and the first two days of the final week were used as project workdays. Throughout the study students had access not only to SFL but also to their textbook (Otto *et al.* 1977) and a shelf of other biology textbooks. Classroom activities and work sessions at the multimedia stations were videotaped daily using four or five small video cameras mounted in out of the way, but not hidden, places. Each had an auxiliary microphone to improve sound quality. The teacher wore a wireless microphone connected to the classroom camera so that his interactions with students could be captured as he moved about the classroom. Each group's SFL NoteBook was collected daily as were *SFL trace* computer files that contained a time log of which parts of SFL students accessed and when.

Resulting knowledge data

On Wednesday of the final week, each project was presented to the class and scored by the teacher. *Project presentations* were also videotaped for later analysis. Selected students were interviewed individually to probe their knowledge of the circulatory system. They were chosen based on identification by the teacher as reasonably successful students and who were both willing and available[2] to be interviewed by the researcher. The semi-structured *interview*, also videotaped, consisted of: a card sort performed by the student to elicit the content and structure of circulatory system knowledge; questions about a newspaper graphic illustrating an experimental alternative to heart bypass surgery to assess the ability to use circulatory system knowledge to understand novel information; and questions about their experiences of learning with SFL. In the *card sort*, students were given rectangles bearing the names of circulatory system components arranged in alphabetical order. They were asked to arrange the cards in any way that made sense to them and to explain why they had arranged them as they had. Since the card sort was conducted at a computer using an object-oriented drawing program, students could add or duplicate cards and create multiple arrangements in a form easily saved for later analysis. Students were also asked to explain a newspaper illustration of an experimental alternative to heart bypass surgery. In addition to probing their understanding of the new technique, they were also asked about the normal blood supply to the heart.

The following day a written *unit test* created by the teacher with some input from the researcher was administered. It consisted of 37 questions using both verbal and pictorial elements to assess students' understanding of the parts, functions and processes of the circulatory system. Because it was clear to both teacher and researcher that Joanne's project, presentation and knowledge were qualitatively superior to that of her classmates, the teacher collected all of Joanne's hand-written project notes after the unit test.

Retention data

Two months later ten self-selected students took a HyperCard-based *video quiz* developed by the researcher to check knowledge retention. Seated at a multimedia workstation, the student clicked a button that played a segment from the videodisc and answered questions about the segment by typing answers or annotating drawings on the screen.

Data analysis

Analysis of the vast amounts of diverse data collected for the larger study drew on case study methods (Merriam 1991) augmented with techniques from cognitive psychology (Cronbach 1985, Cronbach 1991, Ericsson and Simon 1984) and other interpretative traditions in educational research (Erickson 1986, Jaeger 1988). Integration of these methods was achieved within an interactive model of data analysis (Miles and Huberman 1984) that employed the systematic and iterative use of data displays informed by the work of Tufte (1983, 1990). Miles and Huberman advocate creation of data displays that summarize the available data and enable the researcher to search for patterns in the data, which can then be evaluated, reconstructed and re-evaluated. Tufte offers principled and well researched guidelines for the construction of such displays.

The preconceptions test, unit test and video quiz were analysed for all students. Case records were created for selected students. Analysis of student case records proceeded in two phases. During the first phase the written tests, the final version of the project, the classroom presentation and the interview data were analysed to assess a student's knowledge at the beginning and end of the study. In the second phase the student's learning activities were examined by summarizing project plans, videotape data and computer files in calendar displays.

Assessment of prior and post knowledge

All data providing evidence of a student's knowledge (written tests, final project, class presentation and interview) were entered into the student's case record which was segmented to place both question and answer in one segment. Each segment was first coded based on what anatomical part of the circulatory system was the focus. In a second pass, each segment was coded based on whether the segment provided evidence of the student's knowledge of the structure (S) of that part, its function (F), its behaviour (B), or the causal mechanism (M) of the behaviour. *Structure* refers to subcomponents and their spatial relationships. *Function* refers to the role the anatomical part plays in the larger system in which it is embedded. *Behaviour* refers to dynamic processes and changes in structures, while *mechanism* refers to the causes of the behaviour. For example, a model of the circulatory system begins with the structure of the circulatory system, i.e. the heart, blood vessels and blood. To that anatomical/structural model, dynamic behaviour such as the heart pumping blood, blood vessels conducting blood and blood carrying cells and chemicals are added. Together the structures and their interacting behaviours form the mechanism that accomplishes the global function of the circulatory system of carrying cells and chemicals throughout the body (Buckley 1992, Chi *et al.* 1991). However, the heart, blood vessels and blood are themselves dynamic structures with their own components and mechanisms. The emergent behaviour depends not only on the interactions among parts, but also on the state of each part. The heart, for instance, propels blood by the contractions (B) of cardiac muscle (S) stimulated by the pacemaker system (S) and the opening and closing (B) of heart valves (S). The strength of the contraction depends not only on stimulation by the pacemaker, but also on the state of polarization of the Purkinje fibres and the volume of blood in the heart, as well as the health of the cardiac muscle. Each of these components can also be modelled resulting in a multilevel hierarchy of models based on the anatomy of the circulatory system and integrating its physiology down to the biochemical level (Buchanan 1999, Newell 1981).

Segments were then sorted by both codes and the collated segments were considered together in order to judge whether the collected information indicated accurate, inaccurate, or partial knowledge of that part of the circulatory system and whether that knowledge was integrated. The integration judgement was based on consistency across the collated data and upon the student's ability to use more than one component at a time. From analysis of the collated data a display (see Figure 10) was

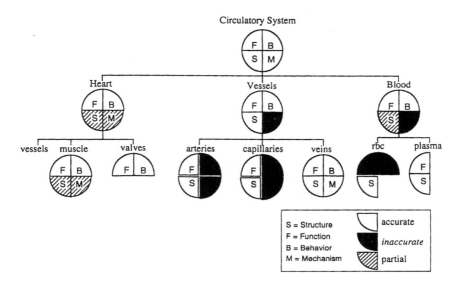

Figure 10 Display of circulatory system knowledge as hierarchy of model components

created to enable visual comparisons of a student's knowledge before and after the study and comparisons across students.

Accurate knowledge is indicated by clear quadrants, inaccurate knowledge by dark gray quadrants and incomplete knowledge by striped quadrants. Separated quadrants represent fragmented knowledge, while integrated knowledge is indicated by circles with four contiguous quadrants. Knowledge need not be accurate or complete to be integrated. Inaccurate knowledge can be integrated in the form of reciprocating misconceptions – pieces of inaccurate knowledge that reinforce each other (Feltovich *et al.* 1988).

The process of considering the collated segments and creating the display provided many opportunities to search for both confirming and disconfirming evidence and to verify the reasoning that entered into decisions about the display. Intercoder agreement among two other coders and the researcher was 67%. The display enables visual comparisons of a student's knowledge before and after the study and comparisons across students. Development of the coding scheme and display is detailed elsewhere (Buckley 1992).

Analysis of learning activities

Description of the learning activities of individual students required triangulation among multiple data sources for each day of the study Videotapes and computer files of each student were summarized in calendar type displays used to tabulate what kinds of data were available for a given student on a given day and to summarize the student's daily in-school learning activities. From the daily summaries, learning episodes were identified for more detailed analysis. Detailed descriptions of learning episodes, some spanning more than one class session, were created from these microanalyses. Thus, within the limitations of the available data, the cases include evidence of the state of the student's circulatory system knowledge before and after the study, the student's learning activities during the three weeks and detailed descriptions of the student's reasoning with and about information during specific learning episodes.

Analysis of representations

Analysis of the learner's interaction with the representations was limited to instances when there was sufficient data in the form of videotapes and computer logs to permit construction of plausible narratives of learning activities and make connections to the learner's knowledge at the end of the study. Representations were identified by examining the computer traces collected by the SFL program during use and, when the learner accessed the video disc contents directly, by identifying segments from the audio portion of the videotape of the work session. While segments without audio cannot be identified from the videotape, such segments were also accessed by the learner when SFL was recording the traces. Representations were analysed for content and the characteristics of each representation and its interface features. The content of each representation was analysed using the same coding scheme used to assess student knowledge. The characteristics of each representation with its interface were analysed using a framework adapted from Goldsmith (1984) (Buckley and Boulter 1999, Buckley and Boulter 2000).

Content analysis

As was done during knowledge assessment, each representation was coded first for which anatomical part of the circulatory system was represented and then what information about the structure, function, behaviour or mechanism of that anatomical unit was included. [. . .]

Table 3 Analytical matrix completed for 'beating heart' video

	Syntactic	*Semantic*	*Pragmatic*
Unity	Colour differences such as white (fat), red (muscle) and dark lines suggest structures, as do rounded shapes. Highlighting when clicked shows boundaries of structures	A larger and smaller chamber are visible as are blood vessels	Recognition enabled by caption and prior knowledge
Location	Rounded shapes provide some depth clues, as does text caption	No scale clues	Prior knowledge that heart is in chest
Emphasis	Slow motion movement. Structures highlighted when clicked	Compelling movements of heart chambers as they fill and empty	Text caption draws attention to dynamic processes
Text parallels	Text caption on computer screen. Pop-up text box on videoscreen when part is clicked	Pop-up text names parts and processes when part is clicked for interpretation	Text caption on computer screen establishes context

Characteristics of representations

An analytical matrix was completed for each representation to capture the relevant visual and semiotic aspects of the representation. The analytical framework devised by Goldsmith (1984) for research on illustrations was adapted for interactive media because it combines both semiotic levels and visual factors (Buckley and Boulter 1999, Buckley and Boulter 2000). Semiotic levels take into account the prior knowledge and interpretation of the user, while visual factors focus on the graphic elements of the representation. Since the representations are embedded in interactive and dynamic media, analysis of the characteristics of the representations included consideration of the interface features. Table 3 presents the analytical matrix for 'beating heart'. Each matrix was then summarized for consideration when constructing the narratives that integrate the findings of this study.

Findings

This classroom-based study sought to address the questions: What is the nature and extent of student learning about the circulatory system when they have access to SFL? How do they go about their learning? How do the representations and interface features in SFL contribute to their learning? The written test scores (Figure 11) provide evidence that students increased their knowledge of the circulatory system over the three week period. However, from analysis of the interviews, projects and presentations, I concluded that the knowledge of the majority of students was still largely fragmented, incomplete, inert and often inaccurate. For example, when asked during the interview to reason about the illustration of an alternative to heart bypass surgery, some students had to be reminded that the heart beats. The one exception was a student who will be called Joanne. Her performance and knowledge at the end of the study was judged by both teacher and researcher to be qualitatively and quantitatively superior to that of her classmates. Therefore, her knowledge and learning activities were exhaustively examined and compared with those of another student, Deanna (Buckley 1992).

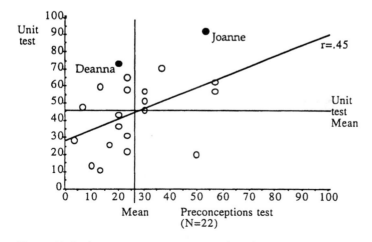

Figure 11 Students' post unit test scores plotted against their preconceptions test scores

Model-building with interactive multimedia

This description of model-building was created from analysis of Joanne's prior knowledge, her knowledge at the end of the study and microanalysis of her learning activities as captured in her project plan, notes and videotapes and computer logs of her work sessions. It documents her learning gains and learning activities.

Joanne was not the most able student in the class according to the teacher. She scored near the top of the preconceptions test scores and at the top of the unit test scores (see Figure 11). She also had the highest score on the video quiz at the end of the year. However, she was not an eager, always motivated, student. For example, in videotapes of early days of the study Joanne can be observed with her head down on the desk – especially when the teacher lectured with the lights dimmed. During the course of this study, however, she demonstrated a clear ability to direct her own learning, which may be why she wanted to work alone, in an early interview she said:

> When you work in a group you don't learn as much . . . Well, you learn how to work with other people. And they might bring up ideas that help you learn and stuff, but then you have people doing this part of the work and people doing that part of the work and you get left out of part of the work so you don't really know that part.
>
> (INT1, 29 March 1990, 38: 40)

This statement is interpreted as evidence of her intentional model-building goal; she wanted all the pieces of information.

Prior knowledge

Based on analysis of just one data source, the preconceptions test, Joanne had some of the components of a working model of the circulatory system at the beginning of the study (see Figure 12). She understood the functions of the major components of the circulatory system, knew that the heart had four chambers and that muscles help pump blood through the chambers but perhaps not the path of blood flow through the heart and body or the role of heart valves. Unlike half of her classmates, she knew of the connection between the digestive and circulatory systems, but her understanding of the exchange of substances in the digestive system was poorly developed,

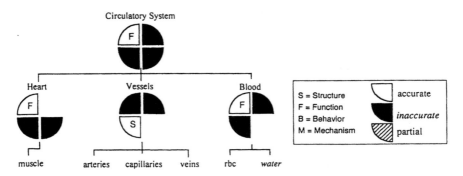

Figure 12 Joanne's knowledge at the beginning of the study from preconceptions test analysis

lacking structures to accomplish the exchange. She wrote on the preconceptions test, 'After the food is broken down it mixes with the blood and carried to the heart where it can be pumped throughout the body'.

Resulting knowledge

Based on evidence collected at the end of the study, Joanne's model of the circulatory system was much more detailed, integrated and useful, even if not entirely accurate. Analysis of her project, presentation, interview and unit test provided evidence that it contained the elements shown in Figure 13. Since the data originate in tasks not specifically designed to elicit a comprehensive mental model of the circulatory system, this diagram is most likely a partial representation of her knowledge at the end of the study.

Joanne's knowledge consisted of information about the structure, function, behaviour and mechanism of many parts of the circulatory system, anchored in an anatomical hierarchy. This hierarchy was evident in both her project and card sort. Joanne's knowledge at the top level of the hierarchy was both integrated and accurate, but at progressively finer levels of detail, her knowledge was less complete, less accurate and less integrated. Some of the inaccuracies were well integrated providing an example of reciprocating misconceptions (Feltovich *et al.* 1988). For example, Joanne believed that red blood cells carry not only oxygen but also food and that they deliver both to the cells by passing through small spaces in the capillary walls.[3] This is an instance of integrating two inaccurate behaviours (that red cells carry food and pass through capillary walls) with an inaccurately scaled model of capillary structure to form a plausible, but inaccurate mechanism.

Joanne was able to use her knowledge to explain the normal functioning of the circulatory system and to understand and explain a newspaper illustration of an experimental alternative to coronary artery bypass surgery which she had not seen before. In her explanation of the illustration we can observe two ways in which her

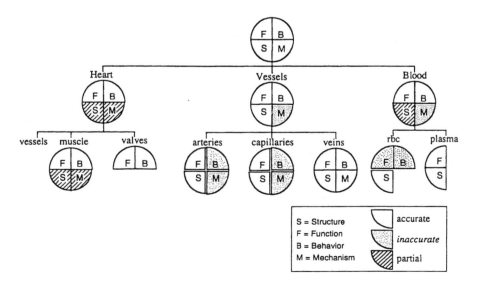

Figure 13 Representation of Joanne's knowledge at the end of the study

model of the circulatory system functioned first, in applying her existing knowledge with ease and second, in reasoning beyond her existing knowledge. When given the illustration and asked how it would work, she responded:

> J: It's just like a cut into it. Just seems like it would let the left ventricle bleed into the heart.
> R: Into the heart?
> J: Yeh, ... like because the blood is already in the left ventricle; right? And that should be the blood that has the oxygen and the food. And so, it's just letting already oxygenated ... blood that has oxygen and food already ... just let it into the heart, so instead of having the coronary artery supply, just having holes let it kind of bleed into the muscle so it gets food and that.

The rapidity with which she applied her knowledge (that the blood in the left ventricle was oxygenated and understood that this procedure would therefore enable oxygen to get to the cardiac muscle) was noticeable, from which it was inferred that her knowledge was well integrated; precompiled, if you will.

She was also asked how the heart was normally supplied with blood:

> There's the coronary artery. And then it's got all these capillaries and stuff that branch out into the muscles of the heart that give it all the food and stuff. And then it goes into ... I suppose, a vein. I'm not sure if it goes into a vein or not. Makes sense that it would but I'm not sure. I just know how it goes in.

This indicates her ability to reason with incomplete knowledge and to extend her general model of blood vessels to the specific instance of the heart's blood supply.

Her ability to explain the normal functioning of the circulatory system and the fluid way in which she understood and explained the experimental alternative to bypass surgery suggests that Joanne had a useful mental model of the circulatory system that included embedded models of many of its components. Important questions to address thus are: How did she develop this model from her fragmented and incomplete knowledge at the beginning of the study? What role did the representations in SFL play?

Learning activities

Joanne's learning activities took place within the context of classroom activities and during voluntary unstructured after school sessions. It was not unusual for students to use the multimedia workstations during their prep periods, after school and occasionally before school – especially in the two days before the projects were due. Based on analysis of her project plan, notes, computer logs and vide otape of classroom and work sessions, Joanne posed questions and sought the answers in the various representations in SFL and textbooks. Her interactions with representations are described and the contribution of the representations examined.

Joanne's project plan and notes provide evidence of the questions she posed as she began planning her presentation From her project plan (Table 4) it can be seen that Joanne focused on parts, purposes, functions, what happens and how organs work together.

After completing the first part of her project plan on Friday, she began the search for information and materials by browsing through several textbooks including the course textbook (Otto *et al.* 1977). Her notes for the day list page numbers of illustrations. On the following class day, Joanne expanded her project plan to include the items shown in Table 5 and listed some project goals (Table 6). Again we see the emphasis on parts and purposes and interactions among parts. The data do not provide specific evidence that browsing the illustrations suggested parts of the circulatory system to be included in her project, but it is plausible.

Interaction with representations

All students in the class saw the images the teacher used when introducing 'Science for Living' and demonstrating its use to the class. Among other things, the students saw compelling images of beating hearts and comparisons of the human circulatory system with those of various animals. Joanne may have encountered these images again during the get-acquainted exercises that took place in small groups. When the teacher lectured on the absorption of food from the small intestine into the blood, the students saw animations (Capra 1957) describing capillaries and substance exchange in the capillaries. Joanne's interaction with the images in these situations was passive; she was not in control of the display.

When Joanne *was* in control of information access, videotapes of work sessions show Joanne intently engaged with the information. Computer logs generated during the get-acquainted task of investigating blood vessels using SFL, show that Joanne looked at every video clip of blood vessels, often stopping or slowing the action and accessing additional text information about the segment. During one after school session, Joanne investigated the heart. Using SFL, she accessed video segments of a rotating beef heart, a heart beating in an open chest, a slow motion video of

Table 4 Joanne's project plan (emphasis added)

Friday	Card
	Introduction and purpose
	Intro to digestion
	Intro to circulatory
	Mouth, blood vessels and other gland. in the mouth, *purposes*
	Esophagus with *functions, parts*
	Stomach and different *parts* of stomach and different *functions*
	How does the circulatory and stomach *work together*
	What happens in the small intestine
	How does heart and intestines *work together*

Table 5 Joanne's project plan (emphasis added)

Monday	Card
	Intro to circulatory
	Parts of blood and *purpose*
	Arteries
	Capillaries
	Veins
	Parts of the heart
	How it pumps

Table 6 Joanne's notes (emphasis added)

Goals
Explain *structure* of organ and importance. Explain *purpose* and *parts* of organ. *How does the circulatory system work with organ?* *What organs interact with the organ and how?* *What about other systems that interact and help the circulatory and digestive systems?*

a beating heart with both an auricle and a ventricle visible and a heart valve functioning *in vivo*. As she had done with blood vessels, Joanne often paused or slowed the play back of these video segments and clicked on the image to access additional textual information. When 'Science for Living' malfunctioned, Joanne began to access the information on the videodisc directly. She spent more than 45 minutes viewing the images quite intently, despite occasional interruptions by other students. Since she was controlling the video disc player directly, no computer log was generated for determining precisely what information she accessed. However, audio from narrated segments provides evidence that Joanne viewed segments explaining the structure and functioning of the heart and heart valves, comparing animal hearts and circulatory systems, the functioning of the heart's pacemaker and showing small pieces of heart muscle beating in a petri dish. She watched intently, replaying some segments, as one expert (Dr. Lawry) displayed and described the exterior and interior anatomy of the beef heart, demonstrated what makes heart sounds, described the path of blood flow on a diagram of the circulatory system and talked about the parts of the heart. She also viewed Dr. Maron's segment on heart disease that describes cholesterol deposition in the coronary artery.

From her comments to a classmate at the next computer, it was inferred that video segments of live phenomena were also part of her viewing. At one point she commented:

> This needs music to go with it. For real, it does. I can sit here and watch this and imagine music. I mean … when they're showing real slow blood cells moving through your veins and stuff, you imagine something slow. And when it's going real fast, you imagine something fast. And when something's beating, you imagine it like scary kind of like.

Viewing these segments directly from the videodisc without the SFL interface denied her access to the additional information embedded in SFL, but from the computer traces it is clear that she had already systematically examined many of these images using SFL.

Joanne spent most of the next class working with books. Her notes (Table 7) for the day and the questions she posed to the teacher reveal the same intense interaction with information. She interrupted her note-taking to pose these questions to the teacher and researcher:

> The heart has two sides, right? Do they fill at the same time; like do you hear both lubs at the same time from the two doors closing?

So the doors do close at the same time. You don't ever hear like screwy beats? ... Is there any time that it can get off beat? *What would happen if the one side of your heart would beat slower than the other?* (emphasis added)

OK, your heart has two different sides with your right atrium and right what ever and ... it's got the two valves between the atrium and the ventricle. Is there ever a time when those valves get off beat with each other and you hear maybe a lub lub dub?

Now it would be like only on one side? The other side cannot keep up and ... what would that be called?

Contributions of the representations

The representations Joanne accessed contributed to the formation and revision of her model of the heart. Joanne's questions can be traced back to the common metaphor, 'the heart is two pumps in one' found both in the textbook and in SFL. Given the textbook metaphor of two pumps, right and left, she questions whether the two pumps might function independently or at least not be properly synchronised. The notion of two pumps is also explicit in the 'Two Pumps' segment shown in Figure 14. The screen displays two insets In one a cardiologist uses the mouse to point to parts of the circulatory system displayed as a diagram in the second inset while he describes (on audio) the flow of blood through the circulatory system. The representation portrays the circulatory system using the lines of the diagram to represent parts of circulatory system. It is an abstract spatial relationship indicating only that the parts are connected in closed loops. The moving arrow cursor directs attention (emphasis) to parts of the circulatory system as it moves over the diagram, while they are named in the audio narration. Together the cursor and the narration (text

Table 7 Notes from the back of Joanne's planning sheets (emphasis added)

Blood picks up all waste chemicals from your cells.
It also delivers needed chemicals to all cells.
1. heart – pushes blood thru [sic] vessels
2. blood vessels – carry blood
3. blood – carrys [sic] chemicals

Heart
2 pumps – left and right
  small top chamber (atrium)
  large bottom chamber (ventricle)
Large muscle (cardiac muscle)
  [p.] 179 Muscle squeezes together blood pumped out
  [p.] 180 muscle at rest blood in the heart
allows blood to only move in one direction
  enters top chamber (3 veins)
    top chambers squeeze; blood enters lower CH
  lower chambers relax allow blood in
    valves from top chambers close
      fill with blood
      squeeze together blood goes out arteries
    * valves keep blood moving in one direction
[p.] 181 right side less muscular because only pumps to lungs

Figure 14 Freeze frame from 'Two Pumps' video segment (SFL 1990)

parallels) describe the flow of blood through the circulatory system (behaviour of the circulatory system) along with some structures and their functions. While reinforcing the notion of two pumps and contributing some information about the structure of the heart, it does not contribute to a model of the behaviour of the heart within the circulatory system. From her questions it is inferred that Joanne at this stage had a mental model of a beating heart that includes the heart valves opening and closing to produce the heart sounds. Which of the representations she accessed could contribute to the formation of this model?

Model formation

From computer logs and videotapes of work sessions Joanne accessed twelve representations of the heart while seeking answers to her questions of parts, purposes and

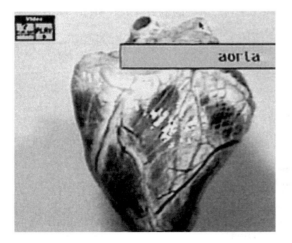

Figure 15 Freeze frame from 'Rotating Beef Heart' video (SFL 1990)

how they work together. She also accessed representations in the textbooks available in the classroom, but the data do not permit identification of the specific representations.

Several representations contain information that relates to her initial questions about parts of the heart (structure). In 'Rotating Beef Heart' (Figure 15) the external structure of the heart can be explored, while in the 'Heart Parts' (Figure 16) segment, a cardiologist opens a heart and describes its internal structure.

In 'Rotating Beef Heart' (Figure 15), a beef heart is shown rotating on a turntable. When the user clicks the 'explore' button on the video control panel at the top left of the screen, the image freezes and the user can click different parts of the heart (structure) which are then highlighted and named in a pop-up text box. The syntactic challenge of discerning the parts is overcome by highlighting the part, while the semantic challenge of naming them is lessened by the close linking of heart structure and parallel text.

In 'Heart Parts' (Figure 16) the screen displays two insets. In one a cardiologist manipulates a beef heart that has been cut open. A close up of the heart and his hands in the second inset shows him touching the interior structures while he names them on audio. Text on the screen also names the structures. The syntactic challenge of discerning parts is somewhat addressed by his fingers touching and manipulating the parts of the heart. This also serves to direct attention (emphasis) while audio and screen text name the parts. However, it is difficult to see the parts clearly.

Neither of these segments contains information about the behaviour of the heart; however, there are some very compelling segments that do. In 'Beating Heart' (Figure 17) a living human heart is shown beating in a chest opened for surgery. The user can explore the image as described earlier. When clicked, the selected part is highlighted and the pop-up text names the part and describes some behaviour. The user can also click the 'slow' button on the video control panel to see the heart beating in slow motion. This allows the user to observe the wave of contraction that causes the chambers to empty and the fluid flow that fills them. Both external structure and behaviour are displayed in this video clip. The syntactic problem is again solved via the interface and the user's actions. In addition, the slow motion playback enables the user to observe the displayed behaviour more closely.

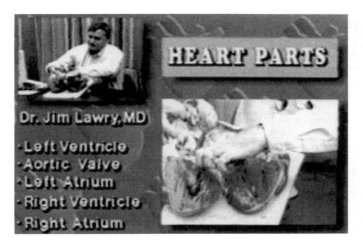

Figure 16 Freeze frame from 'Heart Parts' video segment (SFL 1990)

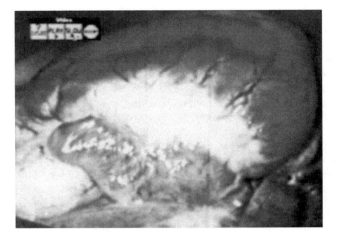

Figure 17 Freeze frame from 'Beating Heart' video segment (SFL 1990)

'Heart Cycle' (Figure 18) represents the internal structures and behaviour of the heart. In one inset the cardiologist is seen manipulating the pump while the other displays a close up of his hands and the pump. On audio Dr. Lowry explains what causes heart sounds while squeezing the pump and slapping the desk to simulate the heart sounds and their place in the heart cycle. The behaviour of the heart is represented by the action of the two hands. The contraction of heart muscle is represented by the hand squeezing the pump while the sound of the closing valve is represented by the other hand hitting the desk. The mechanism or cause of the heart sound is described in the audio text. The temporal sequence is represented, but with two analogies that are not causally linked. The hand squeezing the pump doesn't cause the other hand to hit the desk. Then an animation of the heart cycle is played in the inset. This animation represents the structure and behaviour of the heart with moving lines representing walls and heart valves. Blood flow through the heart is represented as moving wavy lines but the direction isn't clearly one way. Neither the cardiologist's actions nor the

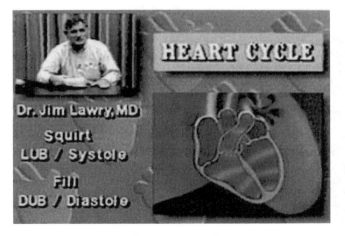

Figure 18 Freeze frame from 'Heart Cycle' (SFL 1990)

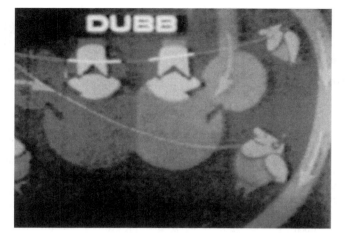

Figure 19 Animation freeze frame from *Hemo the Magnificent* (Capra 1957)

audio text are coordinated with the animation. While the squeezing and slapping do in some sense simulate the behaviour of the heart, only the squeezing maps to the mechanism (contraction of the heart muscle) that causes this behaviour.

An animation (Figure 19) from *Hemo the Magnificent* (Capra 1957) better represents the behaviour and mechanisms of the heart. It is a segment of full screen animation with audio. The heart is represented by lines that move when pushed by four little muscle men. Audio text explains the cause of heart sounds as the closing of the doors between the chambers of the heart. This part of the animation displays the internal structure and behaviour of the heart. Lines are used for the walls of the heart and the valves. Muscle men represent the cardiac muscle. Moving arrows are used to clearly represent blood flowing through the heart in one direction. The audio text draws the analogy of the valves as one way doors that permit the blood to flow only in one direction. This is a reasonable analogy because the sound of the heart valves closing has the same cause as the sound of doors closing and connects with physical intuitions and common experience. Although this segment suggests that the arrows representing blood press on the doors, it doesn't explicitly articulate the differences in blood pressures that cause the valves to open and close.

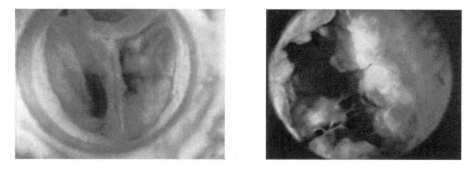

Figure 20 Freeze frame of heart valves (Capra 1957)

This animation is followed by a segment showing 'Heart Valves' *in situ*. Heart valves are shown (Figure 20) opening and closing while the audio track says 'lub' or 'dub' synchronously with the valves closing. This representation of the behaviour of heart valves adds to the animation by allowing the user to observe the phenomenon *in situ*. Because the interaction is passive, some of the information about the phenomenon are not made explicit. Identifying other structures such as the tendons that strengthen the leaflets of the valve (barely visible in the freeze frame on the right) could provide additional information about the structure and mechanism of heart valves.

Together these representations contribute information not only about the internal structures and the behaviour of the heart, but also about part of the mechanism that produces the behaviour of the heart as a whole. Recall that mechanism is defined as the interacting behaviours of the components that produce the emergent behaviour of the whole. For example, cardiac muscle (men) push blood through heart valves that permit blood to flow in just one direction.

Having analysed these representations, we can better understand their contributions to the learner's models of the heart that enabled her to ask questions about the two pumps beating independently. At the end of the learning episode, the teacher suggested that normally both sides contract at the same time. Although we know from the logs that Joanne accessed a segment about the pacemaker system that co-ordinates heart conditions we have no data to provide evidence of her reasoning about it. It was not mentioned by any of the participants during this learning episode. From this episode, it was inferred that Joanne had a model of the heart that included its behaviour and part of the mechanism (the role of heart valves in producing heart sounds and in permitting unidirectional blood flow through the heart). Within the model-based learning framework this sequence is interpreted as testing a model of the heart as two independent pumps, which, judging from the final interview data below, she rejected:

> At the same time . . . blood is filling both the atriums. The one on the right is taking it from the rest of the body, while the one on the left side is taking blood from the lungs. And then after that's filled up, the valves open down to the ventricles at the same time, because I know they close at the same time and the blood flows down to the ventricles.

Model revision

In addition to the purposeful information seeking just described, Joanne devoted nearly two days to 'messing around' with the Life Lab simulation. During this episode she revised her model of heart disease and her model of the heart. In the final interview she described how her understanding of heart disease changed as a result of this learning episode:

> . . . I didn't really know. I just knew that some foods had cholesterol and that if you didn't watch out then you was going to get a buildup in your arteries. But I didn't know what arteries, you know. I thought it was the aorta and thought that's what happened and you just didn't get blood to the rest of your body. That's what I thought, but then the aorta is so big that you'd have to eat pure cholesterol and fat and by that time our coronary artery would [be clogged] so you as wouldn't even have a heart.

Videotape data and computer logs show that Joanne used Life Lab during two consecutive class days and one after school session. The Life Lab simulates a stair climbing stamina test. When using Life Lab, the user sets the input variables on the left side of the screen by choosing foods from a kitchen (fat in diet), the level of smoking; the frequency, duration and intensity of exercise; the height, weight and general health of parents (genetic status); and age. Some of the output variables are visible on the lower right side of the screen: blood pressure, heart rate and an angioscope image displaying a graphical representation of cholesterol accumulation in an unspecified blood vessel. When the simulated StairClimb is run via buttons at the top right of the screen, the television screen displays images of the stairs being climbed. There are also audio outputs in the form of a voice saying, 'You are sweating profusely. You are very tired. You are exhausted. You must stop'. In addition, the user can view three presentations about heart disease, risk factors and prevention given by the cardiologist at the bottom of the screen.

According to computer logs created by SFL, Joanne ran three complete trials and one incomplete trial on the first day. The following day she ran two trials, but without the StairClimb portion of the simulation. Her omission of the Stair Climb suggests that Joanne used the angioscope as the outcome by which she judged her success. Videotape of the after school work session on the same day supports this inference. When the researcher wandered by to peer over her shoulder, Joanne commented:

J: I'm trying to give it the best one, 'cause . . . it seems like [the angioscope] always fills up no matter what.

After Joanne worked diligently at the computer for some time, she said to herself, 'Ah, I found one'. When a classmate sat down to work at an adjacent computer. Joanne explained:

Look. I've finally found somebody who didn't have any cholesterol buildup at all. They had zero fat. They didn't smoke. They exercised until they about dropped. Oh, I didn't do their DNA! Shoot! OK. Well, their DNA's good, too. I mean they are healthy!'

After completing the series of trials, Joanne viewed the three segments describing heart disease, cardiac risk factors and prevention. 'Heart Disease' includes an animated representation very similar to the angioscope display. It shows the gradual deposition of cholesterol in an artery followed by a diagram that identifies the coronary artery as the site where such deposition can contribute to heart attacks. The angioscope displays the effect of risk factors on cholesterol deposition in blood vessels, but does so with minimal anatomical context. In contrast, the heart disease segment begins with a similar representation, displays the process of deposition (behaviour) and uses parallel text on the screen and in audio to identify the coronary artery as the structure where the deposition is taking place. The diagram shown on the right provides further anatomical context by spotlighting (emphasis) where the coronary artery is located (structure) on a drawing of the exterior of the heart.

From this episode it was inferred that providing spatial location information about the coronary artery, in combination with Joanne's focus on the importance of structure, enabled her to revise her general model of cholesterol deposition in arteries to a more specific model of cholesterol deposition in coronary arteries which leads to heart attacks. In a model-based learning framework this is interpreted as revising her model of heart disease by embedding a model of cholesterol deposition in her model of the heart. It was inferred from her reasoning about the novel illustration during the interview that she also revised her model of the heart by adding models of coronary vessels (arteries and capillaries prior to the interview and veins during the interview).

Reciprocating misconceptions

Both of these learning episodes portray positive contributions to learner's mental models of the circulatory system. However, representations may also contribute to misconceptions. Joanne constructed an inaccurate mechanism as the means by which food and oxygen get to the cells of the body. By combining a faulty behaviour of the red cells (carrying food as well as oxygen) with a faulty structure of capillaries (gaps between cells are large enough for red cells to slip out into the tissues), Joanne constructed a pair of reciprocating misconceptions (Feltovich *et al.* 1988). These two misconceptions work together to form a plausible, but inaccurate, mechanism for delivering food and oxygen to cells. The data are insufficient to draw specific links between the representations and the misconception, however, one animation segment is suspect. In 'grocery man/garbage man' (Capra 1957) a scuba diver tows a canister while swimming through a capillary. The canister spews forth oxygen molecules and steaks in one part of the capillary and vacuums up carbon dioxide molecules and banana peels in another. All of the objects pass freely through the gaps in the capillary walls. Although metaphorically correct at some level, the inconsistencies in the scales of the objects portrayed may impede use of the learner's physical intuitions and prior experiences in developing a more accurate understanding of this segment.
[. . .]

Discussion

This chapter has examined a case of model-based learning in which a learner assembled models of the circulatory system and its components from pieces of information accessible in 'Science for Living: the Circulatory System', an interactive multimedia resource prototype. The original questions and larger study were not cast in terms of mental models or model-based learning. Rather a broad range of research and concepts from cognitive psychology, science education and educational technology provided a fertile foundation for developing the initial model of model-based learning that emerged from the SFL project. This case demonstrates that while model-building can take place in the science classroom, the learner must have access to the necessary pieces of information and employ effective learning strategies in interacting with that information. Although we cannot generalize from a single case, we can form an initial model of model-based learning and the roles of learning strategies and representations. It is, however, difficult to consider them independently because they are parts of an interacting system. The role of representations in model-based learning is very much a function of the learner's interaction with them. A wide range of learner characteristics influence this interaction.

The description of Joanne's learning strategies has included the questions she posed and the way in which she interacted with and reasoned about representations. Her plan, activities and notes provide evidence of learning goals and goal-oriented behaviour and hence the intentional nature of her learning (Bereiter and Scardamalia 1989). This case also documents the highly constructive way (Chan *et al.* 1992) in which she interacted with information both in SFL and in other sources. The episode in which she reasons about the heart-is-two-pumps metaphor is but one example. From project plan to project completion Joanne's learning focused on the structure of the circulatory system enriched with the functioning of its component parts, 'how they work together'. This, evidenced from her notes, suggests that Joanne views biology in terms of interacting systems. Others have noted the relationship between interacting systems beliefs and successful science learning (Mandinach 1989, Mandinach and Cline 1989, Schauble *et al.* 1991).

Furthermore, Joanne's learning goals and strategies set the stage for spontaneous model revision while 'messing around' with the Life Lab simulation. Her notes provide evidence that she was alert to the importance of both dynamic processes and anatomical structure. This may have focused her attention on the relevant information in the simulation and associated animations, which she used to revise and elaborate her models of the heart and of coronary artery disease. How she actually integrated the diverse sources of information into her mental model remains unclear. Given her goals and the highly constructive way in which she interacted with information, it is possible that model formation from these diverse sources occurred in the spontaneous, unconscious and simultaneous manner described by Iran-Nejad (1990) as active, dynamic self-regulated learning. While this might seem to conflict with the idea of intentional model-building, it is perhaps facilitated by the focus on structure and behaviour that is central to model-based learning.

In her quest for understanding, Joanne pursued a path not unlike that of a biologist, seeking out structures that cause the observed behaviours. Jacob (1982) describes the development of biological theory:

> Even when an abstract entity such as the gene appears, the biologist will not rest until he has replaced it by material components, particles or molecules, as if, in order to last, a biological theory had to be based on a concrete model.
>
> (Jacob 1982: 14)

This suggests that Joanne's model-building may provide a productive foundation for the development of expertise. She posed questions, sought information from a variety of sources and reasoned about that information, sometimes as if she were conducting a thought experiment (Clement 1993, Gilbert and Boulter 1998). Unlike the scientists in Clement's study, Joanne does not appear to evaluate her model explicitly, although she may employ internal consistency checks that rely on physical intuitions about concrete objects (Clement 1994). Her reasoning resembles reflective theory change (Chinn and Brewer 1993) in that it involves deep processing and explanatory physical mechanisms.

In general, Joanne demonstrated a very productive, generative mode of learning, grounded in the structure of the phenomena and possibly extensible into the development of domain expertise. For example, her mental model provides a good foundation for learning the physiology and pathology of the circulatory system, in part because of its grounding in anatomy (Chawla and Patel 1988, Patel *et al.* 1991). Joanne's model of the circulatory system can become progressively more complex by embedding models within models. With embedded models she can manage the complexity of phenomena without oversimplifying. She can focus on the level of the anatomical hierarchy appropriate for the reasoning in progress and switch levels as needed. Thus her models an progress by encompassing smaller structures and mechanisms such as molecules and ions or by embedding models within larger models of more complex biological systems. Thus, the structure of the phenomena of the domain provides the rationale for a progression of causal models (White 1993, White and Frederiksen 1990).

While this case has illustrated learning behaviours and resources that enabled Joanne to engage in model-building, it does not explain *why* Joanne behaved as she did. Her desire to work alone and her project goals may reflect an intrinsic motivation to understand the phenomenon as opposed to an extrinsic motivation to perform to other's expectations (Bower 1983, Dweck 1984, Entwistle 1988, Lepper and Malone 1987, Nolen 1988). Perhaps her learning activities spring from a learning trait or learning style that favours deep processing over surface processing (Entwistle 1988, Schmeck 1988). Alternatively, perhaps she employed a learned strategy. There is insufficient data to do more than speculate.

Whatever combination of these factors may have motivated her, Joanne used her prior knowledge and the resources of SFL and the classroom very effectively to accomplish her goals and the assigned task, She invested effort (Salomon 1983, Salomon and Globerson 1987) in interacting with the representations in SFL in a highly constructive way (Chan *et al.* 1992), exploring them and associated text systematically.

While access to the representations in SFL may have been an important enabling mechanism for Joanne's learning, it was not sufficient to ensure model-building by the other students in the classroom. As with Joanne, the data do not permit us to say why that was the case. Perhaps it relates to the issues of motivation, learning traits or learning styles discussed earlier. Perhaps it relates to prior knowledge. The limited evidence provided by the preconceptions test does indicate a difference in prior knowledge between Joanne and Deanna, the contrasting case (Buckley 1992). Deanna scored very low (20%) on the preconceptions test, but came second on the unit test scores (73% vs. 92%). It could be that a certain critical mass of knowledge is needed to begin building models. However, in Figure 11 we saw that three others scored as high on the preconceptions test as Joanne (53%) Two of the other three were identified by the teacher as very able students and were among the students selected for case studies; they did not engage in model-building. Perhaps the same learning approach exhibited by Joanne in this case enabled her to retain more of what she had learned earlier (Salomon and Globerson 1987).

The data do permit illustration of the differences between Joanne's learning activities and those of other students. The most obvious one is that Joanne worked alone while the others worked in groups of three or four students. Deanna led three other students in the production of their project and presentation. Perhaps as Joanne stated early on, Deanna didn't get all the pieces of knowledge or information needed to build a mental model.

However, there were also notable differences between Joanne and Deanna in the interpretation of the task, their interaction with information and the use of SFL. Deanna's group conceptualized the task differently and therefore posed different questions. They saw the task as one of describing where food and blood go in the body. Their project described the flow of materials through a sequence of organs, but seldom provided details or mechanisms of the process at that location. The organs were linked by their place in the sequence but not by anatomical structure *per se*. From their project plan and presentation, it was inferred that their goal was to describe behaviour rather than explain the causes of the behaviour (Horwood 1988). Armed with different questions, Deanna's group sought information most often from the textbooks available in the classroom. Consequently they may have had difficulty grasping the dynamic behaviour of the circulatory system and its interacting parts. While there was little difference in the amount of time (~500 minutes) Joanne and Deanna used SFL, there were differences in the way they used it. Deanna's group used SFL primarily as a tool to produce their project and as a source of pictures and video. Of the total time they spent using SFL, 74% as occupied using the NoteBook to produce their project; an additional 17% was lost due to technical difficulties. Two students in the class, one in Deanna's group, were often distracted by such problems. When these students had technical difficulties with SFL, they would abandon the content in favour of engagement with the programming behind SFL. This behaviour distracted the rest of the group as well. Only 6% of usage by Deanna and group involved the information, experts or labs in SFL. When Deanna did focus on the content in SFL, she did not routinely or systematically access the additional information intended to aid comprehension. Instead she quickly clicked through the images seldom lingering over individual images or exploring them. When Deanna's group did engage with the content, they often did so at a low level of constructive activity, such as typing slightly paraphrased text from books into their projects. Although Joanne also used the majority (63%) of her SFL time producing the project, she spent 20% of her time engaged with the content, losing only 4% to technical difficulties. Learning how to use SFL accounted for the remaining 3–4% of SFL usage for both Deanna and Joanne.

Of course, none of these differences operates in isolation. Interactions among group members and with the teacher can have powerful effects on the learning activities of the group (Boulter 1996, Boulter 1997, Salomon and Perkins 1998). The teacher's interactions with Joanne and Deanna differed as well. In the full transcript of the 'heart-is-two-pumps' episode, the teacher encouraged Joanne to seek out the information for herself, while with other groups, including Deanna's, he often gave mini-lectures in response to their questions. Perhaps this reduced their engagement with the information and short-circuited their learning (Salomon and Globerson 1987).

The focus on structure and interacting behaviours is a recurring theme not only in Joanne's goals and knowledge, but also in SFL and in biology research. It was notably absent from the plans and the knowledge of other students in the class. Some had to be reminded that the heart pumps. The use of structure and function in instruction is not new; their use in biology texts and their embodiment in anatomy and physiology classes is ubiquitous in biological and medical education. However, they are seldom used explicitly as the foundation for further learning of the dynamics and causal mechanisms of biological phenomena or embedded in a framework that integrates multiple levels of organization and time scales.

While we cannot generalize from a single case, its rich and systematic description of the resources (structure) and learning activities (behaviour) does support formation of a working model of the cognitive core of model-based learning which can then be used and evaluated in further studies and revised, elaborated or rejected as appropriate.

Implications

Given the importance of models and modelling for science learning as well as for conducting science (Gilbert and Boulter 1998), the research reported in this chapter has implications for the development of theory and future research as well as the design of learning environments.

For theory development

This chapter has described a case of model-building in biology and characterized it as an initial model of the cognitive core of science learning. Giere (1990) describes theories as families of models and the hypotheses that link them to phenomena. Like biological phenomena, the phenomena of classrooms include many levels of organization. In order to construct a family of models to populate a theory of model-based teaching and learning, not only must this model of individual learning be tested, but it must also be embedded within the larger systems of participation in classrooms and other learning contexts. When model-based learning is embedded in a particular context, factors in model-based teaching come into play. In classrooms, the role of the teacher in the selection of phenomena, representations, tasks and in guiding discourse about them is important (Boulter 1992, Boulter 1996). In museums, one must first engage the visitor's attention, but conversations about the exhibits may influence both the attention and the understanding that the visitor takes away from the visit (Gilbert and Priest 1997, Tunnicliffe 1998). In activity centres, inter-actions with phenomena and physical models are also a factor (Falcão *et al.* 1999). The numerous individual and cultural factors that influence learning in science are beyond the scope of this discussion.

By creating models of the structures, behaviours and mechanisms at play in different contexts, we can test, elaborate and revise our basic model of model-based teaching and learning. To this end, research and design experiments (Brown 1992) are currently underway in a field-based ecological inquiry course and a biotechnology course (Boulter *et al.* 1999; see also Gilbert and Boulter 2000). In designing this research we consider carefully the design of the learning environment and data collection methods that can be implemented within the constraints of the classroom.

Design of learning environments

Learning environments, whether they are intelligent tutoring systems, laboratories, museums, activity centres or traditional classrooms, include many elements. This chapter focuses on just two aspects: information resources and learning activities.

Design of information resources. The first issue to be addressed is the target model of the phenomena (Norman 1983). Here the desired outcome is not a list of dis-crete objectives but an integrated model of the desired understanding similar to the dis-play of Joanne's knowledge (Figure 10). For other phenomena the hierarchy may not be based on an anatomical hierarchy but on levels of organization (Miller 1992) that correspond roughly to structures arrayed along a scale of physical size. In an ecologi-cal inquiry course, the hierarchy ranges from the geosphere to atoms and molecules. The extent of the hierarchy to be addressed in the curriculum or research project requires judgement based on the prior knowledge and cognitive development of the learner as well as the constraints of the learning environment. It is hypothesized that it is more effective to facilitate understanding of a few contiguous levels in an inte-grated manner than to present many levels in an incomplete and fragmented way. The use of contiguous levels permits causal explanations and models to be constructed which can then be extended by unpacking the structures and behaviours that interact at the lower level to produce the emergent behaviour of the higher level.

Are the necessary pieces of information available and accessible? This question requires consideration of the aspects (structure, function, behaviour, mechanism) of the phenomenon to be represented, the challenges inherent in particular representa-tions and the role of the interface or other conventions of use in overcoming those challenges. It is hypothesized that a few, excellent, compelling images that, taken together, explicitly represent all the aspects of phenomena needed to achieve the target understanding are more effective than a large, mediocre set with missing compo-nents. Specifically, we try to:

- Make the structure of the phenomenon explicit to the learner. This may require video or diagrams that include explicit aids to interpretation (Kindfield 1993–1994; Lowe 1993);

- When the behaviour of the structure is essential to its functioning, enable learners to see the behaviour of the structure whether it is heart muscle contracting or a molecule changing shape. This is analogous to the oft-repeated demand that textbooks include causal explanations of phenomena rather than descriptions;
- Emphasize the interactive nature of biological systems. Even phenomena that seem static, like the solidity of bones, are in states of dynamic equilibrium; and
- Provide an expanded context in the form of cross references to the larger system in which a phenomenon is embedded and the smaller systems of which it is composed.

Design and implementation of learning activities. Numerous researchers have demonstrated that the task assigned is not always the task accomplished (Bereiter and Scardamalia 1989, Roth and Bowen 1993). In this chapter students' interpretations of the task varied in ways that influenced the questions they posed and sought to answer. Therefore, it is important in assigning tasks that learning goals (both the student's and the teacher's) be considered and negotiated:

- Assign tasks that help students focus on structure and behaviour and on unpacking causal mechanisms. Gobert and Clement (1999) have successfully used a sequence of drawing tasks in which students create spatial, dynamic and causal diagrams of plate tectonics phenomena;
- Enable learners to pursue their own questions about phenomena so that they develop learning goals of increasing their own understanding (Bereiter and Scardamalia 1989, Brown *et al.* 1993, Brown and Campione 1990, Scardamalia *et al.* 1989);
- Involve students in the critical use of representations of all kinds (Mandinach 1989, Mandinach and Cline 1989, Marsh and Boulter 1997, Marsh, Willimont and Boulter 1999). Kindfield (1993–1994) suggests that the use of representations in reasoning and problem solving co-evolve with domain expertise;
- Assign tasks such as creating drawings, maps, posters, web pages, animations or simulations of phenomena that require the learner to interact with information and their own knowledge in order to produce their own representations (Burtis *et al.* 1993, Chan *et al.* 1997, Gobert and Clement 1999).

Regarding methods for studying model-based learning

The decision, based on numerous philosophical and pragmatic considerations, to conduct research in the classroom places constraints on the methods employed. A variety of methods have been used to elicit mental models in laboratory research, but most are too time consuming to administer in the classroom. Continuing the philosophy of minimal interference with normal classroom activities, we design course assignments and learning activities that serve the dual purposes of student assessment and to pose questions, tasks and problems intended to elicit students' mental models which we analyse using the analytical framework described in this chapter. Current data collection includes:

- Eliciting prior knowledge at the very beginning of the course using a paper and pencil representation task. This also serves to activate prior knowledge in preparation for engagement with course content;
- Assigning assessment tasks that include creating representations of their understanding;

- Interviewing a sample of the students at the end of the course to elicit more fully their models of the phenomena and to triangulate with their other representations; and
- Recording classroom discourse for later analysis of reasoning with models and representations as well as for identifying elements of model-based teaching.

For future research

This chapter has documented a case of intentional model-building that focused on the learner's activities and constructive engagement with representations in the accomplishment of a task. Further research is needed to test and elaborate this model of intentional model-based learning by individuals and to embed it in a model of model-based teaching and learning that encompasses the diverse social and cultural contexts in which science learning takes place.

There are unanswered questions that relate to the larger context of science learning. Does model-building explain the performance of successful science students? Is it the primary path to effective science learning or are there others? How does intentional model-building relate to analogical reasoning and the development of alternative conceptions? Can we teach model-building?

Several studies have noted the correlation between epistemology and learning (for example, Gobert and Clement 1999, Posner and Strike 1989, Songer and Linn 1991). They suggest that the epistemology of the learner influences the learner's goals and approach to a task. Does engagement in model-based learning bring about epistemological changes as well as conceptual ones?

While this case has raised questions about the natural occurrence of model-building, whether it is a learning strategy or a learning style, or a function of epistemology or motivation or views of the nature of science, it has highlighted the importance of tasks and engagement with representations. Representations form a critical link not only between learners and phenomena but also between the level of individual learning and the level of collaborative learning among a group of individuals. For this reason, investigations of model-based learning continue with a focus on two questions.

How do different tasks and learning activities influence model-building? Project-based, problem-based, inquiry-based and issue-based science curricula are examples of different approaches developed to help more students learn science. What elements in these curricula facilitate or hinder model-building? What elements of model-based learning might enhance the effectiveness of these curricula?

How do different types of representations contribute to model-based learning? Bruner (1963) posits a progression in learning that includes enactive, iconic and symbolic. Do progressions of model types (for example, concrete, visual, mathematical) that parallel this learning progression facilitate model-building? The critical use of representations and the creation of representations may offer paths by which learners construct models. How do they compare with interactions with the phenomena? How do they function in different domains with different phenomena?

Conclusions

This chapter has presented research that is an example of research that moves beyond lists of misconceptions to examining productive foundations for constructing new understandings (Smith III, diSessa and Roschelle 1993/1994). It has demonstrated that model-based learning can occur in science classrooms. The roles of learning activities and representations in model-based learning were examined by describing the representations with which Joanne interacted while constructing a multimedia project describing how food absorbed in the small intestine is circulated to all the cells of the body. Each representation was analysed in terms of what part of the circulatory system was portrayed, whether the representation included information about the structure, function, behaviour or mechanism of that particular part, how the characteristics of the representation and interface made that information accessible and how the representation contributed to the learner's mental models of the circulatory system at the end of the study. Narratives described the learner's interactions with particular representations and how the representations contributed, both positively and negatively, to specific parts of the learner's mental models. The major contribution of this chapter lies in the logical and empirical linking of the learning goals and resulting knowledge of the learner with the representations to which she had access. The micro-analyses of knowledge, representations and learning activities supported construction of the model-based learning framework, grounded in the multiple literatures of cognitive psychology, science education and educational technology. While there is a need for further research that extends our understanding of model-based learning, the type of learning described in this chapter cuts across educational philosophies, instructional strategies and learning environments and suggests a potentially powerful strategy for organizing science learning of all types.

Notes

1. Storyboards are used in television and film work to plan story line sequences.
2. Some students were not available for interviews due to conflicts with after school jobs and activities.
3. Red blood cells carry oxygen but not food. Molecules from food are carried by the plasma portion of blood. Molecules of oxygen released by the red blood cell and food pass through the spaces in capillary walls, but not red blood cells themselves.

References

Arnaudin, M. W. (1983) Students' alternative conceptions of the human circulatory system. Unpublished Masters paper (Wilmington: University of North Carolina).

Arnaudin, M. W. and Mintzes, J. J. (1985) Students' alternative conceptions of the human circulatory system: a cross-age study. *Science Education*, 69, 721–733.

Arnaudin, M. W. and Mintzes, J. J. (1986) The cardiovascular system: children's conceptions and misconceptions. *Science and Children*, 48–51.

Bereiter, C. and Scardamalia, M. (1989) Intentional learning as a goal of instruction. In L. B. Resnick (ed.) *Knowing, learning and instruction: Essays in honor of Robert Glaser* (Hillsdale, NJ: Lawrence Erlbaum Associates), 361–392.

Boulter, C. (1992) Collaborating to investigate questions: a model for primary science. Unpublished Doctoral (Reading: University of Reading).

Boulter, C. (1996) Discourse and conceptual understanding in science. I. B. Davies (ed.) *Oral Discourse and Education*, Vol. 3 (Dordrecht: Kluwer), 239–248.

Boulter, C. J. (1997) Language, models and modelling in primary science classroom. In J. K. Gilbert (ed.) *Exploring Models and Modelling in Science and Technology Education* (Reading: Faculty of Education and Community Studies, University of Reading).

Boulter, C. J. and Buckley, B. C. (2000) Constructing a typology of models for science education. In J. K. Gilbert and C. J. Boulter (eds) *Developing models in science education* (Dordrecht: Kluwer), 25–42.

Boulter, C. J., Buckley, B. C. and France, B. (1999) Understanding decay: models in biology and biotechnology. Paper presented at the Annual meeting of the National Association for Research in Science Teaching, Boston, Massachusetts, USA.

Bower, G. H. (ed.) (1983) *The psychology of learning and motivation: advances in research and theory*, Vol. 17 (New York: Academic Press).

Branch, C. E., Ledford, B.R., Robertson, B. T. and Robison, L. (1987) The validation of an interactive videodisc as an alternative to traditional teaching techniques: auscultation of the heart. *Educational Technology*, March, 16–22.

Bransford, J., Sherwood, R., Vye, N. and Rieser, J. (1986) Teaching thinking and problem solving. *American Psychologist*, 41, 1078–1089.

Brewer, W. F. (1987) Schemas versus mental models in human memory. In P. Morris (ed.) *Modelling Cognition* (Chichester: John Wiley and Sons), 187–197.

Brown, A. L. (1992) Design experiments: theoretical and methodological challenges in creating complex interventions in classroom settings. *Journal of the Learning Sciences*, 2, 141–178.

Brown, A. L. and Campione, J. C. (1990) Communities of learning and thinking or a context by any other name. *Human Development*, 21, 108–125.

Brown, A. L., Ash, D., Rutherford, M., Nakagawa, K., Gordon, A. and Campione, J. C. (1993) Distributed Expertise in the Classroom. In G. Salomon (ed.) *Distributed cognitions: Psychological and educational considerations* (New York: Cambridge University Press), 188–228.

Bruner, J. S. (1963) *The Process of Education* (New York: Random House).

Buchanan, M. (1999) The heart that just won't die. *New Scientist*, 161, 24.

Buckley, B. C. (1989) Beginning the exploration: Interactive multimedia in science education, unpublished manuscript, Stanford University.

Buckley, B. C. (1992) Multimedia, misconceptions and working models of biological phenomena: Learning about the circulatory system. Unpublished doctoral dissertation, Stanford University.

Buckley, B. C. and Boulter, C. J. (1999) Analysis of representations in model-based teaching and learning in science. In R. Paton and I. Neilson (eds) *Visual Representations and Interpretation* (Liverpool: Springer), 289–294.

Buckley, B. C. and Boulter, C. J. (2000) Investigating the role of representations and expressed models in building mental models. In J. K. Gilbert and C. J. Boulter (eds) *Developing models in science education* (Dordrecht: Kluwer), 105–122.

Bunderson, C. V., Baillio, B., Olsen, J. B., Lipson, J. I. and Fisher, K. M. (1984) Instructional effectiveness of an intelligent videodisc in biology. *Machine-Mediated Learning*, 1, 175–215.

Burtis, J., Scardamalia, M. and Bereiter, C. (1993) Understanding scientific processes through student-generated animations. Paper presented at the annual meeting of the American Educational Research Association, Atlanta.

Capra, F. (1957) *Hemo The Magnificent* [16mm Film] (New York: American Telephone and Telegraph).

Carey, S. (1985) *Conceptual Change in Childhood* (Cambridge, MA: MIT Press).

Chan, C., Burtis, J. and Bereiter, C. (1997) Knowledge building as a mediator of conflict in conceptual change. *Cognition and Instruction*, 15, 1–40.

Chan, C. K. K., Burtis, P. J., Scardamalia, M. and Bereiter, C. (1992) Constructive activity in learning from text. *American Educational Research Journal*, 29, 97–118.

Chawla, A. S. and Patel, V. L. (1988) Causal reasoning about complex physiological mechanisms by novices. Paper presented at the Tenth Annual Conference of Cognitive Science Society, Montreal, Quebec, Canada.

Chi, M. T. H., Chiu, M.H. and deLeeuw, N. (1991) *Learning in a non-physical science domain: The human circulatory system* (Pittsburgh, PA: Learning Research and Development Center).

Chinn, C. A. and Brewer, W. F. (1993) The role of anomalous data in knowledge acquisition: a theoretical framework and implications for science instruction. *Review of Educational Research*, 63, 1–49.

Clark, R. E. and Salomon, G. (1986) Media in teaching. In M. C. Wittrock (ed.) *Handbook of Research on Teaching* (third edn) (New York: MacMillan)

Clement, J. (1989) Learning via model construction and criticism: protocol evidence on sources of creativity in science. In J. A. Glover, R. R. Ronning and C. R. Reynolds (eds) *Handbook of creativity: Assessment, theory and research* (New York: Plenum Press), 341–381.

Clement, J. (1993) Model construction and criticism cycles in expert reasoning. Paper presented at the Fifteenth Annual Meeting of the Cognitive Science Society, Hillsdale, NJ.

Clement, J. (1994) Use of physical intuition and imagistic simulation in expert problem solving. In D. Tirosh (ed.) *Implicit and explicit knowledge* (Hillsdale, NJ: Ablex), 204–244.

Cronbach, L. J. (1985) *Essentials of Psychological Testing* (Fourth edn) (New York: Harper and Row).

Cronbach, L. J. (1991) Methodological studies – a personal retrospective. In R. E. Snow and D. E. Wiley (eds) *Improving inquiry in social science* (Fourth edn) (Hillsdale, NJ: Lawrence Erlbaum Associates), 385–400.

deKleer, J. and Brown, J. S. (1983) Assumptions and ambiguities in mechanistic mental models. In A. L. Stevens and D. Gentner (eds) *Mental Models* (Hillsdale, NJ: Lawrence Erlbaum Associates), 155–190.

Dweck, C. S. (1984) Motivation. In R. Glaser and A. Lesgold (eds) *The Handbook of Psychology and Education Vol. 1* (Hillsdale, NJ: Lawrence Erlbaum Associates), 245–301.

Dwyer, F. M. (1972) *A Guide for Improving Visualized Instruction* (State College, PA: Learning Services).

Dwyer, F. M. (1978) *Strategies for Improving Visual Learning* (State College, PA: Learning Services).

Entwistle, N. (1988) Motivational factors in students' approaches to learning. In R. R. Schmeck (ed.) *Learning Strategies and Learning Styles* (New York: Plenum Press), 21–51.

Erickson, F. (1986) Qualitative methods in research on teaching. In M. C. Wittrock (ed.) *Handbook of Research on Teaching* (New York: Macmillan), 119–161.

Ericsson, K. A. and Simon, H. A. (1984) *Protocol Analysis* (Cambridge, MA: MIT Press).

Falcão, D., Gouvêa, G., Cazelli, S., Valente, M.-E., Queiroz, G., Colinvaux, D., Krapas, S. and Alves, F. (1999) *Models and learning in science museums*. Paper presented at the meeting of the European Science Education Research Association, Kiel, Germany.

Feltovich, P. J., Spiro, R. J. and Coulson, R. L. (1988) The nature of conceptual understanding in biomedicine: the deep structure of complex ideas and the development of misconceptions. In D. A. Evans and V. L. Patel (eds) *Cognitive Science in Medicine* (Cambridge, MA: MIT Press), 113–172.

Fisher, C., Dwyer, D. C. and Yocam, K. (eds) (1996) *Education and Technology: Reflective on Computing in Classrooms* (San Francisco: Jossey-Bass).

Gay, G. (1986) Interaction of learner control and prior conceptual understanding in computer-assisted video instruction. *Journal of Educational Psychology*, 78, 222–227.

Gellert, E. (1962) Children's conceptions of the content and functions of the human body. *Genetic Psychology Monographs*, 65, 293–405.

Gentner, D. and Stevens, A. L. (eds) (1983) *Mental Models* (Hillsdale, NJ: Lawrence Erlbaum Associates).

Giere, R. N. (1990) *Explaining Science* (Chicago: University of Chicago Press).

Gilbert, J. and Boulter, C. (1998) Learning science through models and modelling. In B. Fraser and K. Tobin (eds) *International Handbook of Science Education* (Dordrecht, Holland: Kluwer), 52–66.

Gilbert, J. and Priest, M. (1997) Models and discourse: a primary school science class visit to a museum. *Science Education*, 81, 749–762.

Gilbert, J. K. (1995) The role of models and modelling in some narratives of science learning. Paper presented at the Annual meeting of the American Educational Research Association, San Francisco.

Gilbert, J. K. and Boulter, C. J. (eds) (2000) *Developing models in science education* (Dordrecht: Kluwer).

Gobert, J. D. and Clement, J. J. (1999) Effects of student-generated diagrams versus student-generated summaries on conceptual understanding of causal and dynamic knowledge in plate tectonics. *Journal of Research in Science Teaching*, 36, 39–53.

Goldsmith, E. (1984) *Research into Illustration* (Cambridge: Cambridge University Press).

Horwood, R. H. (1988) Explanation and description in science teaching. *Science Education*, 72, 41–49.

Iran-Nejad, A. (1990) Active and dynamic self-regulation of learning processes. *Review of Educational Research*, 60, 573–602.

Jacob, F. (1982) *The Logic of Life* (Betty E. Spillman, trans.) (New York: Pantheon Books).

Jaeger, R. M. (ed.) (1988) *Complementary Methods for Research in Education* (Washington, D.C.: American Educational Research Association).

Johnson-Laird, P. N. (1983) *Mental Models* (Cambridge, MA: Harvard University Press).

Joseph, J. H. and Dwyer, F. M. (1982) The instructional effectiveness of integrating abstract and realistic visualization. Paper presented at the Annual Meeting of the Association for Educational Communications and Technology, Research and Theory Division, Dallas, TX.

Kapit, W. and Elson, L. M. (1977) *The Anatomy Coloring Book* (New York: Harper and Row).

Kindfield, A. C. H. (1993–1994), Biology diagrams: tools to think with. *Journal of the Learning Sciences*, 3, 1–36.

Kozma, R., Jones, T., Wykoff, J. and Russell, J. (1992) Multimedia, multiple representations and mental models in chemistry. Paper presented at the annual meeting of the American Educational Research Association, San Francisco.

Larkin, J. H. and Simon, H. A. (1987) Why a diagram is (sometimes) worth ten thousand words. *Cognitive Science*, 11, 65–99.

Lepper, M. and Malone, T. (1987) Intrinsic motivation and instructional effectiveness in computer-based education. In R. E. Snow and M. J. Farr (eds) *Aptitude, Learning and Instruction III: Conative and Affective Process Analyses* (Hillsdale, NJ: Lawrence Erlbaum Associates), 255–286.

Lowe, R. (1993) *Successful instructional diagrams* (London: Kogan Page).

Mandinach, E. B. (1989) Model-building and the use of computer simulation of dynamic systems. *Journal of Educational Computing Research*, 5, 221–243.

Mandinach, E. B. and Cline, H. F. (1989) Applications of simulation and modeling in precollege instruction. *Machine-Mediated Learning*, 3, 189–205.

Marchionini, G. (1988) Hypermedia and Learning: Freedom and Chaos. Educational Technology, November, 8–12.

Marsh, G. and Boulter, C. J. (1997) Primary planet perspectives: Part B – Views on orreries from year 5 girls. In C. J. Boulter (ed.) Aspects of primary children's understanding of science (Reading, UK: The New Bulmershe Papers, University of Reading), 64–77.

Marsh, G., Willimont, G. and Boulter, C. J. (1999) Modelling the solar system. *Primary Science Review*, 59, 24–26.

Mayer, R. E. (1989a) Models for understanding. *Review of Educational Research*, 59, 43–64.

Mayer, R. E. (1989b) Systematic thinking fostered by illustrations in scientific text. *Journal of Educational Psychology*, 81, 240–246.

Merriam, S. B. (1991) *Case Study Research in Education* (San Francisco: Jossey-Bass).

Miles, M. B. and Huberman, A. M. (1984) *Qualitative Data Analysis* (Beverley Hills: Sage Publications).

Miller, G. (1992) *Living in the Environment* (Seventh edn) (Belmont, CA: Wadsworth).

Monaghan, J. and Clement, J. (1994) Factors affecting the efficacy of computer simulation for facilitating relative motion concept acquisition and visualization. Paper presented at the Annual Meeting of the American Educational Research Association, New Orleans, LA.

Newell, A. (1981) Summer 1981, The Knowledge Level. *AI Magazine*, 2, 1–20.

Nolen, S. B. (1988) Reasons for studying: motivational orientations and study strategies. *Cognition and Instruction*, 5, 269–287.

Norman, D. A. (1983) Some observations on mental models. In A. L. Stevens and D. Gentner (eds) *Mental Models* (Hillsdale, NJ: Lawrence Erlbaum Associates), 71–14.

Otto, J. H., Towle, A. and Madnick, M. E. (1977) *Modern Biology Teacher's Edition* (New York: Holt, Rinehart and Winston).

Patel, V. L., Evans, D. A. and Groen, G. J. (1988) Biomedical knowledge and clinical reasoning. In D. A. Evans and V. L. Patel (eds) *Cognitive Science in Medicine* (Cambridge, MA: MIT Press), 53–112.

Patel, V. L., Kaufman, D. R. and Magder, S. (1991) Causal explanation of complex physiological concepts by medical students. *International Journal of Science Education*, 13, 171–185.

Porter, C. S. (1974) Grade school children's perceptions of the internal body parts. *Nursing Research*, 23, 384–391.

Posner, G. J. and Strike, K. A. (1989) The conceptual ecology of physics learning. Paper presented at the annual meeting of the American Educational Research Association, San Francisco.

Quiggin, V. (1977) Beginning research: children's knowledge of their internal body parts. *Nursing Times*, 73, 1146–1151.

Roth, W.M. and Bowen, G. M. (1993) An investigation of problem-framing and solving in a grade 8 open-inquiry science program. *Journal of the Learning Sciences*, 3, 165–204.

Rouse, W. B. and Morris, N. M. (1986) On looking into the black Box: prospects and limits in the search for mental models. *Psychological Bulletin*, 100, 349–363.

Salomon, G. (1980) The use of visual media in the service of enriching mental thought processes. *Instructional Science*, 9, 327–339.

Salomon, G. (1983) The differential investment of mental effort in learning from different sources. *Educational Psychologist*, 18, 42–50.

Salomon, G. and Globerson, T. (1987) Skill may not be enough: the role of mindfulness in learning and transfer. *International Journal of Educational Research*, 11, 623–637.

Salomon, G. and Perkins, D. N. (1998) Individual and social aspects of learning. *Review of Research in Education*, 23, 1–24.

Scardamalia, M., Bereiter, C., McLean, R. S., Swallow, J. and Woodruff, E. (1989) Computer-supported intentional learning environments. *Journal of Educational Computing Research*, 5, 51–68.

Schauble, L., Glaser, R., Raghavan, K. and Reiner, M. (1991) Causal models and experimentation strategies in scientific reasoning. *Journal of the Learning Sciences*, 1, 210–238.

Schmeck, R. R. (ed.) (1988) *Learning Strategies and Learning Styles* (New York: Plenum Press).

Smith, E. E. and Lehman, J. D. (1988) Interactive video: implications of the literature for science education. *Journal of Computers in Mathematics and Science Teaching*, fall, 25–31.

Smith III, J. P., diSessa, A. A. and Roschelle, J. (1993/1994) Misconceptions reconceived: a constructivist analysis of knowledge in transition. *Journal of the Learning Sciences*, 3, 115–163.

Songer, N. B. and Linn, M. C. (1991) How do students' views of science influence knowledge integration? *Journal of Research in Science Teaching*, 28, 761–784.

Stewart, J. and Hafner, B. (1991) Extending the conception of problem solving. *Science Education*, 75, 105–120.

Trumbull, D., Gay, G. and Mazur, J. (1991) Charting the complex: research on the use of a hypermedia system. Paper presented at the annual meeting of the American Educational Research Association, Chicago, IL.

Tufte, E. R. (1983) *The Visual Display of Quantitative Information* (Cheshire, CT: Graphics Press).

Tufte, E. R. (1990) *Envisioning Information* (Cheshire, CT: Graphics Press).

Tunnicliffe, S. D. (1998) Boy talk: girl talk – is it the same at animal exhibits? *International Journal of Science Education*, 20, 795–811.

Vosniadou, S. and Brewer, W. F. (1992) Mental models of the earth: A study of conceptual change in childhood. *Cognitive Psychology*, 24, 535–585.

White, B. Y. (1993) Intermediate causal models: A missing link for successful science education? In R. Glaser (ed.) *Advances in Instructional Psychology, Vol. 4* (Hillsdale, NJ: Lawrence Erlbaum), 177–252.

White, B. Y. and Frederiksen, J. R. (1990) Causal model progressions as a foundation for intelligent learning environments. *Artificial Intelligence*, 42, 99–157.

PART III

TRENDS IN SCIENCE EDUCATION AT NATIONAL LEVEL

EDITOR'S INTRODUCTION

This Part is concerned with some issues that may manifest themselves in particular ways in a given nation-state.

In Chapter 8, Aikenhead adopts an anthropological standpoint in defining 'science as being a distinctive culture, with particular beliefs and values, within which nests sub-cultures, e.g. those of physics, biology. Individuals are simultaneously members of a range of cultures, e.g. family, age cohort. Whenever a person moves from one cultural context to other, a degree of cognitive conflict will be experienced as different beliefs co-exist. This may be particularly acute if the conflict is between very different cultures, for example between 'science' and that of a distinctive non-Western ethnic group. The implications are, in the case of students, that they may find conflicts between the values espoused in their home lives and those implicitly adopted in their science classes. Aikenhead introduces the notion of 'culture broker' as someone who eases 'border crossing' between two cultures. The implications are that science teachers may have to act as culture brokers, which implies that they have knowledge of the home cultures from which their students come. Unless this is done, students may abandon science as a value and belief set.

Questions for you to consider might include:

- What evidence is there that some students in science classes experience significant 'border crossings'?
- What evidence is there that some of these 'border crossings' are so stressful as to inhibit students' learning of science?
- What actions can a science teacher take in a class to reduce the conflicts inherent in significant 'border crossings'?
- What adaptations to the science curriculum might a 'Western' nation state consider if it has several 'non-Western' origin ethnic groups in its midst?

One of the major 'border crossings' students may have to face is between science and religious faith. In Chapter 9, Roth (a science teacher) and Alexander (a student) co-author an interview-based exploration of the conflicts that exist between science – here the physical sciences – and the Christian religion, mediated by the teacher who was, in effect, an atheist.

The chapter is very unusual – not only that such a study was conducted at all, but also that an interpretative approach revealed so much detail of the issues involved.

Questions that you may care to ask might include:

- To what extent is it necessary that a science teacher should be aware of the religious affiliations of students in order to teach them effectively?
- What difference might such knowledge have for how teaching takes place?
- What stance should the science curriculum of a national state take in respect of topics where the beliefs implicit in the science run counter to those of a religion professed by citizens?
- In these regards, what distinction can be made between superstitions, e.g. magic, astrology and formalised religion?

In the longer run, those aspects of the science curriculum that become commonplace as a consequence of curricular globalization may well be assessed by means of one of the international comparative measures, or a derivative of it. However, those aspects of the curriculum that retain a distinctly national flavour will need to be assessed in some detail within the nation-state concerned. In Chapter 10, Black discusses the three purposes for assessment – formative (to aid learning), summative (for review, transfer and certification) and summative (for public accountability). He looks at the characteristics of the assessment needed to address each of these three purposes and at the problems encountered in trying to use one instrument for more than one purpose.

Questions that you may care to address might include:

- How may formative assessment be used to support the aims implied in Part II, i.e. significant conceptual development, more effective teacher talk, more learning in socio-cultural contexts, more use of argumentation in classes?
- How may formative assessment be used to support the aims implied in this Part, i.e. supporting 'border crossing', clarifying the relationship between science and religion, increasing family participation in science education?
- What are the strengths and weaknesses in the use of summative assessment for public accountability purposes?
- How can the weaknesses of summative assessment for public accountability purposes be addressed?

CHAPTER 8

SCIENCE COMMUNICATION WITH THE PUBLIC

A cross-cultural event

G.S. Aikenhead

S.M. Stocklmayer, M.M. Gore, C. Bryant (eds) *Science Communication in Theory and Practice* (2001) Dordrecht: Kluwer Academic Publishers, pp. 23–45

Introduction

[. . .]

Cultural anthropology suggests that science communication with the public is a cross-cultural event. If people do not clearly identify the cultures involved in the act of communicating, people risk the quagmire of miscommunication. A critical analytic understanding of the culture of Western science, and of the cultures of various audiences, is a prerequisite to effective science communication with the public. In the first part, I summarise this prerequisite to effective communication, while in the second part, I describe effective communication in terms of culture brokering, illustrated in part by a case study of a recent Canadian science centre exhibit.

A cultural perspective on Western science

Before we can think about the cultural aspects of science communication with the public, we first need to clarify what cultures and subcultures are. Then we need to understand how people cross cultural borders to communicate with each other. Last, we need to become conversant with anthropological research into the ease with which people cross cultural borders. In this section, I develop several key anthropological concepts that are applicable to the realm of science communication with the public.

Culture

Cultural anthropologists such as Geertz (1973, p. 5) have defined culture as

> an ordered system of meanings and symbols, in terms of which social interaction takes place.

This statement accurately describes the scientific community engaged in research, as scientists develop more accurate and sophisticated systems of meanings (theories, models, laws and principles, often expressed symbolically), and as they publish their manuscripts in journals (formal social interaction) to establish the validity of their ordered system of meanings. In addition to communicating through formal publications, social interactions take place in person, by e-mail, by telephone, at conferences, in the lab, in the field, and in bars or at other informal gatherings. According to Geertz's definition, science can be thought of as a culture with its own language and conventional ways of communicating for the purpose of social interaction within the community of scientists,

In an anthropological study of a high-energy physics community, Traweek (1992) described culture in a more detailed way:

> A community is a group of people with a shared past, with ways of recognizing and displaying their differences from other groups, and expectations for a shared future. Their culture is the ways, the strategies they recognize and use and invent for making sense, from common sense to disputes, from teaching to learning, it is also their ways of making things and making use of them.
>
> (pp. 437–438 [. . .])

By treating physicists as working within cultural borders, Traweek discovered some fascinating behaviour and bizarre communication by Japanese high-energy physicists as they negotiated between the subculture of their Japanese national physics community and the subculture of the international physics community. Traweek found that risk taking, power, culture, and subjectivity were all intermingled in ways that encouraged Japanese physicists to conform with their Japanese national physics community. This made it difficult for these Japanese physicists to cross the cultural border into the international community of high-energy physics. Japanese physicists were the target of pejorative humour, sarcasm, and cultural reprisals from their Japanese colleagues. Therefore, Japanese high-energy physicists had to cross into the culture of international physics with great care and subtlety by using humour, selected conformity and politics, so as not to offend their Japanese colleagues in high-energy physics. By recognising the cultural differences between Japanese high-energy physicists and international high-energy physicists, Traweek could better understand the otherwise bizarre communication among some Japanese physicists. Perhaps there is a lesson here for James Watson and Gina Kolata – they should have recognised science as a culture, a culture with borders that must be crossed if outsiders are to understand the communication conventions of that culture, and if insiders are going to communicate effectively with the public.

Consistent with both Geertz's and Traweek's definitions of culture, Phelan, Davidson and Cao (1991) suggested that culture be conceptualised as the

> norms, values, beliefs, expectations, and conventional actions of a group.
>
> (p. 228)

This cogent definition helps to clarify how science is a cultural phenomenon. Science content can be subsumed under 'beliefs'. The communication conventions of scientists are guided by the norms, values, and expectations of the culture of science, and by the specific norms, values, and expectations of the specialty field of the scientist, that is, the his or her paradigm or scientific subculture. Other definitions of culture have guided research in science communication (for example, Banks, 1988; Bullivant, 1981; Ingle and Turner, 1981; Jordan, 1985; Maddock, 1981; Samovar, Porter and Jain, 1981; and Tharp, 1989). From these works one can establish the following list of attributes of culture: communication (psycho- and socio-linguistic), social structures (authority, participant interactions), customs, attitudes, values, beliefs, worldview, skills (psychomotor and cognitive), behaviour, and technologies (artefacts and know-how). In various studies, different attributes of culture have been selected as a focus on a particular interest in multicultural communication. The definition of Phelan *et al.* (1991) of culture (above) is advantageous because it has relatively few categories and they can be interpreted broadly to encompass all anthropological aspects of culture and subculture.

Just as there are paradigms (subcultures) within the culture of science, there are subgroups in everyday life, most commonly identified by race, language, and ethnicity, but which can also be defined by gender, social class, occupation and religion. Consequently, an individual simultaneously belongs to several subgroups; for instance, an oriental female Muslim physicist or a male middle-class Euro-American journalist. Large numbers and many combinations of subgroups exist due to the associations that naturally form among people in society. Each identifiable subgroup is comprised of people who generally embrace a defining set of norms, values, beliefs, expectations, and conventional actions. In short, each subgroup shares a culture, often called a 'subculture' to convey an identity with a subgroup. One can talk about, for example, the subculture of females, the subculture of the middle class, the subculture of the television media, or the subculture of a particular science museum.

Border crossing

An everyday scenario will illustrate the difficulties people can encounter whenever they move between cultures or between subcultures:

> George and Gracie Smith flew from North America to Spain, physically crossing political borders, but not crossing cultural borders. After waiting 45 minutes in a restaurant for their dinner bill to arrive, George finally became vocally irate over the waiter's lack of service. The waiter, in turn, became hurtfully perplexed over the fact that his impeccable manners were not appreciated.

Misunderstandings can arise whenever one of the players does not recognise a cultural border that needs to be crossed for effective communication (Aikenhead, 1996).

People often cross cultural borders so easily that they do not realise they are even there – for example, when people move between the subculture of their friends and the subculture of their family home. But for people whose peer culture is vastly different from their home culture, transitions between friends and home can be psychologically hazardous and these transitions need to be negotiated carefully. Similarly problematic are the border crossings between humanist and scientific subcultures of Western society. This problem was identified by C.P. Snow (1964) in his classic *The Two Cultures*, pointing out the inability of people to speak to one another between these two cultures.

For people who feel at ease in both a humanist and scientific culture, however, border crossing is no problem. Border crossing for them is smooth. When people feel at ease like this, cultural borders seem invisible or nonexistent. It is when people begin to feel a degree of psychological discomfort with another subculture that border crossing becomes less smooth, and needs to be managed. Contributing to their discomfort may be some sense of disquiet with cultural differences or their unwillingness to engage in risk-taking social behaviour (depending on the situation, of course). When the self-esteem of people is in jeopardy (for instance, when playing badminton with players much better than they are or when participating in an unusual social occasion such as wearing a Halloween costume), border crossing could easily be hazardous. People may react in various ways to protect their egos. Even worse, if psychological pain is involved, avoidance is the natural response and border crossing becomes impossible. These descriptors of the ease of border crossing – smooth, manageable, hazardous, and impossible – are categories that Phelan *et al.* (1991) derived from their anthropological study of high school students who had to cross cultural borders between their homes and their school. This category system was helpful to Costa (1995) in her study of students' feelings of ease in science classes. The category system will be helpful in this chapter for understanding the role of a science communicator.

Border crossing into the culture of science can be made smoother for the public if science communicators know the culture of the everyday world of the public, and can contrast that culture with a critical analysis of the culture of science (its norms, values, beliefs, expectations, and conventional actions). But even more, a science communicator must consciously move back and forth between the publics everyday world and the scientists' world – switching norms explicitly, switching values explicitly, switching conceptualisations explicitly, switching expectations explicitly, and switching language conventions explicitly. The role of a science communicator is described in more detail later. [. . .]

Values and norms

One principal component of any culture is its values and norms. Values and norms guide scientists whenever they decide between, for example, competing theories or competing experimental methodologies (Chubin, 1981). Values and norms are learned by the apprentice scientist and they become important aspects to his or her paradigm (Hawkins and Pea, 1987; Kuhn, 1970). Longino (1990) refers to this set of discipline-centred values as constitutive values (for example, parsimony, accuracy, open-mindedness, objectivity, etc.). In contrast to constitutive values, she points to the social context outside of science in which scientists live daily. She refers to these cultural values as contextual values. Her research documented cases in which these contextual values (rather than constitutive values) influenced the decisions taken by scientists over what 'facts' to believe. She concluded that science-as-practised (as opposed to science-as-imagined) is not value-neutral. The value-neutrality of science has also been falsified by other studies (Casper, 1980; Graham, 1981; Snow, 1987; Ziman, 1984). Those who believe in the neutrality of science contend that science is free of contextual values, not constitutive values.

Therefore, science communicators must be aware of the values and norms that are potentially inherent in the language conventions of scientists (their discursive practices). For instance, one constitutive value, scientific objectivity, is often communicated to the public through science textbooks. Textbooks, however, camouflage more subtle contextual values, for example, the value 'technoscience fix' (Carlsen *et al.*, 1994; Factor and Kooser, 1981) – the idea that solutions to societal problems (such as water contamination) only require more scientific knowledge and more innovative technologies.

Moreover, when one examines the constitutive values within science, one discovers differences between the constitutive values espoused by scientists, and the constitutive values actually practised by scientists (Mitroff, 1974). For instance, scientists publicly revere objectivity but many rely on subjective hunches in the privacy of their labs. Holton (1978) explained this apparent conflict in values by distinguishing between two types of scientific activity – 'private science' and 'public science'. Each has a different social setting and therefore a different communication audience. Public science is communicated in journals, conference proceedings, textbooks and news releases, while private science is done in labs and communicated in personal notebooks, letters, e-mails, and informal conversations. Private science communication is not necessarily guided by the same values and norms as communication in the public science arena. For example, subjectivity and closed-mindedness have advantages in private science but never in public science where objectivity and open-mindedness form the cultural expectations. It is interesting that research on scientists who analysed the Apollo moon rock samples in the early 1970's indicated that those who were held in high esteem by their colleagues used conflicting sets of values and norms (values and norms associated with public and private science), while those who were considered mediocre by their colleagues embraced only public science values and norms (Gauld, 1982).

Sociological research into present-day practices of scientists (e.g. Latour, 1987) concurs with Holton and Gauld. Scientific activity embraces two legitimate, dichotomous sets of values (norms and counter-norms). When public-science values and norms define the whole enterprise of science, they propagate myths about the nature of science because they hide the function of the private-science (sometimes guided by, for instance, subjectivity and closed-mindedness). Miscommunication is ripe whenever statements expressed in the social context of private science are repeated in the social context of public science. This distinction may shed light on the mis-communication between James Watson and Gina Kolata. Did Watson neglect to express his enthusiasm in the language conventions of public science (appropriate for the front page of the New York Times)? Did Kolata neglect to recognise Watson's expression as private science? Perhaps both failed to recognise the cultural border between the two subcultures – private science and public science – each with its own set of norms, values, beliefs, expectations, and conventional actions. When people do not see a cultural border to cross, they run the risk of miscommunicating.

Compared with scientists, the general public expresses an even wider array of values and norms, many of which conflict with those embraced by the culture of science. Cobern (1991) explored a way to identify clusters of values that seem to inform the public's general outlook on the world. Drawing upon the work of anthropologist Kearney (1984), Cobern investigated the way that people's worldviews may predispose them to being sympathetic or antagonistic toward the worldviews conveyed by much of Western science. Cobern and Aikenhead (1998) illustrated the ease of communication between a science teacher (Mr Hess) and students who generally shared his worldview toward nature (that is, orderly and understandable, governed by physical forces which can be fully understood by tearing nature apart and analysing the pieces – reductionism). On the other hand, students who possessed alternative worldviews toward nature, such as those formulated on aesthetic or spiritual orientations toward nature, had communication problems with Mr Hess. Worldview is a convenient concept that embodies fundamental

> presuppositions about what the world is really like and what constitutes valid and important knowledge about the world.
>
> (Cobern, 1996, p. 584)

Worldviews are basic culture-laden frameworks from which daily values and norms flow.

In summary, science communication with the public will be more effective when people recognise science as a culture having many subcultures (such as paradigms, as well as private and public subcultures). For both insiders and outsiders to the culture of science, cultural borders must be crossed before effective communication can take place between those two groups. These border crossings can be smooth, managed, hazardous, or impossible, depending upon the cultural differences experienced by individuals, and depending upon their resourcefulness and motivation to cross otherwise hazardous or impossible borders. Scientists are guided by a complex and dynamic set of cultural values and norms, as is the general public. Similarities and differences between these two groups may be better understood by considering their different worldviews.

The culture of science and the public domain

The division between science and the general public manifests the theory/practice dichotomy endemic to Plato's eidos and praxis. This remnant of Greek culture continues to characterise Western thinking today. Western science tends to isolate itself in eidos (idealised pure knowledge), rendering itself superior to praxis (practical knowledge needed for action), according to Platonic Greek tradition. Therefore, understanding science communication predicated on that distinction becomes difficult for people for whom a theory-practice distinction does not exist. The problem can be eased somewhat by the communicator expressing the cultural features found on both sides of this cultural border.

How is scientific knowledge actually used outside the culture of science, in people's commonsense and professional life-worlds, that is, in praxis? A cherished myth in the culture of Western science is the belief that people can directly apply scientific knowledge to their everyday world (Aikenhead, 1980; Layton, 1991; Ryle, 1954; Solomon, 1983). Reality is much different. Based on case study research in the UK, Jenkins (1992) commented that using science in the everyday world is

> no more a straightforward application of the scientific knowledge acquired at school or in other formal contexts than technology is merely applied science. Rather it is about creating new knowledge or, where possible, restructuring, reworking and transforming existing scientific knowledge into forms which serve the purpose in hand. Whatever that purpose (political, social, personal, etc.), it is essentially concerned with action or capability, rather than with the acquisition of knowledge for its own sake.
>
> (p. 236)

This conclusion guides us in helping the general public negotiate what would otherwise be a hazardous border crossing between their everyday culture and the culture of science. One hazard is the fact that scientific knowledge must be deconstructed and then reconstructed in the context of everyday use (Layton, 1991). In the context of teaching science Layton, Jenkins, Macgill and Davey (1993) concluded:

> The nature of the transformation needed is not a matter which has hitherto commanded much attention from science teachers, although it has been a preoccupation of engineers for a century or more. . . . The essence of the problem is that the concepts developed by scientists in their quest for understanding [eidos] do not always map with exactitude onto the design parameters in terms of which practical action has to be planned [praxis]. As a result, for science to articulate with practice, some reworking is often required.
>
> (p. 129)

This communicative challenge has plagued science educators as they contemplate how to communicate with students over the use of science content outside of the classroom. The same challenge exists for all science communicators.

A case in point was a student (Melanie) who found border crossing into the culture of science hazardous when studying the topic of heat (Aikenhead, 1996). In spite of her high motivation to participate in hands-on group activities, Melanie could not cross the cultural border into the science of heat and temperature. Her difficulty may have arisen from her having a worldview at odds with the worldview generally embraced by science. Cobern (1996) argued,

> ... 'it is not that the students fail to comprehend what is being taught, it is simply that the concepts are either not credible or not significant' (p. 601) because 'for students it is aesthetic, religious, pragmatic, and emotional concepts that have scope and force with regard to nature.'
>
> (p. 597)

Thus, a general distaste for mechanistic reductionist concepts (a central feature of a conventional scientific worldview) might explain why students such as Melanie choose not to integrate the scientific concepts of heat and temperature into their everyday notions of hot and cold (Kilbourn, 1980).

In the adult world of consumers, Layton *et al.* (1993) discovered that a scientific understanding of heat energy had no consequence to lay people managing domestic energy problems in their life-world. Layton and his colleagues seriously questioned the objective of science education to teach what is rarely usable in the everyday world. In the words of Wynne (1991):

> ordinary social life, which often takes contingency and uncertainty as normal and adaptation to uncontrolled factors as a routine necessity, is in fundamental tension with the basic culture of science which is premised on assumptions of manipulability and control.
>
> (p. 120)

These lessons from science education apply directly to the communication of science with the public. The more that someone's worldview differs from the one conveyed by Western science, the less smooth (the more impossible) will be their border crossing into the culture of science and, as a consequence, the more they challenge science communicators. Communicating effectively requires a knowledge of one's audience. Challenges can be met more realistically when we recognise that this communication is a cross-cultural event. Cultural gaps must be bridged, not just by content knowledge bridges (that is, the naive belief that the public only needs more accurate knowledge), but by bridges that communicate the norms, values, beliefs, expectations, and conventional actions of scientists (the culture of science).

Some useful distinctions among people in the public domain were identified by Ogawa (1998b) in the context of science education reform in Western countries. He described three types of orientations the public will assume towards science. His first type concerns whether a person understands science (science literacy versus science illiteracy). His second type of orientation addresses a more emotional aspect, whether a person supports science (a pro-science or anti-science position). Ogawa's third type of orientation deals with an ideological belief that scientific knowledge is the only valid form of knowledge to use in any context. This belief, often called 'scientism', privileges scientific knowledge over all other ways of knowing (Nadeau and Désautels, 1984). Thus, Ogawa's third type of orientation consists of pro-scientism versus anti-scientism. In short, Ogawa contends that people's stance toward science will be influenced by how they fit into these three types of orientations. Thus, their receptivity to, and engagement in, scientific communication will vary according to their literacy in science, their support of science, and their allegiance to scientism. Ogawa's scheme generated six orientations of people:

i.   science-literate, pro-science, pro-scientism folk
       ('science believers');
ii.   science-literate, pro-science, anti-scientism folk
       ('science contextualists');
iii.   science-literate, anti-science, anti-scientism folk
       ('authentic anti-scientists');
iv.   science illiterate, pro-science, pro-scientism folk
       ('science fanatics');
v.   science illiterate, pro-science, anti-scientism folk
       ('science vigilantes'); and
vi.   science illiterate, anti-science, pro-scientism folk
       ('neo anti-scientists').

These categories can sensitise science communicators to the challenges that face them and their Western audiences.

Western science and non-Western cultures

Communication barriers are even more pronounced between Western science and non-Western cultures. Researchers have investigated the obstacles encountered when one teaches Western science to non-Western students. Their findings are highly relevant to science communication with the public. Because science tends to be a Western cultural icon of prestige, power, progress, and privilege, the culture of science tends to permeate the culture of those who engage it, with cultural assimilation being one possible negative consequence (Baker and Taylor, 1995; Dart, 1972; Jegede and Okebukola, 1991; MacIvor, 1995; Ogawa, 1995). This assimilation threatens indigenous cultures, thereby causing these people to experience Western science as a hegemonic icon of cultural imperialism (Battiste, 1986; Ermine, 1995; Linkson, 1998). Science communicators in the global village need to extend their cultural sensitivity to a public outside of Western culture.

The encroachment of Western culture occurs, in part, because it is hidden in the Trojan horse of Western science. Different cultures have reacted differently to this encroachment. Aboriginal, Japanese, and Islamic peoples represent three cultural groups that have fought against such assimilation. Each group is discussed here in turn. Emphasis is given to Aboriginal peoples because they are the most underrepresented group in Western science. Nevertheless they must deal with Western scientists in the areas of health, land management, and ethics (MacIvor, 1995; Wolfe, Bechard, Cizek and Cole, 1992). Their perspective helps us understand the cultural borders that most people in the global village must cross before effective science communication can succeed.

Aboriginal cultures

Knudtson and Suzuki (1992) documented various indigenous knowledge systems around the world that describe and explain nature. Aboriginals, they claimed, possess powerful knowledge systems that convey wisdom, a key element missing in Western science, Aboriginal knowledge about the natural world (Aboriginal science) contrasts with Western scientific knowledge in a number of other ways. The following summary of Aboriginal science is based on sensitive and scholarly analyses by Christie (1991), Ermine (1995), Kawagley (1990), Linkson (1998), McKinley (1996), Mitchie, Anlezark and Uibo, (1998), Peat (1994), Pierotti and Wildcat (1997), Pomeroy (1992), and Roberts and Wills (1998). They wrote about the Maori in Aotearoa (New Zealand), the original peoples of Australia, and the First Nations peoples on Turtle Island (America).

Aboriginal and Western science differ in their social goals: survival of a people versus the luxury of gaining knowledge for the sake of knowledge and for power over nature and other people. They differ in intellectual goals: to co-exist with mystery in nature by celebrating mystery versus to eradicate mystery by explaining it away. They differ in their association with human action: intimately and subjectively inter-related versus formally and objectively decontextualised. They differ in other ways as well: holistic Aboriginal perspectives with their gentle, accommodating, intuitive, and spiritual wisdom, versus reductionist Western science with its aggressive, manipulative, mechanistic, and analytical explanations.

The Western world has capitulated to a dogmatic fixation on power and control at the expense of authentic insights into the nature and origin of knowledge as truth (Ermine, 1995).

> They even differ in their basic concepts of time: circular for Aboriginals, rectilinear for scientists.
>
> (p. 102)

Aboriginal and scientific knowledge differ in epistemology. Pomeroy (1992) summarises the difference found on Turtle Island:

> Both seek knowledge, the Westerner as revealed by the power of reason applied to natural observations, the Native as revealed by the power of nature through observation of consistent and richly interweaving patterns and by attending to nature's voices.
>
> (p. 263)

Ermine (1995) contrasts the exploration of the inner world of all existence by his people with a scientist exploring only the outer world of physical existence. He concludes:

> Those who seek to understand the reality of existence and harmony with the environment by turning inward have a different, incorporeal knowledge paradigm that might be termed Aboriginal epistemology.
>
> (p. 103)

Along similar lines, Roberts and Wills (1998) compare a fundamental Maori ontological principle of 'whakapapa', an orientation to the past that connects a person to the creators of the land, with a Western scientific future orientation that embraces a preoccupation with matter and causal mechanisms.

Battiste (1986) explicates a Turtle Island epistemology by giving detail to what Pomeroy (1992) called 'naturequotes voices':

> A fundamental element in tribal epistemology [lies] in two traditional knowledge sources:
> 1. from the immediate world of personal and tribal experiences, that is, one's perceptions, thoughts, and memories which include one's shared experiences with others; and
> 2. from the spiritual world evidenced through dreams, visions, and signs which (are) often interpreted with the aid of medicine men or elders.
>
> (p. 24)

On the one hand, subculture science is guided by the fact that the physical universe is knowable through rational empirical means, albeit Western rationality and culture-laden observations (Ogawa, 1995); while on the other hand, Aboriginal knowledge of nature celebrates the fact that the physical universe is mysterious but can be survived if one uses rational empirical means, albeit Aboriginal rationality and culture-laden observations (Pomeroy, 1992). For example, when encountering the spectacular northern lights, Western scientists would ask, 'How do they work?' while the Waswanipi Cree ask, 'Who did this?' and 'Why?' (Knudtson and Suzuki, 1992). We can learn more about the culture of Western science the more we contrast it with other ways of knowing nature.

The norms, values, beliefs, expectations, and conventional actions of Aboriginal peoples contrast dramatically with the culture of Western science. Western science has been characterised as essentially mechanistic, materialistic, reductionist, empirical, rational, decontextualised, mathematically idealised, communal, ideological, masculine, elitist, competitive, exploitive, and impersonal (Fourez, 1988; Kelly, Carlsen and Cunningham, 1993; Rose, 1994; Snow, 1987). By comparison, Aboriginal sciences tend to be thematic, survival-oriented, holistic, empirical, rational, contextualised, specific, communal, ideological, spiritual, inclusive, cooperative, coexistent, and personal. Based on these two lists, Western science and Aboriginal sciences share some common features (empirical, rational, communal, and ideological). Consequently, it is not surprising that efforts are underway to combine the two knowledge systems into one field called 'traditional ecological knowledge' (Corsiglia and Snively, 1995). While a romanticised version of the peaceful coexistence of an Aboriginal with the environment should be avoided, Knudtson and Suzuki (1992) document the extent to which environmental responsibility is globally endemic to Aboriginal cultures. It is this quality that led Christie (1991), Pierotti and Wildcat (1997), Roberts, Norman, Minhinnick, Wihongi and Kirkwood, (1995), and Simonelli (1994) to define scientific ecology and sustainable Western science in terms of Aboriginal cultures. Simonelli (1994) quoted a Lakota ceremonialist's view of science and technology:

> This is not a scientific or technologic world. The world is first a world of spirituality. We must all come back to that spirituality. Then, after we have understood the role of spirituality in the world, maybe we can see what science and technology have to say.
>
> (p. 11)

Deloria (1992), also of the Lakota nation, challenged Western science's objectivity and validity when he spoke about improving the culture of science by getting scientists to adopt an Aboriginal sense of contextualised purpose.

Differences between the culture of Western science and the cultures of indigenous Aboriginal students help to explain the apparent reticence of students to learn about heat and temperature, or about any other Western science concept (Aikenhead, 1997; Schilk Arewa, Thomson and White, 1995; Sutherland, 1988). The cultural borders around Western science are seldom smooth for Aboriginal peoples. For instance, in an American study of third grade children, Schilk *et al.* (1995) concluded, that the perceptions Indian students had of scientists, largely dictated by popular media, were in direct conflict with their Iroquois values (p. 3):

Interviewer: Do you think you could be a scientist?
Client: That's not something Indians do. I couldn't hurt things or blow things up.

As long as Western prestige, power, progress, and privilege continue to affront the wisdom of traditional knowledge of the land, science communication world-wide will be challenged. More than ever before, science communicators in the 21st century will be engaged in helping both Western scientists and Aboriginal peoples communicate with each other.

Japanese culture

Japanese people, for the most part, resisted the encroachment of Western culture fairly successfully until the mid 19th century, when they were forced by the threat of physical violence to open their country to American commerce and technology (Shelley, 1993). Western science followed in due course. Before this cultural inva-sion, Japanese people had a knowledge of nature, of 'shizen', which encompassed descriptive and explanatory elements as well as cosmological characteristics (Ogawa (1997):

Everything surrounding human life (for example, mountains, rivers, plants, trees, insects, fish or animals) has its own spirit, which can communicate with each other as well as with the people living there. Thus, the special feelings summarised by the 'one-bodiness', which means that human beings and every natural thing are one body in total, are felt by the Japanese.

(p. 176)

Elsewhere Ogawa (1998a, p. 158) asserts that most Japanese feel and are familiar with such spirits. Fortified by a feeling of animism, Japanese people cannot regard natural things as mere objects of value-free inquiry, as Western scientists tend to do. Although the word 'observe' is translated into Japanese by 'kansatsu', that is not an accurate translation because kansatsu connotes a close spiritual-like relationship, much different from the objective relationship presupposed by the Cartesian dualism (the mind/matter dichotomy) that forms a cornerstone to a Western science worldview (Kawasaki, 1996b).

The observer-object relationship connoted by kansatsu is not unique to Japanese culture. Most Aboriginal languages lack a verb 'to observe' with a Cartesian conno-tation. For example, Canadian Plains Cree use the verb 'kanawapamew' to indicate a visual connection to an animate object. The verb changes as the human sense changes to hearing or touching, and as the classification of an object changes to inanimate – connoting a very different relationship. Similarly, feminist writers have critiqued Western science for its hegemonic Cartesian discourse (Rose, 1994;

Scantlebury, 1998). For example, Barbara McClintock's highly successful scientific research, described in Keller's (1983) *A Feeling for the Organism*, supports the view that alternative observer-object relationships can successfully advance Western scientific knowledge.

Discourse is highly dependent upon one's worldview. Because discourse is central to science communication with the public, we need to be sensitive to our own language, to the language of Western science, and to the language of our audience. For instance, to describe scientists observing a distant galaxy requires a different discourse depending upon the audience. An effective communicator should be able to acknowledge the audience's conventional meaning of 'to observe' and then be able to articulate the cultural border that needs to be crossed in order to appreciate what scientists have done when they have 'observed' that galaxy. In short, the science communicator must help an audience cross the cultural border into science sufficiently to engage in the act of communicating.

Returning to the topic of Japanese culture, the accelerated acculturation of Western science that followed the American incursion of 1863 was consciously controlled by the Japanese intelligentsia. They were very much aware of the cultural border between Western nature and Japanese shizen (Kawasaki, 1996a). The cultural border is identified today by such expressions as, 'I may wear a Western suit, but I have a bamboo heart'.

The degree to which Japanese people embrace Western materialism and its ideology of progress, is the degree to which Western assimilation seems to have succeeded (Suzuki and Owa, 1996) However, Japanese people have exhibited a type of acculturation of Western science that protects their bamboo hearts. They transform this foreign element into something quite new.

> The paradox is that Japanese culture through its long history has been able to adopt various components of foreign culture without losing its own identity.
> (Ogawa, 1998a, pp. 142–143)

Thus, Western science is transformed into something different, even though it is still called Western science or 'neo-science' by Ogawa (1997).

This information helps to explain Traweek's (1992) observations of the difficulties experienced by high-energy Japanese physicists when they attempted to move between the subculture of Japanese physics into the subculture of international (Western) high-energy physics, described earlier in this chapter. Perhaps the Japanese high-energy physicists were negotiating the boundary between 'neo-science' and Western science by switching worldviews and values/norms as they crossed the border. Ogawa's analysis also points out that if we wish to communicate Western science to a Japanese public, we must cross two cultural borders: from Western science to a transformed Western science (neo-science), and then to the everyday culture of Japanese society. Corresponding challenges exist for science communicators in societies other than Japan.

Even within Western cultures, Western science was shown (earlier in this chapter) to be transformed into a different knowledge system whenever science is used for practical action (Jenkins, 1992; Layton, 1991; Layton *et al.*, 1993). The similarity to the Japanese transformation of Western science into neo-science is striking.

In summary, science communication is much more complex than transmitting scientific information. One needs to respond to the multiple cultures or subcultures involved, not only within the culture of Western science, but within one's audience. If a science communicator does not realise the culture-laden nature of science as practised in Euro-American institutions (Western science), and the culture-laden nature of its discourse, then he or she runs very high risks of creating misunderstandings in an audience. If a science communicator does not critically analyse his or her own linguistic conventions, and those of his or her audience, then he or she runs very high risks of mis-communicating with the public. Sensitivity to our discourse is fundamental to science communication with the public.

Islamic cultures

The encroachment of Western (Greek) thought into Islam has a very different history from either the attempted colonisation of Aboriginal peoples or the acculturation of Japanese people. The history of Islamic science during the 8th to 12th centuries is largely characterised by a multicultural synthesis involving knowledge and technique from China, India, Greece, and Arabian nations (Krugly-Smolska, 1992).

Today, Islamic nationalism has created several views toward Islamic science, with different sects (or movements) defining Islamic science differently. Sardar (1997) described five competing views. One major issue in this debate is an epistemological issue. It concerns reestablishing the relationship between revelation (knowledge found in the Qur'an) and reason (inductive empirical knowledge).

> Revelation in Islam is above reasoning, but not above reason. Neither is reason above revelation. This subtle relationship was destroyed when Greek thought became dominant in Muslim societies.
>
> (Sardar, 1989, p. 13)

One of Sardar's (1997) five categories of Islamic science – 'mystical fundamentalism' – was the object of interest in Irzik's (1998) analysis of Islamic science in modern Turkey. Irzik contended that in their search for an Islamic science, 'radical intellectuals' reject Western science in terms that parallel critiques by Japanese people (Kawasaki, 1996a) and by Aboriginals (Christie, 1991; Ermine, 1995).

> These [radical] intellectuals also criticize industrialization on the grounds that production for the sake of ever more profits has turned human beings into mere puppets of Capitalist consumer society manipulated by mass media, deprived them of their religious-spiritual values, and enslaved them to the greed for material wealth.
>
> (Irzik, 1998, p. 167)

A significant segment of the global public will likely perceive scientific knowledge generated in Western institutions as laden with Western values and morally bankrupt. Communicators of science must keep in mind the various socially constructed realities of different publics.

For instance, Sardar's (1989) balance of revelation and reason has been replaced in some Islamic quarters by a radical form of Islamic science in which a hierarchy of revelation over reason exists. This hierarchy is dedicated to the principle of unity in which Allah, humankind, and nature (bodies and souls included) exist 'in harmony with the natural order of things' (Irzik, 1998, p. 173).

No matter what the culture, a fundamentalist public anywhere will present a great challenge to effective science communication worldwide. Even in Western cultures, for instance, Ogawa (1998b) pointed out that some of the public (science believers, science fanatics, and neo anti-scientists – described earlier) embrace a pro-scientism ideology called 'scientific fundamentalism' by Sardar (1997). This fundamentalism will be of particular interest to those science communicators who catch themselves inadvertently communicating this fundamentalist scientism without being aware of the ideological baggage attached to their communication, and therefore being surprised by the negative reaction from their audience.

Summary

Communication of science with the public will occur in various cultural contexts each one populated by a different public. Not only are there diverse publics to be considered, but there are pluralistic sciences to be acknowledged. Western science has tended to dominate Aboriginal science, Japanese science, and Islamic science, not because of any intellectual or moral superiority but because Western science is embedded in a culture that has colonised large portions of the planet. Western science has been invested with much more authority then, for instance, everyday common-sense science, not because Western science is necessarily more valid in that context, but because its culture is associated with prestige, power, progress, and privilege. A question of truth is hybridised with a question of social or political privilege. These are some of the ideological features to science communication with the public of which a communicator must be aware.

Culture brokering

Challenges to effective science communication with the public have accumulated throughout this chapter. Potential solutions to these challenges were suggested. These solutions had common features in that they recognised the cultural nature of any science (Western or otherwise), the need to cross cultural borders when communicating science, and the need to be sensitive to the subcultures of the audience. They also recognised the need to acknowledge such cultural components as values, norms, ideologies, histories, epistemologies, and linguistic conventions, on both sides of the cultural border.

Stairs (1995) referred to people who facilitated Canadian First Nations peoples movement between Aboriginal and Euro-Canadian society as 'culture brokers.' A culture broker helps people move back and forth between cultures and helps them resolve any conflicts that might arise.

Communicating science to the public has traditionally been a process of transmitting scientific facts, principles, and triumphs (Dierking and Martin, 1997). This has largely been a one-way process (Layton et al. 1993). By re-conceptualising this communicating process as a two-way cross-cultural event, and by taking on the role of culture broker, a communicator's task changes fundamentally. A culture brokering science communicator acknowledges and respects the cultural perspective of his or her audience, a cultural perspective that has norms, values, beliefs, expectations, and conventional actions, some of which may conflict with those of Western science. The audience's indigenous science is neither ignored nor marginalised. A culture broker will identify the cultural border that separates the public's indigenous culture from the culture of Western science. In addition, the cultural nature of Western science is established, perhaps through an explication of some of its cultural features.

These aspects of culture brokering form a foundation for increasing the effectiveness of communicating Western science to the public; in other words, for increasing the ease with which the public can cross the cultural border into Western science, enough to participate in the communication intended by the science communicator.

This cross-cultural event is made even smoother when a science communicator consciously and explicitly moves back and forth between the culture of Western science and the cultures of the audience (audiences are often multicultural). This can be accomplished verbally, by labeling each side of the cultural border with some type of linguistic marker. This might be achieved, for example, by referring to a group of high-energy physicists as 'a tribe of physicists': by relating stories that serve as defining moments of contrast, such as the newspaper story that began this chapter; and most of all, by making it overtly clear which culture we are communicating in at any given moment, and by making it overtly clear when we cross into another culture. Visual and auditory cues constitute the creative substance of communication while humour is often its winning style.

A realistic goal for culture brokers is to make transitions across borders smoother for our audience by transforming: impossible borders into hazardous ones, hazardous borders into manageable ones, or manageable borders into smooth ones.

When crossing cultural borders, we invariably switch norms, values, beliefs, expectations, and conventional actions. This switching is done overtly for more effective communication. Both the communicator and the audience are aware of the critical changes in language conventions, in epistemology, in worldviews, and in ideology, that accompany the cultural border crossing event. This awareness defines the goal of a culture brokering science communicator.

[. . .]

Conclusion

[. . .] It was Watson himself who did so much towards communicating science effectively to the public when he published *The Double Helix* in 1968. His readers were made aware of the paradigms of practice, the cultural metaphors, the social conventions, and the competitive struggles that characterise science-in-action. His book lay bare for public scrutiny many of Western science's cultural features, even more vividly than subsequent scholarly treatises on the social construction of science (e.g. Latour, 1987; Latour and Woolgar, 1979; Longino, 1990). Watson portrayed fellow scientists as developing an ordered system of meaning and symbols (a helical model for DNA) in the context of social interactions. These social interactions were so poignantly portrayed that some people thought the book should be X-rated.

Latour (1987) criticises journalists who report every new development in technoscience as a breakthrough in the progress of humanity. He points out that they fail to communicate science culture effectively to the public by not, for instance, identifying the ideology of scientism associated with 'technoscience breakthroughs' by asking, for example, 'progress for whom?' A critical analytic understanding of the culture of Western science is a prerequisite to effective communication with the public. Western scientific knowledge and technique must be seen as socially constructed within paradigms of practice, and socially determined by cultural metaphors and conventions, by economic interests, and by competition for privilege and power.

This prerequisite knowledge about Western science was informed [. . .] by such anthropological concepts as culture, subculture, assimilation, acculturation, worldview, and ease of border crossing; and by related concepts such as constitutive and contextual values, norms and counter-norms, public and private science, ideology, and epistemology. [. . .]

Because science is necessarily embedded in a culture, science does not transfer easily into other cultures, including the subculture of everyday praxis in Western nations. This problematic transferability was amplified by communication problems that arose when Western science was taught to a non-Western public. Western science, with its own set of norms, values, beliefs, expectations, and conventional actions, turns out to be only one way of making sense of nature. Not only do we science communicators need to be sensitive to multicultural audiences, but from time to time we will need to consider multiple sciences as well.

Sensitivity and knowledge are prerequisites to becoming an effective culture broker who can help audiences cross the cultural border into Western science, smoothly enough to engage with the science communicator. Culture brokering will be a new role for most communicators. It will take extended practice to cultivate and perfect.

References

Aikenhead, G.S. (1980). *Science in social issues: implications for teaching*. Ottawa, Ontario: Science Council of Canada.

Aikenhead, G.S. (1996). Science education: Border crossing into the subculture of science. *Studies in Science Education*, 27, 1–52.

Aikenhead, G.S. (1997). Toward a First Nations cross-cultural science and technology curriculum. *Science Education*, 81, 217–238.

Baker, D., & Taylor, P.C.S. (1995). The effect of culture on the learning of science in non-western countries: The results of an integrated research review. *International Journal of Science Education*, 17, 695–704.

Banks, J.A. (1988). *Multiethnic education*. 2nd ed. Boston, MA: Allyn & Bacon.

Battiste, M. (1986). Micmac literacy and cognitive assimilation. In I. Barman, Y. Herbert, & D. McCaskell (Eds.), *Indian Education in Canada, Vol. 1: The Legacy*. Vancouver, BC: University of British Columbia Press, 23–44.

Bullivant, B.M. (1981). *Race, Ethnicity and Curriculum*. Melbourne, Australia: Macmillan.

Carlsen, W., Kelly, G., & Cunningham, C. (1994). Teaching ChemCom: Can we use the text without being used by the text? In J. Solomon & Glen Aikenhead (Eds.), *STS education: International perspectives on reform*. New York: Teachers College Press, pp. 84–96.

Casper, B.M. (1980). Public policy decision making and science literacy. In D. Wolfie et al. (Eds.), *Public policy decision making and scientific inquiry: Information needs for science and technology (Report No. NSF-80-21-A6)*. Washington, DC: National Science Foundation.

Christie, M.J. (1991). Aboriginal science for the ecologically sustainable future. *Australian Science Teachers Journal*, 37(1), 26–31.

Chubin, D.E. (1981). Values, controversy, and the sociology of science. *Bulletin of Science, Technology & Society*, 1, 427–436.

Cobern, W.W. (1991). *World view theory and science education research, NARST Monograph No. 3*. Manhattan, KS: National Association for Research in Science Teaching.

Cobern, W.W. (1996). Worldview theory and conceptual change in science education. *Science Education*, 80, 579–610.

Cobern, W.W., & Aikenhead, G.S. (1998). Cultural aspects of learning science. In B.J. Fraser & K.G. Tobin (Eds.), *International handbook of science education*. Dordrecht, The Netherlands: Kluwer Academic Publishers, 39–52.

Corsiglia, J., & Snively, G. (1995). Global lessons from the traditional science of long-resident peoples. In G. Snively & A. MacKinnon (Eds.), *Thinking globally about mathematics and science education*. Vancouver, Canada: University of British Columbia, Centre for the Study of Curriculum and Instruction, 25–50.

Costa, V.B. (1995). When science is 'another world': Relationships between worlds of family, friends, school, and science, *Science Education*, 79, 313–333.

Dart, F.E. (1972). Science and the worldview. *Physics Today*, 25 (6), 48–54.

Deloria, V. (1992). Relativity, relatedness and reality. *Winds of Change, (Autumn)*, 35–40.

Dierking, L.D., & Martin, L.M.W. (Guest Eds.) (1997). Special issue: Informal science education. *Science Education*, 81 (6).

Ermine, W.J. (1995). Aboriginal epistemology. In M. Battiste & J. Barman (Eds.), *First Nations education in Canada: The circle unfolds*. Vancouver, Canada: University of British Columbia Press, 101–112.

Factor, L., & Kooser, R. (1981), *Value presuppositions in science textbooks*. Galesburg, IL: Knox College.

Fourez, G. (1988). Ideologies and science teaching. *Bulletin of Science, Technology, and Society, 8,* 269–277.

Gauld, C. (1982). The scientific attitude and science education: A critical reappraisal. *Science Education, 66,* 109–121.

Geertz, C. (1973). *The interpretation of culture*. New York: Basic Books.

Graham, L.R. (1981). *Between science and values*. New York: Columbia University Press.

Hawkins, J., & Pea, R.D. (1987). Tools for bridging the cultures of everyday and scientific thinking. *Journal of Research in Science Teaching, 24,* 291–307.

Holton, G. (1978). The scientific imagination: Case studies. Cambridge: Cambridge University Press.

Ingle, R.B., & Turner, AD. (1981). Science curricula as cultural misfits. *European Journal of Science Education, 3,* 357–371.

Irzik, G. (1998). Philosophy of science and radical intellectual Islam in Turkey. In W.W. Cobern (Ed.), *Socio-cultural perspectives on science education: An international dialogue*. Dordrecht, Netherlands: Kluwer Academic Publishers, 163–179.

Jegede, O.J., & Okebukola, P.A. (1991). The effect of instruction on socio-cultural beliefs hindering the learning of science. *Journal of Research in Science Teaching, 28,* 275–285.

Jenkins, E.W. (1992). School science education: Towards a reconstruction. *Journal of Curriculum Studies, 24,* 229–246.

Jordan, C. (1985). Translating culture: From ethnographic information to education program. *Anthropology and Education Quarterly, 16,* 104–123.

Kawagley, O. (1990). Yup'ik ways of knowing. *Canadian Journal of Native Education, 17* (2), 5–17.

Kawasaki, K. (1996a). The concepts of science in Japanese and western education. *Science & Education, 5,* 1–20.

Kawasaki, K. (1996b, September). *Kansatsu: The way to produce the Japanese eureka situation*. A paper presented at the international symposium on Culture Studies in Science Education, Ibaraki University, Mito, Japan.

Kearney, M. (1984). *World view*. Novato, CA: Chandler & Sharp Publishers, Inc.

Keller, E.F. (193), *A feeling for the organism*. San Francisco: W.H. Freeman and Co.

Kelly, G.J., Carlsen, W.S., & Cunningham, C.M. (1993). Science education in sociocultural context: Perspectives from the sociology of science. *Science Education, 77,* 207–220.

Kilbourn, B. (1980). World views and science teaching. In H. Munby, G. Orpwood, & T. Russell (Eds.), *Seeing curriculum in a new light: Essays from science education*. Toronto: OISE Press, 34–43.

Knudtson, P., & Suzuki, D. (1992). *Wisdom of the elders*. Toronto, Canada: Stoddart.

Krugly-Smolska, E. (1992). A cross-cultural comparison of conceptions of science. In G.L.C. Hills (Ed.), *History and philosophy of science in science education, Vol. I.* Kingston, Ontario, Canada: Faculty of Education, Queen's University, 583–593.

Kuhn, T. (1970). *The structure of scientific revolutions (2nd Ed.)*. Chicago: University of Chicago Press.

Latour, B. (1987). *Science in action*. Cambridge, MA: Harvard University Press.

Latour, B., & Woolgar, S. (1979). *Laboratory life: The social construction of scientific facts*, London: Sage.

Layton, D. (1991). Science education and praxis: The relationship of school science to practical action. *Studies in Science Education, 19,* 43–79.

Layton, D., Jenkins, E., Macgill, S., & Davey, A. (1993). *Inarticulate science? Perspectives on the public understanding of science and some implications for science education*. Driffield, East Yorkshire, UK: Studies in Education.

Linkson, M. (1998, July). *Cultural and political issues in writing a unit of Western science appropriate for primary aged Indigenous students living in remote areas of the Northern Territory*. A paper presented to the 47th annual meeting of the Australian Science Teachers Association, Darwin, Australia.

Longino, H.E. (1990). *Science as social knowledge. Values and objectivity in scientific inquiry*. Princeton, NJ: Princeton University Press.

MacIvor, M. (1995). Redefining science education for Aboriginal students. In M. Battiste & J. Barman (Eds.), *First Nations education in Canada: The circle unfolds.* Vancouver, Canada: University of British Columbia Press, 73–98.

Maddock, M.N. (1981). Science education: An anthropological viewpoint. *Studies in Science Education, 8,* 1–26.

McKinley, E. (1996). Towards an Indigenous science curriculum. *Research in Science Education, 26,* 155–167.

Michie, M., Anlezark, J., & Uibo, D. (1998, July) *Beyond bush tucker: Implementing Indigenous perspectives through the science curriculum.* A paper presented to the 47th annual meeting of the Australian Science Teachers Association, Darwin, Australia.

Mitroff, I.I. (1974). Norms and counter-norms in a selected group of the Apollo moon scientists: A case study of the ambivalence of scientists. *American Sociology Review, 39,* 579–595.

Nadeau, R., & Désautels, J. (1984). *Epistemology and the teaching of science.* Ottawa, Canada: Science Council of Canada.

Ogawa, M. (1995). Science education in a multi-science perspective. *Science Education, 79,* 583–593.

Ogawa, M. (1997). The Japanese view of science in their elementary science education program. In K. Calhoun, R. Panwar, & S. Shrum (Eds.), *International Organization for Science and Technology Education 8th symposium proceedings, Vol. 2: Policy.* Edmonton, Canada: University of Alberta, 175–179.

Ogawa, M. (1998a). A cultural history of science education in Japan: An epic description. In W.W. Cobern (Ed), *Socio-cultural perspectives on science education: An international dialogue.* Dordrecht, Netherlands: Kluwer Academic Publishers, 139–161.

Ogawa, M. (1998b). Under the noble flag of 'developing scientific and technological literacy.' *Studies in Science Education, 31,* 102–111.

Peat, D. (1994). *Lighting the seventh fire.* New York: Carol Publishing Group.

Phelan, P., Davidson, A., & Cao, H. (1991). Students' multiple worlds: Negotiating the boundaries of family, peer, and school cultures. *Anthropology and Education Quarterly, 22,* 224–250.

Pierotti, R., & Wildcat, D.R. (1997). The science of ecology and Native American tradition. *Winds of Change, (Autumn),* 94–97.

Pomeroy, D. (1992). Science across cultures: Building bridges between traditional Western and Alaskan Native sciences. In G.L.C. Hills (Ed.), *History and philosophy of science in science education, Vol. II.* Kingston, Ontario, Canada: Faculty of Education, Queen's University, 257–268.

Roberts, R.M., Norman, W., Minhinnick, N., Wihongi, D., & Kirkwood, C. (1995). Kaitiakitanga: Maori perspectives on conservation. *Pacific Conservation Biology, 2,* 7–20.

Roberts, R.M., & Wills, P.R. (1998). Understanding Maori epistemology: A scientific perspective. In H. Wautischer (Ed.), *Tribal epistemologies: Essays in the philosophy of anthropology.* Sydney: Ashgate, pp. 43–77.

Rose, H. (1994). The two-way street: Reforming science education and transforming masculine science. In J. Solomon & G. Aikenhead (Eds.), *STS education: International perspectives on reform.* New York: Teachers College Press, pp. 155–166.

Ryle, G. (1954). The world of science and the everyday world. In G. Ryle (Ed.), *Dilemmas.* Cambridge: Cambridge University Press, pp. 68–81.

Samovar, L.A., Porter, R.E., & Jain, N.C. (1981). *Understanding intercultural communication.* Belmont, CA: Wadsworth.

Sardar, Z. (1989). *Explorations in Islamic science.* London: Mansell.

Sardar, Z. (1997). Islamic science: The contemporary debate. In H. Selin (Ed.), *Encyclopaedia of the history of science, technology, and medicine in non-western cultures.* Dordrecht, Netherlands, Kluwer Academic Publishers, 455–458.

Scantlebury, K. (1998). An untold story: Gender, constructivism & science education. In W.W. Cobern (Ed.), *Socio-cultural perspectives on science education: An international dialogue.* Dordrecht, Netherlands: Kluwer Academic Publishers, 99–120.

Schilk, J.M., Arewa, E.O., Thomson, B.S., & White, A.L. (1995). How do Native American children view science? *Cognosos, 4* (3), 1–4.

Shelley, R. (1993). *Culture shock.* Portland, Oregon: Graphic Arts Center Publishing Co.

Simonelli, R. (1994). Sustainable science: A look at science through historic eyes and through the eyes of indigenous peoples. *Bulletin of Science, Technology & Society*, *14*, 1–12.

Snow, C.P (1964). *The two cultures*. New York: Menton Books.

Snow, R.E. (1987). Core concepts for science and technology literacy. *Bulletin of Science Technology Society*, *7*, 720–729.

Solomon, J. (1983). Learning about energy: How pupils think in two domains. *European Journal of Science Education*, *5*, 49–59.

Stairs, A. (1995). Learning processes and teaching roles in Native education: Cultural base and cultural brokerage. In M. Battiste & J. Barman (Eds.), *First Nations education in Canada: The circle unfolds*. Vancouver, Canada: University of British Columbia Press, 139–153.

Sutherland, D.L. (1998). *Aboriginal students' perception of the nature of science: The influence of culture, language and gender*. Unpublished PhD dissertation, University of Nottingham, Nottingham, UK.

Suzuki, D., & Oiwa, K. (1996). *The Japan we never knew*. Toronto, Canada: Stoddart.

Tharp, R. (1989). Psychocultural variables and constraints: Effects on teaching and learning in schools. *American Psychologist*, *44*, 349–359.

Traweek, S. (1992). Border crossings: Narrative strategies in science studies and among physicists in Tsukuba science city, Japan. In A. Pickering (Ed.), *Science as practice and culture*. Chicago: University of Chicago Press, 429–465.

Watson, J. (1968). *The double helix*. New York: Signet.

Wolfe, J., Bechard, C., Cizek, P., & Cole, D. (1992). *Indigenous and Western knowledge and resources management system*. Guelph, Canada: University of Guelph.

Wynne, B. (1991). Knowledge in context. *Science, Technology and Human Values*, *16*, 111–121.

Ziman, J. (1984). *An introduction to science studies: The philosophical and social aspects of science and technology*. Cambridge: Cambridge University Press.

_____

CHAPTER 9

THE INTERACTION OF STUDENTS' SCIENTIFIC AND RELIGIOUS DISCOURSES

Two case studies

Wolff-Michael Roth and Todd Alexander

International Journal of Science Education (1997) 19(2), 125–46

[. . .]

When students come to school they often bring understandings which actively interfere with the curriculum offered by the formal educational setting. Much research has been conducted to try to understand how everyday talk about phenomena developed prior to instruction interferes with the science talk students encounter in school.[1] This literature is commonly described by labels such as misconceptions', 'alternative frameworks', 'naive conceptions', 'phenomenological primitives', and 'conceptual change'. Other sources of interference with science instruction are less charted. Thus, although the discourses of science and that of fundamentalist Christians have often been incommensurable at the institutional level, religious discourse has rarely been studied as a potential interference with the learning of scientific discourse at the individual level.

We engaged in this study to construct an understanding how religious discourse interacts with scientific classroom discourse in some students but not others. In this study, some students made conflicting claims in their scientific and religious discourses which they could not resolve. These conflicts interfered with learning science. Other students developed mechanisms which allowed them to eschew such conflicts, and others did not experience any conflicts. We expanded a framework developed for the analysis of scientists' discourse to make it suitable for the analysis of scientific and religious discourse. Although there appear to be marked conflicts between scientific and religious discourses in other cultures (e.g., conflicts between Islam and science (Anees 1995)), 'religion' in this study refers to public and personal dimensions of Christian faith. [. . .]

Background

The boundary between science or technology and religion has long been the site of individual, institutional and cultural conflict. In order to minimize the conflict at the institutional level, some countries, such as the USA, have elevated the separation of church and state to a fundamental principle enshrined in their constitutions (O'Connor and Ivers 1988) while other countries such as the former USSR have consistently suppressed any role for religion. This separation at the institutional level was also formally pronounced on behalf of organized science by the National Academy of Science (NAS) (1984:6) in *Science and Creationism*. NAS took the position that 'religion and science are separate and mutually exclusive realms of human thought whose representation in the same context leads to misunderstanding of both scientific theory and religious belief'.

Although the differences between scientific and fundamentalist Christian discourses have been argued repeatedly in court, little research exists with respect to whether or not such differences might interfere with students' appropriation of school science talk. In spite of the formal separation between science and religion, many people do not make such a separation at the personal level (Lawson and Wester 1990, Lawson and Worsnop 1992). Hence, when there is a conflict between their scientific and religious knowledge students have difficulties learning the subject matter of their curriculum. Students with strong commitments to creationist discourse about the beginning of the universe are less prone to understand evolutionary biology than their peers. It is alarming then that a large number of students and university administrators favour the teaching of creationism. Research conducted in several public universities in Ohio showed that between 80 and 94% of the students favoured the instruction of creation science (Bergman 1979, Fuerst 1984). A survey of approximately 28% of the Ohio school board presidents revealed that more than 52% want creation science to be taught alongside the theory of evolution, and do not believe that this means introducing religion (Zimmerman 1991).

We can then expect to have students who employ religious discourses that they and their parents regard as incompatible with canonical scientific classroom discourse. These religious discourses may be even more problematic for science instruction than students' intuitive and mundane discourse about natural phenomena ('misconceptions') which are not linked to religious explanatory schemes. The research presented in the chapter arose from these concerns. In the context of high school science, we wanted to understand the interaction of scientific and religious discourses, and students' management of conflicting knowledge claims within and across discourse domains.

Study design

This chapter was developed from a data base established in the context of a two-year longitudinal study of physics students' views about knowing and learning. The larger study was concerned with physics students' ontological, epistemological and sociological claims about the nature of physics knowledge, the evidence they mustered in support of these claims and their views of learning. The entire data base contains more than 25,000 pages of transcripts (interviews and class discussions), student essays and short responses. Four reports, each co-produced by an outside university researcher not directly involved with the students, dealt with various aspects of the data base (Lucas and Roth 1995, Roth and Roychoudhury 1993, 1994, Roth and Lucas 1995). The present chapter, co-authored by the teacher and one of the students deals with the interaction of students' scientific and religious discourses.

Participants and setting

From a cohort of 46 students enrolled in a junior-level physics course, 23 enrolled in and completed a senior level physics course. Seven students, according to their own accounts, had strong religious commitments. One of these students, Todd[2], is the second author of this study. The principal author and teacher of all physics courses at the school taught both the junior and senior year physics courses. At the time, his preparation included an MSc in physics and a PhD in science education, research experience in both fields, and ten years of experience teaching science, mathematics and computer science.

This chapter is unusual for educational research in that it is co-authored by a teacher and a senior high school student. This collaboration came about in the following way. During one of our many conversations, Todd had asked if he could participate in the study as a researcher, for he was interested in how others talked about science and religion. We came to an immediate agreement to work jointly on data analysis, writing the manuscript, and conducting member check interviews with other students. We jointly presented different aspects of our work at international conferences. Our collaboration was facilitated by a relationship of trust that we had built over three years. While we do not deny the differences between our life experiences and expertise in educational research, these differences were not used to set up a relationship based on differences in power. By using individual voices, we set apart instances where we speak with our individual voices.

Science and religion at school

At the time of the interviews, we were associated with a private all-boys' school (Grades 4 to 13) in central Canada. In terms of academic standards, the students in this school are not much different from those attending the surround public schools. Boarding was compulsory for juniors and seniors. Daily chapel attendance was compulsory for all students irrespective of religion or denomination. Although the chaplain was an ordained minister of the Anglican Church (Church of England), the services were non-denominational and deemed appropriate for the collective of faiths in the student body which included Christians, Muslims, Hindus, Sikhs, Jews and Buddhists. Each morning, the 15-minute service consisted of a hymn (from the Anglican hymn book) and reflections, usually presented by an ordained priest, but at least once a week presented by a senior student. Senior students were the chapel wardens, responsible for assuring order and keeping attendance. The chapel choir was made up of students from all grades. Until their junior year, students attended a compulsory course in religion. These courses, part of the requirements stipulated by the Ministry of Education, focused on various world religions without prioritizing any one of them.

The senior author along with 50% of the faculty, also lived on the school grounds and was associated with a residence. This provided the authors with many opportunities to meet formally and informally after school to complete this project. Like the majority of faculty (approximately 90%), Roth did not attend the chapel services which were optional for teachers.

Todd and Brent, along with 21 other students attended the elective junior and senior physics courses taught by the senior author. In both the junior and senior physics courses, about 70% of class time was devoted to experiments. Most of the research questions were student-framed; students planned and conducted the experiments, interpreted their data and submitted reports. The only conditions were that they had to deal with the content matter specified by the Ministry of Education and that they were convincing (not necessarily 'right') in terms of design and results. The remaining class time was spent on reviewing textbook materials and questions, preparing collaborative concept maps and discussing supplementary readings. These included essays, individual chapters and books such as 'Objectivity in science' (Suzuki 1989), such as 'What every school boy should know' (Bateson 1980) and *Inventing Reality: Physics as Language* (Gregory 1990). These texts raised questions about the objectivity and rationality of scientific inquiry and knowledge taken for granted in the students' science textbooks. Finally, to meet the provincial requirements for proficiency in physics content, the students read the pertinent textbook chapters on their own and completed about six end-of-chapter questions per week.

The teacher took a very personal stance to knowing and learning. He provided students with continuous feedback on their work, including the essays. The students received an 'A' for the completion of an essay, but were not required to espouse any one particular worldview. The same stance was evident in the whole-class discussions of readings. Each discussion was intended as a forum, an opportunity for students to talk through important and difficult issues in an environment of trust. For the teacher, it was not an issue of indoctrinating students to a different kind of truth but presenting knowing as something personal. Elsewhere (Roth and Lucas, 1993), more detailed evidence is provided of the non-dogmatic nature of the class discussion and response to student essays.

Teacher and his beliefs

It has been argued that students' and teachers' epistemological commitments interact and contribute to the classroom climate (Roth and Roychoudhury, 1993, 1994). In the following paragraphs, the teacher writes about his beliefs.

WMR: My discourse was an important aspect of the setting in which students developed over the two years.[3] To avoid the dangers of merely labeling my discourse as *agnostic* or *atheist*, we decided that I should provide a brief description.

The knowledge which we take as shared with others is socially constructed and legitimated within and across cultures. As an educator and social scientist, I am a member of a culture which engages in a continuous and continuously changing discourse to establish new explanatory resources. The meanings of concepts are not fixed, nor can they be considered as the same for all people. Idiosyncratic variations in our discourses (used to account for 'scientific concepts' or 'religious beliefs') have to be considered the norm rather than the exception. There is no need for the notion of a god as a discursive resource to explain the origin, purpose and destiny of mankind. On the other hand, although I do not use a god as a discursive resource, I consider myself (and am considered by others) as spiritual. Through mankind, the universe inspects itself self-reflexively.

In my physics courses, I discussed with students the problematic of objectivity, the occasional character of scientific knowledge, the discursive practices of scientists and the historical changes in scientific discourses. From these discussions the students constructed different understandings of my spiritual/religious commitments. Some, like Todd, felt that I was committed neither to formal religion nor to atheism, but that I was deeply spiritual. Others, like Brent, thought I was a 'complete atheist'.

Science and religion: psychosocial setting

The two case studies featured in this chapter are based on the interviews with and essays written by two students, Todd (second author) and Brent.

Todd: Having been brought up in a household where science and religion were both part of daily life, it was easy for me to bring the two beliefs together. This coexistence of science and religion continued at our school where both chapel services and science are part of the daily experience. Thus, for me, the notion of God became all-encompassing including science and the knowledge constructed through its procedures. At the school, I liked very much and did well in all my subjects, including sciences—biology, chemistry and physics. Besides sciences, I also took a keen interest in philosophy, poetry and fine art all of which were part of my course work towards graduation. I was one of the chapel wardens, and a member of the chapel choir. In my conversations with Michael, the senior author, I came to know that my discourse could be labeled 'social constructivist'. While this might be surprising, I do have a significant spiritual-religious life. These labels, however, like so many, do not express my specific discourse at the time of the study. (I elaborate on science and religion below.) My contribution also presented us with a problem which we had to resolve as we wrote this chapter. I often felt tempted to change or add to my earlier written and spoken statements. Michael, on the other hand, felt that the chapter should be about high school students' discourse rather than a story of my changing discourse in the process of our inquiry. That is a different story which I would like to tell in another place. So we decided to present my views as we reconstructed them together from the essays, formal interviews, personal notes and informal conversations at the time I attended Grade 12.

Brent: In his last two years at school, Brent was a moderately successful student; his grade point average was about one-half standard deviation below the mean. He was less successful in his two sciences, chemistry and physics: barely passed one and failed the other. Brent had selected these science courses in part because of his parents' wish that he become a medical doctor ('My parents sort of pushed me'). In order to enter the prerequisite science programme, he had to complete the senior-level physics and chemistry courses. He had a keen interest in theatre arts, a subject in which he received an 'A', and was actively involved in several drama productions at the school. During the two years at the school, he repeatedly talked about his deep religious commitments and the conflicts he experienced as he learned chemistry and physics. His peers also knew him as an avid debater with respect to religious issues. Brent was also a chapel warden and a member of the chapel choir.

Brent's parents had a very strong influence. Brent indicated that both in his church and home he was 'scared into' the belief that he would go to hell unless he believed in God. Physics and chemistry, on the other hand, taught him that he was merely made of atoms, indicating that there was no afterlife. He considered science teachers to be atheists who refuse to belief in God and who indoctrinate students, attempting to make them believers of science.[4] On the basis of such tensions, paired with the observation that some of the high-achieving students were not religious at all, he concluded that science was only for atheists. He constantly felt caught between his parents and church on the one hand, and school science on the other. For as long as he could remember, his parents did not help him to overcome the conflicts he felt between scientific and religious knowledge claims, and merely told him to believe in a supreme being.

Data and analysis

Data and interpretation

The data sources for Todd and Brent included three formal interviews (lasting between 45 and 75 minutes) and nine reflective essays (from 4 to 7 single-spaced type written pages) on the nature of scientific and personal knowledge, the nature of physics and views on learning science. Over the two years we developed a close relationship; we met up three times per week and kept personal notes and journal entries, which became part of the data. In our conversations we talked about epistemology, litera- ture and poetry, cosmology, religion and philosophy. We included in our data base articles by scientists publishing in *Zygon* (from the Greek meaning 'yoke'), an inter- disciplinary journal with the mission to bridge science and religion.

We independently read and annotated all data, then met to discuss our emerging constructions, This process was repeated, followed by the construction of a first draft of the manuscript which became the basis for further discussions. The present chapter emerged as the product of recurrent cycles of writing and collaborative reflections. During our reading of the data, we recognized the variability of students' discourses, which led in some cases to seemingly contradictory statements. For example, Brent stated that knowledge is socially constructed, that is, a function of social and cultural contingencies and that it is absolute, a mirror of nature. From a traditionally psycho- logical and sociological perspective, this made him an unreliable source of information (Gilbert and Mulkay 1984). However, developments in social psychology and the sociology of scientific knowledge during the past ten years allowed us a different reading of such variability in discourse.

Construction of the analytic framework

In classical measurement theory, views and attitudes are treated as unitary constructs which should lead people to answer specific interview questions (or questionnaires) in consistent ways across time within the same context, or at the same time but across contexts (Edwards and Potter 1992, Potter and Wetherell 1987). The notions of internal reliability and test–retest validity of questionnaires are built on this assump- tion. However, recent analysis of scientific discourse provided ample evidence for the variability of scientists' views and accounts within and across contexts (Gilbert and Mulkay 1984). These interpretive variations in participants' discourse arise as accounts are produced to do different things in different contexts. Accordingly, speakers' accounts should not be taken as evidence for individual beliefs. Rather than attempting to identify participants' elusive unitary attitudes, we constructed a framework through the analysis of the organization of discourse in relation to its function and context. Individuals' talk about 'their' ideas and beliefs should therefore be taken as state- ments that reflect what generally count as ideas and beliefs; this talk should not be taken as expressions of things in individual person's minds (Edwards and Potter 1992, Pollner 1987, Potter and Wetherell 1987). This talk about ideas, beliefs, and actions depends in many different ways on speaking individuals' interpretations of their present context.

When speakers make claims or statements that may be considered tenuous, they support these statements by making others which, in the context of the conversa- tion, they consider to be unquestionable. These unquestionable statements are called 'discursive resources' and the domain from which they are drawn are called 'inter- pretive repertoires' (Gilbert and Mulkay 1984). Gilbert and Mulkay introduced the empiricist repertoire to classify statements that invoke the infallibility of experiments in support of claims that scientific knowledge is true and impartial; they intro-duced the contingent repertoire to classify statements that invoke the contextual influences of social, material and cultural nature in support of claims that know-ledge is not true and impartial. However, these two epistemological claims about scientific knowledge are incompatible. To mediate incompatible claims, scientists used a form of argument Gilbert and Mulkay called the truth-will-out-device (TWOD). Accordingly, scientists argued that in spite of the contingencies, truth will eventually come out.

Because of our interest in scientific *and* religious discourse, we needed to modify Mulkay and Gilbert's framework. Beginning with Todd and Brent's data, we constructed the rational and subjective repertoires which apply to scientific and reli-gious discourse. By means of the constant comparative method (Strauss 1987), we tested and modified our initial framework to include the discursive devices described below. As a final test, we selected all those articles from the past four years of *Zygon* by physicists writing about the relationship of science and religion (Pannenberg 1988, Peacocke 1991, Reich 1990, Sperry 1991). Based on these analyses, we modified the framework so that it was also applicable to the writings of these scientists and prac-ticing Christians.

Our analytic framework, in contrast to all others with which we are familiar, is commensurable with our pragmatist view of knowing (Rorty 1989). Equally important, this framework does not do violence to participants by constructing them as 'irrational', 'illogical', or 'inconsistent' on the basis of what others view as incompatible statements.

Credibility

This study satisfies a number of criteria required to establish the credibility of inter-pretive research (Guba and Lincoln 1989). Both authors lived at the school, interacted with each other and students in a variety of contexts, and built trust between them-selves and other students; this satisfied the criterion of prolonged engagement.[5] As part of the larger two-year study, we interacted extensively to identify the perti-nent issues which deepened our study due to persistent observation. A university science educator and a fellow science teacher with no interest in the project served as peer debriefers who engaged with us in extended discussions to formulate and refine our knowledge claims. Through our collaborative work in the interpretation of the data sources and the writing of the project, as well as through other conver-sations concerning art, philosophy, religion, science, literature and poetry, we ascertained our mutual positions and constructions. As a result, we present joint constructions arising from the progressive subjectivity in our interactions. Being partic-ipant and co-investigator allowed Todd to ascertain the emerging constructions as a member check. As a final check, Brent read a draft manuscript and subsequently discussed it with us. He fully agreed with our characterization of his talk about science and religion, and expressed his hope that this manuscript might lead to changes in science teaching that would help other students like himself.

Interpretive repertoires and discursive mediation devices: framework for understanding scientific and religious discourse

Past research in science education treated beliefs, attitudes and attributions as unitary psychological constructs which can be measured by means of appropriate instruments (questionnaires, survey, interview, etc.). Variations in participants' discourse (on selections of items on questionnaires) were then treated as unwanted phenomena. They also led investigators to construct their participants as irrational, illogical, or as holders of compartmentalized knowledge and beliefs (Potter and Wetherell 1987). We took a different route here. Rather than granting the existence of unitary beliefs *a priori*, we avoided the construction of irrational participants by using interpretive repertoires to account for all of the discourse, including variations.

Interpretive repertoires

When we asked participants to talk about controversial issues (evolution versus creation, abortion, euthanasia) they drew on two realms for answers—science and religion. When we asked participants to characterize the knowledge claims made by the authorities in the two realms, they drew on the *rational* and *subjective* repertoires. The rational repertoire was introduced to classify statements that referred to the rationality of scientific and religious pursuits. The subjective repertoire was introduced to classify statements that referred to social and personal contingencies which make scientific and religious knowledge claims less than reliable (Figure 21). The following quotations illustrate two claims to rationality in the scientific enterprise (Quadrant 1).

> *Social construction*: [Physics] tries to model the universe because scientists understand that they can't really know what nature and science really is, but, so I guess the closest they can get is to make a model of it, a representation of what it is. And I think as long as the math part of it, as long as that is accurate and your predictions that you get from using your mathematical model, as long as those are accurate, it doesn't—I don't think it matters.

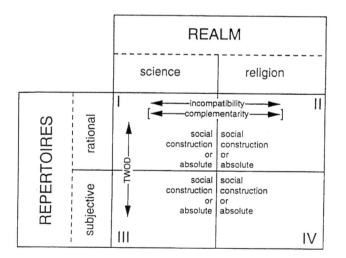

Figure 21 The analytic framework of interpretive repertoires. In each Quadrant, knowledge claims are absolute or socially constructed. 'TWOD', 'incompatibility' and 'complementarity' are devices that mediate the relationship between cells in order to avoid the conflict apparent between two contradictory knowledge claims

Absolute: Do scientific laws and theories exist before they are discovered by scientists? How could one propose that Newton's laws of motion did not exist before he discovered them? It is obvious that these laws exist in nature, and scientists discover them. In retort to this question, one could ask, 'Was there no gravity on Earth before Newton clearly defined it?' Of course there was.

Students talked about the Christian God and formal religious organizations. Typical student statements that illustrate the rational in religious discourse (Quadrant II) were:

Social construction: In contrast to the personal experience of God, there are also the socially constructed organized religions and their practices. Because of their negotiated character these practices vary across denominations and religions.

Absolute: God exists, because of all the miracles that he has done and everything from the past and the history says in the Bible . . . When I hear what other people think how the Earth was created, I say, 'well that is wrong' . . . I would think that religion is completely by the book of God, is not artificial, because I have grown up that way.

The existence of a subjective repertoire is based on the observation that students talked about personal and social contingencies of scientific and religious knowledge claims that cannot be publicly accounted for in rational terms. As before, these knowledge claims may be absolute or socially constructed. Examples of the subjective dimensions in students' talk about science (Quadrant III) are:

Social construction: Well that's—the social environment will create the biases—it's the way a scientist or any person has been brought up that will shape his thoughts, his mind and this will influence. There was—last year we read this essay by David Suzuki. And he cited an example of thinking that I think it was, white men are more intelligent than black men because [they had bigger brains].

Absolute: Science is based on fact and the knowledge will not change because of his or her social environment. Man constantly searches for numerical answers. Therefore if he is affected by his surroundings, he will no longer be scientific.

Students who talked about the personal dimensions of religion did so in absolute terms. Thus, a typical statement was 'I think truth lies within ourselves, in no one else; you can't run your life based on a book, you just have to look within yourself'. Among the students, there was nobody who felt that the personal experience in the religious–spiritual domain was a matter of construction. However, the teacher's view (stated in the design section) that even one's personal experience is mediated by discursive practices of the community within which one participates is an example of the social construction of personal dimensions of religion.[6]

Discursive mediation devices

To mediate conflicting statements that arise from two statements—such as 'scientific knowledge is true' (Quadrant I) and 'society influences scientists' knowledge claims' (Quadrant III)—some individuals use discursive mediation devices. Previous research showed that scientists employed the truth-will-out-device (TWOD). This discursive device allows scientists to claim the objectivity of their knowledge claims while maintaining influences of contingent (subjective) nature. We found that some of our students used the same device, The following student statement is an illustration of TWOD:

> Presuppositions do, I mean, they do delay scientists finding the absolute truth. Scientists are approximating truth, I think, and then such as more recent, scientists they are getting more and more close, and eventually we could [could know the truth] if the world doesn't end before. An example, see Bohr's model of the atom. He had this model that had orbitals, like the set distances; it had orbitals, and they were all circular. And the mechanical, the quantum mechanical [model], it disproved it. But I mean, it took a long time to disprove it.

When we included the second discourse domain, religion, we found that there was a new potential conflict in knowledge claims (Quadrants I and II). Students argued that both scientific and religious authorities made claims to absolute knowledge. In some instances, these knowledge claims were contradictory. Brent, for example, was so torn by these contradictions that it interfered with his learning. Others had developed a device similar to the TWOD. We called it the incompatibility device (Figure 21). Accordingly, two knowledge claims were incompatible so that an individual drew either on one or the other realm to deal with controversial issues. For example, Ian said that institutional science and religion were incompatible and he kept the domains clearly separate in his accounts. When he talked about issues in which both realms might be concerned, Ian usually decided to privilege one realm over time other. On abortion and euthanasia, he used a religious argument to support his pro-life stand. On issues connected with genetic engineering he talked about the potential good emerging from the scientific enterprise. In this separation of the two realms, Ian chose the solution of many scientists.

The framework outlined so far is sufficient to classify students' scientific and religious discourse which we set out to understand. The analysis of published articles in *Zygon* revealed that our model was not entirely sufficient to account for all of the discursive variations. Some scientists used one other device to deal with conflicting claims of science and religion that was not used by our students. The complimentarity device (Figure 21) allows an individual to look at the object of inquiry (such as abortion or euthanasia) from two mutually exclusive viewpoints and integrate these through a dialectical and hermeneutic process. With the inclusion of this discursive mediation device, the presented analytic framework was comprehensive and general enough to cover students' and scientists' discourse. Our analyses showed that students—as did the scientists publishing in *Zygon* and those interviewed by Gilbert and Mulkay (1984)—used interpretive repertoires to support their claims. When two repertoires led to conflict, discursive mediating devices were invoked. These devices included the TWOD and incompatibility devices, and, in the case of some scientists, the complementarity device. To flesh out how discourses about science and religion interact, we now present two case studies.

Two case studies of scientific and religious discourse

The variability in the students' discourse was an immanent feature of the interviews with, and essays by, Todd and Brent. We observed discourse variations which in some cases became apparent as contradictions in one and the same interview. In the following sections, we will first account for Todd's discourse under the heading of 'Science and religion at peace'. Todd presented his views about knowing in science and religion, and finished by outlining how he integrated both discourses. As joint authors, we situated his views in a cultural, historical, scientific and spiritual context. In a similar structure, we accounted for Brent's scientific and religious discourses under the heading of 'Science and religion in conflict'. The selected excerpts in both instances are—with minor stylistic variations from the original—from our data. Todd and Brent read the excerpts to make sure that they accurately represented what they intended to say.

Science and religion at peace

Science

Over the course of his junior and senior years, Todd's view about science and scientific knowledge changed. Whereas he initially talked about the existence of scientific truths, the absoluteness and infallibility of scientific knowledge and the possibility of objectivity, his current discourse is radically different. His view of the nature of science as an effort to construct explanatory schemes which are negotiated in a social forum of the scientific community is not unlike that presented in recent developments in the history and philosophy of science, social studies of science, and epistemology (Hesse 1980, Knorr-Cetina 1981, Rorty 1979, von Glasersfeld 1987). Thus, although there is a world which is experientially real, it is impossible to know such a world as it really is. He argued that constructions are useful in dealing with this world, but we can never know the functional relationship between this knowledge and the world. As a community, scientists construct language games (Wittgenstein 1968) which are deconstructed when they are no longer viable in the light of sufficient new experimental evidence. In terms of our framework, Todd described scientific knowledge as socially constructed (Quadrant I, Figure 22a).

Todd: Science is a language game. It allows us to talk about the world in a community of knowers which shares a common language. This language allows us to create tools—concepts and theories—to talk about this world, predict and explain events, and thus create our knowledge of this world. We are now forced to ask ourselves, what shape do these tools and truths take and how are they used by us. The answer takes us to the beginning of one of my essays where I stated that it is 'with words, with sounds, all joyful, playful and obscene' on which scientific knowledge is based. The language we create and use to describe our observations becomes the tool itself. By changing the language we not only change the law and principles science is stating but we also change a previously accepted truth and effectively make a new one. Thus, it is language and the way in which we choose to define the phenomena we observe that is at the core of our knowledge; it is through these words that we arrive at the images and ideas that allow us to predict and explain our observations. This holds true for everything in our lives, it is through our language that we communicate our ideas, thoughts, and feelings, and it is also through them that we are able to learn through the recreation of our perceptions within our minds.

When the personal and subjective come to bear on the realm of science, measurements, procedures and interpretations have to be considered tentative until, in the light of new evidence, they are revised, The social and subjective also lead to specific sociocultural rather than universal interpretations of scientific experiments such as brought forth by science in communist USSR or Nazi Germany. But the subjective also accounted for the shifts in 'social truths' over time. That which is accepted today as valid knowledge may be error tomorrow, and the outrageous and unacceptable ideas of today become the truths of tomorrow.[7] Because scientific knowledge is socially constructed and always tentative, such variations in truth value are characteristic features of the epistemology; they do not conflict with Todd's discourse (Quadrant III, Figure 22a). But while scientific knowledge is socially constructed (an epistemological claim), Todd makes absolute statements about the existence of the world (an ontological claim).

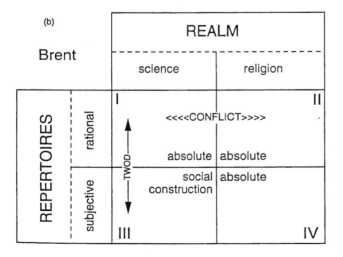

Figure 22 The interpretive repertoires of two students, Todd and Brent. Brent does not have a device to mediate the conflicting claims in Quadrants I and II. TWOD permits him to reconcile conflicting claims arising from the repertoires in Quadrants I and III

Todd: I find myself asking continually, does not the way in which we choose to describe what is occurring in fact create our reality? Now that we have progressed in science to a point that we are determining the relationship of things that are no longer visible to us and are at times almost unimaginable, it seems that reality becomes what man makes it. The way in which we describe things and think they are becomes what is real for us, until a time that a new and better way is thought of to replace the old; this in turn becomes our new reality. But this language has not only such a descriptive quality to be used in understanding the phenomenal world, but can also be used reflexively, to think about our thinking, language, and knowledge. It lets us conceive of our knowledge as being constructed, and as having a precarious relationship with that which it describes, including language itself ... Although I believe that the world is constructed, a construction mediated by language, figural models, and perceptions, I do not consider myself a solipsist. I believe that there is a world in which we are thrown, a world which we sense as experientially real, about which we have no doubt.

Religion

For Todd, knowledge claims shared within organized churches are like those of other institutions; they are negotiated within communities. That is, these knowledge claims bear the same marks as those in other public arenas such as science, art, or music (Quadrant II, Figure 22a).

Todd: In contrast to the personal experience of God, there are also the socially constructed organized religions and their practices. Because of their negotiated character these practices vary across denominations and religions.

The subjective repertoire of religious knowledge allowed Todd to take account of the personal knowledge of God. He left no doubt that personal knowledge of God (an epistemological claim) has absolute status ('absolute' in Quadrant IV, Figure 22a). With his religious discourse, Todd took a position that Christian theology began to develop during the Age of Enlightenment, and then in England particularly during the second half of the last century. According to this position, the Bible should not be read literally, but as an allegory or account of the universe from the perspective of a people at the time of the writing of Genesis, about 3000 years ago (Kenkel 1983, Pannenberg 1988). Accordingly, creation and evolution are not incompatible, but are different ordering stories that make sense in their respective contexts. In fact, the evolutionary changes in the animate world can be viewed as a continuous creation of a world in which God is immanent (Peacocke 1991:462). But in this view, God is not some kind of spiritual gas permeating the universe like the nineteenth century ether, but 'all-that-is in its actual processes *is* God, manifest in his mode as continuous creator ... we could say that the world is *in God*, that there is nothing in the world *not* in God'. Such an understanding of God and His relationship to the world Peacocke calls 'pan*en*theism' which views God as including and penetrating the whole universe so that every part exists in Him, but that God transcends this world, is more than, and not exhausted by, the universe. As for evolution, it is a process of emergence in which God's work can be seen at work, continuously creating in and through the material world.

Todd: Religion and God are part of a spiritual realm of human beings. Our experience with God is always a personal one. This experience has an ontology similar to the reality of material objects and events phenomena: it is experientially real. But in addition, this personal experience is also the only source of truth and permits me to make truly ethical and moral decisions. The experience of God is a spiritual one which includes all the wonders of human existence; it includes all those things like love, beauty, truth and goodness which cannot be explained by science, and may have no place in science. I mean, just look at intangible things, like love and beauty. I think that equates to God for me. You do not understand why, but you know that these things exist. You know certain things are beautiful, and you know you love certain things, but you cannot explain why, you just do. It's like beauty: if you are sitting at night down by the lake, having a beer or a smoke or whatever. All of a sudden the sun goes down, and the colors appear in the sky and on the horizon. It is beautiful, that is IT, that is beauty, you cannot say why, you can't define it. In my view, God is not a material or physical being, and cannot be perceived or described in any way. Whenever I think of God I get a picture of nothing, but try to think of nothing, and that's God, and that's: well think of nothing that's as close as you can get to everything, and that gives you God. If you are infinite then there is no such thing as change, but is all-encompassing, so we can't apply change to infinite things, I mean that's like saying is God good-looking, or is God plain, or, I don't know, tall, we can't apply the term to infinite things. The essence is that things came from God, and they are part of God, God doesn't have two hands, doesn't have a face, doesn't have a mind, God just is.

Integration of science and religion

Because the notion of social construction allows multiple viewpoints of the same 'object', Todd did not experience conflict bringing the two realms together in the process of rational discourse. He could draw on all repertoires without experiencing conflict for answers to difficult decisions; therefore, Todd did not need a mediating device such as TWOD, incompatibility, or complementarity (see Figure 22a).[8] The religious discourse provided Todd with an important spiritual resource for making difficult decisions in this world. Like others (Postman 1992), Todd indicated that a scientific or technological rationality cannot provide the necessary ethical dimension for making informed choices about dealing with issues such as abortion, euthanasia, AIDS, or genetic engineering. Scientific and technological rationality always are subvervient to market or political pressures, while the religion-informed, personal ethic provides 'true' standards. With a number of theologians, particularly those in the tradition of his own Anglican Church, Todd believes that an ethic has to be contingent on the particulars of each situation. Thus, rather than seeking an absolute, immutable and dogmatic ethic, he favored a situational ethic (Fletcher 1966). This ethic is not informed by either scientific or religious dogma but by the specific relationships of the individual case in its sociocultural, economic, scientific and spiritual context.

Todd: I believe that my non-literal understanding of the Biblical creation story interfaces with my conception of an immaterial God that revealed itself to Moses as an entity without image. God's presence is immanent in the universe as creation, and evolution is the process by which the world is continually transformed. Although in this view, God does not actively intervene in the physical world, God and the associated spirituality are resources for me to deal with ethical problems. As a scientist or doctor (see note 2), I will draw on these resources within myself where I relate to God. I find that when we have problems, we draw on our religion not on science.

Science is there just for man to use, but there is not the energy in it: like when we have problems and difficulties we draw on our religious and spiritual sides, and when we have problems we look at our religious side. We are not looking for a textbook, we do not read a book about it: we look into ourselves.

Science in and of itself does not have an ethic, it is value neutral ready for man to use for the betterment of man. To overcome this lacuna of value neutrality in decisions involving man and the world, we have to use our personal, religious and/or Spiritual resources for dealing with the ethical and moral dimensions of decision making. Because of its personal nature, this spirituality leads to an ethic which is very case-based and differs from decision maker to decision maker. Euthanasia and abortion need to be case related, that is the only way that decisions would be made for one person on a case. As a doctor, I will know before an operation. I can see both sides, all the arguments, and I ride the fence pretty much to all of them; if I disagree with an abortion then I would not perform it; if I disagreed with euthanasia then I would not perform it. I would make a decision case by case because these are not black and white issues. Just like with genetic engineering, it is not a black and white subject. Here too, every decision would be very situational. I mean, it is totally situational, both are prime examples, with huge gray areas and I think for me I would be very internally very case related.

Science and religion in conflict

Science

Brent described science as a human effort that yields absolute truths (Quadrant I, Figure 22b). He used the subjective repertoire in the realm of science to account for the errors due to the emotional engagement and personal investments of the scientists in the products of their labor (Quadrant III, Figure 22b). Here, Brent encountered a problem; he had to account for the difference between the absolute truths generated by scientists and the erroneous knowledge they produce because of their personal engagement. In this case, Brent made use of the TWOD which assures that the ill-constructed aspects of scientific knowledge will be weeded out. He suggested that erroneously accepted scientific work will be re-evaluated in the future. The facts will decide and weed out wrong explanations so that the truth will come out. This has the effect that over time, scientific knowledge more and more approximates truth.

Brent: The statement 'the social environment of a scientist will influence the content of the knowledge he or she proposes is debatable but I would have to agree because of the fact that wherever a scientist will live, he or she will alter their observations and knowledge . . .

We talked about Suzuki's essay on objectivity in science. People seemed to assume that there is no truth. But I disagree. Science does approximate truth. It only adds on to more questions which needed to be answered. As days have passed from Socrates to Newton thoughts which have been expressed in public, slowly make us realize that *this is what the world is made of*.[9] More and more people begin to add on, or reliably explain a dilemma precisely as the days flow by. Science is what people say how the world is built. To a degree, science may lead a path towards truth, but are we accurate enough to say that science is a true fact? We can say that science provides us with true facts, explanations to what the truth really is; and science is but one way to resolve a question which needs to be answered. Yes, in fact I am saying that science is reality and no other belief more and more approximates truth.

Religion

Brent said that religious knowledge claims are rationally accountable and based on the Bible and the existence of God. Knowledge claims shared by the members of churches therefore have an absolute status (Quadrant II, Figure 22b). These claims are supported by the Bible and members' knowledge of God's existence:

Brent: We know of God because he reveals himself in a very understandable way. We know that God exists, because of all the miracles that He has done in the past. History and the Bible say that He is the person that made the Red Sea go apart, He is the one who multipled the bread and the wine. This is why we believe that there is God. This is the reason why Christianity is probably one of the most popular religions there ever was. There are a lot of people, even Muslims and others believing in God. All in all, God in any religion has become the main focus and that's why people assume that there is a God, because more people believe it.

Religion, I find it very hard to understand how I believe in God; I can't touch Him, I can't see him. But then the Bible says, 'this woman was blind, and she touched his clothes and she was able to see again. She touched him, and she was able to see again'. I want something like that, I want something to believe in. God put Adam and Eve on earth, so that is one reason that there is logic behind the existence of [physical] forces. There are forces and similar things, created by God, that keep Adam and Eve down there, gravity and whatever, they say, that's all.

In accordance with his need for concrete experience, Brent took most of the Biblical accounts as literal descriptions. In this, he resembled many fundamentalist Christians who engage in the legal debate of science *versus* religion although his own Presbyterian church does not promulgate such discourse. Besides the literal truth of the Bible, Brent's discourse shared two other features with that of those fundamentalist Christians who argued against science in court: the irreconcilable differences between religion and science, and the superiority of biblical wisdom over scientific knowledge (Gieryn *et al.* 1985). First, religion stands against science as in an engagement of two armies trying to conquer each other, or like two orators vying for the audience's approval. Any positive acknowledgement of the viability of a scientific account for the present state of the universe could only come at the expense of biblical authority, a victory for science and ultimately the devil. He often used military metaphors to describe his discussions on science and religions ('I put up a big fight', 'I shot down his argument') or qualified statements as more or less persuasive ('I put up a pretty good debate', 'his argument would be a lot more diverse than mine', 'the listener would find it more convincing'). Second, faith in the Bible is more valuable than scientific knowledge because only religion is able to provide man with purpose and ethico-moral standards. However, Brent's own accounts were little informed by the ongoing discussion of creation science *versus* evolution (such as his own account about the age of the earth) so that he did not and could not make use of fundamentalists' discursive strategies (O'Connor and Ivers 1988, Overton 1983). He recognized this lack of persuasiveness, and for that reason always found himself in the position of the underdog in discussions with teachers or groups of peers.

Comparing Brent's and Todd's talk about God's relationship with creation, we notice that Brent stressed the externality of the creative acts—He is creating something external to Himself—while Todd held a reformed view (Peacocke 1991), where God is immanent in and of the creation.

Brent's discourse about his personal religious experience transpired certainty. His knowledge claims equal the absolute status of the church's public knowledge claims (Quadrant IV, Figure 22b).

Brent: I need to see or touch in order to believe, and this causes me some pain. For I have asked God for signs or something like that. Moses and people like that they got their sign. Whereas I am just a little boy—I feel like I am a little boy now—who does not have a God because he didn't give me the sign. I believe in God—I think I believe in God—and that there is an afterlife for me. There is actually something there for me, so that I wouldn't got to hell and I will be up there with the angels, or something like that ... To be 100% sure that there is God or something from physics, to be a 100% sure that there is something, I need to touch it. If it is something like that, I want to see it, I want to touch it.

Science and religion

The following excerpts from Brent's interviews and essays illustrate the conflicts arising from the absolute truth claims of science and religion as rational enterprises.

Brent: From my perspective there are no similarities between science and religion at all. Science says that something else did it, and my religion says that God did it all. Religion and science, they do not connect. People might say that they do, but they don't connect at all. It is really like an apple and an orange, or an apple and a coconut whatever you want to take; science and religion don't just connect in a way that they can work with each other. There is nothing in science that says anything about God, there is nothing in science at all; and there is nothing in religion that says anything about science. So how can they associate if they don't mention anything at all? For myself, that is logical enough. There is nothing at all. Chemistry and physics, however, they do connect, because chemistry needs physics and physics needs chemistry in some ways; religion never says anything about science and science never says anything about religion, that is the way I think.

Physics offends my beliefs, probably because of something that I have grown up with all my life. Science completely goes against what God has created, the so-called power person who created everything; and people who are in the sciences are saying that 'you know, it wasn't him at all'. To me that is a direct insult. In a way, I could take that very lightly, but I just can't accept the fact that science and religion go together. In science, I feel like I am drawn away from religion and that really worries me a lot, because I feel I am being taken away from what I have been a part of, which is religion. If I go towards religion, I feel like I am not giving science a chance at all, and therefore I feel like I am not giving science a chance and I can't see myself doing that, because I am a person of morals.

I have to refute your claim that the universe was created four billion years ago. I think that the earth has been created 50,000 years ago, by my belief that is probably the only firm foundation that I have, I think it is 50,000 and not five million. I don't see what possible proof scientists could have that the earth is like 50 billion, how they can say it takes 50 billion years for fossils. When I hear you and other people talk about how the Earth was created, by referring to the theories of Big Bang and evolution, I say, well that is wrong. I believe that you are wrong and I am right—I am right because God has taught me so; and you are wrong because God did not bring you up that way, you are misinterpreting what the world actually is.

Brent's scientific and religious discourses both included accounts of concrete experiences. Lacking concreteness easily led Brent to doubts and disbelief. While he accepted scientists' (and technologist') authority, he found himself at a loss when it came to abstract concepts or theories. He associated many of his problems in learning science with the irreconcilable conflicts between the religious discourse – which he learned at home from his parents and in church and the scientific discourse to which he was introduced at school.

Conclusions

This study allowed us to explore the complexities in students' scientific and religious discourse. Our analysis in terms of interpretive repertoires accounted for students' talk in different contexts. The strength of our analytic scheme of interpretive repertoires lies in the fact that it accounts for the conflicts in discourse without constructing individuals as 'irrational', and it accounts for the discursive strategies used to resolve these conflicts.

Our analysis suggests that science teachers may have to consider helping students to develop discursive mediation devices; these would allow students to deal with conflicting situations. Cobern (1993:949) pointed out that science classroom learning environments 'can be improved, especially with regard to students who typically do not do well or who do not like science, if teachers are aware of students' world views' (p. 949). The questions that remain to be addressed are related to whether science teachers *recognize* the necessity of incorporating teaching strategies that would help students deal with their conflicting discourses. The teacher in this study always found time to discuss questions related to the epistemology of science. These discussions can easily be broadened to touch on the issues presented here. Other science teachers frequently say that they do not have enough time to cover the required content. In such cases, an alternate solution would be for schools to offer a special course that allows students to engage in a philosophy-of-wisdom inquiry in which the discourses of music, literature, drama, politics, science, religion and philosophy are treated at the same level (Maxwell 1992); that is, none of the discourses should dominate at the expense of the others. Such a course would allow students to discuss some of the key problems we face, but which are traditionally addressed only from a scientific–technological perspective without yielding viable solutions. Among these problems are all those which potentially threaten the survival of mankind on our planet.

At this point, we deem it important to assert that the most serious danger for both science and religion comes from the corruption of both scientific and religious habits of thought. Science and religion, particularly those in the Jewish, Catholic and many classical Protestant traditions, share the traits that they 'make objective demands upon self, require discipline and method, and rigorously attack self-deception' (Novak 1983:34). These virtues are all but abandoned by a new rising culture which shows a blatant naïveté with respect to the purpose and method of science and indulges in the occult, magic, astrology and other similar pursuits as a substitute for science and religion. We notice that decline in traditional religion has not resulted in a decline of superstition, totemism, and magic, but has given rise to new forms of pursuing them. By providing students avenues and opportunities to integrate traditional scientific and religious discourses, we may yet turn the tide to help both survive.

It needs to be emphasized that we are not advocating that every student, or every scientist, should become a Christian, or follow some other credo. We illustrated that there are ways in which science and religion can be accommodated by one and the same person without leading to problematic and incoherent constructions of Self. Although we are not claiming that science should be replaced by religion and ethics, there is a definite place for a high school course in which science, religion, philosophy, arts and other subjects are treated as parallel forms of inquiry towards the development of a 'good world'. Such a course would also allow students to experience science as but one form of inquiry, with a limited realm of applicability. Such a course needs to be truly interdisciplinary, in which no single discourse is privileged, such as in some 'science in society' courses, where scientific discourses dominate at the expense of the social and humanistic discourses.

Notes

1. Because of the problems associated with mapping talk and text onto underlying cognitive representations (Edwards and Potter 1992), this chapter takes as its central tenet the primacy of language as a reality-constituting practice. Rather than focusing on underlying 'beliefs' and 'conceptions', we studied students' discourse. This aspect of our approach is explained in greater detail in the section on interpretive repertoires.
2. Todd, the co-author of this chapter, is identified by his real name throughout the manuscript. He currently studies medicine at the University of Western Ontario. This chapter was drafted while he was still a high school student. Brent and Ian are the pseudonyms for two other students.
3. It was also implicit in the conceptualization and design of the study, was part of the ecology of the interview situations, and unavoidably determined the reading of the data sources.
4. Incidentally, Feyerabend (1991) suggested that scientific discourse shares some features with orthodox discourse in some Christian denominations.
5. We both lived in the same residence. One of us was head boy, a senior student representative, the other served in an advisory and supervisory position. Our positions entailed daily contacts which often evolved into prolonged discussions on topics that ranged from the strictly academic to the personal, aesthetic and ethico-moral.
6. For an interesting account of the discursive construction of Self see Edwards and Potter (1992).
7. As a graduate student, Louis de Broglie made the proposal to treat matter as wave. This proposal is said to have been treated as outrageous by professors and graduate students at de Broglie's institution until Einstein, during a visit to de Broglie's institution, recognized it as a major advance in theoretical physics.
8. Todd maintained that evolution and creation, for example, are different but socially constructed ordering stories. We use the complementarity principle when speakers invoke different descriptions to explain a phenomenon, all of which may they regard true depending on the context.
9. The emphasis is Brent's.

References

Anees, M.A. (1995) Islam and scientific fundamentalism. *Technoscience*, 8(1), 21–2.
Bateson, G. (1980) *Mind and Nature* (Toronto: Bantam).
Bergman, J. (1979) The attitude of university students toward the teaching of creation and evolution in the schools. *Origins*, 6, 60–70.
Cobern, W.W. (1993) College students' conceptualizations of nature: an interpretive world view analysis. *Journal of Research in Science Teaching*, 30, 935–51.
Edwards, D. and Potter, J. (1992) *Discursive Psychology* (London: Sage).

Feyerabend, P.K. (1991) *Three Dialogues on Knowledge* (Oxford: Blackwell).

Fletcher, J.F. (1966) *Situation Ethics. The New Morality* (Philadelphia: Westminster).

Fuerst, P.A. (1984) University student understanding of evolutionary biology's place in the creation/evolution controversy. *Ohio Journal of Science*, 84, 218–28.

Gieryn, T.F., Bevins, G.M. and Zehr, S.C. (1985) Professionalization of American scientists: public science in the creation evolution trials. *American Sociological Review*, 50, 392–409.

Gilbert, G.N. and Mulkay, M. (1984) *Opening Pandora's Box: A Sociological Analysis of Scientists' Discourse* (Cambridge: Cambridge University Press).

Gregory, B. (1990) *Inventing Reality: Physics as Language* (New York: Wiley).

Guba, E. and Lincoln, Y. (1989) *Fourth Generation Evaluation* (Beverly Hills: Sage).

Hesse, M. (1980) The strong thesis of sociology in science, in M. Hesse (ed.), *Revolutions and Reconstructions in the Philosophy of Science* (Bloomington: Indiana University Press).

Kenkel, A. (1985) A case against scientific creationism: a look at content issues, *Science Education*, 69, 59–68.

Knorr-Cetina, K.D. (1981) *The Manufacture of Knowledge: An Essay on the Constructivist and Contextual Nature of Science* (Oxford: Pergamon).

Lawson, A.E. and Weser, J. (1990) The rejection of non-scientific beliefs about life: effects of instruction and reasoning skills. *Journal of Research in Science Teaching*, 27, 589–606.

Lawson, A.E. and Worsnop, W.A. (1992) Learning about evolution and rejecting a belief in special creation: effects of reflective reasoning skill, prior knowledge, prior belief and religious commitment, *Journal of Research in Science Teaching*, 29, 143–66.

Lucas, K.B. and Roth, W.-M. (1995) A discursive approach to student epistemologies: two case studies. Paper presented at the annual conference of the Association for Science Education Research of Australia, Bendigo, Victoria.

Maxwell, N. (1992) What kind of inquiry can best help us create a good world? *Science Technology and Human Values*, 17, 205–27.

National Academy of Sciences, Committee on Science and Creationism (1984) *Science and Creationism: A View from the National Academy of Sciences* (Washington: National Academy Press).

Notar, M. (1983) False foes. *Society*, 20, 2, 32–35.

O'Connor, K. and Ivers, G, (1988) Creationism, evolution and the courts. *Political Science and Politics*, 21, 10–17.

Otterton, W.R. (1983) The decision in McLean *v.* Arkansas Board of Education. *Society*, 20, (2), 3–12.

Pannenberg, W. (1988) The doctrine of creation and modern science. *Zygon*, 23, 3–21.

Peacocke, A. (1991) God's action in the real world. *Zygon*, 26, 455–76.

Pollner, A. (1987) *Mundane Reason: Reality in Everyday and Sociological Discourse* (Cambridge: Cambridge University Press).

Postman, N. (1992) *Technopoly: The Surrender of Culture to Technology* (New York: Knopf).

Potter, J. and Wetherell, M, (1987) *Discourse and Social Psychology: Beyond Attitudes and Behaviour* (London: Sage).

Reich, K.H. (1990) The relation between science and theology: the case for complementarity revisited. *Zygon*, 25, 369–89.

Rorty, R. (1979) *Philosophy and the Mirror of Nature* (Princeton: Princeton University Press).

Rorty, R. (1989) *Contingency, Irony, and Solidarity* (Cambridge: Cambridge University Press).

Roth, W.-M. and Lucas, K.B. (in press). From 'truth' to 'invented reality': a discourse analysis of high school physics students' talk about scientific knowledge. *Journal of Research in Science Teaching*.

Roth, W.-M. and Roychoudhury, A. (1993) About knowing and learning physics: the perspectives of four students. *International Journal of Science Education*, 15, 27–44.

Roth, W.-M. and Roychoudhury, A. (1994) Physics students' epistemologies and views about knowing and learning. *Journal of Research in Science Teaching*, 31, 5–30.

Sperry, R.W. (1991) Search for beliefs to live by consistent with science. *Zygon*, 26, 237–58.

Strauss, A.L. (1957) *Qualitative Analysis for Social Scientists* (New York: Cambridge University Press).

Suzuki, D. (1989) *Inventing the Future. Reflections on Science, Technology, and Nature* (Toronto: Stoddart).

von Glasersfeld, E. (1987) Learning as a constructive activity. In C. Janvier (ed.) *Problems of Representation in the Teaching and Learning of Mathematics* (Hillsdale: Erlbaum), 3–17.

Wittgenstein, L. (1968) *Philosophical Investigations* (Oxford: Blackwell).

Zimmerman, M. (1991) The evolution–creation controversy: opinions of Ohio school board presidents. *Science Education*, 75, 201–14.

CHAPTER 10

PURPOSES FOR ASSESSMENT

P. Black

Testing: Friend or Foe? (1997) London: RoutledgeFalmer, pp. 24–36

Introduction

Assessments may be conducted to serve several different purposes. In this chapter, the main types of purpose will be discussed in three main sections, concerned respectively with the support of learning, with reporting the achievements of individuals, and with satisfying demands for public accountability. These three sections will be followed by consideration of the interactions, supportive or conflicting, between these purposes.

It is important to match the selection and use of assessment methods to the particular purpose which the assessment is meant to serve and a distinction has to be made at the outset between the purposes and the instruments and procedures that might be used. For example, the same test questions may be used for quite different purposes, and, conversely, a single purpose might be served by combining the results obtained from a range of different types of assessment. Furthermore, assessments may be carried out by many different agencies, from the teacher in the classroom to a committee mounting an international survey. [...]

Support of learning

Formative assessment

The importance of this function is expressed in the following passage from a USA author:

> ... the teacher has need of constant information about what the student knows and the strategies being used to process and comprehend new concepts ... By imbedding diagnostic instruction in instructional activities, teachers can preserve the integrity of assessment tasks (the wholeness of tasks and natural learning context) and protect instructional time that would otherwise be diverted to testing ... There is general agreement that external packaged tests will not solve the problem of what teachers need to know about student learning.
>
> (Shepard, 1992)

The issue is also emphasized, in a different way, in the following extract, ... from the TGAT report:

> Promoting children's learning is a principal aim of schools. Assessment lies at the heart of this process. It can provide a framework in which educational

objectives may be set, and pupils' progress charted and expressed. It can yield a basis for planning the next educational steps in response to children's needs. By facilitating dialogue between teachers, it can enhance professional skills and help the school as a whole to strengthen learning across the curriculum and throughout its age range. (DES, 1988)

Taken together, these extracts cover a number of different points about the uses of assessment to improve learning. Outstanding is the principle that feedback is essential to the conduct of effective teaching. No system, mechanical or social, can adjust and adapt as it performs its task without that frequent information about the operation of its system which is needed to modify the input in the light of the actual — rather than the intended or imagined — progress of the system. This is particularly important in any enterprise where the response may be very variable and unpredictable — which is surely true of most classrooms.

Effective teaching ought to vary in pace and style according to the needs of the learners. Teachers need to go slowly, or repeat what has been done, when difficulties of their pupils become apparent. They need also to differentiate their teaching as they collect evidence that some have grasped ideas and want to go ahead, whereas others are trapped in confusions so that they are unable to go ahead. Whilst some differentiation may be achieved by setting, which can be a matter for controversy, all agree that even within a group chosen on the basis of a particular band of achievements, there will be a wide range of understandings and of rates of progress. Teachers need sound information on which to base differentiation decisions, and insofar as remedial action can be taken, its efficacy also needs to be checked. Individualized learning schemes are set up on the extreme view that pupils may be so different that each has to work at his or her own pace. However, the outstanding characteristic of such schemes is that assessment of attainment becomes the keystone in determining the progress of each pupil's learning work.

Ideally, assessment should provide short term feedback so that obstacles can be identified and tackled. This is particularly important where the learning plan is such that progress with this week's work depends on a grasp of the ideas discussed last week. Such assessment is generally called **formative**. It is clear that formative assessment is the responsibility of the classroom teacher, but others, in the school or outside, can support such work by providing training and methods.

All formative assessment is to a degree diagnostic, and the term **diagnostic** assessment is also used. Although it is hard to distinguish diagnostic from formative by dictionary definitions, in practice the two are used with different emphases, even though their ranges of application overlap. Standardized tests, constructed and refined by experts, are often used in a school to help identify special and extreme learning difficulties. The need here is for expert precision because the learning problems might be both deep and general, so that the type of adjustment that can be made on the spot in a normal classroom cannot possibly meet the special need. Such tests are said to be diagnostic. Thus diagnostic assessment is an expert and detailed enquiry into underlying difficulties, and can lead to radical re-appraisal of a pupil's needs, whereas formative assessment is more superficial in assessing problems with particular classroom work, and can lead to short-term and local changes in the learning work of a pupil.

Curriculum, pedagogy and the formative function

Because formative assessment is intended as the feedback needed to make learning adaptive and thereby more effective, it cannot simply be added as an extra to an existing, non-interactive, scheme of work. The feedback procedures, and more particularly their use in varying the teaching and learning programme, have to be built into the teaching plans, which thereby will become both more flexible and more complex. This is emphasized very strongly by Linn (1989):

> ... the design of tests useful for the instructional decisions made in the classroom requires an integration of testing and instruction. It also requires a clear conception of the curriculum, the goals, and the process of instruction. And it requires a theory of instruction and learning and a much better understanding of the cognitive processes of learners.
>
> (p. 5)

This quotation opens up further issues. The teacher has to decide what to assess, and to interpret the pupil's work in terms of a need that might require attention. In one topic, the fact that a pupil has not yet grasped a particular idea might not matter, in that it will be encountered again later and until then that grasp will not be needed. In another topic, a particular understanding may be an essential basis for work in the immediate future, so that the pupils will be disabled unless the present difficulty can be dealt with now. Judgments about what can be left and about what has to be grasped now are rarely clear cut. Thus, the practice of formative assessment has to be informed by a model that is quite detailed, in that it has to provide some guidance about the ways in which a pupil might progress in learning, linked to a clear conception of the curriculum and its learning goals. The reactions against multiple choice testing [...] were in part driven by the realization that they could not give useful information in relationship to new models of learning.

A different issue is raised by the above quotation from the TGAT report in its use of the phrase 'by facilitating dialogue', which follows from the statement 'a framework in which ... and pupils' progress charted and expressed', and which leads to hopes for strengthening the whole work of the school. The formulation of a policy about learning, and interaction between teachers and others about the framing and implementation of such policy, requires a language in which learning aims and achievements can be discussed. Such language must be linked to concrete examples, both of pupils' achievements and of teachers' actions in learning, for without this it will be merely abstract and idealistic with little practical effect. Formative assessment should provide those examples, develop this language, and enrich and so give meaning to the shared understanding of ideas and policies about learning.

All of these arguments should make clear that the improvement of formative assessment is a complex enterprise, yet one which should be at the heart of any policy which aims to improve pupils' learning, and which will also be at the heart of the enterprise of classroom teaching. It would be optimistic to assume that teachers usually have sound information about the progress of their pupils' learning — the evidence is that this is far from being the case. Many practical issues also arise, concerned with the collection, analysis, recording and interpretation of data for formative assessment and with the adaptations of classroom practice that may have to ensue. [...]

Certification, progress and transfer

Summative assessment within a school

Whenever pupils move so that responsibility for their learning is transferred from one teacher to another, information should also be transferred so that the new teacher can plan work and guide each pupil appropriately. The information needed for this purpose will depend on how the work in the new class is related to the old. If there is close continuity, then the formative information about recent progress and immediate needs that the old teacher would have needed is also needed by the new.

However, the new teacher might also need an overview of each pupil's recent achievements and progress in order to be able to anticipate the progress and needs of each, which might affect the organization of the new classroom and the distribution of learning tasks. If the new work is very different from the old, for example if it involves a fresh start in which the subject is tackled afresh at a more sophisticated level than hitherto, then here again the information needed is more general — an overview of the pupil's earlier achievement which might help predict capacity to profit from the new learning programme.

Thus, on transfer the need for **summative** assessment arises. The term implies an overview of previous learning. This could be obtained by an accumulation of evidence collected over time, or by test procedures applied at the end of the previous phase which covered the whole area of the previous learning. Beneath the key phrases here, 'accumulation' or 'covered', lies the problem of selecting that information which is most relevant for the summative purpose. The principles of selection might depend on one's beliefs about what matters for the next phase of learning in the subject (and might therefore differ between different curriculum subjects) and might also depend on the particular transition that is involved.

As argued above, for transfer between classes in the same school, with a high degree of continuity, the difference between assessment for the formative purpose and for the summative might be rather small. Indeed, within the work of one year group, a teacher might gather formative evidence and supplement it with a comprehensive test in order to review and to decide on structural changes — for example to change the grouping of pupils. This might be seen as a weak form of summative assessment, happening quite frequently, and there would be a close link, and a difference of degree rather than of kind, between the teacher's formative and summative work.

However, transfer between different stages of schooling and between different teachers imposes new requirements. If it is to be an effective communication, the assessment information has to be formulated with a structure and a language that reflects a shared understanding between those who are communicating. It will not be enough that the two teachers communicating are working to a common scheme of work. It will be necessary also that the information satisfies three further criteria:

- It has to be adequately detailed. To say that a pupil has a grade C in science may convey little: a profile which showed any variations in this grade between (say) practical investigative work, learning of facts, and tackling of numerical problems would be far more useful.
- The two teachers have to be working to common criteria for grading. Given a report by a pupil on a practical investigation, one of the teachers might have given it a B and the other a D because they worked to different criteria — one teacher giving priority to orderly structure and clarity of expression in a report, the other to the quality of scientific thinking revealed in the investigation design and in the interpretation of the results.
- There should also be a shared procedure for determining standards of grading. Two teachers could be using the same criteria but have different standards for interpretation of the conventional grades in terms of marks — a decision by one to give (say) a B grade might be seen by the other as far too generous.

Transfer between and out of schools

These problems are more difficult to overcome if a summative assessment is to help guide the transfer of pupils between institutions — for example, between primary and secondary school, or from secondary school to a sixth-form college. Communication of criteria and standards will be less informal, so more priority has to be given to clear and agreed documentation. In addition, for each of the examples mentioned, several different schools will be sending pupils to the same higher institution. Unless these schools are working to common schemes and produce assessments on a shared basis the summative assessment information will be worthless. Thus, either different schools have to cooperate closely and accept constraints on their freedom to work in their own ways, or curricula and assessment have to be formally established and operated by external agencies. This is one of many examples where each school's own desire for its freedom of manoeuvre has to be reconciled with constraints which can be justified by the broader needs of their pupils.

Transfer to a new type of school can place a pupil in a very different type of learning environment. It will then be more difficult to predict, on the basis of previous achievements, how that pupil will progress in the new school. Ideally, the success of primary schools in predicting secondary progress ought to be investigated by monitoring the secondary school progress, so that their summative assessments can be improved. A great deal of such analysis used to be carried out when an examination at 11 (the 'eleven-plus') was widely used in England and Wales to determine the type of secondary school to which a pupil was to be directed. This analysis was used to modify procedures for interpreting the test — and school assessment — data to maximize the efficiency of prediction.

Such considerations also bear on the large discontinuities involved when pupils move either out of school into employment, or to further and more advanced study, whether at ages 16, or 18, or on completion of an undergraduate degree course. Here there may be very little direct link between the learning work, which might be the subject for any assessment and the future needs. The issue is further complicated because these future needs may be very diverse, ranging over various types and levels of further education and over many different types of employment. It is clearly almost impossible to imagine that a single grade can give information useful for all these purposes.

A set of grades obtained over several subjects may be a better guide. If, within each subject, the results were a profile reflecting success in meeting different types of demand, the user would have an even better chance of looking selectively at what was needed for his purpose. It might help to add to this information quite different assessments cutting across the boundaries of school subjects; possible assessments of so-called 'core skills' and assessments of personality characteristics are possible additions here. Overall, the need is for multi-dimensional data, but whilst such complexity can guard against simplistic judgments, it can also make demands on those using the information to study and understand its structure and its terminology, and also to keep up with the inevitable frequent changes.

Within this context, public examinations can be considered in relation to their function of certificating individuals. As will be discussed below, such examinations also have a function in judging teachers and schools for accountability purposes. In the UK, the national curriculum tests for ages 7, 11 and 14, the General Certificate for Secondary Education (GCSE); the Advanced-level (A-level), the National Vocational Qualifications (NVQ) and many others for older school pupils, and university degree examinations, are all in this category. These examinations are clearly summative, but they may also contribute to teachers' formative work, by helping each teacher to check standards and by providing good examples of assessment tasks. In principle, such certification systems can use teacher assessments as part of their evidence. In some countries, the responsibilities are left entirely in the hands of teachers, in others teachers' judgments play no part. In most countries, external and school based assessments are combined in a variety of ways. [. . .]

Overall issues

The certification purpose of assessment raises three main issues:

- The assessment has to be as effective as possible in relation to its purpose. Here, the precise requirements can differ a great deal across this category — from transfer between infants and juniors at age 7 to the transition to employment of a university student on graduation. Each transfer requires its own methods, and what is generally lacking is research data, on the relationship between assessment results and subsequent attainments, which could be used to improve those methods.
- There have to be choices about who is to control the process and who is to carry it out. Here are included choices about the local or national control and about whether this control is general and flexible or close and detailed. Closely linked to such choices is the assignment of responsibility to teachers and schools, or to external agencies, or to a combination of these.
- Decisions have to take account of the costs implied. The cost of public examinations is a significant item in the budgets of secondary schools, and for all schools summative assessments which have to work to shared external standards bear a high cost in terms of the time of classroom teachers and of school managements.

Accountability

Accountability and test results

Schools have a responsibility to the public who fund them. One aspect of the discharge of that responsibility is to provide evidence that they are indeed promoting the learning of their pupils. An economical way to do this is to provide aggregation of the results of their pupils' performance in the various public examination systems which their pupils have to take for their own personal needs — i.e. those discussed in the previous section.

Assessment data will have to be detailed if they are to be a useful guide. However, such data on their own cannot provide valid guidance. A school working with pupils of poor educational background in an area of social deprivation where parental support is limited may be producing results which are below a national average but which, in the circumstances of that school, represent an outstanding achievement. Thus, data on the achievements on intake of the pupils, and on the catchment area and the pupils' home backgrounds, will also have to be considered in making any judgment or taking any action on assessment results. More generally, a wide range of data are needed if the achievements of the pupils in any one school are to be interpreted.

This is not to say that poor outcomes and real needs are to be hidden by some form of manipulation. Distinctions have to be made here — again in relation to the purpose for which the information is to be used. If the poor results of a school can be shown to be related to a low budget and to large class sizes, the policy guidance is that action has to be taken on the resource determinants. If the performance and careers of the teachers in that school are to be judged, then allowance has to be made in the light of the factors which constrain them. If a parent has to decide whether or not to send her child to that school, then the judgment involves different considerations again. An alternative school may produce much better results, but if it also has a very favourable intake, it could be that for a given pupil of average attainment, that school may not do as well for that pupil as one which appears to have less impressive test results.

There has been much controversy about whether or not it is fair to publish school test results in 'league tables'. The justification that they can guide parental choice is a weak one, insofar as comparisons made without allowance for the many features which affect the results can be misleading and so lead to inappropriate choices. Many have argued that it would be fairer to schools and more helpful to parents to publish 'value-added' data, comparing intake test results with later attainments. However, a school's circumstances can affect its pupils' capacity to make progress as well as their starting points. Such complications will not be pursued further here — the general problems of judging school effectiveness raise issues beyond the scope of this book (see Gray, 1996).

Helping schools to improve

It may be natural to think of comparisons, but the public interest ought also to focus on whether certain agreed standards have been reached. Here the question of uniformity of assessments across schools becomes important. The detail and multidimensionality of reporting will also matter if the assessment is to indicate where the particular strengths and weaknesses of each school may lie. This last point raises the larger question of how those responsible for schools may act on the information about their work that assessment results may provide.

However, this question implies two assumptions. The first is that the assessment data are suitable for this purpose. For example, if a particular set of primary schools adjust their summative reporting to meet needs agreed with a particular secondary school, these reports may not be comparable with those in another district, even in the same urban area, so that comparisons cannot be made. Similarly, where the demands of local employment are quite specific, the adjustment of information to meet the needs of the local community may be in tension with a demand for uniform standards and for comparison with other schools.

Problems of interpreting results for policy purposes can arise within a school. Most secondary schools undertake careful examination of GCSE and A-level results. Such reviews can be helped by data on the average performances over the country in each particular subject and, where entry to a given subject examination is limited because it is a matter for optional choice, by comparisons of the general attainment of those pupils who enter for that particular subject. Because there can be quite marked differences between the entry groups for different subjects — some, for example, attracting the more capable, or repelling all but the most capable and committed, comparisons of performances between one subject and another have to be made with care, whether they are to apply at the level of school departments or nationally (see Fitzgibbon, 1996). Comparisons in relation to national assessment can be helped again by national data, both for test results as a whole and at the level of individual items. (Software for this purpose has been produced by the UK School Curriculum Assessment Authority.)

Sampling surveys

Another way in which assessments which might inform policy can differ from those for individual certification lies in the possibilities of sampling. To produce an overall picture of a nation's performance, it is not necessary to test every pupil within a given age group. The APU in the UK, for example, tested only about 2 per cent of each of three age groups. Moreover, even that gave sample sizes of about 12 000 for each test, whereas for any one set of questions it could be shown that a sample of about 500, if carefully distributed over different types of school and different regions, could give an adequately stable average. What was in fact done was to give about thirty different sets of questions to different selected sets of pupils. This made it possible for the surveys to explore a wider range of attainments in greater detail than would be possible with a test which would have to be the same for every pupil. In consequence, the data obtained were far richer, far more interesting and useful to teachers, and have been more relevant to policy debates than public examination data have ever been, or than the national assessment test data are proving to be (Black, 1990; Gipps and Stobart, 1993, pp. 34–36, 40–42). This approach, of giving different tests to different and restricted samples to enhance the value of the data, is known as **matrix light sampling**. It has been used in several countries, notably the USA, Australia and New Zealand, as well as in the UK's APU surveys. The issues here bear on the content and construct validity of assessment results. [. . .]

If the accountability to be secured is that of individual schools, it might still be possible to produce information that is less costly and more informative by giving different tests to different samples of pupils rather than by giving them all the same test. However, this could only be the case for large schools where any one age cohort would be large enough for the purpose.

Interactions between purposes

The choices which will distinguish or adapt assessments to their purposes may be made at several levels:

- At the outset, the particular set of test items or procedures may be chosen to fit to the purpose.
- Then the way in which these are administered and marked may differ according to the purpose.
- The ways in which the outcomes may be analysed or combined could also vary with the purpose.
- Finally, a particular purpose may require its own specific interpretation of that assessment data.

The three elements to be addressed here are assessment methods, assessment agencies and the purposes. One testing method carried out by a single agency might serve more than one purpose and would thereby be economical. If on the other hand, the methods to be used for different purposes have to be completely different, or the interests of different agencies are in tension or even opposed, then separation is required.

Certification with accountability

One example is the possibility that tests given to all pupils for the certification purpose could provide all that is needed for the accountability purpose. Most of the arguments which bear on this possibility have been touched upon in the previous section in the discussion of sampling surveys. Sample surveys can provide better quality information at lower costs than the certification tests for every pupil, but if the certification test for all is a priority and has to be used, then the sampling survey comes as extra expense. The cost is not only financial. External assessments create work for teachers whilst making it more difficult for them to get on with their normal tasks. Thus, it was understandable, although regrettable, that with the coming of national testing for all at 7, 11, and 14 in the UK, the national surveys of the APU were discontinued in spite of the loss of the detailed information that the surveys alone could provide. Here it can be seen that the two purposes are in tension, so that to give priority to the one is to reduce a system's capacity to serve the other.

Formative with summative

A second and more notable example is the possibility that assessment by teachers might serve both the formative and summative purposes for their pupils and so remove the need for operation of separate agencies and procedures to serve the certification purpose. Some have laid stress on the differences between the formative and summative purposes, and have argued that the assessment instruments and procedures needed for the one are so different from those for the other that neither can flourish without clear separation. On the other side, it can be argued that the two functions are two ends of the same spectrum and that there is no sharp difference, and that if the two functions are separated, then teachers' assessment work will be devalued. [. . .]

Purposes in tension?

More will be said about these tensions in later chapters, for they raise more extensive technical arguments, whilst also moving into issues which are matters of public and political priority. What should be clear is that, in this second example as in the first, the two purposes are in tension. The time and effort needed by teachers if they were to bear the whole of the certification role would be extensive and might make it harder for them to develop and implement improved formative assessment. On the other hand, where very important decisions are based on wholly external tests, both pupils and teachers have to direct their work to meet the narrow range of demands which economical external testing can provide — and the model of teachers' own assessment inevitably becomes one of using examples of the external tests to train pupils, thereby weakening teachers' own formative assessment practices.

Whilst some degree of tension is inevitable, there can also be synergy. Instruments developed and trialled carefully by experts for certification and accountability exercises can be used by teachers to enrich their own range of questions used for the formative work. The work a teacher might have to do with peers to ensure common external standards when contributing to a certification process directed by an outside agency might well help that teacher towards a better appreciation of the aims and standards to which she should be working in her own formative assessment.

Summary

* The three main purposes of assessment are
  - formative, to aid learning,
  - summative for review, transfer and certification, and
  - summative for accountability to the public.

- The practice of formative assessment must be closely integrated with curriculum and pedagogy and is central to good quality teaching.
- The formative and summative labels describe two ends of a spectrum of practice in school-based assessment rather than two isolated and completely different functions.
- There are different levels of summative activity; summing up may be needed:
  - during the progress of work in one class,
  - on transfer between classes in a school,
  - for transfer between two schools, or between school and employment or further and higher education.
- The results of assessment and testing for accountability should:
  - be related to common criteria and standards,
  - be linked with comprehensive and detailed data on the schools intake and context, for otherwise the data will be unfair and misleading,
  - be designed and communicated so that they can serve the improvement of schools,
- Sample surveys may be a more efficient way of informing policy for the improvement of learning than blanket testing of all pupils.
- There are tensions between the different purposes of assessment and testing, which are often difficult to resolve, and which involve choices of the best agencies to conduct assessments and of the optimum instruments and appropriate interpretations to serve each purpose.

Bibliography

Airasian, P.W. (1991) *Classroom Assessment*, New York: McGraw Hill. Chapter 1.
Gipps, C.V. (1994) *Beyond Testing: Towards a Theory of Educational Assessment*, London: Falmer. Chapter 3.
Gipps, C. and Stobart, G. (1993) *Assessment. A Teachers' Guide to the Issues*, London: Hodder and Stoughton. Chapter 2.
Salvia, J. and Ysseldyke, J.E. (1991) *Assessment*, Boston: Houghton Mifflin. Chapter 1.
Stiggins, R.J. (1994) *Student-Centered Classroom Assessment*, New York: Merrill/Macmillan. Chapters 3 and 4.
Wood, R. (1991) *Assessment and Testing*, Cambridge: Cambridge University Press. Chapters 8 (diagnostic assessment), 17 (aptitude testing) and 18 (personnel selection and assessment).

References

Black, P.J. (1990) 'APU science – the past and the future', *School Science Review*, 72, 258, pp. 13–28,
Department of Education and Science (DES) (1988) *National Curriculum: Task Group on Assessment and Testing: A Report*, London: Department of Education and Science.
Fitzgibbon, C.T. (1996) *Monitoring Education: Indicators, Quality and Effectiveness*, London: Cassell.
Gifford, B.R. and O'Connor, M.C. (eds) (1992) *Changing Assessments: Alternative Views of Aptitude, Achievement and Instruction*, Boston and Dordrecht: Kluwer.
Gipps, C. and Stobart, G. (1993) *Assessment. A Teachers' Guide to the Issues*, London: Hodder and Stoughton.
Goldstein, H. and Lewis, T. (eds) (1996) *Assessment: Problems, Developments and Statistical Issues*, Chichester and New York: John Wiley.
Gray, J. (1996) 'The use of assessment to compare institutions', in Goldstein, H. and Lewis, T. (eds) *Assessment. Problems, Developments and Statistical Issues*, Chichester and New York: John Wiley, pp. 121–33.

Linn, R.L. (1989) 'Current perspectives and future directions', in Linn, R.L. (ed.) *Educational Measurement*, 3rd edn., London: Collier Macmillan, pp. 1–10.

Shephard, L.A. (1992) 'Commentary: What policy makers who mandate tests should know about the new psychology of intellectual ability and learning', in Gifford, B.R. and O'Connor, M.C. (eds) *Changing Assessments: Alternative Views of Aptitude, Achievement and Instruction*, Boston and Dordrecht: Kluwer, pp. 301–28.

PART IV

SOME INITIATIVES FROM WITHIN SCIENCE EDUCATION

EDITOR'S INTRODUCTION

This Part includes some of the ideas for the future of science education that have recently come from the community of science education researchers and curriculum developers.

In Chapter 11, Hodson sets out a radical agenda for science education that is designed to address the ills from which it currently suffers. He starts by reviewing the trends in the science curriculum over recent decades and notes that, in broad terms, they have not met the ambitions of their advocates. He then analyses what he sees to be the essential conflict looming within education in general and science education in particular: that which I summarise as being between 'education for a corporate state' and 'education for democracy'. In advocating a sharp shift towards science education for democracy ('science education for citizenship'), he sees four desirable trends. First, the evolution of 'science, technology, society and environment' courses. Second, more emphasis on the affective aspects in science education (see also Chapter 4). Third, a greater emphasis on informal education. Fourth, and perhaps most importantly, the explicit pursuit of 'political literacy', through the adoption of real-world, issue-based, context-centred, approaches to curriculum construction. He then sets out a convincing argument for the structure of and elements to be included in such a curriculum. Finally, Hodson reviews the inevitable barriers to change that will be met.

Questions for you to address might include:

- How long do you think 'normal science education', as currently practised globally, can survive?
- To what extent do you think that a greater emphasis on 'science education for citizenship' is called for in your nation-state?
- What challenges might the average science teacher meet in trying to implement a real-world, issue-based, context-centred, science curriculum?
- How could these challenges be met?

This theme of 'science education for citizenship' is carried forward in Chapter 12, in which Gough looks at the currently uneasy relationship between science education and environmental education. She portrays the range of curricular arrangements between the two and uses case study material from Australia to show that the aims of neither are being met satisfactorily. She goes on to advocate a reappraisal of both – the ideas about science education echo those of Hodson – while pointing to the gains that would ensue if the project is carried through. As I put it, for science education the issue is 'change or the curriculum perishes'; for environmental education the issue is 'change or we all may physically perish'.

Questions for you to address might include:

- What would have to change in science education, as currently practised, to accommodate environmental education?
- What would have to change in environmental education, as currently practised, to accommodate science education?
- What are the curricular consequences if these changes do not take place?
- What might the curricular consequences be if these changes do take place?

CHAPTER 11

TIME FOR ACTION

Science education for an alternative future

Derek Hodson

International Journal of Science Education (2003) 25(6), 645–70

Then and now

The shifting emphases of science education debate over the past 30–40 years are clearly reflected in the numerous slogans and rallying calls that have gained prominence, including 'Being a Scientist for a Day' (from the early Nuffield science projects in the United Kingdom), 'Learning by Doing', 'Process, not Product', 'Science for All', 'Less is More', 'Children Making Sense of the World' and 'Science as a Way of Knowing'. From the early 1990s onwards, much debate has centred on another slogan: the notion of 'Scientific Literacy' and how to achieve it – a debate that shows little sign of slowing down or reaching resolution.

Although the attainment of scientific literacy has been almost universally welcomed as a desirable goal, there is still little clarity about its meaning (Jenkins, 1990; Eisenhart, Finkel & Marion, 1996; Galbraith, Carss, Grice, Endean & Warry, 1997; DeBoer 2000; Kolsto 2000; Laugksch 2000; Tippens, Nichols & Bryan, 2000) and little agreement about precisely what it means in terms of curriculum provision. While some see scientific literacy as the capacity to read newspaper and magazine articles about scientific and technological matters with a reasonable level of understanding, others see it as being in possession the knowledge, skills and attitudes essential to a career as a professional scientist, engineer or technician. While some argue for a broadening of the knowledge base of the science curriculum to include greater consideration of the interactions among science, technology and society (the STS emphasis), others urge curriculum decision makers to concentrate on the knowledge and skills deemed (by some) to be essential to continued economic growth and effective competition within the global marketplace. If it is correct that most people obtain their knowledge of contemporary science and technology from television and newspapers (National Science Board, 1998; Select Committee, 2000), then the capacity for active critical engagement with text is not only a crucial element of scientific literacy, it is perhaps the *fundamental* element. In that sense, education for scientific literacy has striking parallels with education in the language arts (Hewson, 2002; Norris & Phillips, in press). But what else should be regarded as crucial? Understanding the nature of science? Knowledge of the major theoretical frameworks of biology, chemistry and physics, and their historical development? Awareness of the applications of science? Ability to use science in everyday problem solving?

In one early attempt at clarification, Pella, O'Hearn and Gale (1966) suggested that scientific literacy comprises an understanding of the basic concepts of science, the nature of science, the ethics that control the scientist in his [sic] work, the inter-relationships of science and society, the interrelationships of science and the humanities, and the differences between science and technology. A quarter century later, *Science for All Americans* (American Association for the Advancement of Science (AAAS), 1989, p. 4) defined a scientifically literate person as

> one who is aware that science, mathematics, and technology are interdependent human enterprises with strengths and limitations; understands key concepts and principles of science; is familiar with the natural world and recognizes both its diversity and unity; and uses scientific knowledge and scientific ways of thinking for individual and social purposes.

More recently, the Organization for Economic Cooperation and Development's (OECD) Programme for International Student Achievement (PISA) proposed that a scientifically literate person is

> able to combine science knowledge with the ability to draw evidence-based conclusions in order to understand and help make decisions about the natural world and the changes made to it through human activity.
>
> (OECD, 1998, p. 5)

There are strong echoes here of Arons' (1983) emphasis on the ability to

> discriminate, on the one hand, between acceptance of asserted and unverified end results, models, or conclusions, and on the other, understand their basis and origin; that is, to recognize when questions such as 'How do we know?' 'Why do we believe it?' 'What is the evidence for it?' have been addressed, answered, and understood, and when something is being taken on faith.
>
> (p. 93)

Similar capabilities have sometimes been included in the notion of *intellectual independence* (Munby, 1980; Aikenhead, 1990; Norris, 1997). Without such capabilities, citizens are 'easy prey to dogmatists, flimflam artists, and purveyors of simple solutions to complex problems' (AAAS, 1989, p. 13) – including, one might add, some otherwise respectable scientists, politicians and commentators, who intimidate through their facility in a mode of discourse unfamiliar to many citizens.

Running alongside this debate about the goals of science education and the curriculum content required to achieve them has been a parallel debate about the design and implementation of better teaching and learning methods. While there have been some dissenters, it is probably fair to say that the dominant psychological influence on the science curriculum during the 25 years that *IJSE* has been published has been the constructivist view of learning and the pedagogy that is claimed to derive from it. Indeed, in many parts of the world, the promotion and acceptance of constructivism is such that it now has the characteristics of a 'new orthodoxy' of science education (Fensham, 1992), despite some strenuous criticisms that it neglects the rationality of science (Matthews, 1993) and over-emphasizes the rationality of learning (West & Pines, 1983). This latter point is of crucial significance because it leads directly to arguments for a greatly enhanced role for the affective and social dimensions of learning. Much attention in recent years has also been directed towards the development of more effective laboratory work and more extensive use of fieldwork (Wellington, 1998), and efforts to integrate formal classroom-based teaching with informal learning (museums, science centres, etc) and various forms of community-based learning (Helms, 1998; Pedretti, 2002).

During this same period, our views about science itself have undergone substantial revision. Recent scholarship in the history, philosophy and sociology of science has effected a major shift from the view that scientific knowledge is universal, coherent, objective and unproblematic towards recognition that it is sometimes uncertain, contentious and unable to provide clear, unambiguous answers to many important questions. There is increasing recognition among science educators that science is a product of its time and place, inextricably linked with its sociocultural and institutional location, and profoundly influenced by its methods of generation and validation.

In reflecting on the impact of these slogans, trends and movements in science education, there is much cause for satisfaction. The Science for All movement has led to a broadening of the student population exposed to science in the later years of schooling. There is also more science in the curriculum of primary (elementary) school than ever before. The STS movement has ensured some broadening of the scope of science education and, to some extent, has broadened the conception of science itself. Students now study something about the ways in which scientists work and the methods by which knowledge is created and validated. There is increasing recognition of the need to look at the wider social, political, economic and ethical issues that surround the practice of science. While issues of inequity related to gender and ethnicity have not always been solved, at least they have been raised. Teaching and learning methods have been extended in interesting new directions: there is now much less emphasis on the acquisition of factual knowledge via direct instruction and correspondingly greater emphasis on active learning; there are more opportunities for students to engage in their own scientific investigations; teachers are beginning to use assessment and evaluation practices inspired by notions of authentic assessment, performance-based assessment and educative assessment.

However, while much has been achieved, there is still considerable cause for concern. Many students still do not learn much of what we intend: their scientific knowledge and their capacity to use that knowledge effectively and purposefully fall well short of our intentions; their understanding of the nature and methods of science are often incoherent, distorted and confused. The motivation for science that is so apparent in the early years of schooling often dissipates as students progress through secondary school, leading many to drop out of science at the earliest opportunity. In many educational jurisdictions, the imposition of strict new assessment regimes have led to the absurd situation in which teachers seem to spend almost as much time measuring student competence in science as they do in developing it.

What of the future?

While we can be certain that the curriculum will change over the next 25 years, perhaps only a fool would attempt to predict the directions of that change. Nonetheless, we can identify some of the many factors that will drive that change, including the changing nature of society and the expectations that society has for education (and for science and technology education in particular), increasing ethnic diversity of the school population, rapid advances in science and technology, changes in our understanding of how students acquire and develop complex scientific understanding, increased awareness of the significance of the affective and social dimensions of learning, the impact of new technologies on classroom practice, shifts in the relative influence afforded to different stakeholders in education (students, parents, teachers, scientists, business interests), and so on.

While it may be unwise to predict, we may still choose to speculate on possibilities, or, the more usual province of university-based science educators, advocate particular changes. The proposals I outline in this chapter are located in some discernible trends: principally, the broadening conception of STS to include environmental education (STS becomes STSE), extending the definition of scientific literacy to encompass a measure of political literacy, prioritizing the affective, and making much greater use of informal and community-based learning opportunities. More importantly, perhaps, the proposals are driven by a commitment to address the social, cultural and environmental 'fallout' from the current North American concern to link business interests, economic growth and scientific literacy.

First, an observation: in previous generations, we have been able to predict the kind of knowledge, skills and attitudes that students currently in school would need for a lifetime of employment. Now, for the first time in history, we are educating students for life in a world about which we know very little, except that it will be characterized by substantial and rapid change, and is likely to be more complex and uncertain than today's world. For some, this is an exciting prospect; for others, it is profoundly disconcerting, even frightening. The question I pose is: 'What kind of science education is appropriate as preparation for this relatively unknown world?' It is important to emphasize that the concerns and proposals discussed in this chapter relate to science education in Western, industrialized societies. While many similar general concerns arise for science education in the developing world, the specific local matters that usually take precedence are outside the scope of the chapter.

We live in a very different world from the world of 1978. In the quarter century since issue 1 of *IJSE* appeared, science has lost much of the innocence and purity afforded to it by the creators of the major curriculum advances of the 1960s – PSSC, *Chem Study* and BSCS in the United States, and the various Nuffield and Schools Council courses in the UK. A succession of human and environmental tragedies have sometimes cast science in the role of villain; disturbing social changes and deep ethical concerns arising from scientific and technological innovations have caused science to be viewed by many as a potential threat to familiar and comfortable ways of life; the increasing commercialization, industrialization and militarization of science have shown once and for all that science is not value-free and disinterested. The merger of science and technology into technoscience, the appropriation of the knowledge-making capacity of science to promote the interests of the rich and powerful, and the usurping of the scientific and technological endeavour for the goal of ever-increasing levels of material consumption, have profoundly changed the sociopolitical and moral-ethical contexts of scientific and technological practice. To what extent has the school science curriculum responded to these changes? To what extent have curriculum makers addressed the level of cynicism and disaffection for science and technology created by these changes, with its adverse impact on enrolment in science and engineering?

The principal response, of course, has been the development of STS courses (Solomon & Aikenhead, 1994; Yager, 1996). However, while there have been some notable successes, STS materials have often

> lacked an adequate theoretical foundation and have served a limited, if valuable, function of supporting and enriching otherwise conventional school science courses.
>
> (Jenkins, 2002, p. 19)

School science courses, especially in the later years, continue to be dominated by the basic disciplines of physics, chemistry and biology. There is very little in the way of integration and, in many countries, scant attention given to the earth sciences and environmental science. Consequently, in 1997 and 1998, the Nuffield Foundation funded a series of 'closed seminars' and 'open meetings' of science educators in an attempt to formulate a more comprehensive vision of science education and what it can and should achieve, The Report, *Beyond 2000: Science Education for the Future* (Millar & Osborne, 1998), concludes that the National Curriculum for England and Wales has failed to meet the needs of contemporary society, much less anticipated the needs of future society. The authors acknowledge that

> the changing curricular position of science has not been accompanied by corresponding change in the *content* of the science curriculum ... This has remained fundamentally unaltered and is, essentially, a diluted form of the 1960s GCE curriculum,
>
> (p. 4)

that is, an abstract, academic curriculum. Among the ten recommendations for change is the proposal that scientific knowledge be presented as a number of 'explanatory stories' – '*inter-related sets of ideas* which, taken together, provide a framework for understanding an area of experience' (p. 13, emphasis in original). There should be more emphasis on technology and the applications of science; greater attention should be given to the social processes used to generate, test and scrutinize knowledge claims; teachers should employ a wider range of teaching and learning approaches, including the use of case studies of historical and current issues; new and broader approaches to assessment should be devised and implemented in order to focus attention on the more important aspects of learning. Throughout the document, the case for the importance of scientific literacy (largely defined in terms of conceptual and methodological knowledge, with some sociocultural dimensions) is strongly and repeatedly made, thus reinforcing the view of some critics that this is yet another attempt to rescue a conventional science education in crisis rather than a commitment to radically reshape the nature and purpose of the curriculum.

> Our view is that the primary and explicit aim of the 5–16 science curriculum should be to provide a course which can enhance 'scientific literacy', as this is necessary for all young people growing up in our society, whatever their career aspirations or aptitudes ... school science education should aim to produce a populace who are comfortable, competent and confident with scientific and technical matters and artefacts. The science curriculum should provide sufficient scientific knowledge and understanding to enable students to read simple newspaper articles about science, and to follow TV programmes on new advances in science with interest. Such an education should enable them to express an opinion on important social and ethical issues with which they will increasingly be confronted. It will also form a viable basis, should the need arise, for retraining in work related to science or technology in their later careers.
>
> (Millar & Osborne, 1998, p. 9)

In his highly provocative work, *The Myth of Scientific Literacy*, Shamos (1995) argued that the pursuit of universal scientific literacy is a futile goal because its elements (as briefly outlined in documents such as *Beyond 2000* and *Science For All Americans*) are so wide ranging that they cannot be achieved – and certainly not for everyone. Moreover, he declared, scientific literacy in any of the senses relating to science content isn't necessary anyway. Most people can get along perfectly well without scientific knowledge or can easily access it when the need arises. Indeed, many people who are otherwise successful in their lives proudly proclaim their ignorance of, and lack of interest in, science. After all, many people use VCRs, drive cars and deploy computers with little or no understanding of the science that underpins their manufacture and operation. Perhaps the consequence of life as an 'ignorant consumer' is precisely why we need to ensure universal scientific literacy, though I have much sympathy for Layton, Jenkins, MacGill & Davey (1993) when they describe a very different kind of scientific literacy, what they call 'practical knowledge in action'. The science needed for solving the problems of everyday life, they argue, is very different in form from that presented via the school curriculum. This strand of argument has prompted Peter Fensham (2002) to state that it is 'time to change drivers for scientific literacy' and to abandon the traditional ways of identifying science content knowledge for the school curriculum. More in line with Fensham's recommendation would be a curriculum designed in accordance with the findings described by Law (2002) arising from a study in which she and her co-researchers asked leading scientists, health care professionals, local government representatives, managers and personnel officers in manufacturing industry, and the like, about the kind of science and the kind of personal attributes and skills that are of most value in persons employed in their field of expertise.

In speculating about or advocating for the future school science curriculum, there are two questions to consider. First, 'Is scientific literacy necessary?' Second, 'Is it sufficient?' Perhaps life in the 21st century will demand higher levels of scientific literacy than were previously required of citizens. Perhaps not. What is clear is that ordinary citizens will increasingly be asked to make judgements about matters underpinned by science knowledge or technological capability, but overlaid with much wider considerations. Those without a basic understanding of the ways in which science and technology are impacted by, and impact upon, the physical and the sociopolitical environment will be effectively disempowered and susceptible to being seriously misled in exercising their rights within a democratic, technologically-dependent society. It is this concern for the vulnerability of the scientifically illiterate to the blandishments of politicians and corporate advertizing that leads directly to my next consideration: the social, cultural and environmental 'fallout' from the current drive to link business interests, economic growth and scientific literacy.

Corporatism versus democracy?

In recent years, the economic argument for scientific literacy has become the predominant one in North America. It is both powerful and persuasive, as illustrated by the Government of Canada's (1991) attempt to establish a link between school science education and a culture of lifelong learning as the key to the country's prosperity.

> Our future prosperity will depend on our ability to respond creatively to the opportunities and challenges posed by rapid change in fields such as information technologies, new materials, biotechnologies and telecommunications . . . To meet the challenges of a technologically driven economy, we must not only upgrade the skills of our work force, we must also foster a lifelong learning culture to encourage the continuous learning needed in an environment of constant change.
>
> (Government of Canada, 1991, pp. 12, 14)

The power of a particular discourse is located in the ways in which it determines how we think about society and our relations with others, and in its impact on how we act in the world. Lankshear, Gee and Hull (1996) use the term *fast capitalist texts* to describe the business and management books, company policy documents and media pronouncements which have now become mainstream popular cultural interpretations of the 'proper' nature of work and commerce in newspapers, magazines, radio and television. Language has been transformed by industry and corporate business leaders into a sociotechnical device capable of creating and sustaining new social relationships between managers and workers, and imposing particular capitalist values on workers. In other words, transnational businesses have created and sustained a discourse that serves their immediate and future needs, and have extended this discourse to schools and the education system. In order to design, develop, optimize, produce and market goods and services for the global marketplace, industry claims to need a flexible, 'just-in-time' and compliant workforce, which it is the education system's job to provide. Seemingly, at least in Ontario, the corporate world has been successful in exerting its will on the school curriculum, as witness this statement from the Ministry of Education and Training (2000, p. 3):

> The new Ontario curriculum establishes high, internationally competitive standards of education for secondary school students across the province. The curriculum has been designed with the goal of ensuring that graduates from Ontario secondary schools are well prepared to lead satisfying and productive lives as both citizens and individuals, and to compete successfully in a global economy and a rapidly changing world.

The pressures exerted by business and industry on schools to provide more 'job ready' people can be seen as part of an overt sociotechnical engineering practice in which new capitalism is creating 'new kinds of people by changing not just their overt viewpoints but their actual practices' (Lankshear *et al.* 1996, p. 22). It is reengineering people in its own image! Indeed, there are many who view these developments as symptomatic of a dangerous trend, both for individuals and for society as a whole, part of what Bencze (2001) calls

> an *apprenticeship for consumership* – that is, creation of a large mass of . . . citizens who simultaneously serve as loyal workers and voracious, unquestioning consumers.
>
> (p. 350)

In similar vein, Apple (1993) states that in this new economy-driven educational climate, students are no longer seen as people who will participate in the struggle to build and rebuild the social, educational, political and economic future, but as consumers; freedom is

> no longer defined as participating in building the common good, but as living in an unfettered commercial market, with the education system . . . integrated into the mechanisms of such a market.
>
> (p. 116)

When school presents students, almost daily, with a language that promotes economic globalization, increasing production and unlimited expansion, identifies technology with unfettered 'progress', work with money and excellence with competition and 'winning at any cost', it is implicated in the manufacture and maintenance of what Bowers calls the *myths of modernity*:

that the plenitude of consumer goods and technological innovation is limited only by people's ability to spend, that the *individual* is the basic social unit ... and that science and technology are continually expanding humankind's ability to predict and control their own destiny.

(Bowers, 1996, p. 5, emphasis added)

At risk here are the freedoms of individuals, the spiritual well-being of particular societies, and the very future of the planet. In Edmund O'Sullivan's (1999, p. 27) words:

Our present educational institutions which are in line with and feeding into industrialism, nationalism, competitive transnationalism, individualism, and patriarchy must be fundamentally put into question. All of these elements together coalesce into a world view that exacerbates the crisis we are now facing.

Little of the world's poverty, injustice, terrorism and war will be eliminated, and few of current environmental crises (ozone depletion; global warming; land, air and water pollution; increasing deforestation and desertification; loss of biodiversity) will be solved, without a major shift in the practices of Western industrialized society and the values that currently sustain them. Interestingly, one of the keys to ameliorating the current situation may lie in increased levels of scientific literacy among the world's citizens – but a different kind of scientific literacy. As the authors of *Benchmarks for Scientific Literacy* (AAAS, 1993) suggest,

People who are literate in science ... are able to *use* the habits of mind and knowledge of science, mathematics, and technology they have acquired to think about and make sense of many of the ideas, claims, and events that they encounter in everyday life.

(p. 322, emphasis added)

The authors of *Science For All Americans* (AAAS, 1989, p. 12) direct attention towards scientific literacy for a more socially compassionate and environmentally responsible democracy when they state that science can provide knowledge 'to develop effective solutions to its global and local problems' and can foster 'the kind of intelligent respect for nature that should inform decisions on the uses of technology' and without which, they say, 'we are in danger of recklessly destroying our life-support system'. Regrettably, they don't go on to suggest that scientific literacy also includes the capacity and willingness to act in environmentally responsible and socially just ways. This component is also absent from the definition proposed by the Council of Ministers of Education (1997, p. 4) to guide curriculum construction throughout Canada:

scientific literacy is an evolving combination of the science-related attitudes, skills, and knowledge students need to develop inquiry, problem-solving, and decision-making abilities, to become lifelong learners, and to maintain a sense of wonder about the world around them.

Because, they say, 'it conveys more clearly a flavour of science education for action as well as for personal enlightenment and satisfaction', the Scottish Consultative Council on the Curriculum (SCCC, 1996, p. 15) adopted the term *scientific capability* instead of scientific literacy. Scientific capability is described in terms of five distinct, but clearly interrelated, aspects: scientific *curiosity* – an enquiring habit of mind; scientific *competence* – ability to investigate scientifically; scientific *understanding* – understanding of scientific ideas and the way science works; scientific *creativity* – ability to think and act creatively; and scientific *sensitivity* – critical awareness of the role of science in society, combined with a caring and responsible disposition. Hence, becoming 'scientifically capable' involves considerably more than the acquisition of scientific skills, knowledge and understanding. It also involves the development of personal qualities and attitudes, the formulation of one's own views on a wide range of issues that have a scientific and/or technological dimension, and the establishment of an underlying value position. In the words of the SCCC (1996, p. 15),

> a person who is scientifically capable is not only knowledgeable and skilled but is also able to draw together and apply her/his resources of knowledge and skill, creatively and with sensitivity, in response to an issue, problem or phenomenon.

It is interesting and extremely disappointing that a document purporting to be action-oriented does not include preparation for sociopolitical action by students in its definition of scientific capability. If we are to tackle the crisis (crises) that O'Sullivan identifies, we need a much more overtly politicized form of science education, a central goal of which is to equip students with the capacity and commitment to take appropriate, responsible and effective action on matters of social, economic, environmental and moral-ethical concern.

It is timely, then, that the pendulum of education policy in England and Wales may now be moving away from a focus on producing a suitably educated workforce towards a wider socialization and development role. The so-called Crick report, responding to what the authors perceived as 'worrying levels of apathy, ignorance and cynicism about public life' (Qualifications & Curriculum Authority (QCA, 1998, p. 8)), has recommended the immediate implementation of *education for citizenship* comprising three strands: social and moral responsibility, community involvement and political literacy.

> We aim at no less than a change in the political culture of this country both nationally and locally: for people to think of themselves as active citizens, willing, able and equipped to have an influence in public life and with the critical capacities to weigh evidence before speaking and acting; to build on and to extend radically to young people the best in existing traditions of community involvement and public service, and to make them individually confident in finding new forms of involvement and action among themselves
>
> (QCA, 1998, p. 8)

This radical agenda would require a very different conception of scientific literacy – one in which emphasis is not just on scientific knowledge and skills, but on the clarification of problems and negotiation of possible solutions through open, critical dialogue and active participation in democratic mechanisms for effecting change. As McConnell (1982) remarked, some twenty years ago,

> Public decision making by citizens in a democracy requires an attitude of attentiveness; skills of gaining and using relevant knowledge; values of which one is

aware and to which one is committed; and the ability to turn attitudes, skills and values into action.

(p. 13)

The curriculum proposals outlined in this chapter are designed to achieve these goals.

Politicizing the science and technology curriculum

One of the absurdities of some current curriculum initiatives is that they utilize elements of the history, philosophy and sociology of science to show how scientific inquiry is influenced by the sociocultural context in which it is located but do not use this understanding to politicize students. Many teachers avoid confronting the political interests and social values underlying the scientific and technological practices they teach about, and seek to avoid making judgements about them or influencing students in particular directions. This makes little or no sense. First, it asks teachers to attempt the impossible. Values are embedded in every aspect of the curriculum: content, teaching/learning methods and assessment/evaluation strategies are selected using criteria that reflect and embody particular value positions, whether teachers recognize it or not. Moreover, values can be promoted as much by what is omitted from discussion as by what is included. Second, it mistakes the very purpose of the science component of education for citizenship: ensuring a level *critical* scientific and technological literacy for everyone as a means to bring about social reconstruction. The purpose of such an education is to enable young citizens to look critically at the society we have, and the values that sustain it, and to ask what can and should be changed in order to achieve a more socially just democracy and to ensure more environmentally sustainable lifestyles. This view of science education is overtly and unashamedly political. It takes the Advisory Group on Education for Citizenship and the Teaching of Democracy in Schools (QCA, 1998) at its word not just education *about* citizenship, but education *for* citizenship.

> ... citizenship education is education *for* citizenship, *behaving and acting as a citizen*, therefore it is not just knowledge of citizenship and civic society; it also implies developing values, skills and understanding.
>
> (p. 13, emphasis added)

Politicization of science education can be achieved by giving students the opportunity to confront real world issues that have a scientific, technological or environmental dimension. By grounding content in socially and personally relevant contexts, an issues-based approach can provide the motivation that is absent from current abstract, de-contextualized approaches and can form a base for students to construct understanding that is personally relevant, meaningful and important. It can provide increased opportunities for active learning, collaborative learning and direct experience of the situatedness of scientific and technological practice. In the Western contemporary world, technology is all pervasive; its social and environmental impact is clear; its disconcerting social implications and disturbing moral-ethical dilemmas are made apparent almost every day in popular newspapers and TV news bulletins. In many ways, it is much easier to recognize how technology is determined by the sociocultural context in which it is located than to see how science is driven by such factors. It is much easier to see the environmental impact of technology than to see the ways in which science impacts on society and environment. For these kinds of reasons, it makes good sense to use problems and issues in technology and engineering as the major vehicles for contextualizing the science curriculum. This is categorically not an argument against teaching science; rather, it is an argument for teaching the science that informs an understanding of everyday technological problems and may assist students in reaching tentative solutions.

In constructing a new science and technology curriculum for the 21st century, my inclination is to provide a mix of local, regional/national and global issues focusing on seven areas of concern: human health; food and agriculture; land, water and mineral resources; energy resources and consumption; industry (including manufacturing industry, the leisure and service industries, biotechnology, and so on); information transfer and transportation; freedom and control in science and technology (ethics and social responsibility). Although my focus is science education in the Western world, it is apparent that very similar concerns impact curriculum debate in the developing world (Lee, 1992; Vlaardingerbroek, 1998; Dillon, 2002). Indeed, science teachers in Botswana regard 'reducing the spread of HIV/AIDS' as the principal goal of science education, while 'promoting environmental awareness and an active interest in preserving and maintaining the natural environment', 'promoting healthy diet and avoidance of drugs' and 'promoting human population control' are ranked third, fourth and fifth (Vlaardingerbroek, 1998).

As argued elsewhere (Hodson, 1994), the kind of issues-based approach I am advocating can be regarded as comprising four levels of sophistication.

- *Level 1*: Appreciating the societal impact of scientific and technological change, and recognizing that science and technology are, to some extent, culturally determined.
- *Level 2*: Recognizing that decisions about scientific and technological development are taken in pursuit of particular interests, and that benefits accruing to some may be at the expense of others. Recognizing that scientific and technological development are inextricably linked with the distribution of wealth and power.
- *Level 3*: Developing one's own views and establishing one's own underlying value positions.
- *Level 4*: Preparing for and taking action.

At the simplest level, case studies of the societal impact of inventions such as the steam engine, the internal combustion engine, the printing press or the computer can be used to bring about an awareness that science and technology are powerful forces that shape the lives of people and other species, and impact significantly on the environment as a whole. They can also be used to show that scientific and technological developments are both culturally dependent and culturally transforming. In other words, science is a product of its time and place and can sometimes change quite radically the ways in which people think and act. For example, the science of Galileo, Newton, Darwin and Einstein changed our perception of humanity's place in the universe and precipitated enormous changes in the way people address issues in politics, economics and history. This 'Level One awareness' also includes recognition that the benefits of scientific and technological innovations are often accompanied by problems: hazards to human health, challenging and sometimes disconcerting social changes, environmental degradation and major moral–ethical dilemmas.

Much of STS and environmental education, while recognizing these adverse features of development, is currently pitched at the level where decision-making in science and technology is seen simply as a matter of reaching consensus or effecting a compromise. In contrast, the intention at Level Two is to enable students to recognize that scientific and technological decisions are taken in pursuit of particular interests, justi-fied by particular values and sometimes implemented by those with sufficient economic or political power to override the needs and interests of others. As a consequence, the advantages and disadvantages of scientific and technological developments often impact differentially on society. Case studies can be used to achieve a level of critical scientific literacy that recognizes how science and technology serve the rich and the powerful in ways that are often prejudicial to the interests and well-being of the poor and powerless, sometimes giving rise to further inequalities and injus-tices. Such studies help students to see that material benefits in the West (North) are often achieved at the expense of those living in the Developing World. It is here that the radical political character of the curriculum begins to emerge. Those curricula that take the trouble to address the symptoms of Third World poverty (malnutrition and famine, inadequate sanitation, and diseases such as rickets, tuberculosis and cholera) usually neglect to include a sociopolitical and historical analysis of its cause. Often, they treat the issue of poverty as a consequence of climatic harshness, overpopulation and ignorance. By contrast, the approach advocated here would recog-nize the role played by Western governments and business interests in controlling the production and distribution of resources. Students would quickly recognize that critical consideration of scientific and technological development is inextricably linked with questions about the distribution of wealth and power. Moreover, they would begin to see the ways in which problems of environmental degradation are rooted in societal practices and in the values and interests that sustain and legitimate them.

Level Three is concerned primarily with supporting students in their attempts to formulate their own opinions on important issues and to establish their own value positions, rather than with promoting the 'official' or textbook view. It focuses much more overtly on values clarification, developing strong feelings about issues, and actively thinking about what it means to act wisely, justly and 'rightly' in particular social, political and environmental contexts (Beck, 1990, 1993). This phase has much in common with the goals of Peace Education (Hicks, 1988) and Global Education (Selby, 1995). It begins with the fostering of self-esteem and personal well-being in each individual, and extends to respect for the rights of others, mutual trust, the pursuit of justice, cooperative decision-making and creative resolution of conflict between individuals, within and between communities, throughout the world. It is driven by a deep commitment to anti-discriminatory education exposing the common roots of sexism, racism, homophobia, Eurocentrism and Westism (or Northism) in the tendency to dichotomize and generate a sense of *other*; working actively to confront the 'us and them' mentality that invariably sees 'us' as the norm, the desir-able and the superior. It culminates in a commitment to the belief that alternative voices can and should be heard in order that decisions in science and technology reflect wisdom and justice, rather than powerful sectional interests (Maxwell, 1984, 1992).

The final (fourth) level of sophistication in this issues-based approach is helping students to prepare for and take responsible action. Socially and environmentally responsible behaviour will not necessarily follow from knowledge of key concepts and possession of the 'right attitudes'. It is almost always much easier to proclaim that one cares about an issue than to do something about it! The keys to the trans-lation of knowledge into action are *ownership* and *empowerment*. Those who act are those who have a deep personal understanding of the issues (and their human and environmental implications) and feel a personal investment in addressing and solving the problems. Those who act are those who feel personally empowered to effect change, who feel that they can make a difference, and know how to do so.

Preparing students for action necessarily means ensuring that they gain a clear understanding of how decisions are made within local, regional and national government, and within industry, commerce and the military. Without knowledge of where and with whom power of decision-making is located, and awareness of the mechanisms by which decisions are reached, intervention is not possible. Furthermore, the likelihood of students becoming active citizens is increased substantially by encouraging them to take action *now* (in school), and by providing opportunities for them to do so. Suitable action might include conducting surveys of dump sites, public footpaths and environmentally sensitive areas, generating data for community groups such as birdwatchers and ramblers, making public statements and writing letters, organizing petitions and consumer boycotts of environmentally unsafe products, publishing newsletters, lobbying local government officials, working on environmental clean-up projects, creating nature trails, assuming responsibility for environmental enhancement of the school grounds, monitoring the school's consumption of energy and material resources in order to formulate more appropriate practices, and so on. It is not enough for students to learn that science and technology are influenced by social, political and economic forces; they need to learn how to participate, and they need to experience participation. It is not enough for students to be armchair critics! As Kyle (1996, p. 1) puts it:

> Education must be transformed from the passive, technical, and apolitical orientation that is reflective of most students' school-based experiences to an active, critical, and politicized life-long endeavour that transcends the boundaries of classrooms and schools.

It is easy to see the potential for politicization in the seven areas of concern listed above: Human Health (for example, health goals in North America versus Third World, priorities in health spending, gender issues relating to 'body image'); Land, Water and Mineral Resources (for example, land usage issues, including Aboriginal land rights and efforts to formulate an Antarctic Treaty, water pollution, sustainable consumption); Food and Agriculture (politics of starvation, factory farming, genetically modified food); Energy Resources (renewable energy sources, politics of the petroleum industry, consumption and lifestyle issues); Industry (employment considerations versus environmental impact, sustainability issues, automation); IT and Transportation (data protection issues, cultural imperialism, emission controls); Ethics (genetic engineering; Third World organ donors, Hippocratic oath for scientists and engineers). It is also relatively easy to see how these areas of concern lend themselves to treatment at the four levels of sophistication. At level 1, students are made aware of the societal and environmental impact of science and technology and alerted to the existence of alternative technologies, with different impact. At level 2, they are sensitized to the sociopolitical nature of scientific and technological practice. At level 3, they become committed to the fight to establish more socially just and environmentally sustainable practices. At level 4, they acquire the knowledge and skills to intervene effectively in decision-making processes and to ensure that alternative voices, and their underlying interests and values, are brought to bear on policy decisions. Some of the issues addressed through this curriculum will be global (ozone depletion, acid rain, global warming), some will be local (factory-based pollution, road construction, loss of recreational space), but the common element should be *sustainability*. How can economic and scientific/technological development be maintained in a way that values and protects the natural and social environment? As will be argued later, this challenge is as much social as it is scientific-technological.

In advocating a 4-level model, my intention is not to suggest that all action is delayed until the final years of schooling. Rather, that students proceed to whatever level is appropriate to the topic in hand, the learning opportunities it presents and the stage of intellectual and emotional development of the students, bearing in mind the simple class management principle of investing each topic with a degree of variety. In some areas of concern it is relatively easy for students to be organized for action; in other areas it is more difficult. It is also the case that, for some topics, level 3 is more demanding than Level 4. For example, it is easier to take action on recycling than to reach a considered and critical judgement of recycling versus reduced consumption versus alternative materials.

Elements of curriculum

Perhaps I can clarify what I have in mind by addressing the four major components of such a curriculum.

- *Learning Science and Technology*: acquiring and developing conceptual and theoretical knowledge in science and technology, and gaining familiarity with a range of technologies.
- *Learning About Science and Technology*: developing an understanding of the nature and methods of science and technology, an awareness of the complex interactions among science, technology, society and environment, and a sensitivity to the personal, social and ethical implications of particular technologies.
- *Doing Science and Technology*: engaging in and developing expertise in scientific inquiry and problem solving; developing confidence and competence in tackling a wide range of 'real world' technological tasks.
- *Engaging in Sociopolitical Action*: acquiring the capacity and commitment to take appropriate, responsible and effective action on matters of social, economic, environmental and moral-ethical concern.

To an extent, items 3 and 4 can be combined by engaging students in science/technology problem-solving situations that have a community dimension, as described by Sutti (1991), Paton (1994), Albone, Collins and Hill (1995), van Marion (1995, 1998), Cunniff and McMillen (1996), Helms (1998), Lee and Roth (2002), Roth (2002), Roth and Lee (2002). Many students will already be aware of politically active organizations such as Greenpeace, the Sierra Club, World Wildlife Fund and Earthwatch. Education at level 4 includes both a study of what these organizations are trying to achieve and the methods they employ. Much can be learned that is applicable to local contexts.

While space precludes a detailed consideration of each of these elements, one or two important points can be made. As Fensham (1990) and Layton *et al.* (1993) have observed, the conceptual understanding needed to address issues in technology and engineering is often somewhat different from the abstract, idealized knowledge of conventional science courses. Moreover, the precise relationship between the theoretical knowledge of science (knowing *that*) and the practical knowledge of technology (knowing *how*) is not always simple and straightforward. The history of science and technology reveals four possibilities: science precedes technological application (technology as applied science); technology precedes the science that eventually explains it; scientific development and technological development are entirely independent; scientific and technological development are mutually dependent and interactive.

Layton (1988) makes the point that even when technology is 'just' applied science, there is still lots more to do. He gives the example of Perkin's development of mauve, and says that its translation into a commercial product required 'knowledge, skills and personal qualities very different from those needed for the test tube oxidation of aniline' (p. 371). At the outset, mauve would not take evenly on large batches of cloth, there was no suitable mordant for cotton, raw materials were not readily available, handling concentrated nitric and sulphuric acids on a 'factory scale' presented all manner of engineering problems, there were problems of marketing associated with consumer reluctance, and so on. Notions such as optimization, feedback modelling, systems analysis, critical path planning and risk assessment have to be included whenever science is applied to these 'real world' situations.

Of course, real world problems are rarely the simple matters of cause and effect portrayed in traditional science curricula; rather, attempts at solution often reveal layers of increasing complexity and uncertainty that cannot be contained within a particular disciplinary framework. Problems in science and technology become inextricably linked with considerations in economics, politics, aesthetics and moral philosophy. In general, a scientific solution is valid/acceptable if it conforms to the rationality of science – i.e., if it has observational or experimental support, if it is internally consistent, if it is consistent with other accepted theory. It helps if it is elegant and parsimonious, though those criteria may not be considered essential. In technology, a solution has to work, of course, but it also has to be efficient, cost-effective, durable, possibly aesthetically pleasing, and so on. There may also be critical considerations relating to social and environmental impact. Technologies are rarely 'good' in an absolute sense. Rather, they are good from some perspectives, less good (or even undesirable) from others. In that case, whose perspective is to count, whose interests are to be served, whose values are to be upheld? One person's acceptable risk or cost is another person's intolerable hazard, social disruption or cultural insensitivity. Technology is inescapably a social activity, determined by the prevailing distribution patterns of wealth and power. The curriculum should acknowledge these realities. The extent to which technology can have social, political, economic and environmental impact well beyond that imagined by scientists and engineers is well illustrated in Nye's (1990) book *Electrifying America*:

> In the United States electrification was not a 'thing' that came from outside society and had an 'impact'; rather, it was an internal development shaped by its social context. Put another way, each technology is an extension of human lives: someone makes it, someone owns it, some oppose it, many use it, and all interpret it. The electric streetcar, for example, provided transportation, but there was more to it than that. Street traction companies were led into the related businesses of advertising, real estate speculation, selling surplus electrical energy, running amusement parks, and hauling light freight. Americans used the trolley to transform the urban landscape, making possible an enlarged city, reaching far out into the countryside and integrating smaller hamlets into the urban market. Riding the trolley became a new kind of tourism, and it became a subject of painting and poetry. The popular acceptance of the trolley car also raised political issues. Who should own and control it? Should its workers unionize? Did the streetcar lead to urban concentration or diffusion, and which was desirable? Like every technology, the electric streetcar implied several businesses, opened new social agendas, and raised political questions. It was not a thing in isolation, but an open-ended set of problems and possibilities.

(pp. ix–x)

Dealing with complex 'real world' problems requires a significant shift from the traditional approaches of scientific problem solving. Traditional mechanistic thinking, with a simple linear chain of cause and effect ascertained through close experimental control, is no longer appropriate. What is needed is a shift to a more holistic, systems style of thinking able to deal with complex webs of relationships, multiple interdependencies, feedback systems and unpredictability. In Capra's (1982) words,

> we are trying to apply the concepts of an outdated world view the mechanistic world view of Cartesian-Newtonian science – to a reality that can no longer be understood in terms of these concepts. We live today in a globally interconnected world, in which biological, psychological, social, and environmental phenomena are all interdependent. To describe this world appropriately we need an ecological perspective which the Cartesian world view does not offer.
>
> (pp. 15–16)

As indicated earlier, the curriculum proposals outlined here are unashamedly intended to produce activists: people who will fight for what is right, good and just; people who will work to re-fashion society along more socially-just lines; people who will work vigorously in the best interests of the biosphere. It is here that the curriculum deviates sharply from STS courses currently in use. The kind of scientific literacy under discussion here is inextricably linked with education for *political literacy* and with the ideology of education as social reconstruction. The kind of social reconstruction I envisage includes the confrontation and elimination of racism, sexism, classism, and other forms of discrimination, scapegoating and injustice; it includes a substantial shift away from unthinking and unlimited consumerism towards a more environmentally sustainable lifestyle that promotes the adoption of appropriate technology. There are two major aspects to this element of the curriculum: *political education* and *values education*. It is to the latter that I now turn my attention.

Changing values and changing lifestyle

Science and technology education has the responsibility of showing students the complex but intimate relationships among the technological products we consume, the processes that produce them, the values that underpin them and the biosphere that sustains us. Failing to do so, on spurious grounds of disciplinary purity or rigour, is simply reinforcing the status quo and contributing to the problems. As Martin Luther King said, in a somewhat different context, 'If you are not part of the solution, you are part of the problem'. In an issues-based curriculum oriented towards sociopolitical action, it is not appropriate to regard environmental problems as matters of careless industrialization and inexpert management of natural resources. Such an approach ignores the underlying causes of the problems – the values underpinning industrialization and the exploitation of natural resources. It is dangerously misleading because it suggests that science itself can solve the problems by simple technical means. In that sense, the approach depoliticizes the issues, thereby removing them from the 'realm of possibility' within which ordinary people see themselves as capable of intervention. As a consequence, dealing with environmental problems is left to experts and officials, and ordinary citizens are disempowered. Education for sociopolitical action entails recognizing that the environment is not just a 'given', but a social construct. It is a social construct in two senses. First, we act upon and change the natural environment, and so construct and reconstruct it through our social actions. Few parts of the planet are free of mankind's intervention. Continuing rainforest clearance in countries such as Brazil and Indonesia in pursuit of short-term economic gain is the most spectacular example, of course, but even the large 'unspoiled' areas of European countryside show the indelible imprint of previous generations of agricultural workers. Second, we perceive the environment in a way that is dependent on the prevailing sociocultural framework. Our concept of environment itself is a social construct, and so could be different. Indeed, many indigenous peoples do perceive it in significantly different ways (Knudtson & Suzuki, 1992). Joe Cole, a character in Jenny Diski's (1987) novel *Rainforest*, states:

> There is no nature, only Nature – an imaginary state of man's own invention, a realm of concept and language. That is man's place and it is nowhere except inside his head; a mirror image of a distorted fantasy he calls Mankind ... Nature is a conceit: a man-made garden in which we wander to relax and preen, as we nod to one another in passing, and congratulate ourselves on being us. We created Nature so that we might take pride in how far we have ventured beyond it.
>
> (pp. 54–55)

Environmental problems are not problems 'out there' in our surroundings, but problems 'in here' (in our heads), in the way we choose to make sense of the world. They are pre-eminently social problems – problems of people, their lifestyles and their relations with the natural world. Indiscriminate clearance of tropical rainforest for non-forest use brings about local problems of erosion, floods and fuel wood shortage, and global problems related to global warming, climate change and loss of biodiversity. While science provides an understanding of the value of the forest, it doesn't contribute much to solving the problems. Solutions will be found, if at all, by dealing with issues relating to poverty (both individual and national), patterns of land ownership, terms of international trade and burgeoning populations. In those countries where birth rates *have* declined, the factors have not been more (scientific) understanding of fertility, but availability of cheap/free contraceptives, less dependence on children as a source of labour and as insurance against old age or accident, decreased child mortality, and greater educational and employment opportunities for women.

By encouraging students to recognize the ways in which the environment is socially constructed, we can challenge the notion that environmental problems are 'natural' and inevitable. If environment is a social construct, environmental problems are social problems, caused by societal practices and structures, and justified by society's current values. It follows that solving environmental problems means addressing and changing the social conditions that give rise to them and the values that sustain them. Science education for sociopolitical action is inescapably an exercise in values clarification and values change. Environmental problems will not just 'go away', nor will they be solved by a quick 'technical fix' while we blithely maintain our profligate lifestyle. We have to change the way we live; the planet can no longer sustain our present (Western) way of life, Changing our way of life entails changing our values. Acid rain, global climate change, toxic waste, the threat of nuclear holocaust, ozone depletion, loss of biodiversity, increasing deforestation and desertification are all located in our impoverished values. As Ernst Schumacher said in his book *Small is Beautiful*, some thirty years ago, we have to reject our current values of bigger, faster and more powerful, our current preoccupation with higher production and wealth generation, in favour of an orientation towards 'the organic, the gentle, the non-violent, the elegant and beautiful' (Schumacher, 1973, p. 29).

A crucial element in this politicized science education is rejection of the notion of *technological determinism* – the idea that the pace and direction of technological change are inevitable and irresistible. We *can* control technology or, rather, we can control the controllers of technology. We can, and should, promote the notion of technological choice, whereby citizens decide for themselves the kind of technology they will and will not use. Addressing alternative values rooted in ecofeminism and/or in the perspectives of indigenous peoples lays the groundwork for a serious consideration of alternative, more environmentally sustainable and appropriate technologies – which Budgett-Meakin (1992) characterizes as technologies which are sensitive to local social, cultural and economic circumstances, capitalize on local skills, ingenuity and materials, make sparing and responsible use of non-renewable resources, and are controlled by the community, thereby resulting in increased self-respect and self-reliance. Adoption of appropriate technology entails rejection of any technology that violates our moral-ethical principles, exploits or disadvantages minority groups, or has adverse environmental impact. The goal is a *humanized* technology: a technology more in harmony with people and with nature, a technology that is energy and materials conserving – that is, based on renewable resources and recycling, and on durability rather than in-built obsolescence and deterioration. Many science curricula promote the view that energy production based on oil or coal consumption, 'hydro' or nuclear power are the only viable alternatives, dismissing the use of wind, solar, tidal and biomass energy production as 'cranky', economically disadvantageous or hopelessly futuristic. Whose interests are being served by failing to make students aware of alternatives and, therefore, likely to demand alternatives? Certainly not those of the wider global community or of the planet as a whole. What is at issue here is not short-term economic gain but longterm environmental health.

It is now a well-worn cliché to say that we live in a global village, and that what we do in our own backyard can impact quite significantly on people living elsewhere in the world. What is also true is that our actions now impact on the lives of future citizens. The ethics of previous generations have dealt almost exclusively with relations among people alive at the same time. In startling contrast, contemporary technology makes an urgent issue of relations with those as yet unborn. In recognizing this new reality we would do well to heed the wisdom of the First Nations people of North America.

> Treat the Earth well. It was not given to you by your parents; it was loaned to you by your children. We do not inherit the Earth from our ancestors, we borrow it from our children.

It is not too much of an exaggeration to say that the degree to which young citizens incorporate sustainable practices in their professional and personal lives will determine the quality of life for future generations. The science curriculum has a crucial role to play in teaching them how to exercise the enormous power of technology responsibly, carefully and compassionately, and in the interests of *all* living creatures. The time is long past when 'alternative technology' can and should be (falsely) equated with the somewhat pejorative term of 'alternative lifestyle'.

The most fundamental element in this values shift is the rejection of *anthropocentrism*, identified by Smolicz and Nunan (1975), some quarter century ago, as one of the ideological pivots of Western science and science education. Many scholars have argued that anthropocentric thinking, and the consequent objectification of nature, is the root cause of the global environmental crisis (Corcoran & Sievers, 1994; Russell & Bell, 1996). By objectifying nature, people absolve themselves of any moral responsibility for the care and preservation of the natural environment and justify their continued exploitation of natural resources and other life forms. The pervasiveness of anthropocentrism is evident in our common everyday language: we subdue Mother Nature, conquer virgin territory, rape the countryside, achieve mastery over the elements, manage, exploit and control natural resources. To effect the kind of shift in society that I am advocating, we need to replace this anthropocentrism with a *biocentric* ethic comprising the following elements: all things in the biosphere have intrinsic value and an equal right to exist alongside humans; the natural world is not just a resource for human use; all life forms are inextricably interconnected (Russell, 1997). Adopting such an ethic means having respect for the intrinsic value of all livings things, cultivating a sense of compassion and caring towards both human and nonhuman species, having a concern for maintaining the existence of biological and cultural diversity, and challenging and rejecting all forms of discrimination. Appreciating interconnectedness means acquiring an understanding of the relationships that exist between all natural and human made systems, recognizing that all human actions have consequences that will affect a complex global system that includes human and nonhumans species, having an awareness of and acting on choices to maintain an ecologically sound and humane lifestyle. Laszlo (2001) describes the inculcation of this clutch of values as developing a 'planetary ethic' – an ethic which 'respects the conditions under which all people in the world community can live in dignity and freedom, without destroying each other's chances of livelihood, culture, society and environment' (p. 78). Laszlo is at some pains to state that abiding by a planetary ethic does not necessarily entail major sacrifices or self-denying behaviour. Striving for excellence, beauty, personal growth, enjoyment, even comfort and luxury is still possible, provided that we consider the consequences of our actions on the life and activity of others by asking:

- Is the way I live compatible with the rights of others?
- Does it take basic resources from them?
- Does it impact adversely on the environment?

Changing pedagogy

Clearly, values cannot and should not be imposed on students from outside. They must be fostered from within. But how? What changes in pedagogy are necessary to effect such a radical shift in student values? It is well documented that informal learning experiences can sometimes be more effective than formal schooling in bringing about awareness of issues, attitudinal shifts and willingness to engage in sociopolitical action (Ramey-Gassert & Walberg, 1994; Rennie & McClafferty, 1996; Jeffrey-Clay, 1999; Pedretti, 2002). Informal learning experiences are particularly well positioned to facilitate the affective and social components of learning (Alsop & Watts, 1997; Meredith, Fortner & Mullins, 1997). They can provide the fusion of the cognitive, affective and social that is too often absent in the classroom but is essential to the kind of radical shift in attitudes and values on which sociopolitical action depends. It is also well established that education *in* and *through* the environment can play a substantial role in assisting the reordering of values and the development of new ones. Gough (1989), for example, describes how the kind of experiences advocated by the Earth Education movement (van Matre, 1979) can be utilized in re-orienting students' environmental understanding.

Some years ago, Woolnough and Allsop (1985) talked about the importance of students 'getting a feel for phenomena' through hands-on experiences in the laboratory as a prerequisite for conceptual understanding. What I am advocating here is 'getting a feel for the environment' – building a sense of ecological relationships through powerful emotional experiences 'in the field'. The key emphases are: sharpening the senses; building key ecological concepts – not just as analytical abstractions but as tools for *seeing* and *understanding*; providing opportunities for solitude; making learning a joyful and magical experience. We should aim to give all students the opportunity to experience the silence and majesty of the forest, mountains and seashore. By learning to be sensitive to the spirituality of the caves, volcanoes and trees – rather than seeing them merely as products of erosion, the outcome of geo-thermal activity and resources for making paper or furniture – children can recover what many indigenous peoples around the world have never lost: a sense of unity between humanity and the environment. Literature, art, photographs and movies are both a useful substitute for, and a powerful adjunct, to outdoor experiences; they can play a significant role in shifting students' values. Russell and Hodson (2002) suggest that *whalewatching* and other ecotourist activities can be even more effective in preparing the ground for a shift from anthropocentrism to biocentrism and humane education. As Paul Shepard (1982) says, maturity of thought (*wisdom* rather than mere knowledge) arises from connecting with the Earth in the early years of childhood. Without close contact with the natural environment, he argues, we become *infantile adults*: wanting everything now and new; careless of resources and waste; unable to empathize with 'others'; prone to violence when frustrated; despising age and denying human natural history.

Barriers and resistance

Making the kind of changes to the curriculum advocated in this chapter will not be easy. Much that I have suggested is likely to be disturbing to science teachers, severely testing both their competence and confidence. Traditionally, science education has dealt with established and secure knowledge, while contested knowledge, multiple solutions, controversy and ethics have been excluded. Accommodating to what some teachers will perceive as loss of teacher control and direction will be difficult. Indeed, to teach this kind of issues-based curriculum science teachers will need to develop the skills and attitudes more commonly associated with the humanities and language arts.

Of course, not all of the issues to be addressed in such a curriculum will be global or even regional; many of the most compelling issues are local. This requires a much greater degree of curriculum flexibility and local decision making than many educational jurisdictions currently favour. These changes raise concerns about assessment and evaluation. Conventional assessment methods do not cope very well when there is no clearly defined outcome, no certain and unambiguous solution; when the curriculum is extended to include sociopolitical action, evaluation is as much about what the community learns from an activity as what the students learn. Clearly, much work will be needed to develop appropriate assessment and evaluation strategies.

Because this approach diverges so markedly from traditional images of science education, it may be strenuously resisted by universities and by the community of scientists. Parents may see it as a 'soft option' to 'proper' science (i.e., abstract, theoretical science assessed by conventional means). Delamont (1990) cautions that attempts to change the image of science could undermine public confidence in science and so have adverse effects on the funding of research. Change may even be resisted by students. They, too, have expectations of science lessons, and sometimes act to restore the familiar when teachers attempt radical change. The problems for science teachers intent on radical change are neatly summed up by Lakin and Wellington (1991, p. 187):

> They don't expect reading and discussion or drama and role play – they do expect Bunsen burners and practical work. They don't want to find out that science is not a set of facts, that theories change, and that science does not have all the answers – they want the security of a collection of truths which are indisputable.

As Jenkins (1992) remarks,

> these expectations are not simply an aspect of the hidden curriculum of science . . . They are fostered by the unproblematic presentation of science in the media, burnished by members of the scientific community, and form part of the wider attempt to insulate science from influences that are keen to threaten its 'neutrality' and independence.
>
> (p. 562)

There may be teachers, educational administrators and members of the wider community who perceive the capacity for effecting social change that is located in a body of students who are critically literate in science and technology, and sufficiently politically literate to ensure that their voices are heard, as a threat rather. The more successful this form of education, the more opposition it may generate.

It is clear that radicalizing science education along these lines is a formidable undertaking. Hence it is unlikely to be achieved by conventional strategies for curriculum reform. A curriculum that aims to achieve a critical scientific and technological literacy must, in my view, be based on a model of curriculum development that seeks to encourage and support teachers in becoming critically literate about their own educational practice. Action research is probably the only coherent and viable way of addressing the issues of curriculum evaluation, curriculum development and professional development/teacher education that are central to the implementation of this radically new form of science education. Action research creates and sustains a supportive, critical environment in which groups of teachers who are familiar with the students, the locality and the school environment work together on theoretical and practical issues related to the design and implementation of a new science curriculum in a critical and supportive environment. A fundamental principle underpinning this approach is that all curriculum knowledge should be regarded as problematic, and open to continuous and rigorous scrutiny, critical appraisal and revision. Because we live in such a rapidly changing world our work as curriculum builders is never finished. Action research also assumes that teachers can acquire the expertise necessary for effective curriculum development by refining and extending the practical professional knowledge they already possess through critical collaborative activity supported by researcher/facilitators. Such was the rationale underlying a series of action research projects aimed at addressing five key aspects of science and technology education in Ontario.

- Introduction of an STSE approach into the primary and secondary curriculum
- Gender issues
- Presentation of a more authentic view of science through the curriculum
- Multicultural and antiracist science education

- The problems of teaching science in elementary school
- The nature of technology education and its relation to science and environmental education

In each case, groups of teachers (many of whom gained academic credit for their involvement) worked with a researcher/facilitator over two academic terms. Hodson, Bencze, Nyhof-Young, Pedretti and Elshof (2002) describe each project in detail and state what was learned about science and science education, and about action research. The authors formulate some guidelines for action researchers in science education and conclude with a chapter that looks at what else is necessary if we are to bring about significant and radical curriculum change in our school science programmes. Even when teachers and teacher educators embrace the kind of science curriculum I have outlined, there may still be much to do to convince the wider public of its desirability and efficacy. As I have argued elsewhere (Hodson, 1999), legitimating and establishing education for sociopolitical action necessitates extensive community involvement and has much in common with notions of 'participatory research' (Hall & Kassam, 1988) – matters that are well beyond the scope of this chapter.

References

Aikenhead, G.S. (1990) Scientific/technological literacy, critical reasoning, and classroom-practice. In S.P. Norris & L.M. Phillips (eds.), *Foundations of literacy policy in Canada*. Calgary, AB: Detselig.

Albone, A., Collins, N., and Hill, T. (1995) *Scientific research in schools: A compendium of practical experience*, Bristol: Clifton Scientific Trust.

Alsop, S. and Watts, M. (1997) Sources from a Somerset village: A model for informal learning about radiation and radioactivity. *Science Education*, 81, 633–650.

American Association for the Advancement of Science (AAAS) (1989) *Science for all Americans*. A Project 2061 report on literacy goals in science, mathematics, and technology. Washington, DC: AAAS.

American Association for the Advancement of Science (AAAS) (1993) *Benchmarks for scientific literacy*. Oxford: Oxford University Press.

Apple, M.W. (1993) *Official knowledge: Democratic education in a conservative age*. New York: Routledge.

Arons, A.B. (1983) Achieving wider scientific literacy. *Daedalus*, 112, 91–122.

Beck, C. (1990) *Better schools: A values perspective*. Lewes: Falmer Press.

Beck, C. (1993) *Learning to live the good life*. Toronto: OISE Press.

Bencze, J.L. (2001) Subverting corporatism in school science. *Canadian Journal of Science, Mathematics and Technology Education*, 1(3), 349–355.

Bowers, C.A. (1996) The cultural dimensions of ecological literacy. *Journal of Environmental Education*, 27(2), 5–11.

Budgett-Meakin, C. (1992) *Making the future work. Appropriate technology: A teacher's guide*. London: Longman.

Capra, F. (1982) *The turning point: Science, society, and the rising culture*. New York: Simon & Schuster.

Corcoran, P. and Sievers, E. (1994) Reconceptualizing environmental education: Five possibilities. *Journal of Environmental Education*, 25(4), 4–8.

Council of Ministers of Education, Canada (1997) *Common framework of science learning outcomes*. Toronto: CMEC Secretariat.

Cunniff, P. and McMillen, J. (1996) Field studies: Hands-on, real-science research. *Science Teacher*, 63(6), 48–51.

De Boer, G.E. (2000) Scientific literacy: Another look at its historical and contemporary meanings and its relationship to science education reform, *Journal of Research in Science Teaching*, 37, 582–601.

Delamont, S. (1990) A paradigm shift in science education? *Studies in Science Education*, 18, 153–158.

Dillon, J. and Tearney, K. (2002) Reconceptualizing environmental education: Taking account of reality. *Canadian Journal of Science, Mathematics and Technology Education*, 2(4), 467–483.

Diski, J. (1987) *Rainforest*. Harmondsworth: Penguin.

Eisenhart, M., Finkel, E., and Marion, S.F. (1996) Creating the conditions for scientific literacy: A re-examination. *American Educational Research Journal*, 33, 261–95.

Fensham, P.J. (1990) Practical work and the laboratory in science for all. In E. Hegarty-Hazel (ed.), *The student laboratory and the science curriculum*. London: Routledge.

Fensham, P.J. (1992) Science and technology. In P.W. Jackson (ed.), *Handbook of research on the curriculum*. Washington, DC: AERA/Macmillan.

Fensham, P.J. (2002) Time to change drivers for scientific literacy. *Canadian Journal of Science, Mathematics and Technology Education*, 2(1), 9–24.

Galbraith, P.L., Carss, M.C., Grice, R.D., Endean, L., and Warry M. (1997) Towards scientific literacy for the third millennium: A view from Australia. *International Journal of Science Education*, 19, 447–67.

Gough, N. (1989) From epistemology to ecopolitics: Renewing a paradigm for curriculum, *Journal of Curriculum Studies*, 21, 225–241.

Government of Canada (1991) *Prosperity through competitiveness*. Ottawa: Minister of Supply and Services Canada.

Hall, B.L. and Kassam, Y. (1988) Participatory research. In J.P. Keeves (ed.), *Educational research methodology and measurement: An international handbook* (pp. 150–155). Oxford: Pergamon Press.

Helms, J.V. (1998) Science and/in the community: Context and goals in practical work. *International Journal of Science Education*, 20, 643–653.

Hewson, P.W. (2002) Literacy and scientific literacy: A response to Fensham. *Canadian Journal of Science, Mathematics and Technology Education*, 2(2), 207–13.

Hicks, D. (1988) *Education for Peace: Issues, principles and practice* (London: Routledge).

Hodson, D. (1994) Seeking directions for change: The personalisation and politicisation of science education. *Curriculum Studies*, 2, 71–98.

Hodson, D. (1999) Going beyond cultural pluralism: Science education for sociopolitical action, *Science Education*, 83 (6), 775–796.

Hodson, D. with Bencze, L., Nyhof-Young, J., Pedretti, E. and Elshof, L. (2002) *Changing Science Education Through Action Research: Some Experiences from the Field*. Toronto: Imperial Oil Centre for Studies in Science, Mathematics and Technology Education, OISE/UT, in association with University of Toronto Press, pp. 361.

Jeffrey-Clay, K.R. (1999) Constructivism in museums: How museums create meaningful learning environments. *Journal of Museum Education*, 23, 3–7.

Jenkins, E. (1990) Scientific literacy and school science education. *School Science Review*, 71 (256), 43–51.

Jenkins, E.W. (1992) HPS and school science education: remediation or reconstruction? In S. Hills (ed.), *History and philosophy of science in science education*, Vol 1. Kingston: Queen's University.

Jenkins, E.W. (2002) Linking school science education with action. In W.-M. Roth & J. Desautels (eds.), *Science education as/for sociopolitical action*. New York: Peter Lang.

Knudtson, P. and Suzuki, D. (1992) *Wisdom of the elders*. Toronto: Stoddart.

Kolsto, S.D. (2001) Scientific literacy for citizenship: Tools for dealing with the science dimension of controversial socioscientific issues. *Science Education*, 85(3), 291–310.

Kyle, W.C. (1996) Editorial: The importance of investing in human resources. *Journal of Research in Science Teaching*, 33, 1–4.

Lakin, S. and Wellington, J.J. (1991) *Teaching the nature of science. A study of teachers' views of science and their implications for science education*. Sheffield: Division of Education, University of Sheffield.

Lankshear, C., Gee, J.P., and Hull, G. (1996) *The new work order: Behind the language of the new capitalism*. Boulder, CO: Westview Press.

Laszlo, E. (2001) *Macroshift: Navigating the transformation to a sustainable world*. San Francisco, GA: Berrett-Koehler.

Laugksch, R.C. (2000) Scientific literacy: A conceptual overview. *Science Education*, 84(1), 71–94.

Law, N. (2002) Scientific literacy: Charting the terrains of a multifaceted enterprise. *Canadian Journal of Science, Mathematics and Technology Education*, 2(2), 151–176.

Layton, D. (1988) Revaluing the T in STS. *International Journal of Science Education*, 10, 367–378.

Layton, D. Jenkins, B., MacGill, S., and Davey, A. (1993) *Inarticulate Science?* (Driffield: Studies in Education).

Lee, M.N.N. (1992) School science curriculum reforms in Malaysia: World influences and national context. *International Journal of Science Education*, 14(3), 249–261.

Lee, S. and Roth, W.-M. (2002) Learning science in the community. In W.-M. Roth & J. Desautels (eds.), *Science education as/for sociopolitical action.* New York: Peter Lang.

Matthews, M.R. (1993) Constructivism and science education: Some epistemological issues. *Journal of Science Education and Technology*, 2, 359–370.

Maxwell, N. (1984) *From knowledge to wisdom.* Oxford: Basil Blackwell.

Maxwell, N. (1992) What kind of inquiry can best help us create a good world? *Science, Technology & Human Values*, 17, 205–227.

McConnell, M.C. (1982) Teaching about science, technology and society at the secondary school level in the United States: An educational dilemma for the 1980s. *Studies in Science Education*, 9, 1–32.

Meredith, J., Fortner, R.W., and Mullins, G.W. (1997) Model of affective learning for nonformal science education facilities. *Journal of Research in Science Teaching*, 34, 805–818.

Millar, R. and Osborne, J. (eds.) (1998) *Beyond 2000: Science education for the future.* London: King's College London School of Education.

Ministry of Education and Training (2000) *Ontario curriculum, grades 9 to 12: Program planning and assessment.* Toronto: Queen's Printer for Ontario.

Munby, H. (1980) Analyzing teaching for intellectual independence. In H. Munby, G. Orpwood and T. Russell (eds.), *Seeing curriculum in a new light: Essays from science education.* Toronto: OISE Press.

National Science Board (1998) *Science and engineering indicators – 1998.* Arlington, VA: National Science Foundation.

Norris, S.P. (1997) Intellectual independence for nonscientists and other content-transcendent goals of science education. *Science Education*, 81, 239–258.

Norris, S.P. and Phillips, L.M. How literacy in its fundamental sense is central to scientific literacy. *Science Education.* 87(2), 224–240.

Nye, D.E. (1990) *Electrifying America: Social meanings of a new technology, 1880–1940.* Cambridge, MA: MIT Press.

Organization for Economic Cooperation and Development (OECD) (1998) *Instrument design: A framework for assessing scientific literacy.* Report of Project Managers Meeting. Arnhem: Programme for International Student Assessment.

O'Sullivan, E. (1999) *Transformative learning: Educational vision for the 21st Century.* London: Zed Books.

Paton, R. (1994) Algal production systems for wastewater treatment (an example of school-based research). *Journal of Biological Education*, 28(1), 53–62.

Pedretti, E. (2002) T. Kuhn meets T. Rex: Critical conversations and new directions in science centres and science museums. *Studies in Science Education*, 37, 1–42.

Pella, M.O., O'Hearn, G.T., and Gale, C.W. (1966) Referents to scientific literacy. *Journal of Research in Science Teaching*, 4, 199–208.

Qualifications and Curriculum Authority (QCA) (1998) *Education for citizenship and the teaching of democracy in schools.* London: QCA.

Ramey-Gassert, L. and Walberg, H.J.I. (1994) Re-examining connections: Museums as science learning environments. *Science Education*, 78, 345–363.

Roth, W.-M. (2002) Taking science education beyond schooling. *Canadian Journal of Science, Mathematics and Technology Education*, 2(1), 37–48.

Roth, W.-M. and Lee, S. (2002) Scientific literacy as collective praxis. *Public Understanding of Science*, 11, 1–24.

Rennie, L.J. and McClafferty, T. (1996) Science centres and science learning. *Studies in Science Education*, 27, 53–98.

Russell, C.L. (1997) Approaches to environmental education: Toward a transformative perspective. *Holistic Education Review*, 10(1), 34–40.

Russell, C.L. and Bell, A.C. (1996) A politicized ethic of care: Environmental learning from an ecofeminist perspective. In K. Warren (ed.), *Women's Voices in Experiential Education*. Dubuque, IA: Kendall Hunt.

Russell, C.L. and Hodson, D. (2002) Whalewatching as critical science education? *Canadian Journal of Science, Mathematics and Technology Education*, 2(4), 485–504.

Schumacher, E.F. (1973) *Small is beautiful: A study of economics as if people mattered*. London: Blond & Briggs.

Scottish Consultative Council on the Curriculum (SCCC) (1996) *Science education in Scottish schools: Looking to the future*. Broughty Ferry: SCCC.

Selby, D. (1995) *Earthkind: A teacher's handbook on humane education*. Trentham: Trentham Books.

Select Committee on Science and Technology House of Lords (2000) *Science and society*. 3rd Report, Session 1999–2000. London: HMSO.

Shamos, M. (1995) *The myth of scientific literacy*. New Brunswick, NJ: Rutgers University Press.

Shepard, P. (1982) *Nature and madness*. Athens, GA: University of Georgia Press.

Smolicz, J.J. and Nunan, E.E. (1975) The philosophical and sociological foundations of science education: The demythologizing of school science. *Studies in Science Education*, 2, 101–143.

Solomon, J. and Aikenhead, G. (eds.) (1994) *STS education: International perspectives on reform*. New York: Teachers College Press.

Sutti, A. (1991) The water analysis project: An alternative model for environmental study. In OECD/CERI, *Environment, schools and active learning*, pp. 59–65. Paris: OECD.

Tippens, D.J., Nichols, S.E., and Bryan, L.A. (2000) International science educators' perceptions of scientific literacy. In S.K. Abell (ed.), *Science teacher education: An international perspective*. Dordrecht: Kluwer.

Van Marion, P. (1995) Contracts between schools and institutions outside the school in environmental education: Problems and promising experiences. In F. MacDermott (ed.), *Proceedings of the conference on the exchange of experiences in environmental education in Great Britain and the Nordic countries*. Bradford: European Research and Training Centre on Environmental Education.

Van Marion, P. (1998) Experimental data collected by school classes. In H. Bayrhuber (ed), *Proceedings of the 1996 conference on European researchers in didaktik of biology*. Kiel: University of Kiel.

Van Matre, S. (1979) *Sunship Earth: An acclimatization program for outdoor learning*. Martinisville. In: American Camping Association.

Vlaardingerbroek, B. (1998) Challenges to reform: Botswana junior secondary school science teachers' perceptions of the development functions of science education, *International Journal of Educational Reform*, 7(3), 264–270.

Wellington, J. (ed) (1998) *Practical work in school science: Which way now?* London: Routledge.

West, L.H.T. and Pines, A.L. (1983) How 'rational' is rationality? *Science Education*, 67, 37–39.

Woolnough, B.E. and Allsop, T. (1985) *Practical work in science*. Cambridge: Cambridge University Press.

Yager, R.E. (ed.) (1996) *Science/technology/society as reform in science education*. Albany, NY: State University of New York Press.

CHAPTER 12

MUTUALISM

A different agenda for environmental and science education

Annette Gough

International Jouranl of Science Education (2002) 24(11), 1201–15

Introduction

Environmental education as a formal education movement has its origins in the concerns about environmental degradation and decreasing quality of life expressed by scientists in the 1960s (see, for example, Carson 1962, Ehrlich 1968, 1969). Thus, in the wake of publicity and political actions attending these concerns, environmental education initially entered school curricula in the early 1970s through science education (Gough 1997: 15). Indeed, at that time there was a broad acceptance in society that threats to human well-being and the environment could be countered through further scientific research and the application of technology. Such a belief is exemplified in the *Tbilisi Declaration* (UNESCO 1978: 24), which states that 'Education utilising the findings of science and technology should play a leading role in creating awareness and a better understanding of environmental problems'. More recently, UNESCO has emphasized the link between environmental education and science education by changing the subtitle of its publication *Connect* from the 'UNESCO-UNEP environmental education newsletter' (as it was from 1976 to 1996) to the 'UNESCO international science, technology and environmental education newsletter' (since 1997).

In its early formulations, the explicit aims of environmental education were often concerned with stimulating a sense of individual responsibility for the physical and aesthetic quality of the total environment based on a knowledge of general ecological principles, an understanding of the impact of human society on the biosphere, and an awareness of the problems inherent in the environmental change. The underlying belief seemed to be that 'if you provide people with accurate information about a situation, their values, attitudes, and behaviour change for the better' (McInnis 1975: 54), and this belief was enacted in the curriculum development strategies used by environmental educators. For the most part, they simply translated scholarly scientific material into subject matter to be taught and learned, generally through science education, because the construction of school environmental knowledge in the science curriculum was seen to be a direct outcome of scientific production.

However, as a result of forums such as the UNESCO-UNEP Belgrade workshop (1975) and the Tbilisi conference (UNESCO 1978), the goals and objectives for environmental education changed during the 1970s to emphasize more explicitly values and attitudes clarification, decision-making skills and an action component. The reports from these forums also recognized that the traditional formulations of the academic disciplines are individually inadequate for achieving the aims of environmental education, and instead proposed an interdisciplinary approach rather than a new or separate subject. For example, in one of the papers from the Belgrade workshop Buzzati-Traverso (1977: 13) argued that:

> the field under discussion is vast and multifaceted; it should be approached with a holistic attitude in that man [*sic*] and the innumerable components of his [*sic*] physical and cultural environment should be examined together in order to identify the complex and often hidden interactions which determine the pattern of human concerns.

These aspects of environmental education did not sit comfortably with conventional representations of science in science education as an objective, rational and value free search for 'one true story' (Harding 1986: 193), and some science educators began to question the relationship between science education and environmental education. For example, Hall (1977: 76) claimed that 'science teachers will do environmental education a grave disservice if they try to take it over'. Others, including Greenall (1979) and Fensham and May (1979), argued for a closer relationship between environmental education and a reformed science education that they envisaged as being distinctly different from the version practised in classrooms of the period. Lucas (1980: 1) adopted a different stance, expressing concern that 'too many science educators seem to believe that their discipline is the vehicle for environmental education'. He saw an 'omnipotent disciplinary chauvinism' (1980: 6) in assertions that science teachers could teach topics on society (beyond the social issues that arise from the application of science) – 'will their worldviews as empirical experimenters seriously distort the nature of historical understanding and aesthetic judgement?' – and yet concluded that 'science educators must not ignore the other forces acting to promote environmental wisdom, and must begin to look beyond the confines of their own and other educational literature for inspiration for research and practice' (1980: 21). Robottom (1983) also argued that science education is a limited vehicle for environmental education. At that time, as now, many environmental educators were concerned with the political character of environmental problems and the implications of this for the type of education they were advocating. Their argument was that science and environmental education were incompatible and that environmental education could more appropriately be implemented in curriculum areas other than science, because the science curriculum of the time was inhospitable to engaging with social issues.

Concerns about the relationship between science education and environmental education have continued into the 1990s. For example, Webster (1996: 82) argues that:

> Science, like economics, has been reformed through the promotion of investigative science and the contextualisation of science. The contexts are often social, utilitarian concerns: health, science in everyday life, a nod to environment, and industry. Content still dominates, as does experimentation. As in economics, the hidden values and assumptions about the way the world works remain largely unexplored.

Ashley (2000: 275) similarly discusses the limitations of current science education practices and argues that 'A scientific education for all that is more likely to result in [a more responsible attitude to science] therefore has to be a key objective for environmental education.'

The apparent distance between environmental education and science education in school curricula in Australia increased in the 1990s when the national curriculum nominally separated them into two distinct key learning areas: *Science* and *Studies of Society and Environment* (SOSE) (AEC 1994a, b). Science education was given a limited role in environmental education, with the main environmental education emphasis expected to come through SOSE. However, SOSE is often implemented in schools without an 'environment' component, and environment rarely rates a mention in the science curriculum. The structure of the national curriculum was repeated at the state level in Victoria (Board of Studies 1995, 2000a), Also in Victoria, in the late 1980s, the senior secondary subject *Environmental Science* was relocated from the Science group to become a humanities subject, *Environmental Studies*, and, according to Fensham (1990), its status diminished accordingly. However, in 1998, the subject again was recategorized and renamed for offer as *Environmental Science* (Board of Studies 2000b), in the Science learning area from 2001; at the same time a new subject was created, *Outdoor and Environmental Studies* (Board of Studies 2000c), within the Health and Physical Education (H&PE) learning area. These developments in Victoria over the past two decades are discussed here as instances of the power structures involved in controlling and reforming school curricula.

In this chapter I argue that both science educators and environmental educators need to rethink the relationships between science education and environmental education. If we are to achieve sustainable development then science education must have a role in encouraging ecological thinking (instead of being kept at a distance) and environmental education must move on from the insecure relationships that accompany the abstract arguments for it to adopt 'a holistic approach, rooted in a broad interdisciplinary base' (UNESCO 1978: 24). Over the past 30 years, the relationship between science education and environmental education can be characterized in biological terms as variously being distant, competitive, predator–prey and host–parasite. A rethought relationship could well be a mutualistic one that meets the needs of both to continue to survive in a changing world. As I discuss in the following section, today's students have different priorities and interests from those of the past. Traditional science education is becoming a threatened species while students become more concerned about the environment within a context of a marginalized environmental education. A different relationship between the two educations could enhance their mutual survival.

Student interest in science education and environmental education

One reason for developing a different relationship between science education and environmental education arises from the need to respond to students' declining interest in science despite their increasing levels of environmental concern. In Australia and elsewhere in the Western world there is widespread concern about decreasing student participation in upper secondary science courses. An even greater concern is that while there has been a national increase in participation in upper secondary school education in recent decades, there has not been a proportional increase in participation in science education at the same level (Dekkers and De Laeter 1997). Indeed, Dekkers and De Laeter (1997) report that while enrolments in biology, chemistry and physics increased from 1976 to 1992, they declined quite dramatically (approximately 20%) between 1992 and 1995 (see Table 8 for recent Victorian statistics). There has been an increase in enrolments in some alternative public examination science subjects during this period, particularly food technology, science for life, health education and marine studies, especially by females, who make up 64% of enrolments, but the total number of students studying science subjects is still declining.

A number of explanations can be offered for students' declining interest in studying science subjects, many of which are beyond the scope of this chapter. However, from recent research conducted in Victorian secondary schools (Gough *et al.* 1998, 1999) it would seem that while students come to secondary school from primary school interested in studying science, the content of the science curriculum is a strong negative influence and students rapidly lose interest in pursuing further studies in science beyond the compulsory years (i.e. beyond Year 10). Science education curriculum at lower secondary levels is in urgent need of change if we are to retain student interest in science studies in and beyond the compulsory years. Environmental education might be an appropriate emphasis for rekindling students' interest in the relevance of science, because young people are concerned about the state of the environment.

Recent research by the Environment Protection Authority (EPA) in New South Wales (Australia) indicates that 77% of 15–24-year-olds are concerned about environmental problems (EPA 1994) and that the environment is a higher priority for attention by government for females in the 15–24-year-old age group (EPA 1997). The environment is also a higher priority for attention by government for both males and females in the 15–24-year-old age group (EPA 1997: 50). In the earlier survey (1994: 45), lack of education was mentioned by 86% of respondents as a cause of environmental problems, and in the more recent survey (1997: 15) 'education about the environment' was considered to be the most important initiative that the New South Wales state government could implement over the next few years.

In a recent national survey of school students (Ainley *et al.* 1998: 114) 72% of primary school students and 43% of secondary school students felt that 'in the future ... we will look after the environment better', although some (26% of primary students and 49% of secondary students) thought that 'in the future ... the world's environment will get worse'. Ainley *et al.* (1998, pp. 115–118) could find only slight contributing factors to this decline in optimism, such as students from non-English-speaking backgrounds indicating a greater optimism than students from an English-speaking background, and students in Year 5 who intended to complete secondary schooling were slightly more optimistic than their peers who intended to leave at Year 10. Perhaps by developing a more mutualistic relationship between the science education and environmental education, students might develop a greater optimism for the future of the environment by increasing their knowledge and skills related to the environment.

Science education and environmental education nationally and in Victoria

The arguments put forward nearly two decades ago for science education being a 'limited vehicle' for environmental education focused upon traditional practices of Western science education (grounded in Western understandings of science). I regret that, in many ways these arguments seem to be as reasonable today as they were then. As I discuss below, while there have been changes to the rhetoric of science education at some levels, there have been and continue to be very powerful forces resisting the types of changes to current science education practices that many environmental educators desire. In addition, we need to move discussion beyond the 'wish it would be', and 'logically it should be', to an analysis of how certain power structures have resisted change.

In Australia, environmental education has been included in the national goals for schooling for over a decade. In April 1989, the Australian Education Council proposed 10 common and agreed national goals for schooling in Australia, entitled the *Hobart Declaration*, which include the need to develop in students 'an understanding of and concern for balanced development and global environment' (AEC 1994a: 43). This was updated in the April 1999 *Adelaide Declaration* (*National Goals for Schooling in the Twenty-first Century*) where one of the goals states that 'when students leave school they should . . . have an understanding of, and concern for, stewardship of the natural environment, and the knowledge and skills to contribute to ecologically sustainable development' (as quoted in Environment Australia 2000: 6). Similarly, the recent Victorian policy statement on environmental education (Department of Education 1998a: 4) includes the following goals for programs in environmental education:

• to foster in students an appreciation of the environment, their relationship with it and their responsibility for its future; and
• to develop in students the knowledge, skills, attitudes, values and commitment to initiate individual and collective responses that are environmentally responsible.

However, while these goals are consistent with the *Tbilisi Declaration* (UNESCO 1978) they are advisory only and neither enforceable nor accountable in curriculum reforms at the state level.

The marginalization of environmental education P-10[1]

The descriptions of science education curriculum in documents such as *A Statement on Science for Australian Schools* (AEC 1994a) and the Victorian *Curriculum and Standards Framework: Science* (Board of Studies 1995, 2000a) present a view of science that is virtually indistinguishable from the conventional views of science contained in documents of the early 1980s. However, statements of the rationale for science education have changed. Two decades ago, Lucas (1980, pp. 20–21) challenged science educators to 'not ignore the other forces acting to promote environmental wisdom' and to 'begin to look beyond the confines of their own and other educational literature for inspiration for research and practice'. As the following examples demonstrate, science education appears to have adopted goals and principles that promote environmental wisdom, but there is little evidence of the science educators who write these statements looking to other literatures for inspiration. Also, science is still represented largely as being disengaged from broader social issues.

The national science curriculum position statement (AEC 1994a: 6) includes the principle that effective learning experiences in science should complement the learning that occurs in other learning areas (such as *Studies of Society and Environment*). The statement also asserts that problems concerning the environment, economic development and global sustainability are among the most pressing facing the world today, and notes that 'Whether we can solve these problems depends partly on science and partly on the political, social and economic forces that shape local and global action' (AEC 1994a: 6). This argument is grounded in the UNESCO discourses and indicates that there is scope for the development of environmental education within a science curriculum.

The goals of science education spelt out in the statement reflect a different view of science education from that traditionally practised in schools (AEC 1994a: 5), These include developing

- students' understanding and appreciation of the evolutionary nature of scientific knowledge and the nature of science as a human endeavour, its history, its relationship with other human endeavours and its contribution to society; and
- students' abilities to make decisions that include ethical consideration of the impact on people and the environment of the processes and likely products of science.

Unfortunately, there is little evidence to date that these goals have been taken into account in science curriculum development activities at the state level. Some reasons for this resistance are discussed below.

In Victoria, the Science Curriculum and Standards Framework (CSF II) (Board of Studies 2000a) reduces science education to a list of curriculum foci and learning outcomes and indicators to be achieved and reported upon to parents. However, in contrast with the earlier version (Board of Studies 1995), the current overview of CSF II (Board of Studies 2000d) describes a place for environmental education in the curriculum:

Environmental education in the CSF encompasses three major components:

- Education about the environment, which focuses on key knowledge and understanding of the ecological functioning of the environment. This is located primarily within the Science and SOSE key learning areas.
- Education in the environment. This provides for students to experience the environment and develops positive attitudes and values towards steward-ship of the environment. Opportunities for education in the environment are found especially in SOSE and Health and Physical Education.
- Education for the environment, which focuses on students taking action for the protection or conservation of the environment. This includes the devel-opment of skills to enable students to be active and informed participants in environmental decision-making policy. This is located primarily in the SOSE, Science and H&PE key learning areas.

Specific references to environmental education are indicated by the use of the icon [p. 234] in the text,

The possibilities for implementing environmental education in each of the three named key learning areas of the curriculum are indicated by a small icon (a leaf – see Figure 23) placed alongside relevant examples of contexts and learning activities or skills, processes and procedures within a curriculum focus at each level in a strand. However, the icon is easily overlooked and, in any case, heeding its meaning is discretionary. Indeed, the icon appears only 32 times in a listing of over 400 examples and in most instances signals trivial activities and procedures of questionable pertinence to environmental education. These include:

- 'tell a story about how to look after a pet or farm animal' (Level 1, Board of Studies 2000a: 18);
- 'map the location of world volcanic activity and relate it to earthquake zones' (Level 4, Board of Studies 2000a: 34);

- 'map HAZCHEM signs in a school or shopping precinct and recommend a counter disaster plan' (Level 5, Board of Studies 2000a: 40);
- 'summarise the extraction, processing and use of a mineral or fuel by constructing an annotated flow chart, using computer graphics' (Level 6, Board of Studies 2000a: 54).

Such token gestures do little to reduce the marginalization of environmental education in science curriculum.

It is also significant that the Overview statement (Board of Studies 2000d) is not included in the Science CSF II (Board of Studies 2000a) but is available only as a separate document or on the Board's website. Thus many science teachers may be unaware of its existence. Moreover, although the Science CSF II notes that a special reference to environmental education is designated by the leaf icon (Board of Studies 2000a: 3), the document provides no explanation as to what environmental education is.

In Science, there are only five learning outcomes (out of a total of 54) that have environmental content, and none of these has indicators that go beyond education about the environment. The belief appears to be that 'science can make its contribution to education *for* the environment merely by careful choice of environmentally related topics for existing science courses' (Lucas 1980: 11). Apart from teaching this content, a science teacher can easily minimize consideration of environmental issues (and ignore teaching in or for the environment), and most do so because they feel pressured to cover the curriculum as it stands. This is despite the high levels of student interest in the environment (and low levels of interest in science), as discussed earlier in this chapter.

Figure 23 Leaf symbol for insertion in the text (shown exact size as in Board of Studies 2000a)

The rhetoric–reality gap between the overview statements on the importance of environmental education in science education and the curriculum outcomes statements in science framework documents, and between the content taught by teachers and the interests of students, raises once more the spectre of science education as a limited vehicle for environmental education at the P-10 level. Despite all the research and literature related to making science education more relevant to society's needs for a scientifically literate citizenry (and the significance of environmental education for achieving this), as well as meeting students' interests, most science education practices continue much as they were in the early 1980s (and before). There are several explanations for this.

First, the global trend in the past decade or so for standardized curriculum documents with specified content and reportable learning outcomes has meant that teachers no longer have the discretion to plan their own curriculum to the extent they once could. In Victoria from 1987 until 1995, the only science curriculum statement was a non-prescriptive framework that accepted that 'any school can only teach a sample of all the knowledge, skills and experiences related to science' (Malcolm 1987: 35) within a platform that included the statement that 'science education should be concerned with environmental management, and the survival and quality of life for all' (Malcolm 1987: 9). The openness of this framework meant that teachers could develop a localized curriculum consistent with the goals and objectives of environmental education, and many did so (see, for example, Malcolm 1988). However, with the introduction of the CSF and its requirements to report to parents on the achievement of the specified learning outcomes, teachers believed that they had lost the option of planning a local curriculum and retreated to teaching science from textbooks that covered the science learning outcomes and little else.

Second, the content of the science curriculum specified in the new P-10 curriculum statements has been very much influenced by scientists and their priorities for tertiary studies rather than by student interests or educational issues (such as recognition that schools 'can only teach a sample of all the knowledge').

Third, environmental education is seen by many science teachers as yet another pressure for inclusion in an already overcrowded curriculum, and as an area in which they may have little interest.

Fourth, many science teachers are, in Lucas's terms, 'disciplinary chauvinists' who place a higher priority on teaching content from their own disciplinary specialization rather than engage the interdisciplinary or cross-disciplinary demands of environmental science.

As a final and most significant point, the question remains as to whether science teachers understand environmental education as it is understood by environmental educators. The examples cited above from CSF II suggest that those who control the science curriculum have only a very superficial understanding of environmental education. Indeed, such representations of environmental education for science educators reinforce the view that science is a limited vehicle for environmental education within the current curriculum.

A senior secondary case study in environmental science

Environmental education was introduced as a separate subject in the curriculum at the senior secondary level in Victoria in 1975. Initially entitled 'Agricultural and Environmental Science', it became 'Environmental Science' in 1977. In 1991 it moved from being a science to being in the 'Earth Studies' field of study (and subsequently the SOSE key learning area) and entitled 'Environmental Studies' (Board of Studies 1994). From 2001 there are two environmental education subjects at the senior secondary level: 'Environmental Science' (a science subject, Board of Studies 2000b) and 'Outdoor and Environmental Studies' (a health and physical education subject, Board of Studies 2000c). In this section I will focus upon 'Environmental Science' in its various incarnations. This subject is rare in the Australian situation with only Tasmania offering a similar subject at this level.

The 'Environmental Science' (and 'Environmental Studies') course outlines have always been multidisciplinary in their approach. 'Environmental Studies' draws on both natural and social sciences to develop an understanding of different environments and provide a context for investigating strategies for conservation management (Board of Studies 1994, Mitchell 1999). 'Environmental Science' is a broadly based science subject, which draws on the traditional disciplines of biology, chemistry and physics and applies their concepts in environmental contexts. It focuses on developing an understanding of natural ecosystems and human impact upon them as well as the application of environmental science to ecologically sustainable development and environmental management (Board of Studies 2000b). Much control has been exerted to ensure that the subject is acceptable to scientists and science teachers

Table 8 Enrolments in VCE science subjects and environmental studies in 1992, 1995 and 2000

Subject	Enrolment year		
	1992	1995	2000
Biology	15,183	10,918	10,749
Chemistry	10,737	8,503	8,316
Physics	10,176	7,106	7,808
Psychology	7,831	9,428	12,117
Environmental studies	980	826	662

whereas the study design for 'Outdoor and Environmental Studies' (Board of Studies 2000c) has been allowed to be more holistic in its approach.

Since its inception, however, 'Environmental Science' has been a marginalized subject within the senior curriculum. Although accepted for entry purposes as a science by the major universities in Victoria in the 1980s, the subject has never reached anywhere near the level of enrolments of any of the traditional senior science subjects and, indeed, has declined in enrolments during the 1990s (see Table 8).

Fensham (1990) and Mitchell (1999) have documented various aspects of the seemingly constant battle for survival that has faced the subject since the late 1980s. The arguments for abolishing it have had two main themes. First, there have been attempts 'to hoist environmental education on its own petard ... that there is a weakness in a sectional and optional subject approach' (Fensham 1990: 18). Instead of a separate subject, opponents have argued that the environment should be included as a factor in other subject areas. Supporters of the separate subject have countered that, until the ideal of an environmental ethic overarches 'the whole curriculum and indeed the life and practice of the school and educational system ... environmental subjects need to exist to exemplify what environmental education is' (Fensham 1990: 18). From 2001, in Victoria, the senior secondary subjects of biology, chemistry, economics and geography are to have a strengthened environmental orientation and there will be two environmental subjects: 'Outdoor and Environmental Studies' and 'Environmental Science'. While the student enrolments are traditionally much higher in the former subjects, it remains to be seen what the numbers will be for these two new subjects (their predecessors had approximately 1550 and 660 respectively in 2000). Until we achieve the ideal of an environmental ethic, we are going to need both approaches, and we will need to work on raising the level of acceptability of the environmental subjects and bring them in from the margins.

The second argument focused on the overlap of subject matter between Environmental Science and other subjects such as geography and biology and some of the other sciences. As Fensham (1990: 23) notes, 'except for Psychology which at this point is very individually oriented', Physics, Chemistry and Biology 'quite explicitly refer both to the importance of the sciences for solving social and environmental problems and to the problems that the application of science in the form of various technologies have caused'. However, as with the Science CSF II, the focus in these subjects is on education *about* the environment rather than *for* the environment, i.e. on facts and concepts rather than the values, cognitive tasks and social skills that characterize environmental education. The current study design for Geography (Board of Studies 2000e) is very like that of the old Environmental Studies (Board of Studies 1994), but that is because Geography has expanded its territory to include studies *for* the environment as well as its traditional focus on studies *about* and *in* the environment.

Although the traditional sciences have also declined in enrolments during the 1990s (the increase in Physics enrolments in 2000 is an interesting change in trends), Psychology has continued to grow in popularity. Various explanations can be offered for the growth in popularity of Psychology compared with the other science subjects but these are beyond the scope of this chapter. However, from an environmental education perspective, the future enrolments in Environmental Science are the significant figures. These will be affected by the number of universities that are willing to accept Environmental Science as a legitimate science subject for pre-requisite entry purposes and the number of schools that are willing to offer the subject, as well as student interest in the new subject. Environmental educators will monitor the future of this subject with interest as it is an attempt to address some of the mutualistic concerns raised in this chapter.

Science education and environmental education as mutualism

Science education needs environmental education to reassert itself in the curriculum by making science seem appropriate to a wider range of students and making it more culturally and socially relevant. Environmental education needs science education to underpin the achievement of its objectives and to provide it with a legitimate space in the curriculum to meet its goals because they are very unlikely to be achieved from the margins.

An examination of educational politics over recent years indicates that environmental education continues to be a priority for environment ministries but not education ministries (see e.g. Environment Australia 2000) whereas science education is a perennial priority in education ministries (Gough 1997, Department of Education 1998b). Even where there is an environmental education policy from an education ministry (Department of Education 1998a), it is advisory rather than mandatory. Thus, from both science education and environmental education perspectives it would seem politically astute to forge a new, mutually beneficial relationship between the two areas.

A science education which is mutually respectful of environmental education bears little resemblance to that criticized by Robottom (1983), but accepts Lucas's (1980) challenge to look elsewhere for inspiration for research and practice. As a starting point, this different agenda for environmental science education will involve some integration of the sciences, will be problem orientated, will consider the scientific aspects of real systems (not abstracted ones), and will (finally) recognize the need for contributions from other disciplines (Fensham 1978, Lucas 1980) rather than being separate from them. However, developing a new relationship will also involve more than this – as the lack of success of past attempts to develop environmental education within the P-10 science curriculum and to create a popular senior secondary environmental science curriculum in Victoria testify. A new environmental science education will need to take account of:

- critiques of traditional science education from feminist, post-colonialist and anti-racist perspectives (see e.g. Harding 1993, 1998, Brickhouse 1994, Gough 1998);
- critiques of traditional science education from cultural and constructivist perspectives (see e.g. Aikenhead and Jegede 1998, and Bencze 2000 respectively);
- declining interest of students in studying science at school (Dekkers and De Laeter 1997);

- frequent calls for increasing the scientific literacy of the general public (Shahn 1988, Willis 1990, Jenkins 1992, 1994);
- discussions of the role of science in environmental discourse (Hajer 1995); and
- research that explores differences between the youth of today and previous generations (Gough 1999).

It will also need to consider significant reports, such as *Our Common Future* (WCED 1987), which envisage a positive role for science and technology and a relationship between scientific knowledge and environmental education. For example, 'our technology and science gives us at least the potential to look deeper into and better understand natural systems' (WCED 1987: 1), 'the promotion of sustainable development will require an organized effort to develop and diffuse new technologies' (WCED 1987: 87) and 'unless action is taken to accumulate biological knowledge, valuable information . . . will be lost forever' (WCED 1987: 88). Education is given the task of providing 'comprehensive knowledge, encompassing and cutting across the social and natural sciences and the humanities, thus providing insights on the interaction between natural and human resources, between environment and development' (WCED) 1987: 113).

The science education that can have a relationship with environmental education (and sustainable development) is not necessarily that currently practised, but a reconstructed form, which incorporates a more mutualistic relationship, could well be what is needed.

Some science educators have recognized the possibilities of forging a different relationship between science and environmental education. For example, Jenkins voices the challenge that 'perhaps most difficult of all, however, is constructing science courses which will help empower young people as future citizens in ways that existing science courses are widely seen as having failed to do so' (1992: 243) and notes that 'environmental education exposes with particular clarity the complex interactions among social, economic, personal and other value positions associated with almost any environmental issue' (1994: 606). He believes that it is fundamental for students to be engaged with genuine practical reasoning in order to experience a science education for action, so there is a need for a local context or community of practice to make the experiences genuine, and without this the activity is reduced to its technical dimension. The local context also provides the opportunity for generation of local knowledge informing and empowering action. Privileging local knowledge also helps to destabilize notions of the universal status of scientific knowledge.

In Jenkins's proposal there is a vital connection between science education and environmental education. Environmental education should have an *in* the environment component, an *about* the environment component and a *for* the environment component (Lucas 1979). Through Jenkins's science education for action there is the potential to realize all of these dimensions. Such a proposal might be threatening to those who practise traditional science education, but as the numbers of disinterested students in class increase and the total numbers of students studying science decline, the alarm bells should be triggered that change is needed in science education practices. Adopting an environmental education approach may be just what science education needs. However, the task is to convince those who control the school curriculum and those who teach science in classrooms that science education needs to change. The most recent review in Victoria gave recognition to a place for environmental education in the science curriculum (Board of Studies 2000a), which had not been there previously (Board of Studies 1995). However, as I have discussed above, there is a need for much more reform if environmental education is to become any more than advisory in the science curriculum.

Conclusion

The origins of this chapter lie in my interest in developing a different relationship between environmental education and science education as distinct from the previously characterized limited one. Rather than accepting that science education is something static and, in its traditional form, incompatible with environmental education, I have explored arguments for reconstructing science education to make it more appealing to senior secondary students, more consistent with calls for scientific literacy (or science for action) and compatible with critiques of traditional science education forthcoming from feminists, post-colonialists and others. Similarly, environmental education cannot be seen as something static, monumentalized at Tbilisi and never to be changed. This too must take into account critiques and changes, such as in the light of Agenda 21.

Rather than accepting the confines of traditional science education and its rejection of values and action which make it unattractive to many, the challenge is to change the science education curriculum so it can have a mutually beneficial relationship with environmental education. Not a simple task, but a worthwhile one – for all!
[. . .]

Notes

1. The Australian education system separates the last two years of (post-compulsory) secondary schooling from the preceding (compulsory) years (P-10) and I will follow this convention here. However, the emphasis in my discussion in this section is on the lower secondary years (7–10).

References

Aikenhead, G. and Jegede, O. (1998) Cross-cultural science education: a cognitive explanation of a cultural phenomenon. *Journal of Research in Science Teaching*, 36, 268–288.
Ainley, J., Batten, M., Collins, C. and Withers, G. (1998) *Schools and the Social Development of Young Australians* (Melbourne: Australian Council for Educational Research).
Ashley, M. (2000) Science: an unreliable friend to environmental education? *Environmental Education Research*, 6, 269–280.
Australian Education Council AEC (1994a) *A Statement on Science for Australian Schools* (Canton: Curriculum Corporation).
Australian Education Council AEC (1994b) *A Statement on Studies of Society and Environment for Australian Schools* (Canton: Curriculum Corporation).
Bencze, J.L. (2000) Democratic constructivist science education: enabling egalitarian literacy and self-actualization. *Journal of Curriculum Studies*, 32, 847–865.
Board of Studies (1994) *VCE Environmental Studies Study Design* (Carlton: Board of Studies).
Board of Studies (1995) *Curriculum and Standards Framework: Science* (Carlton: Board of Studies).
Board of Studies (2000a) *Curriculum and Standards Framework II: Science* (Carlton: Board of Studies).
Board of Studies (2000b) *VCE Environmental Science* (Carlton: Board of Studies).
Board of Studies (2000c) *VCE Outdoor and Environmental Studies* (Carlton: Board of Studies).
Board of Studies (2000d) *Curriculum and Standards Framework II: Overview* (Carlton: Board of Studies). Available online: http://www.bos.vic.edu.au/csf/csfII/overview.htm (10 January 2001).
Board of Studies (2000e) *VCE Geography* (Carlton: Board of Studies).
Brickhouse, N. (1994) Bringing in the outsiders: reshaping the sciences of the future. *Journal of Curriculum Studies*, 26, 401–416.
Buzzati-Traverso, A. (1977) Some thoughts on the philosophy of environmental education. In *Trends in Environmental Education* (Paris: UNESCO), 13–19.

Carson, R. (1962) *Silent Spring* (Greenwich, CT: Fawcett).

Connect. UNESCO International science, technology and environmental education newsletter (1997–present day), formerly UNESCO-UNEP environmental education newsletter (1976–1996).

Dekkers, J. and De Laeter, J.R. (1997) The changing nature of upper secondary school science subject enrolments. *Australian Science Teachers' Journal*, 43, 35–41.

Department of Education (1998a) *Investing in the Future.' Environmental Education for Victoria's Schools* (Melbourne: Department of Education).

Department of Education (1998b) *Science Engineering Technology Strategy: SET for Success* (Melbourne: Department of Education).

Ehrlich, P.R. (1968) *The Population Bomb.* (New York: Ballantyne).

Ehrlich, P.R. (1969) *Eco-catastrophe!* (San Francisco, CA: City Lights Books).

Environment Australia (2000) *Environmental Education for a Sustainable Future: National Action Plan* (Canberra: Environment Australia).

Environment Protection Authority (1994) *Who Cares About the Environment?* (Sydney: Environment Protection Authority).

Environment Protection Authority (1997) *Who Cares About the Environment in 1997?* (Sydney: Environment Protection Authority).

Fensham P.J. (1978) Stockholm to Tbilisi – the evolution of environmental education. *Prospects*, VIII, 446–455.

Fensham P.J. (1990) Developments and challenges in Australian environmental education. *Australian Journal of Environmental Education*, 6, 15–27.

Fensham P.J. and May, J.B. (1979) Servant not master – a new role for science in a core of environmental education. *Australian Science Teachers' Journal*, 25, 15–24.

Gough, A. (1997) *Education and the Environment: Policy, Trends and the Problems of Marginalisation* (Melbourne: Australian Council for Educational Research).

Gough, A. (1998) Beyond Eurocentrism in science education: promises and problematics from a feminist poststructuralist perspective. In W.F. Pinar (ed.) *Curriculum: Toward New Identities* (New York: Garland), 185–210.

Gough, A. (1999) Kids don't like wearing the same jeans as their mums and dads: so whose 'life' should be in significant life experiences research? *Environmental Education Research*, 5, 383–394.

Gough, A., Matthews, R. and Milne, G. (1998) *Science: Some Preliminary Research on Years 7–10* (Burwood: Deakin University Faculty of Education for the Science and Technology Taskforce, Department of Education, Victoria).

Gough, A., Marshall, A. and Milne, G. (1999) *Report of Feasibility Study for a Secondary Science Multimedia Resource for Years 7–8* (Burwood: Deakin University Faculty of Education for Department of Education, Victoria).

Greenall, A. (1979) Innovations in science education – CDC's Environmental Education Project. *Australian Science Teachers' Journal*, 25, 41–46.

Hajer, M.A. (1995) *The Politics of Environmental Discourse* (Oxford: Oxford University Press).

Hall, W. (1977) Where next for environmental education? In R.D. Linke (ed.), *Education and the Human Environment* (Canberra: Curriculum Development Centre), 65–76.

Harding, S. (1986) *The Science Question in Feminism* (Ithaca, NY: Cornell University Press).

Harding, S. (1993) Introduction: Eurocentric scientific illiteracy – a challenge for the world community. In S. Harding (ed.), *The 'Racial' Economy of Science.' Toward a Democratic Future* (Bloomington, IN: Indiana University Press), 1–29.

Harding, S. (1998) *Is Science Multicultural? Postcolonialisms, Feminisms, and Epistemologies* (Bloomington, IN: Indiana University Press).

Jenkins, E.W. (1992) School science education: towards a reconstruction. *Journal of Curriculum Studies*, 24, 229–246.

Jenkins, E.W. (1994) Public understanding of science and science education for action. *Journal of Curriculum Studies*, 26, 601–611.

Lucas, A.M. (1979) *Environment and Environmental Education: Conceptual Issues and Curriculum Implications* (Melbourne: Australian International Press and Publications).

Lucas, A.M. (1980) Science and environmental education: Pious hopes, self praise and disciplinary chauvinism. *Studies in Science Education*, 7, 1–26.

Malcolm, C. (1987) *The Science Framework P-10* (Melbourne: Ministry of Education (Schools Division), Victoria).

Malcolm, S. (1988) *Local Action for a Better Environment* (Ringwood: Malcolm).

Mitchell, F. (1999) Environmental science at Years 11 and 12 – a short history. Paper presented at 'Southern Crossings', the international conference of the Australian Association for Environmental Education, Sydney, 14–18 January.

McInnis, N. (1975) The dilemma. In R.J.H. Schafer and J.F. Disinger (eds), *Environmental Education: Perspectives and Prospectives* (Columbus, OH: ERIC), 54–56.

Robottom, I. (1983) Science: A limited vehicle for environmental education. *Australian Science Teachers' Journal*, 29, 27–31.

Shahn, E. (1988) On scientific literacy. *Educational Policy and Theory*, 20, 42–52.

UNESCO (1978) *Intergovernmental Conference on Environmental Education: Tbilisi (USSR), 14–26 October 1977. Final Report* (Paris: UNESCO).

Webster, K. (1996) The secondary years. In J. Huckle and S. Sterling (eds), *Education for Sustainability* (London: Earthscan), 72–85.

Willis, S. (1990) *Science and Mathematics in the Formative Years* (Canberra: Australian Government Publishing Service).

World Commission on Environment and Development WCED (1987) *Our Common Future* (Oxford: Oxford University Press).

PART V

MANAGING CHANGE IN SCIENCE EDUCATION

EDITOR'S INTRODUCTION

The theme of this Part is the gap that always seems to open up between a change that somebody wishes to bring about in an educational system and what actually happens.

Chapter 13 is a synopsis of Fullan's extensive experience in the field. He argues that an educational change fails, as it often does, for some combination of three reasons. First, because many changes are usually far too rational to survive in an irrational world. Logic is always assumed to be superior to psychologic, which is not the case. Second, because changes fail to take into account the local context and culture into which they are to be introduced. It is not necessarily that people are perverse, but that they have often amassed a great deal of experience that tells them (often all too correctly!) that a change will not work. Third, the change, as presented, is often far more complex than the description of it that is provided by its sponsors. Things are assumed that should not be. Fullan argues that the way a change is perceived by an individual sits in one of four quadrants. These are whether that person: is in a position of relevant authority or not; is the initiator of the change or is responding to its introduction. He sets out a set of very useful criteria that, taken together, govern the likelihood of the change's success.

Questions that you may care to ask might include:

- Think of a proposed change in science education of which you have had direct experience and which failed to take place. Why did that happen?
- Thinking of that same failed change, how did you see it in respect to the four quadrants? To what extent does that positioning explain its failure?
- Imagine a change in science education that you would wish to bring about. What would you do to ensure that it had the greatest chance of being successful?
- Think of a change in science education that you would wish to see fail. What would you do to give your wish the greatest chance of prevailing?

One major key to successful change in science education is the instigation of suitable teacher professional development. In Chapter 14, Bell and I present a model of this process based on a long-term teacher development project in New Zealand. Individuals went through three phases of personal development: from coming to see some aspect of their teaching as problematic, through being willing to deal with the restraints in changing that practice, to feeling empowered to make a change. At the same time, they were going through a sequence of social changes: from coming to see that their social isolation was problematic, through changing their perception of collaborative work, to feeling able to initiate collaborative ways of working with other science teaching. The progression in these two aspects was paralleled by a sequence of changes in professional development itself: from feeling able to try out new ideas, through feeling able to adapt those ideas for a particular class, to being able to initiate other changes.

Questions you may care to address might include:

- Can you think of a change in science education during which you underwent personal development?
- To what extent did that same change involve you undergoing social change to some degree?
- To what extent was the overall effect of these changes such that you could, with hindsight, see yourself as having undergone professional development?
- Think of a change in science education that you welcome and in which you will be involved. How might you best prepare yourself to bring about that change?

CHAPTER 13

PLANNING, DOING, AND COPING WITH CHANGE

M. Fullan

The New Meaning of Educational Change 3rd edn (2001) New York: Teachers College Press, pp. 95–112

> Few, if any, strategies can be purely deliberative, and few can be purely emergent. One suggests no learning, the other, no control.
>
> (Mintzberg 1994, p. 25)

For the growing number of people who have attempted to bring about educational change, "intractability" is becoming a household word. Being ungovernable, however, is not the same as being impervious to influence. And the inability to change *all* situations we would ideally like to reform does not lead to the conclusion that *no* situation can be changed.

The picture of change that has been evolving [. . .] needs to be considered from the point of view of what, if anything, can be done about it. To do this, I treat four major aspects of the problem of planning educational change: "Why Planning Fails," "Success Is Possible," "Planning and Coping," and "The Scope of Change."

Why planning fails

> We trained hard . . . but it seemed every time we were beginning to form up into teams we were reorganized. I was to learn later in life that we tend to meet any situation by reorganizing, and what a wonderful method it can be for creating the illusion of progress while producing confusion, inefficiency, and demoralization.
>
> (Gaius Petronius, A.D. 66 cited in Gaynor, 1977)

Understanding why most attempts at educational reform fail goes far beyond the identification of specific technical problems such as lack of good materials, ineffective professional development, or minimal administrative support. In more fundamental terms, educational change fails partly because of the assumptions of planners, and partly because solving substantial problems is an inherently complex business. These two issues are explored in the next two subsections.

Faulty assumptions and ways of thinking about change

There are three interrelated reasons why most planning fails. It is hyperrational; it fails to take into account local context and culture; it is dangerously seductive and incomplete. In a word, the assumptions of policymakers are frequently *hyperrational*

(Wise, 1977, 1988). One of the initial sources of the problem is the commitment of reformers to see a particular desired change implemented. Commitment to *what should be changed* often varies inversely with knowledge about *how to work through a process of change*. In fact, as I shall claim later, strong commitment to a particular change may be a barrier to setting up an effective process of change, and in any case they are two quite distinct aspects of social change. The adage "Where there's a will there's a way" is not always an apt one for the planning of educational change. There is an abundance of wills, but they are *in* the way rather than pointing the way. As we have seen, a certain amount of vision is required to provide the clarity and energy for promoting specific changes, but vision by itself may get in the way if it results in impatience, failure to listen, etc. Stated in a more balanced way, promoters of change need to be committed and skilled in the *change process* as well as in the change itself.

Lighthall's (1973) incisive critique of Smith and Keith's (1971) famous case study of the failure of a new open-concept elementary school provides strong support for the hypothesis that leadership commitment to a particular version of a change is negatively related to ability to implement it. Lighthall states [. . .] that educational change is a process of coming to grips with the *multiple* realities of people, who are the main participants in implementing change. The leader who presupposes what the change should be and acts in ways that preclude others" realities is bound to fail Lighthall describes Superintendent Spanman's first speech to the Kensington school faculty.

> Spanman's visit to Kensington School was to make a presentation to the 21-member faculty. It was not for the purpose of discussing with them their joint problems of creating a whole new kind of education. His purpose was to express to the faculty parts of his reality; it was not to exchange his for theirs. Inasmuch as it was the faculty who were to carry the educational goals and images of his reality into action—that is, to make much of his reality their realities, too—and inasmuch as no person responds to realities other than his own, Spanman's selection of a one-way form of communication was self-defeating. In order for his reality to become part of theirs he would have to have made part of theirs his.
>
> (p. 263)

Innovators who are unable to alter their realities of change through exchange with would-be implementers can be as authoritarian as the staunchest defenders of the status quo. This is not to say that innovators should not have deep convictions about the need for reform or should be prepared to abandon their ideas at the first sign of opposition. Rather [. . .] innovators need to be open to the realities of others: sometimes because the ideas of others will lead to alterations for the better in the direction of change, and sometimes because the others' realities will expose the problems of implementation that must be addressed and at the very least will indicate where one should start.

Lighthall documents how the superintendent and principal at Kensington continually imposed only their own realities and how their stance led in a relatively short time to disastrous results. Lighthall (1973) observed: "The tendency is widespread for problem-solvers to try to jump from their private plans to public implementation of these plans without going through the [number of realities] necessary to fashion them in accordance with problems felt by the adult humans whose energy and intelligence are needed to implement the plans" (p. 282). Sarason (1971) states it another way "An understandable, but unfortunate way of thinking confuses the power (in a legal or organizational chart sense) to effect change with the process of change" (p. 29). In short, one of the basic reasons why planning fails is that planners or decision makers of change are unaware of the situations faced by potential implementers. They introduce changes without providing a means to identify and confront the situational constraints and without attempting to understand the values, ideas, and experiences of those who are essential for implementing any changes.

But what is wrong with having a strong belief that a certain aspect of schooling should be changed? Is it not appropriately rational to know that a given change is necessary, and to make it policy, if one is in a position to do so? [. . .] Aside from the fact that many new programs do not arise from sound considerations, there are other more serious problems. The first problem is that there are many competing versions of what should be done, with each set of proponents equally convinced that their version is the right one. Forceful argument and even the power to make decisions do not at all address questions related to the process of implementation. The fallacy of rationalism is the assumption that the social world can be altered by seemingly logical argument. The problem, as George Bernard Shaw observed, is that "reformers have the idea that change can be achieved by brute sanity."

Wise (1977) also describes several examples of excessive rationalization, as when educational outcomes are thoroughly prescribed (e.g., in competency-based education) without any feasible plan of how to achieve them. Wise characterizes the behavior of some policy makers as wishful thinking: "When policy makers require by law that schools achieve a goal which in the past they have not achieved, they may be engaged in wishful thinking. Here policy makers behave as though their desires concerning what a school system should accomplish, will in fact, be accomplished if the policy makers simply decree it" (p. 45). Wise goes on to argue that even if rational theories of education were better developed—with goals clearly stated, means of implementation set out, evaluation procedures stated—they would not have much of an impact, because schools, like any social organization, do not operate in a rational vacuum. Some may say that they should, but Wise's point is that they do not, and wishing them to do so shows a misunderstanding of the existing culture of the school.

The second missing element is the failure of reformers to go to the trouble of treating local context and culture as vital. Micklethwait and Wooldridge (1996) remind us that policymakers often impose ideas without taking into account local context, and that they are very vulnerable to quick fixes:

Senge and associates (1999) make a similar point:

> The fundamental flaw in most innovators' strategies is that they focus on their innovations, on what they are trying to do—rather than on understanding how the larger culture, structures, and norms will react to their efforts.
>
> (p. 26)

In *What's Worth Fighting for Out There*, Hargreaves and I (1998) argued that we need to take a very different planning approach to so-called resisters because (1) they may have some good ideas, and (2) you ignore them at your peril if they stay around for implementation. There are, in other words, good technical and political reasons for taking resisters more seriously. In some cases, resistance may be a source of learning. Resisters may be right. They may have "good sense" in seeing through the change as faddish, misdirected, and unworkable (Gitlin & Margonis, 1995). Thus, resistance to change can be instructive. As Maurer (1996) observes:

Often those who resist have something important to tell us. We can be influenced by them. People resist for what they view as good reasons. They may see alternatives we never dreamed of. They may understand problems about the minutiae of implementation that we never see from our lofty perch atop Mount Olympus.

(Maurer, 1996, p. 49)

In a similar vein, according to Heifetz (1994), a counterintuitive rule of thumb is required in order to reject "one's emotional impulse . . . to squash those in the community who raise disturbing questions. Consequently, an authority should protect those whom he [or she] wants to silence. Annoyance is often a signal of opportunity" (p. 271). It is a mistake for principals to go only with like-minded innovators. As Elmore (1995) puts it: "[S]mall groups of self-selected reformers apparently seldom influence their peers" (p. 20). They just create an even greater gap between themselves and others that eventually becomes impossible to bridge.

This is not to say that resistance should carry the day, but rather that we need more powerful and sensitive strategies to help instigate the learning and commitment that is necessary for actual implementation and sustained impact.

A third serious flaw concerns the seductive nature of planning when one is aching for a clear solution to urgent problems. Our first guidelines for action for principals (and all leaders) is "steer clear of false certainty" (Hargreaves & Fullan, 1998, p. 105). In times of great uncertainty there is an understandable (but dangerous) need to want to know what to do.

Stacey, the "complexity theorist," explains why:

We respond to the fact that situations are uncertain and conflictual with a rigid injunction that people be more certain and more consensual . . . This denial of uncertainty itself allows us to sustain the fantasy of someone up there being in control and, perhaps, of things turning out for the best if we simply do what we are told, and so it protects us for a while from anxiety. However, because that defensive response involves dependency and a flight from reality, it hardly ever works.

(Stacey, 1996b, pp. 7–8)

Management, leadership, and change gurus can bring about especially seductive kinds of dependency. Their charismatic authority promises people a way out of the chaos that they feel. Gurus cultivate dependent disciples rather than independent thinkers. In his study of the guru phenomenon, psychiatrist Anthony Storr (1997, p. 223) notes that this is because gurus need the reassurance and sense of certainty that having disciples gives them so they can cope with and put aside their own inner doubts. What disciples get out of the relationship is the comfort of someone else taking responsibility for their decisions. Storr eloquently warns us that "the charisma of certainty is a snare which entraps the child who is latent in us all." Disciples of modern gurus, he concludes, are "looking for what they want in the wrong place." I think this is also what Peter Drucker was getting at when he allegedly said, "[P]eople refer to gurus because they don't know how to spell charlatan."

False certainty also occurs when you think you have a good idea, but it turns out that it is incomplete. In Hill and Celio's (1998, pp. 1–10) words, reform theories often have "zones of wishful thinking"; that is, for the reform to be successful certain things have to happen "that the reform needs, but cannot cause." In further work, Hill, Campbell, and Harvey (2000) analyze seven competing reform proposals:

standards-based, teacher development, new school designs, decentralization and site-based management, charter schools, school contracting, and vouchers.

In addition to the problem of multiple, disconnected innovation, [...] Hill, Campbell, & Harvey conclude:

> We learned that there is a plausible case for each of the proposals: each addresses a real problem and would probably cause real changes in public education if fully implemented.
>
> But we also found that none of the proposals was sufficient because none could deliver all of the changes its proponents intended unless other changes which the proposal itself could not deliver, occurred at the same time. For example, reforms based on teacher training do not create incentives to overcome some teachers" reluctance to put in the time and effort to improve their knowledge and skills. In a similar vein, reforms such as vouchers do not in themselves guarantee that there will be a plentiful supply of high-quality independent school providers or that enough teachers and principals to run such schools exist.
>
> (p. 23)

We have, of course, now wandered into the next topic—solving today's educational problem is complex; it *is* rocket science.

Complex problems

Solving complex problems on a continuous basis is enormously difficult because of the sheer number of factors at play. It is further complicated because the *sine qua non* of successful reform is whether *relationships improve*; in fact, we have to learn how to develop relationships with those we might not understand and might not like, and vice versa (Fullan, 2001).

Chaos or complexity theorists put it best:

> Most textbooks focus heavily on techniques and procedures for long-term planning, on the need for visions and missions, on the importance and the means of securing strongly shared cultures, on the equation of success with consensus, consistency, uniformity and order. [However, in complex environments] the real management task is that of coping with and even using unpredictability, clashing counter-cultures, disensus, contention, conflict, and inconsistency. In short, the task that justifies the existence of all managers has to do with instability, irregularity, difference and disorder.
>
> (Stacey, 1996a, pp. xix–xx)

Stating the case more fully (and dauntingly), Stacey argues:

A complexity theory of organization is built on the following propositions:

- All organizations are webs of nonlinear feedback loops connected to other people and organizations (its environments) by webs of nonlinear feedback loops.
- Such nonlinear feedback systems are capable of operating in states of stable and unstable equilibrium, or in the borders between these states, that is far-from-equilibrium, in bounded instability at the edge of chaos.
- All organizations are paradoxes. They are powerfully pulled towards stability by the forces of integration, maintenance controls, human desires for security

and certainty, and adaptation to the environment on the one hand. They are also powerfully pulled to the opposite extreme of unstable equilibrium by the forces of division and decentralization, human desires for excitement and innovation, and isolation from the environment.

- If the organization gives in to the pull to stability it fails because it becomes ossified and cannot change easily, If it gives in to the pull to instability it disintegrates. Success lies in sustaining an organization in the borders between stability and instability. This is a state of chaos, a difficult-to-maintain dissipative structure.
- The dynamics of the successful organization are therefore those of irregular cycles and discontinuous trends falling within qualitative patterns. Fuzzy but recognizable categories taking the form of archetypes and templates.
- Because of its own internal dynamics, a successful organization faces completely unknowable specific futures.
- Agents within the system cannot be in control of its long-term future, nor can they install specific frameworks to make it successful, nor can they apply step-by-step analytical reasoning or planning or ideological controls to long-term development. Agents within the system can only do these things in relation to the short term.
- Long-term development is a spontaneously self-organizing process from which new strategic directions may emerge. Spontaneous self-organization is political interaction and learning in groups. Managers have to use reasoning by analogy.
- In this way managers create and discover their environments and the long-term futures of the organizations.

(p. 349)

The positive side, or if you like, the "solution" involves developing learning organizations. In their new field book, Senge and colleagues (2000) argue that fiat or command can never solve complex problems; only a learning orientation can:

This means involving everyone in the system in expressing their aspiration, building their awareness, and developing their capabilities together. In a school that's learning, people who traditionally may have been suspicious of one another—parents and teachers, educators and local business people, administrators and union members, people inside and outside the school walls, students and adults—recognize their common stake in the future of the school system and the things they can learn from one another.

(Senge et al., 2000, p. 5)

Complex indeed! Anything else is tinkering.

Success is possible

Recognizing the limitations of planning is not the same thing as concluding that effective change is unattainable. But in order to determine if planned educational change is possible, it would not be sufficient to locate situations where change seems to be working. We would need to find examples where a setting has been *deliberately transformed* from a previous state to a new one that represents clear improvement. We need to know about the causes and dynamics of how change occurs.

Over the past decade there have been a number of clear examples of how school districts and schools improved the quality of education through a process of deliberate change. The good news is that we have well-documented cases at the school level [. . .], at the district level [. . .], and recently at the state level [. . .]. The bad news is twofold. First, the successful examples are still in the minority in the sense that only a small proportion of schools, districts, and states have been successful in their attempts. The second worry is more disturbing. There is reason to believe that hard-won successes over a period of 5 to 10 years cannot be sustained under current conditions; furthermore, it appears that the accomplishments are real, but superficial. In other words, even the successful cases cannot be expected to last or to be deep.

Be that as it may, successful change is possible in the real world, even under difficult conditions. And many of the reasons for the achievements can be pinpointed. There are classrooms, schools, communities, districts, and states that have altered the conditions for change in more favorable, workable directions. Not every situation is alterable, especially at certain periods of time; but it is a good bet that major improvements can be accomplished in many more settings than is happening at present.

Planning and coping

We have come to the most difficult problem of all. What can we actually do to plan for and cope with educational change? This section contains an overview of the assumptions, elements, and guidelines for action. Additional specific implications for particular roles and agencies (e.g., teacher, principal, superintendent, and federal or state/provincial agencies) [are discussed in later chapters of the original publication]. First, I introduce the topic by indicating some of the basic issues and by noting that advice will have to vary according to the different situations in which we find ourselves. Second, I provide some advice for those who find that they are forced to respond to and cope with change introduced by others. Third, the bulk of the section is addressed to the question of how to plan and implement change more effectively.

In general, there are four logical types of change situations we could face as individuals. These are depicted in Figure 24. There are many different specific roles even

		Authority position	
		YES	NO
Relation to change effort	Initiator or promoter	I Planner (e.g., policymaker)	II Planner (e.g., developer)
	Recipient or responder	III Coper (e.g., principal)	IV Coper (e.g., teacher)

Figure 24 Change situations according to authority position and relation to the change effort

within a single cell that cannot be delineated here, but people generally find themselves in one of the four situations depending on whether they are initiating/promoting a change or are on the receiving end, and whether or not they are in authority positions. I start with coping, or being on the receiving end of change (cells III and IV), because this is the most prevalent situation.

Those in situations of having to respond to a particular change should assume neither that it is beneficial nor that it is useless; that much is clear from the previous analysis. The major initial stance should involve *critical assessment*, that is, determining whether the change is desirable in relation to certain goals and whether it is "implementable"—in brief, whether it is worth the effort, because it *will* be an effort if it is at all worthwhile. Several criteria would be applied. Does the change address an unmet need? Is it a priority in relation to other unmet needs? Is it informed by some desirable sense of vision? Are there adequate (not to say optimal) resources committed to support implementation (such as technical assistance and leadership support)? If the conditions are reasonably favorable, knowledge of the change process outlined in previous chapters could be used to advantage—for example, pushing for technical assistance, opportunities for interaction among teachers, and so on. If the conditions are not favorable or cannot be made favorable, the best coping strategy consists of knowing enough about the process of change so that we can understand why it doesn't work, and therefore not blame ourselves; we can also gain solace by realizing that most other people are in the same situation of nonimplementation. In sum, the problem is one of developing enough meaning vis-à-vis the change so that we are in a position to implement it effectively or reject it, as the case may be.

Those who are confronted with unwanted change and are in authority positions (cell III) will have to develop different coping mechanisms from those in nonauthority positions (cell IV). For the reader who thinks that resisting change represents irresponsible obstinacy, it is worth repeating that nonimplementable programs and reforms probably do more harm than good when they are attempted. The most responsible action may be to reject innovations that are hound to fail and to work earnestly at those that have a chance to succeed. Besides, in some situations resistance may be the only way to maintain sanity and avoid complete cynicism. In the search for meaning in a particular imposed change situation, we may conclude that there is no meaning, or that the problem being addressed is only one (and not the most important or strategic) of many problems that should be confronted. The basic guideline is to work on coherence by selecting and connecting innovations, thereby reducing disjointed overload while increasing focus. [. . .]

We should feel especially sorry for those in authority positions (middle management in district offices, principals, intermediate government personnel in provincial and state regional offices) who are responsible for leading or seeing to implementation but do not want or do not understand the change—either because it has not been sufficiently developed (and is literally not understandable) or because they themselves have not been involved in deciding on the change or have not received adequate orientation or training. The, psychiatrist Ronald Laing captures this situation in what he refers to as a "knot":

> There is something I don't know
> that I am supposed to know.
> I don't know what it is I don't know,
> and yet am supposed to know,
> And I feel I look stupid
> if I seem both not to know it

and not know *what* it is I don't know.
Therefore, I pretend I know it.
This is nerve-wracking since I don't
know what I must pretend to know.
Therefore, I pretend I know everything.
(R. D. Laing, *Knots*, 1970)

This is a ridiculous stance, to be sure, as painful as it is unsuccessful. It can, of course, be successful in the sense of maintaining the status quo. Depending on one's capacity for self-deception, it can be more or less painful as well. In any case, teachers know when a change is being introduced by or supported by someone who does not believe in it or understand it. Yet this is the position in which many intermediate managers find themselves, or allow themselves to be. Those in authority have a need for meaning, too, if for no other reason than that the change will be unsuccessful if they cannot convey their meaning to others.

Planning and implementing change

The implications for those interested in planning and implementing educational change (cells I and II) are very important, because we would all be better off if changes were introduced more effectively. It is useful to consider these implications according to two interrelated sets of issues: What *assumptions* about change should we note? How can we plan and implement change more effectively?

The assumptions we make about change are powerful and frequently subconscious sources of actions. When we begin to understand what change is as people experience it, we begin also to see clearly that assumptions made by planners of change are extremely important determinants of whether the realities of implementation get confronted or ignored. The analysis of change carried out so far leads me to identify ten "do" and "don't" assumptions as basic to a successful approach to educational change.

1. Do not assume that your version of what the change should be is the one that should or could be implemented. On the contrary, assume that one of the main purposes of the process of implementation is to *exchange your reality* of what should be through interaction with implementers and others concerned. Stated another way, assume that the successful implementation consists of some transformation or continual development of initial ideas.
2. Assume that any significant innovation, if it is to result in change, requires individual implementers to work out their own meaning. Significant change involves a certain amount of ambiguity, ambivalence, and uncertainty for the individual about the meaning of the change. Thus, effective implementation is a *process of clarification*. It is also important not to spend too much time in the early stages on needs assessment, program development, and problem definition activities— school staff have limited time. Clarification is likely to come in large part through reflective practice.
3. Assume that conflict and disagreement are not only inevitable but fundamental to successful change. Since any group of people possesses multiple realities, any collective change attempt will necessarily involve conflict. Assumptions 2 and 3 combine to suggest that all successful efforts of significance, no matter how well planned, will experience an implementation dip in the early stages. Smooth implementation is often a sign that not much is really changing.

4. Assume that people need pressure to change (even in directions that they desire), but it will be effective only under conditions that allow them to react, to form their own position, to interact with other implementers, to obtain technical assistance, etc. It is all right and helpful to express what you value in the form of standards of practice and expectations of accountability, but only if coupled with capacity-building and problem-solving opportunities.
5. Assume that effective change takes time. It is a process of "development in use." Unrealistic or undefined time lines fail to recognize that implementation occurs developmentally. Significant change in the form of implementing specific innovations can be expected to take a minimum of 2 or 3 years; bringing about institutional reforms can take 5 or 10 years. At the same time, work on changing the infrastructure (policies, incentives, and capacity of agencies at all levels) so that valued gains can be sustained and built upon).
6. Do not assume that the reason for lack of implementation is outright rejection of the values embodied in the change, or hard-core resistance to all change. Assume that there are a number of possible reasons: value rejection, inadequate resources to support implementation, insufficient time elapsed, and the possibility that resisters have some good points to make.
7. Do not expect all or even most people or groups to change. Progress occurs when we take steps (e.g., by following the assumptions listed here) that *increase* the number of people affected. Our reach should exceed our grasp, but not by such a margin that we fall flat on our face. Instead of being discouraged by all that remains to be done, be encouraged by what has been accomplished by way of improvement resulting from your actions.
8. Assume that you will need a *plan* that is based on the above assumptions and that addresses the factors known to affect implementation. Evolutionary planning and problem-coping models based on knowledge of the change process are essential.
9. Assume that no amount of knowledge will ever make it totally clear what action should be taken. Action decisions are a combination of valid knowledge, political considerations, on-the-spot decisions, and intuition. Better knowledge of the change process will improve the mix of resources on which we draw, but it will never and should never represent the sole basis for decision.
10. Assume that changing the culture of institutions is the real agenda, not implementing single innovations. Put another way, when implementing particular innovations, we should always pay attention to whether each institution and the relationships among institutions and individuals is developing or not.

Finally, do not be seduced into looking for the silver bullet. Given the urgency of problems, there is great vulnerability to off-the-shelf solutions. But most external solutions have failed. The idea is to be a critical consumer of external ideas while working from a base of understanding and altering local context. There is no complete answer "out there."

The scope of change

There are many dilemmas and no clear answers to the question of where to start. The reader who by now has concluded that the theory of educational change is a theory of unanswerable questions will not be too far off the mark, Harry Truman (and later Pierre Trudeau) said, "We need more one-armed economists," because they were frustrated at the advice they kept getting: "On the one hand ... on the other hand" the same can be said about the scope of educational change efforts. No one knows for sure what is best. We are engaged in a theory of probing and understanding the meaning of multiple dilemmas in attempting to decide what to do.

Sarason (1971) identified many of the underlying issues:

> A large percentage of proposals of change are intended to affect all or most of the schools within a system. The assumption seems to be that since the change is considered as an improvement over what exists, it should be spread as wide as possible as soon as possible. The introduction of new curricula is, of course, a clear example of this. What is so strange here is that those who initiate this degree of change are quite aware of two things: that different schools in the system can be depended on differentially to respond to or implement the proposed change, and that they, the sources . . . do not have the time adequately to oversee this degree of change. What is strange is that awareness of these two factors seems to be unconnected with or to have no effect on thinkings about the scope of the change.
>
> (pp. 213–214)

In later work Sarason (1990) maintains that we still have not learned to focus our efforts on understanding and working with the culture of local systems:

> Ideas whose time has come are no guarantee that we know how to capitalize on the opportunities, because the process of implementation requires that you understand well the settings in which these ideas have to take root. And that understanding is frequently, faulty and incomplete. Good intentions married to good ideas are necessary but not sufficient for action consistent with them.
>
> (p. 61)

Above all, planning must consider the preimplementation issues of whether and how to start, and what readiness conditions might be essential prior to commencing. Implementation planning is not a matter of establishing a logical sequence of steps deriving from the innovation or reform at hand.

Two points put the problem of scope in perspective. First, in some situations it may be more timely or compatible with our priorities to concentrate on getting a major policy "on the books," leaving questions of implementation until later. In other words, the first priority is initiation, not implementation. Major new legislation or policies directed at important social reforms often fit this mode—for example, new legislation on desegregation, special education, or restructuring. There is no answer to the question of whether this is more effective than a more gradual approach to legislation, but it should be recognized that implementation is then an immediate problem. Sarason and Doris (1979), in commenting on special education legislation, warn us: "To interpret a decision . . . as a 'victory' is understandable but one should never underestimate how long it can take for the spirit of victory to become appropriately manifested in practice" (p. 358). Much social policy legislation is vague on implementation; some vagueness may be essential in order to get the policy accepted, but nonetheless it means that implementation can be easily evaded. In the face of major value or power resistance, it is probably strategically more effective in the short run to concentrate our energies on establishing new legislation, hoping that in the long run the pressure of the law, the promotion of implementation through incentives and disincentives, and the emergence of new implementers will generate results.

Second, we have reached a stage, face-to-face with urgent need, and equipped with great knowledge of the dynamics of change, where *large-scale reform* must become the agenda—reform which simultaneously focuses on local development and larger system transformation (Fullan, 2000a). In other words, the focus of planning has shifted in recent times, where the most advanced systems are trying to figure out how to coordinate state policy and local development in order to transform large numbers of schools.

We conclude, then, as Mintzherg, Ahlstrand, and Lampei (1998) have, that "strategy formation is complex space":

> Strategy formation is judgmental designing, intuitive reasoning, and emergent learning; it is about transformation as well as perpetuation; it must involve individual cognition and social interaction, cooperation as well as conflict; it has to include analyzing before and programming after as well as negotiating during; and all of this must be in response to what can be a demanding environment. Just try to leave any of this out and watch what happens!
>
> (p. 372–373)

[. . .]

References

Elmore, R. (1995). Getting to scale with good educational practice. *Harvard Educational Review*, 66(1), 1–26.

Fullan, M. (2000a). The return of large scale reform. *The Journal of Educational Change*, 1(1), 1–23.

Fullan, M. (2001). *Leading in a culture of change*. San Francisco: Jossey-Bass.

Gaynor, A. (1977). As study of change in educational organizations. In L. Cunningham (Ed.), *Educational administration* (pp. 28–40). Berkeley, CA: McCutcham.

Gitlin, A. & Margonis, F. (1995). The political aspect of reform. *The American Journal of Education*, 103, 377–405.

Hargreaves, A. & Fullan, M. (1998). *What's worth fighting for out there*. New York: Teachers" College Press; Toronto, Ontario, Canada: Elementary School Teachers" Federation; Buckingham, UK: Open University Press.

Heifetz, R. (1994). *Leadership without easy answers*. Cambridge, MA: Harvard University Press.

Hill, P., Campbell, C., & Harvey, J. (2000). *It takes a city*. Washington, DC: Brookings Institute.

Hill, P. & Celio, M. (1998). *Fixing urban schools*. Washington, DC: Brookings Institute.

Lighthall, F. (1973, February). Multiple realities and organizational nonsolutions: An essay on anatomy of educational innovation. *School Review*, 255–287.

Maurer, R. (1996). *Beyond the wall of resistance*. Austin, TX: Bard Books.

Micklethwait, J. & Wooldridge, A. (1996). *The witch doctors: Making sense of management gurus*. New York: Random House.

Mintzberg, H. (1994). *The rise and fall of strategic planning*. New York: Free Press.

Mintzberg, H., Ahlstrand, B., & Lampei, J. (1998). *Strategy safari: A guided tour through the wilds of strategic management*. New York: Free Press.

Sarason, S. (1971). *The culture of the school and the problem of change*. Boston: Allyn & Bacon.

Sarason, S. (1990). *The predictable failure of educational reform*. San Francisco: Jossey-Bass.

Sarason, S. B. & Doris, J. (1979). *Educational handicap, public policy, and social history*. New York: Free Press.

Senge, P., Kleiner, A., Roberts, C., Ross, R., Roth, G., & Smith, B. (1999). *The dance of change*. New York: Doubleday.

Smith, L. & Keith, P. (1971). *Anatomy of educational innovation: An organizational analysis of an elementary school*. New York: Wiley.

Stacey, R. (1996a). *Strategic management and organizational dynamics* (2nd ed.). London: Pitman.

Storr, A. (1997). *Feet of clay: A study of gurus.* London: HarperCollins.

Wise, A. (1977). Why educational policies often fail: The hyperrationalizaton hypothesis. *Curriculum Studies, 9*(1), 43–57.

Wise, A. (1988). The two conflicting trends in school reform: Legislative learning revisited. *Phi Delta Kappan, 69*(5), 328–333.

CHAPTER 14

A MODEL FOR ACHIEVING TEACHER DEVELOPMENT

B. Bell and John Gilbert

Teacher Development: A Model from Science Education (1996) London: RoutledgeFalmer, pp. 5–37

The learning of the teachers involved in the research project, the Learning in Science Project (Teacher Development), is analysed in this chapter. The data were analysed to give an overview of the adult learning process as it relates to the teachers' learning or teacher development in the study. The model, based on an earlier version (Bell and Gilbert, 1994) has three central features. First, it is possible to describe three main types of development for the teachers involved in the research — social, personal and professional development. Social development as part of teacher development involves the renegotiation and reconstruction of what it means to be a teacher (of science, for example). It also involves the development of ways of working with others that will enable the kinds of social interaction necessary for renegotiating and reconstructing what it means to be a teacher of science. Personal development as part of teacher development involves each individual teacher constructing, evaluating and accepting or rejecting for himself or herself the new socially constructed knowledge about what it means to be a teacher (of science, for example), and managing the feelings associated with changing their activities and beliefs about science education, particularly when they go 'against the grain' (Cochran-Smith, 1991) of the current or proposed socially constructed and accepted knowledge. Professional development as a part of teacher development involves not only the use of different teaching activities but also the development of the beliefs and conceptions underlying the activities. It may also involve learning some science.

Secondly, the teachers' development was occurring within the context of the effective components of a teacher-development programme. These effective components were support, feedback, and reflection and not an overall specified programme such as the particular in-service programme run in any one year of the research. The data are being reported to describe the learning process of the teachers, not a particular programme.

Thirdly, there is a loose and flexible sequence implied in the model which describes the main aspects of learning for each teacher with respect to time. Different situations (confirmation and desiring change, reconstruction and empowerment) are described only to highlight facets of the teacher development process. These situations are not intended to be discrete. There is much interaction between the learning tasks in each type and each situation, and the teachers' learning activities may not indicate a movement 'forward'. For example, the teachers throughout their learning continued to clarify the problematic nature of their teaching. It was not something carried out just at the beginning of the programme.

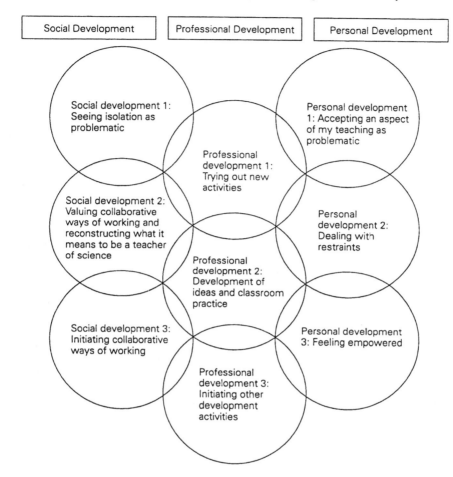

| Social Development | Professional Development | Personal Development |

Social development 1: Seeing isolation as problematic

Personal development 1: Accepting an aspect of my teaching as problematic

Professional development 1: Trying out new activities

Social development 2: Valuing collaborative ways of working and reconstructing what it means to be a teacher of science

Personal development 2: Dealing with restraints

Professional development 2: Development of ideas and classroom practice

Social development 3: Initiating collaborative ways of working

Personal development 3: Feeling empowered

Professional development 3: Initiating other development activities

Figure 25 A model of teacher development

The model

The model is described and explained with respect to the teacher development that occurred as part of the research. The quotations given are to illustrate the overview only. Full details of the data and data analysis are given in Bell (1993a). A diagrammatic representation of the model is given in Figure 25.

Initial personal development

As part of this initial personal development, a teacher was aware, however inchoately, and accepting of a professional dissatisfaction or problem. This aspect of development was usually private, having been self-initiated and sustained before the teacher engaged with the teacher development on offer. For example, one teacher commented on her reasons for joining the programme:

Because I wasn't happy with how I was presenting things. The kids were getting good marks. But I wasn't happy, I just didn't like it, I wasn't getting to every kid in the class, you could see their eyes glazing over ... So I was looking for something new and I didn't really know what I was looking for. I wanted a new approach to the same stuff but I wanted to be able to present it in a different way that was going to break through those barriers.

(11/I2/91)

Another teacher commented that her reasons for joining the programme were:

... the kids were obviously not responding to what I was doing very much. They were sitting there being very lethargic and it was coming from me and not from them. And they were sort of sponges, I suppose, and really didn't see where they were going or any relevance.

(1/I3/90)

[The first part of the transcript code indicates the teacher who is quoted: the second part indicates the interview (I), survey (S), programme session (P) or meeting (M) in which that comment was made; and the last part indicates the year.]

Prior to the teacher development programme, the teachers had decided that the broad type of activity offered might help overcome the dissatisfaction or problem, and the risk of joining the group and the programme had been taken. The dissatisfaction may have been with the learning of students in the classroom, not feeling competent or confident to implement the new curriculum, or feeling stagnant with respect to their own growth and learning. Hence, the teachers saw the development activities as providing opportunities for their self-initiated growth, overcoming a professional problem, exploring an interesting avenue or helping implement new policy.

In deciding to take the risk of publicly acknowledging the need for improvement or help with changing, the teacher had considered the broad content of the activity, the credibility of the facilitator and, for some teachers who knew each other already, the other group members. The teachers entering the teacher development activities associated with the research project, were seeking new teaching suggestions that work, new theoretical perspectives with which to think about their teaching, to improve the learning in their classrooms, to feel better about themselves as a teacher, and to learn how to put new ideas into action. This personal development may have been as a result of school-development discussions and initiatives or as a result of the individual teacher's deliberations. It involved the clarification and awareness of the problem rather than an experience of being 'wound up' over possible problems.

A few of the teachers who joined the teacher development programme (as 'volunteers') had not undergone the personal development as described above. Therefore, whilst they attended the programme at the onset, they were not necessarily engaged in the learning, change and development initially. They may have been nominated for the programme by the school management, rather than the initiative coming from them; they may have gone along with peer pressure, for example when the rest of the science department volunteered and they didn't want to be on the outside of the group; or they may have joined the programme to enhance their CV for promotion rather than to improve learning in their classrooms.

In these instances the individual personal development had not occurred before the programme commenced and their personal development needs had to be addressed within the programme, by both the facilitator and the other teachers. This usually involved helping the teachers to value their overall teaching competence, and to view only one aspect, that which was the focus of the programme, as problematic. No progress was made until this personal development was undertaken.

Initial social development

Before joining a teacher development programme, the teachers were also aware that their isolation in the classroom was problematic. While being the only adult in a classroom can feel safe from negative criticisms and pressures to change, it does not provide the new ideas, support and feedback necessary for teacher development (Hargreaves, 1992). In addition, while joining a teacher development programme involved taking some risks, the expected benefits of working with other teachers to improve teaching and learning were perceived as greater. The teachers who engaged with the teacher development programme were to varying degrees seeking to work with other teachers:

> I didn't have another teacher in my school that was on the course which was perhaps a disadvantage, looking back on it, and so I tended to use other people at our weekly sessions in that respect to give me confidence because I found it was really quite scary to leave your textbooks behind, to leave your dictatorship from the front behind, to risk having chaos in your classroom, to try something new. So I found the weekly sessions really quite good and the discussions.
>
> (11/M1/90)

> Certainly the big group situation, listening to other teachers, other practising teachers — that was a big plus, to hear how other teachers coped with certain circumstances, to hear that other teachers had the same sorts of difficulties and what they had tried and what successes and failures they have had. But they certainly had more credibility for me than reading it in a book.
>
> (7/I5/91)

The opportunities to discuss their teaching with other teachers and to collectively renegotiate what it means to be a teacher of science were seen positively and as helpful for change.

Initial professional development

The teachers appreciated clarifying the problematic aspect of their teaching. But while they appreciated clarifying an aspect that is problematic, they also needed to feel that their teaching overall was not problematic. The facilitator helped by communicating that they were perceived as competent teachers who were developing, rather than as teachers who were struggling. Valuing their ideas about teaching, by giving time in the sessions for them to talk about what they were doing in the classroom, was part of this communication. It would appear that aspects of the initial personal development still needed to be addressed in the programme sessions.

The teachers were also encouraged to adopt the role of teacher-as-researcher. They valued finding out more information from their students and about their teaching, for example, what views of floating and sinking the students had and how many times in a lesson they asked the girls and the boys to answer their questions. This additional information helped them to clarify the problem they may have perceived in their teaching.

The teachers were also asked to adopt the role of teacher-as learner so that they viewed their professional development as learning rather than as a remedial process. A supportive atmosphere helped to ease the uncomfortable feelings associated with learning — feeling incompetent or inadequate — and the uncomfortableness of getting in touch with feelings associated with prior experiences and beliefs. Part of the programme was given to enabling the teachers to learn about the change process. Gaining this metacognition was supportive in that it helped the teachers to understand what was happening for them.

From the beginning of the programme, the teachers were given new teaching activities to use in the classroom, with the expectation that they would use the activities when they felt ready, and that they would have an opportunity to talk about their use of them in a sharing session. Using the new activities required prior planning, visualizing what it might be like to use the activity, preparation of new resources and being convinced that the new activity was needed and would work. The activities were small in scope — an activity not a unit of work or whole teaching sequence; were short in duration, for example, ten to thirty minutes in length; could be done with a wide range of students, for example, across age and attainment groups; were not part of the official teaching and therefore could be done with a small group of students, rather than the whole class; and involved a change of teacher and student performance.

Another important feature of the new teaching activities was that they were seen as likely to lead to better learning conditions, to better classroom management, to 'feeling better about myself as a teacher', and to better learning outcomes (Bell, 1993a, pp. 154–214). The new activities could be understood, talked about with colleagues, and reflected on. However, the activities were also able to be used by the teachers as technicians and as novices rather than experts. Examples of the activities used were an interview-about-instances on burning and a survey based on a piece of research on students' alternative conceptions of burning (Biddulph, 1991). These activities helped the teachers to find out more about their students' thinking. In doing so, they were clarifying a problematic aspect of their teaching, adopting the role of teacher-as-researcher, and using a new teaching activity — one that can be used by a teacher who takes into account students' thinking.

The use of new teaching activities led to talking and thinking about the new teaching activities. The teachers wanted to talk about how the activities went for them. Initially, the discussions were about the concerns the teachers had with getting the activities to work with respect to classroom management and resource management. For example:

> As far as operating the interactive teaching within the school I think we may have to look at getting resource materials together to take some strain off staff and how we actually operate our lab technicians.
>
> (1/I5/90)

Later on, the discussions tended to be more about the educational issues involved in using the activities; for example, the issue of assessment:

> ... I really think the assessment area is one that still needs work. How do we actually go about it and do something in a sort of objective assessment way. We have said we all feel that the kids are doing better, we feel that this is going on and that sort of thing. We have no real measure of it and that is a wee bit of a problem, I think, because there would be those who wouldn't accept that sort of analysis.
>
> (1/I12/91)

The other teachers valued listening to whether or not the activities worked in the classroom, and discussing concerns and problems arising from their use. For example:

> Well I think the camaraderie of that big group was a strong factor in all (our) development. The sharing of ideas, the realization that others had the same sorts of problems and also the chance to look at a problem from a different angle, to hear someone else's point of view on a particular problem, someone else's solution to a particular problem.
>
> (7/I1/90)

The talking went on in the sharing sessions through the telling of anecdotes (Bell, 1993a, pp. 279–319). The discussion arising helped the teachers to clarify their existing ideas on teaching, the role of the teacher, learning and learners. It also enabled new theoretical perspectives on science education to be introduced. For example, the findings of the interviews and surveys about burning (Biddulph, 1991) were shared with the rest of the group in the sharing sessions and the facilitator's questions helped the teachers to clarify their ideas about 'better' learning (Bell and Pearson, 1992). The notions of children's science and constructivist views of learning were also introduced and reflected on over many sessions. In addition, the discussions raised the problem of what to do next; for example, how does the teacher interact with a student who views burning as a process in which things disappear. Problematic aspects of teaching were able to be clarified.

A priority for the teachers was the development of a supportive atmosphere — one in which they felt encouraged to use the new activities; felt that their knowledge and expertise were valued and were seen as useful contributions; felt that their concerns about the possibility of judgments and put-downs were allayed; perceived that the feedback given was supportive and helpful; were able to share their problems and concerns publicly; felt supported; and found that their feelings associated with change were attended to in a non-threatening way. For example:

> I found the discussion quite essential really because it is — you need a bit of raw courage to go out of the security of a textbook and go into something that is totally unknown and the first time I tried I really didn't have a good experience at all. But because of the encouragement of the group and you get various ideas from various people around the group, then you think well I will have another go. It really gave you the support that you needed.
>
> (11/M1/90)

The second personal development

As the teacher development continued, the teachers developed further in a personal way. Each individual teacher had to construct and evaluate for himself or herself, an understanding of the socially reconstructed knowledge of what it means to be a teacher of science. This second phase of personal development also involved dealing with restraints; in particular, attending to the feelings and concerns of behaving differently in the classroom and changing their ideas about what it means to be a teacher of science. Their concerns included fear of losing control in the classroom; amount of teacher intervention; covering the curriculum; knowing the subject; meeting assessment requirements: relationships with students; and appraisal.

Fear of losing control in the classroom

Many teachers get a sense of worth and competence from keeping control in the classroom and having a reputation amongst colleagues of being a teacher who has good classroom control. Using new activities made some teachers feel that they had little or no control. This was indicated in the classroom by an increased noise level; for example:

> The things that you notice initially, especially when you are starting things up, is the amount of noise level that you get and have to be tolerant of. Generally speaking it is constructive noise though. If you come from a situation where you have taught very much teacher dominated, you are very much in control. It is quite difficult to get over, first thing.
>
> (15/M2/91)

Other occurrences that may suggest less control were more movement around the room by students; students making decisions about curriculum content and activities within a broad framework; students challenging the teachers' ideas and being perceived as challenging their authority; and the teachers not being able to plan in the same way as before and feeling that they did not quite know where they were going and what to expect. The teachers were probably still in control but they did not feel like they were. Developing their notions of what it means to be in control in the classroom and attending to the associated feelings were important.

Amount of teacher intervention

In changing roles in the classroom, a teacher may feel uncertain and insecure about the new amount and kind of teacher involvement in giving students the information and the 'right' answers. A lesser amount of intervention resulted in some teachers feeling that they were irresponsible, not helping students and not doing their job — teaching — properly. Also, how to respond to students who have constructed the 'wrong' answer or are doing the 'wrong' things was of concern. These. feelings associated with what it feels like to be helping or not helping students to learn, needed to be attended to.

Covering the curriculum

Most teachers are rightly concerned about their responsibilities to students, parents, employers and the Government to ensure that the prescribed curriculum is covered. When using new teaching activities, the teachers had concerns and needed reassurance that the curriculum was being covered and that the students were not being disadvantaged; for example:

> It was more that their questions, what they were interested in, (were) not necessarily what the scheme said that we had to cover or the syllabus says we have to cover. It was more the fact that it is all very well answering questions, and I can see that they have learned, but if they still don't know, at the end of the year when they come to the common test and they go into the fourth form, all of the things that the syllabus says they should know, then I am not doing my job as a teacher according to the rules.
>
> (16/12/91)

The teachers sought evidence and confirmation that the curriculum was being covered, or that an initially reduced 'pace of coverage' could be redressed later because the quality of learning was improved. Only then, did they feel that they were being responsible and able to be accountable.

Knowing the subject

Many teachers (primary and secondary) feel insecure about their knowledge of the science content in the curriculum. In using a new teaching activity, the teachers had to learn new aspects of the topic or answer unexpected questions from the students. For example, a primary teacher commented:

> It (knowing the science) does, it affects it (my teaching of science) quite a bit. I avoid it if I can. Even the science unit I am doing now I had to go away and re-think. It was presented to me — why don't you try bubbles etc. The whole time it was going on I thought I don't even understand what I am really doing here. There were some great processes going on and the kids were experimenting with the sort of mixtures they should make and I understood the sorts of things that would make bubbles break, etc. But I didn't really understand the actual whole idea of the bubble and what formed it. And so I went away and read that water has a film and then it all fitted in.
>
> (3/I1/90)

Developing teaching strategies to address these incompetencies in the classroom and attending to the feelings of inadequacy associated with not always knowing the answer, needed to be given time in the teacher development programme.

Meeting assessment requirements

Teachers will not continue to develop and use new teaching activities if they feel that they are unable to meet requirements for assessment and reporting using these new teaching activities. These requirements may be school-based ones such as reporting to parents or using common science department tests. They may be national requirements such as the New Zealand national examination of the School Certificate, sat by students aged 15 years. Given that teacher performance may be judged on examination or test results, it was important that the teachers felt confident that this aspect of their responsibilities and duties was addressed. For example, one teacher commented:

> It is the same with School Certificate, We are going to get our exam marks for School Certificate (SC) looked at because at the moment we are doing a bit of a drive on trying to raise our expectations and improve our exam results. And there is one way in which I can do it, I can turn around and you can rote learn your information in SC. You can go through heaps of questions SC, we can lift those marks alright doing a very traditional method of teaching. And if that then raises our School Certificate marks then that is going to be looked at and say 'you have done a good job'. Hopefully we can also do it through an interactive or a constructivist teaching approach but ...
>
> (1/I11/91)

If this aspect was not addressed, the teachers felt insecure and unwilling to continue to use a new approach and they may have re-evaluated the facilitator's credibility.

The teachers needed to feel confident about new learning outcomes, such as learning-to-learn skills and how to assess these skills. Not all teachers initially felt this was a worthwhile learning outcome, in comparison with content-learning outcomes, and needed time and support to develop their ideas about learning in science and to attend to the feelings associated with this.

Relationships with the students

Of concern to most teachers is their relationship with their students. Most teachers want to be both personally liked and professionally respected by their students. A new teaching activity was evaluated in terms of its effect on the teacher–student relationships. In some cases the feelings associated with a change in the relationship were positive; for example, the students saying that the teacher is more on a par with them now. The changes could also invoke negative feelings, such as feeling not useful when the students were becoming more independent at answering their own questions using a variety of resources other than the teacher; or feeling negative in response to the students challenging the ideas of the teacher more or complaining about not getting so many notes. For example:

> My fifth form has been quite critical that I don't give them notes. One of the other teachers has got everything on OHPs (overhead projector transparencies) and he wanders in, plonks down the OHP, turns the thing on and there is all your notes and they feel very secure. They have got the notes, they are going to learn them in that note form and they are very secure. They don't like coming to me because I don't give them notes like that at all. They write up their experiments, and their conclusion to their experiments, formulate their notes but they don't like it like that because they have got to think and they would rather just turn the handle. So you have got to teach them to actually think . . . And that means there is more effort on their part and they don't like having to put the effort in. So I have had a certain amount of resistance, from the exam classes particularly. 'Just give me the answers'. 'No, you go and find them out'. And they don't like that.
>
> (11/13/91)

The feelings associated with the change in teacher–student relationships needed to be attended to by the teachers,

Appraisal

A new teaching activity may not produce the evidence required by the Government or the employers for the existing techniques of teacher appraisal. For example, members of the New Zealand Education Review Office or a principal may judge the performance of a teacher on the quality of the student workbooks or notebooks. These may be used to assess if the content of the curriculum has been covered and if the students have learnt the curriculum content. One secondary teacher commented:

> (How would you feel if an Inspector had come in and looked at the books, what would have been your response?) Yes, I might have felt slightly uncomfortable. I actually was aware that a couple of times during each unit I would make sure that we did some very solid written book work, sort of intersperse it in there. Just tidy up what we have been doing and then we get something on paper. I think that was also to satisfy parents and students because they like,

particularly this school, it is a working-class area and work is book work. Work is having a lot of tidy things on paper. So I do it, you balance it out.

(8/I3191)

Using a new teaching activity therefore induced negative feelings in some teachers if the new teaching activity did not result in books full of student notes. These feelings needed to be attended to if further teacher development was to occur.

Addressing and resolving the above concerns had both a cognitive and an affective aspect. It appeared to the researchers that it was most crucial to address the affective dimensions if teacher development was to continue. Moreover, the development was both personal and social, in that the culture of what it means to be a teacher was being challenged and renegotiated by the group. Each individual teacher was having to position himself or herself with respect to the newly reconceptualized culture. The extent to which each teacher was able to do this determined their level of engagement in the change process.

In the programmes run as part of the research, these concerns or constraints were attended to in the sessions. First, the facilitator attempted to communicate that these restraints were concerns to be attended to and that teachers' expressions of concern were not being viewed as giving excuses for not changing. Secondly, the teachers received suggestions from the facilitator and the other teachers on ways to get around the restraints. For example, one teacher shared how she got the students to compare their before and after-concept maps with the learning objectives in the national curriculum for that topic. The students were able to give feedback to the teacher that they felt the curriculum content had been covered in their learning activities. At times, the concerns were addressed in a specific workshop activity. However, most of these concerns were addressed when they arose in the telling of anecdotes in the sharing sessions.

The second social development

As the programme continued, the teachers' comments indicated that they were valuing collaborative ways of working. As the trust, support and credibility of the facilitator and other teachers became established, the teachers felt more able to contribute and more comfortable with contributing to the programme activities. They were more likely to share with the group anecdotes about what was happening in their classrooms, to give support and feedback to other teachers, to offer suggestions for new teaching activities, to suggest solutions to problems, and to voice their opinions and views. They were contributing to developing and sustaining collaborative relationships. The value the teachers placed on these relationships is evident in their comments on the sharing sessions and talking with other teachers; for example:

Yes, I have been quite amazed at the techniques that various people have. I reckon discussion in a large group like that is really invaluable. Like last year we had two special science people telling us everything they knew and they were very experienced but they still didn't have all the answers as a group of twelve, fifteen would have, obviously. And also what you'll find, is what I have noticed, myself, personally, is with these teachers, they are really good teachers . . ., they were really top of their field. Most of them are authors of books and as a role model I found them really good but you didn't see the problems that you could have, whether they were hiding the problems or they just didn't come across the problems — even still you just weren't told about some problems that can happen ... we had quite a bit of talk about problems in the classroom, and hitches and that is what I find, the hardest part for me is the trip-ups you have along the way and how do you deal with them. I think that is what teachers want to know.

(4/15/90)

Well initially I was quite insecure. To try something new, when you have always got the idea at the end of the year with those magic marks, is quite a courageous thing, if you like and so the fact that we went back every week and could get support — being in a little school I don't get much support from other teachers. But to go back there and have a group of teachers accepting what I said was a big plus because being part time I wasn't — well I was here most of the time but I wasn't accepted totally as a real teacher. Whereas at the course I was, And when I said something people were interested to hear. So I think the fact that it ran over several weeks was quite important, that you got this reinforcement each week and you thought 'Oh well, that was a mess that first one but I will have another go.'

(11/12/91)

The collegial relationships were important as they provided opportunities for listening, contributing, discussing, supporting, giving feedback and reflecting on their teaching. In doing so, the teachers were renegotiating and reconstructing their shared knowledge about what it means to be a teacher of science.

The second professional development

The teachers continued to develop their ideas about science, science education and professional development and to develop their classroom activities. They were engaging in cognitive development and the development of classroom practice. With respect to their cognitive development they were:

- clarifying their existing concepts and beliefs about science education — teaching, learning, the roles of the teacher, learners, the curriculum, the nature of science;
- obtaining an input of new information by listening and reading;
- constructing new understandings by linking the new information with existing ideas;
- considering, weighing up and evaluating the newly constructed understandings;
- accepting or rejecting the new constructions;
- using newly accepted understandings in a variety of contexts and with confidence; and
- reconstructing what it means to be a teacher of science.

With respect to the development of their classroom practice, they were:

- obtaining new suggestions for teaching activities;
- considering them, visualizing and planning for their use in the classroom;
- adapting and using the new activities;
- sharing their classroom experiences with others and obtaining feedback about the use of the activities;
- evaluating the new teaching activities;
- receiving support.

In particular, the teachers were more able to go beyond their classroom management of the new activities, and develop new ways of interacting with the students' thinking. The development of the teachers' classroom activities in this phase was usually to make use of the opportunities created by the use of the new activities to interact with the students' thinking.

The main characteristic of this phase of professional development was that the two aspects of professional development were more connected. The teachers were reflecting on their classroom actions, not just as to whether they worked in terms of classroom management and within school restraints, but as to whether the actions matched their new theoretical ideas. The teachers were also planning for new action in that they were able to initiate or generate new teaching activities by considering the theoretical ideas and by taking into account their students' thinking. They continued to seek new teaching suggestions from the other teachers. Their repertoire of strategies to use in response to students' thinking was growing and they were using the new teaching ideas in new contexts.

The reflection-in-action that the teachers did in the classroom was also changing. Their thinking about their teaching and their role in the classroom, and the thinking underlying their decisions and actions were more in line with a constructivist view of learning. For example, a teacher commented on something be was reflecting on:

> . . . I think the term science teacher is a misnomer for me. I am more of a science educator. There is a difference. I have many colleagues who are good science teachers. They plan really good lessons, with lots of 'teachem workem' slots, have well presented materials, manage their students and resources well and get good test marks. But their students are asked to *remember* a whole lot of new stuff and not much effort is made to link the material being covered to *personal* experiences of the students. I feel I am more of an educator because I try to educate the student from where the student is at the moment in their thinking.
>
> (14/S3/91)

The teachers were changing from being technicians using new activities to teachers who had a constructivist view of learning and who took into account students' thinking. They were not only able to use the new activities from a classroom management point of view but were also able to respond to, and interact with, the students' thinking. Being a teacher who had a constructivist view of learning was becoming a way of thinking and behaving for the teachers, rather than the implementation of some new teaching activities. They were trialling activities and thinking in the classroom to reconstruct what it means to be a teacher of science.

The third personal development

Towards the end of the programme, the teachers' comments indicated that they were feeling more empowered to be responsible for their own development.

Developing a sense of trust is part of this personal development. Developing a trust that things will balance out over a longer period of time (the teaching year, rather than in one lesson) was important. The teachers often expressed a concern that there was not enough time to use a new teaching activity all the time. The time spent on one topic might be more than with the former teaching activities and there was a concern that all topics in the curriculum might not be covered. Some teachers also felt that the time and energy they had to put into using a new teaching activity were too great, limiting their use of the activity to once or twice a week or to some topics only.

These concerns decreased as the teachers evaluated the new teaching over a period of time and learnt to trust the new teaching. Discussion of what more experienced teachers had found was helpful. For example, teachers who have a constructivist view of learning, in contrast to technicians who are just using teaching activities based on a constructivist view of learning, comment that although the time spent on one topic seems to be longer, they find, at the end of the year or in the following year, that the students have retained the new learning. There is less time spent on revision and revisiting previous learning, and the students appear to recall the new concepts more readily in their later learning activities. Although more time is spent during learning, time is saved in later learning. Also, as the teachers developed further they realized that being a teacher who has a constructivist view of learning, was about the way they think and the way they respond to students' thinking in the classroom, not just about the overt activities they do in the classroom. When the teachers moved from being a technician using specific activities to being a teacher responding to and interacting with students' thinking, they commented that they gained rather than expended energy.

It appeared that to continue to develop professionally, the teachers also had to develop their trust in the students — to be more trusting that the students would have ideas on the topic being taught in science, that they would contribute to the discussions in the lesson, that they would learn the content of the curriculum, and that they would continue to take responsibility for their own learning. For example, a secondary teacher commented on students' contributions to the lesson:

> Well just the expectations of the pupils now that when they come into the room I will expect contributions from them.
>
> (8/15/91)

The teachers had to develop personally to be able to stand back and let go. There was personal development in attending to the feelings of apparent loss of control and not being centre stage. Some of the teachers had to consider other kinds of feedback, such as indicators of learning, to maintain their sense of self-worth as a teacher.

Some of the teachers commented that they felt that they were relying more on the students in their teaching. Now that they were acknowledging and valuing the students' knowledge and expertise, they sought their ideas out more and they felt they needed to consult with students more. They no longer felt that they could teach without knowing what the students were thinking. For example:

> It is neat to see the kids actually respond. You sometimes don't acknowledge that they — well I guess lots of teachers don't acknowledge that they actually have some knowledge already and they have experiences and they are involved with people who have had experiences, especially in this (unit on) health and disease. It was interesting the depth of knowledge that collectively the class had.
>
> (5/13/91)

Their personal development involved not only this greater respect for what the students brought to the lesson, but also attending to feelings associated with this — feelings that they were still competent teachers even if they felt they had to consult and rely on the students more.

They also commented that the experience of contributing in the programme sessions was empowering for them as staff members. They had felt empowered by having the opportunity to contribute to the group discussions, as well as having others listen to, and respond to, their ideas and opinions, and felt that they could voice their ideas without having to always be 'right'. They did not feel so uncomfortable if someone disagreed with their ideas. They were more able to acknowledge that different people could have different ideas from them and that this did not decrease their self-worth. This personal development had enabled them to contribute more to staff debates. Many had become more involved in school management, such as being on working parties formulating new school policies and in local and national debates, for example, over bulk funding and draft curricula. A beginning teacher commented:

> The deputy principal is really keen on getting the whole school working on mixed ability teaching, so in fact, I have been roped in as an expert, a local expert on mixed ability teaching because of the work that we have been doing and 'constructivist' teaching.
>
> (14/I4/91)

The sense of empowerment was accompanied by a greater congruence between their personally constructed knowledge and the socially constructed knowledge of what it means to be a teacher of science.

The third social development

As the teachers developed more, they began to actively seek and initiate the activities and relationships with other teachers which they felt fostered their own development. The activities were initiated in the sessions and outside the programme time. For example, one teacher asked for specific help when she felt a new teaching activity had not worked. She was asking her colleagues to work collaboratively with her on the problem. Other teachers commented on conversations they had had with colleagues in the gym, over the telephone, in the staffroom, in the car travelling to and from the programme sessions, and in planning a conference presentation together on the new teaching activities. For example:

> I have got to know three or four other teachers, women teachers very well, so a network has been set up. We frequently ring one another on the phone. We wouldn't have known one another as well and we are a support network. There are various problems that we have that I know now there is somebody I can talk to of a like mind. It has been personal contacts with other teachers.
>
> (7/I2/91)

Subsequent professional development

Some of the teachers took initiatives to continue their development after the end of the programme run as part of the research project, by doing some form of curriculum development or facilitating teacher development programmes themselves. For example, some became involved in writing a unit of work for the school scheme or a teacher's guide on one topic. Others introduced a colleague to the new teaching activities and facilitated the use of activities by the colleague in his or her classroom. Some applied for contract jobs to facilitate regional teacher development programmes for the Ministry of Education. They viewed writing and facilitating as additional ways to receive new theoretical and teaching ideas, support, feedback and further opportunities for talking with other teachers and for reflection. While they were giving, the teachers valued what they were receiving from the teachers with whom they were working. They were using the reconstructed knowledge about being a teacher of science.

Progression in the teacher development

There was a loose and flexible sequence implied in the model which describes the main aspects of learning for each teacher with respect to time. This progression is reported here to help raise the metacognitive awareness of the teachers about their own learning, and to guide the planning and actions of facilitators. The progression is here described as three situations:

Situation 1: confirmation and desiring change

In this first situation, the teachers to varying degrees shared a dissatisfaction with an aspect of the current culture of science teaching. They also had to establish themselves and feel valued and accepted within the group. A component of this involved a checking that their teaching and views of teaching were at least partly within the collectively agreed to knowledge of what it means to be a teacher of science. Receiving validation of themselves as competent professional teachers was an aspect of the confirmation.

The key aspects of the first situation were joining the group and using new and small teaching activities in their classrooms. Teachers undertook these two key activities so long as their respect from their colleagues in the programme and in the schools) was not endangered. A part of engaging in the change process was the group and the programme activities confirming and affirming them. The teachers had to establish or reinforce their self-esteem at the personal level. The changes therefore focused on an aspect of themselves, their teaching, and their position and standing with their peers.

In teacher-development programmes where this confirmation does not occur, the teachers are likely to feel excluded from the group, unvalidated as a teacher, and a threat to their self-esteem. They are also likely to be unaccepting of any reconstruction of what it means to be a teacher of science. Disengagement is highly likely. Given the short duration of most in-service programmes, many teachers in in-service programmes do not get the opportunity to progress beyond the confirmation stage. That is, they join the group, learn about some new teaching suggestions and begin trialling them.

Situation 2: reconstruction

In the reconstruction situation, the teachers were considering and reflecting on new teaching activities and new theoretical ideas; experimenting in the classroom with new teaching, learning and assessment activities; and taking initiatives to adapt materials for their own use. As a consequence they were also having to deal with the feelings associated with the change process and with being different to the commonly accepted culture of teaching. They were, reconceptualizing and renegotiating what it means to be a teacher of science within the group. They were using the support and feedback of the group and confirming the trust in the group.

Situation 3: empowerment

In the empowerment situation, the teachers were accepting of the changes that they had explored and the reconstructed social knowledge of what it means to be a teacher of science. In accepting the changes, the teachers had a new platform of beliefs from which to operate and maybe to change their world. This platform was empowering in that it gave a basis for making decisions about what to do and not to do. The new socially constructed knowledge about what it means to be a teacher of science had been largely accepted by the teachers.

With respect to the personal dimension, the teachers were gaining strength in knowing who they were as teachers, and from having a trust, conviction, and faith in, and an ownership of, their ideas and beliefs. There was a match between their own views of themselves as teachers of science and the newly socially constructed view. At the social level, they were setting up new situations and seeking out new groupings, to support and continue their development. With respect to professional development, they were showing competency in the classroom with the new strategies, being realistic, and establishing the limitations and strengths of their new activities.

Not a stage model of teacher development

The progression outlined above is a development of the purposes for which the teachers are seeking support from teacher development programmes. The progression in our model does *not* mean that a stage model of teacher development is being advocated, even though one of the major approaches to the description of teacher development relies on the notion of 'stages' For example, Leithwood (1992) has summarized three stage models which appear relevant to teacher learning: the development of professional expertise; psychological development; and career-cycle development. According to Kohlberg (1970), stages imply a number of distinct, qualitatively different structures that perform the same function at various points in the development of an individual. The different structures for a given function form an invariant sequence of development, which can be accelerated or retarded, but not changed. Each structure is a whole, with the sequence being an hierarchical integration: higher stages incorporate the structures which characterize the lower stages.

Burden (1990) has summarized some of the weaknesses in all stage models. The stages are often too imprecisely defined to be readily reconcilable with behaviour, so they cannot be empirically tested. Individuals can be found who develop in a way which is not predicted by the model, for example, by omitting (or 'jumping') stages. Such models often do not describe what is actually involved as an individual moves 'upwards' to the next stage, so that support for that transition cannot be given readily. Given the small groups who are surveyed in the production (as opposed to the confirmation) of stage models, it may well be that they are artefacts of sampling. As very few longitudinal studies on individuals are carried out, it may also be that the 'stages' are just a categorization scheme rather than implying actual progression by an individual. Arguably the greatest weakness in the use of stage models to describe teacher development is that they are insensitive to the circumstances of the life of the individual teacher.

In our view, the nature of the learning that any individual achieves is influenced by their perception of the circumstances of their life: their personal history, their present activities, and their more realistic hopes for the future. To be effective, any teaching that is provided must recognize these influences. The greatest influence on the learning of teachers (as a special group of learners) is the 'school climate' or 'school ethos' in which they work. Although this metaphor has been criticized for its width and imprecision (Finlayson, 1987), it is generally used. The pattern perceived by an individual teacher in a given school — of opportunities, expectations and inhibitions, rewards and punishments — both moulds and shapes what is done and not done, and when, how and why professional decisions are taken (for example, Zeichner, Tabachnick, and Densmore, 1987; Sikes, 1985; Tickle, 1989). Accordingly, we are not promoting the given model as a stage model of teacher development; rather, we see it as loosely describing a progression to aid teachers and facilitators in monitoring change.

Discussion

Our analysis of the descriptive data reported in this chapter highlights certain aspects of teacher development:

Learning

Teacher development can be viewed as teachers learning, rather than as others getting teachers to change. In learning, the teachers were developing their personally and socially constructed beliefs and ideas about science education and about what it means to be a teacher of science, developing their classroom practice and attending to their feelings associated with changing. Another aspect of the teacher development was learning about professional development and change processes, and how they themselves learn. Metacognition was thus a part of the teacher development process, as was reconceptualizing what teacher development is.

   Learning in the teacher-development process can be viewed as a purposeful inquiry. The teachers were inquiring into, or investigating, an aspect of their teaching — an aspect that they saw as problematic and wished to change.

Social, personal and professional development

The teacher development of the teachers in the research project can be described as social, personal and professional development. Social development involved working with, and relating to, other teachers and students to reconstruct the socially agreed knowledge about being a teacher of science. Personal development involved attending to feelings about the change process, about being a teacher and about science education, and reconstructing one's own knowledge about being a teacher of science. Professional development involved changing concepts and beliefs about science education and changing classroom activities. These three aspects were interactive and interdependent. The process of teacher development can be seen as one in which social, personal, and professional development is occurring, and one in which development in one aspect cannot proceed unless the other aspects develop also.

   Professional development included the teachers using new teaching activities in the classroom. The contributions from the teachers and the facilitator about new teaching activities initially needed to be ideas for new teaching strategies rather than written resources, such as teachers' guides. For example, initially the teachers found it more helpful to learn about a new way to find out what their students were thinking, such as brainstorming, than to receive a teacher's guide on the teaching of 'energy'. The teacher development programmes had a focus on new teaching activities and on being a teacher. Aspects related to learning, science and the curriculum arose from these two foci.

Teacher development programmes can be seen as having two components. One is the input of new theoretical ideas and new teaching suggestions. This tends to be present in current teacher-development programmes and is usually done in more formal situations, such as seminars and lectures. The second component is trying out, evaluating and practising these new theoretical and teaching ideas over an extended period, and in a collaborative situation where the teachers are able to receive support and feedback, critically reflect, and renegotiate and reconstruct what it means to be a teacher of science. In our experience, this second component tends to be underplayed in many in-service programmes and tends to occur through more informal modes such as telephone conversations, conversations in the staffroom, sharing anecdotes and visiting each other's classrooms. Both components are important if all three aspects of teacher development — social, personal, and professional — are to occur.

Professional development also involved the teachers developing their personally and socially constructed beliefs and ideas about science education, the teaching and learning process and teacher development. The teachers brought to the teacher development programmes different ideas, beliefs, experiences, concerns, interests and feelings. They had different starting points in the development process and achieved different outcomes, within the broad goals of the programme, even though they had attended the same programme. The teacher development programmes had both anticipated and unanticipated outcomes, and the facilitators needed to be prepared for both. Therefore, the teacher development activities were designed so as to acknowledge, incorporate, and address (rather than ignore) the teachers' prior ideas, beliefs, experiences, concerns, interests and feelings about science and science education.

Personal development was an essential aspect of the teacher development. Learning experiences can be set up to help the teachers develop professionally but the personal development, which often occurs outside of a programme, cannot be so readily facilitated. The personal development appeared important in the process in that personal and social development were intertwined, personal development preceded the professional development, the pace of personal development influenced the pace of professional development, and the personal development was often influenced by factors outside the professional and teaching work of the teacher. The restraints mentioned in the second phase of personal development can be viewed as cultural constraints (Tobin, 1990), but dealing with the feelings of teaching 'against the grain' (Cochran-Smith, 1991) to go beyond the restraints was an individual and affective process, done with the support of colleagues. For many teachers, the social development enabled the personal development.

Taylor (1991, p. 21) suggested that 'radical pedagogical reform might require teachers to engage in the renegotiation of the culture of teaching, rather than going it alone'. The social development is seen as necessary for this renegotiation. Through talking with other teachers, the culture of teaching for the teachers in the study was being renegotiated (Tobin, 1993). The social communication and interaction among the teachers were important in the teacher-development process.

A part of the social development was working with other teachers in ways to provide a forum for discussing and reconstructing what it means to be a teacher of science The teachers developed ways of working with, and relating to, other teachers and students from whom they trusted and received support and feedback. The isolation of the classroom was valued less, and collaborative ways of working were valued more for the support and feedback they gave. Social development can be facilitated to a certain extent by facilitating a contrived collegiality (Hargreaves, 1992), but true collaborative ways of working originate from the teachers valuing them as ways of fostering their own and others' development.

Teacher development was helped when the teachers were able to talk with each other about what they were doing in the classroom, as an integral and key part of the programme. For example, the sharing sessions were structured around the use of anecdotes (Bell, 1993a, pp. 279–319). It was not something to be left to chance before or after any meetings. Thus, for instance, the discussion about classroom activities was focused around a task of using a new teaching activity in the classroom. During this talking, the teachers were able to decide what to talk about and not just be on-task in response to a facilitator-initiated activity.

However, the isolation in the classroom is not necessarily problematic. For women teachers working in a hostile environment, isolation may be a sane response to the stress resulting from their experienced powerlessness, disenfranchisement, and professional frustration in a male-orientated curriculum, administration and school environment (Robertson, 1992). A woman teacher joining a group of teachers who are insensitive to gender differences, may not feel supported, encouraged or in a situation of mutual trust. The feedback she would most likely receive may not be helpful in terms of professional, personal or social development.

The classroom can also be a source of teacher development (Thiessen, 1992) and the social development involves the changing of the relationships between the teachers and the students. Here, it is the students who are providing the source of feedback and support for the teacher. When a school culture does not encourage collegial relationships between teachers, a teacher may prefer to work with the students rather than a group of teachers. But in this situation, the teacher is not isolated in her or his development, just isolated from other teachers.

For this overview, the three aspects of teacher development — social, personal, and professional—and the three phases within each have been separated from each other to highlight the multifaceted nature of teacher development. However, the data indicate that the three aspects and the three phases overlap considerably and it has to be acknowledged that the matrix of nine subsets of the process has its limitations.

Empowerment

The teacher development process can be viewed as one of empowerment for ongoing development, rather than one of continued dependency on a facilitator. The aims, activities and facilitation of a programme were planned for teachers to experience this empowerment. The programmes enabled teachers to feel included as part of the group; contribute to the programme and feel that their contributions were valuable to the programme, for example, feeling that their opinions, ideas, teaching activities, suggestions in decision- making, and initiatives were worthwhile; experience competency in teaching; develop a sense of ownership towards their own development; address their concerns and needs; volunteer for the programme or an aspect of the programme; negotiate the content and form of the programme; determine the pace and nature of the changes; reconceptualize their view of teacher development; view themselves as learners; innovate and be creative, rather than only implement given strategies; and feel that the changes are possible and beneficial in the current school and political situation.

At the outset of the teacher development programmes, the facilitator had a strong say regarding the programme sessions to meet the perceived expectations of the teachers. The teachers had been invited to participate in the research and the teacher development programme — it was not initiated by them. Also, other teacher development programmes at the time were very much directed by the person running them. Thus, initially, suggested teaching activities were given to the teachers according to what material was available to implement the findings of the previous research into students' learning. However, as indicated by the model, the facilitator did not maintain this directive position and the teachers increasingly determined the agenda of the meetings as the programme progressed.

The teachers appreciated being given space to decide, for themselves, the pace and nature of the changes they would make to their teaching in the classroom, within the broad framework of the programme. For example, the teachers felt their development was hindered if they were told by the facilitator to try a specific activity in the classroom before the next session. They felt their development was supported if the facilitator gave them a range of activities to try out over the time of several sessions. They were then able to select which activity they would try given the contexts in which they were teaching. Teachers appreciated the opportunity to manage the risk involved in changing what they did in the classroom.

The teachers were able to contribute to the programmes by talking about what they are doing in the classroom, providing their ideas and opinions for discussion, giving support and feedback, and negotiating the content and ways of doing the activities. The teachers gained as much from each other as they did from the facilitator. The act of contributing was seen as empowering by the teachers. Merely responding to the facilitator's questions or directions was seen as a contribution of lesser value. Once the teachers contributed, they were able to be given support and feedback, which are important to their development.

The desired teacher development was not achieved by trying to force the teachers to change. Although the facilitator was explicit about her expectation that the teachers would try out new activities in the classroom, and although the programme had a structure and goals, the precise direction of any change was not predetermined by the facilitator. The teachers needed to be convinced about the need for change, and to determine the direction of the change, before they would engage in development activity in such a way that they would learn.

Empowerment can also be viewed as the teachers being empowered to act on their world, to change or reconstruct the socially constructed knowledge about teaching science. In this emancipatory sense, teacher development is about helping teachers to critique beliefs underlying different educational policies and teaching approaches, to clarify their own beliefs and commitments in science education and to act in ways congruent with their own beliefs and commitments. In the teacher-development programmes run as part of the research project, the teachers were volunteers and there was no legal requirement for them to change, which is in contrast with teacher development programmes run to implement new policy or curricula. The teachers were able to choose whether to come on the programme or not, and whether to use the new teaching activities or not once they had learnt about them. However, the programme can be criticized in that only one view of learning (and teaching) — a constructivist view — was presented and focused on.

For teacher development to continue beyond a particular programme, the teachers had to have been supported to reach the third aspect of their personal and social development. This took time and could not be neatly orchestrated for within the tight timelines set by some administrators wanting to implement new policies.

In summary, the analysis of the research findings suggests that teacher development can be conceptualized as social, personal and professional development. When all three aspects are addressed, as in the teacher-development programmes run as part of the research project, teacher development is promoted (Pearson and Bell, 1993). [. . .]

References

Bell, B. (1993) *Taking into Account Students' Thinking: A Teacher Development Guide*, Hamilton, Centre for Science and Mathematics Education Research, University of Waikato.

Bell, B. and Gilbert, J. (1994) 'Teacher development as personal, professional and social development', *Teaching and Teacher Education*, 10, 5, pp. 483–97.

Burden, P. (1990) 'Teacher development', in Houston, W. (Ed) *Handbook of Research on Teacher Education*, New York, MacMillan, pp. 311–28.

Cochran-Smith, M. (1991) 'Learning to teach against the grain', *Harvard Educational Review*, 61, 3, pp. 279–310.

Finlayson, D. (1987) 'School climate: An outmoded metaphor?', *Journal of Curriculum Studies*, 19, 2, pp. 163–73.

Hargreaves, A. (1992) 'Cultures of teaching: A focus for change', in Hargreaves, A. and Fullan, M. (Eds) *Understanding Teacher Development*, New York, Teachers College Press, pp. 216–40.

Kohlberg, L. (1970) *Moral Development*, New York: Holt, Reinhart and Winston.

Leithwood, K, (1992) 'The principal's role in teacher development', in Fullan, M. and Hargreaves, A. (Eds) *Teacher Development and Educational Change*, London, Falmer Press, pp 86–103.

Pearson, J. and Bell, B. (1993) *The Teacher Development that Occurred*, Report of the Learning in Science Project (Teacher Development). Hamilton, Centre for Science and Mathematics Education Research, University of Waikato.

Robertson, H. (1992) 'Teacher development and gender equity', in Hargreaves, A. and Fullan, M. (Eds) *Understanding Teacher Development*, New York, Cassell and Teachers College Press, pp 43–61.

Sikes, P. (1985) 'The life cycle of the teacher', in Ball, S. and Goodson, I. (Eds) *Teachers' Lives and Careers*, London, Falmer Press, pp. 27–60.

Taylor, P. (1991) 'Collaborating to reconstruct teaching: The influence of researcher beliefs', Paper presented at the annual meeting of the American Educational Research Association, Chicago, April 3–7.

Thiessen, D. (1992) 'Classroom-based teacher development', in Hargreaves, A. and Fullan, M. (1992) (Eds) *Understanding Teacher Development*, New York, Teachers College Press, pp 85–109.

Tickle, L. (1989) 'New teachers and the development of professionalism, in Holly, M. and McLoughlin, C. (Eds) *Perspectives on Teacher Professional Development*, London, Falmer Press, pp. 93–118.

Tobin, K. (1990) 'Social constructivist perspectives on the reform of science education', *Australasian Science Teacher Journal*, 36, 4, pp. 29–35.

Tobin, K. (1993) 'Referents for making sense of science teaching', *International Journal of Science Education*, 15, 3, pp. 241–54.

Zeichner, K., Tabachnick, R. and Densmore, K. (1987) 'Individual, institutional and cultural, influences on the development of teachers' craft knowledge', in Calderhead, J. (Ed) *Exploring Teachers' Thinking*, London, Cassell, pp. 21–59.

International Journal of Science Education

EDITOR

John K. Gilbert, *University of Reading, UK*

International Journal of Science Education is firmly established as the authoritative voice in the world of science education. It bridges the gap between research and practice, providing information, ideas and opinion It serves as a medium for the publication of definitive research findings. Special emphasis is placed on applicable research relevant to educationa practice, guided by educational realities in systems, schools, colleges and universities.

The journal publishes peer-reviewed general articles, papers on innovations and developments, research reports and book reviews. Each volume contains a Special Issue devoted to a topic of major interest and importance, guest-edited by an acknowledged expert. Recent Special Issues have featured environmental education and policy and practice in science education.

The journal has an international readership of science education researchers and science educators worldwide.

This journal is also available online. Please connect to www.tandf.co.uk/online.html for further information.

To request a sample copy please visit: **www.tandf.co.uk/journals**

SUBSCRIPTION RATES
2003 – Volume 25 (12 issues)
Print ISSN 0950-0693
Online ISSN 1464-5289
Institutional: US$1169; £709
(includes free online access)
Personal: US$407; £248 (print only)

Taylor & Francis
Taylor & Francis Group

For further information, please contact Customer Services at either:
Taylor & Francis Ltd, Rankine Road, Basingstoke, Hants RG24 8PR, UK
Tel: +44 (0)1256 813002   Fax: +44 (0)1256 330245   Email: enquiry@tandf.co.u
Website: www.tandf.co.uk
Taylor & Francis Inc, 325 Chestnut Street, 8th Floor, Philadelphia, PA 19106, U!
Tel: +1 215 6258900 Fax: +1 215 6258914 Email: info@taylorandfrancis.cor
Website: www.taylorandfrancis.com

tsed